Crossing the Line

A Memoir in Two Parts

Part One: The Awakening of a Good Ol' Boy
Part Two: The War Years, 1941-1945

By Cecil A. Alexander
with Randy Southerland

Cecil A. Alexander
with Randy Southerland

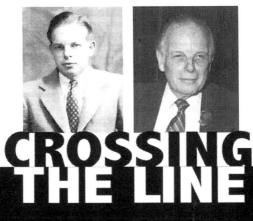

CROSSING THE LINE
A Memoir - Part One

The Awakening of a Good Ol' Boy

Table of Contents

Dedication

To Helen, who has been my rock throughout my "third act",
and her family

To Hermi and our "offs": Terri, Judy, Doug, and their spouses —
Herb, Phil, Ed and Anne — the fathers, step-father, and mother,
of my precious grandchildren: Alex and his wife Sara, Rachael, Jed, Wilson, Julian, my
great-grandchildren, Hannah and Asher,
and those who are yet to come

Acknowledgements

I am forever grateful to my wonderful wife of 27 years, Helen, who has encouraged me every step of the way in the writing of this memoir. When things were darkest for me, she brought me back to life.

I am indeed a very lucky man to have spent so many happy years with two outstandingly beautiful, bright, loving and supportive women – two women, Helen and Hermi, who were the best of friends – by my side, in my life.

My children and their spouses, my grandchildren and even my great-grandchildren (although they couldn't know it) have provided valuable perspective and inspiration as long as I've known them. My "bonus kids" – Helen's children, their spouses, and grandchildren – have been very supportive as well.

I am grateful to my nephew Roman L. Weil, Jr., who flew across the country from the west coast with his grandson, Conrad Laesch, age 6, for a 24-hour stay, because Conrad wanted to meet me. Roman's children, their mother Cherie Buresh Weil, and their spouses Lexie and Brad Laesch, Lacey and David Ogbolumani, and Sandy and Anne Weil, have likewise made special trips because their children – Lily and Greta Laesch, Isabella and Emeka Ogbolumani, and Charlie, Bailie and Adeline (Allie) Weil – wanted to meet the old man. I'm also appreciative of my niece Judith Alexander Weil Shanks for her exhaustive research into family history that culminated in a touching and interesting book, published in 2011, *Old Family Things - An Affectionate Look Back*, from which I borrowed some images for this book. Most of my sister's children and grandchildren came to celebrate my 90th birthday with me. Thank you Carol Weil and Jerry Maltz, Ken Weil and Pam Wilcut, Caitlin and Jed Smith, Liz and Drew Alexander, and Julia Shanks. And thanks to Therese's husband Richard Lansburgh and daughter Deborah Adler for being there then and on so many other occasions, both tragic and joyful.

Thank you to all who came to celebrate on the occasion of my 90th birthday. Too many to list, to my delight, your presence was very much appreciated.

To Stephen Moore, I owe much gratitude for all the ways in which he supported me and chronicled my life in words and photographs. Bruce Logan has provided me with videos of important events in my life and chronicled things for me without my even knowing about it at the time.

Drs. David Apple and Ed Laughlin, both first-rate orthopedic surgeons, did a brilliant job of putting me back together following the wreck in 1983. In more recent years, I have many support people to thank for helping to nurture my health, keeping me going well into my 90s and listening graciously to poems I have memorized and enjoy reciting. Dr. Shep Dunlevie, Dr. Preston Stewart, Dr. John Cantwell and Dr. Michael Haberman have provided fine guidance and offered the gift of unhurried time together, sharing stories, thinking things through in ways that have meant much to me. Dr. Dickie McMullan, my ophthalmologist, is someone I always look forward to sharing some time with.

Julie Fowler of Visiting Nurse Health System (VNHS) has been a source of great comfort, gentle care and just enough toughness, as have Annie Keener and Krista Osborne. They all inspire me to keep moving.

Diana Broome has devotedly kept Helen, me and our books organized and out of trouble even while she is the Aquatics Director at the YMCA. She has helped arrange and produce countless parties and considered us family over many years, as we have her. I also thank Jane Burke, a talented singer and choral director at St. Mark United Methodist Church, who helped keep the books and the household running smoothly for a long time.

Caregivers have made it possible for me to stay at home with Helen and the cats and I owe them all a huge debt of gratitude. Janet Caldwell, Della Carroway, Llana Clarke , Shurlan Forbin, Precious Johnson, Betty Parham, Annlie Salina, Percy Sichalwe and Sharone Williams, you have cared for me with skill, tenderness and good humor and I know how fortunate I am to have had you in my life.

Robert Barrow has been my right and left hand on many occasions over the years as an invaluable help to Helen and me, assisting in so many ways to keep our home a lovely place.

I feel very grateful to my daughter Judy and my son-in-law Ed who have been living in the house with Helen and me for a while, helping to manage and oversee the household. They make me feel well taken care of.

I am very appreciative of Randy Southerland, Fred DuBose and my daughter Judy for the roles they played in the creation of this book. I also thank Eugene (Gene) Patterson and Melissa Fay Greene for their kind words and am humbled by their expressions of support.

A team of proofreaders, some family and some friends of Judy's stepped up at the very end of getting this book to publication to clean up the details. Thanks so much to my grandson Jed Augustine, Kate Blakeslee, Heather Fenton, Kim Salyer Griffin, Ceci Aaron Haydel, Bruce Logan, Kerry Munger Livingston, Alex Millkey, Lacey Weil Ogbolumani, Rana Roop, Frances Fowler Slade, Susan Mumpower-Spriggs, Cherie B. Weil, and Nell Ziroli.

This work by San Francisco artist and calligrapher Colleen Molloy was commissioned by and given to me by my children after the wreck that took the life of my wife, and their mother, Hermi.

The quotes are from Winston Churchill excerpted from speeches made in 1941 and 1932.

These became and remain my words to live by.

Cecil A. Alexander, 2012

"A profile in courage: the life of Cecil Alexander, Jr., a hero in war and a visionary in peace. In World War II, Alexander flew 60 bombing missions and was twice honored with the Distinguished Flying Cross. In peacetime, he studied at Georgia Tech, Yale, M.I.T., and Harvard with the brightest minds of his generation in architecture and design, and then returned home to help build a new Atlanta. In Alexander's vision, Atlanta should become a city modern in its skyline and modern in its thinking. The creation of uniquely beautiful buildings and the struggle for racial equality went hand-in-hand for Alexander, serving his conviction that it was possible to live bigger, and better, and more justly. He is a founding father not of old-time Terminus, but of today's dazzlingly contemporary, international, harmoniously diverse city."

Melissa Faye Greene
Author Praying for Sheetrock, The Temple Bombing, Last Man Out,
There Is No Me Without You, No Biking in the House Without a Helmet

"My relationship with Cecil Alexander, one of the great souls of Atlanta, one of the great spirits of the South, began as we were leaders in the Black-Jewish Coalition and fashioned a lasting friendship between us that created inroads into the community at large. It was such a pleasure, such an honor, such a *blessing* to see Cecil and to spend time with him at his home. He is 94 years young and still devising ways to build a better world. I just hope when I'm 94 that I still have what it takes to take the long, hard look. To never give up, never give in, to never get lost in a sea of despair."

Congressman John Lewis
August 15, 2012 - Speaking at The Breman Museum, Atlanta,
on the occasion of the 30th anniversary of the Black-Jewish Coalition

"The courage that propelled Cecil Alexander through 60 missions flying Marine dive bombers over the Pacific is built into Atlanta's bricks now. His demanding decency laid moral sills under modern Atlanta as well as the tall buildings he designed. He risked his living in the 1950s and 60s to defy the popular little men whose racism tried to block his vision of an upright Atlanta. He steadied the hand and watched the back of the great Mayors Bill Hartsfield and Ivan Allen who leaned on him for unfrightened leadership in the private sector, and got it. Some men hesitated in that time when Atlanta had to decide whether to be great. Cecil Alexander stood up, and said, 'Follow me.' "

Eugene Patterson
1950s and 60s Editor, The Atlanta Constitution

Introduction

My Road to a Wider World

One day in June 1967, I sat in the office of Atlanta Mayor Ivan Allen. We were discussing his Housing Resources Committee, which I chaired, when the phone rang. The strained voice of a police officer issued from the desk phone: "Mayor Allen, a white policeman shot and killed a black man and wounded a boy at the Dixie Hills housing development. There's a very angry group of men gathering in the parking lot in front of the strip shopping center and I thought you should know."

Concern crossed the mayor's face, but his voice stayed steady and calm. "Thanks. I'll look into it."

Helen Bullard, his brilliant political adviser, was sitting next to the mayor's sprawling oak desk. He pointed his finger at her and then at me. "I want you two to drive over to Dixie Hills and check things out," he said, "then come back and tell me whether I should go." Go we did, as would the mayor, who, as you'll learn in Chapter 9, "The Transformation of a Good Ol' Boy," handled the crisis with the kind of aplomb rarely seen. If the mayor saved the day, I was catapulted into a phase of my life that was both a culmination of 40-odd years of preparation to fight for racial justice and a beginning.

First, though, let me say I believe it's a mistake to call people of my age "the greatest generation." That title belongs to those in 1776 who pledged their lives, their fortunes, and their sacred honor to form this nation. Millions in my generation lived through volatile, tragic, catastrophic, and violent times with a few rewarding moments of glory and tranquility, but we met the challenge not because we were great but because we had no choice.

In only one instance can I claim my experience and challenges were different from those faced by all but a few of my peers. That was my transformation from a Southerner with the traditional paternalist attitude toward blacks to a dedicated advocate for civil rights — an experience that has given me the temerity to write these pages. My memoir will, I hope, reveal an aspect of that chaotic era not usually discussed. I also hope it will reveal my motivations as I took part in the wrenching struggle.

The story would not be complete without the significant events and encounters that shaped my life. Chapters are devoted to, among other reminiscences, my youth in Atlanta; my education in New England; my active involvement in Atlanta's politics and government; my long career as an architect; and glimpses of the triumphs and tragedies of my personal life. Part Two of *Crossing the Line*, titled *The War Years*, covers my time as a World War II Marine dive-bomber pilot in the Pacific and my history as a soldier (with a wife) on the mainland.

While recalling the best of years of my life has been a joy, writing this book wasn't always a happy experience. Too many people intertwined with my life are dead, and too many dreams remained dreams. The chapter "My World Ripped Apart" recounts the horrible wreck that killed my first wife and injured me for life. "A Flag for all Georgians" traces one of my forays into race relations when I designed a new flag for Georgia that minimized the Confederate Cross; it flew over the Georgia Capitol Building for two years until a Republican governor replaced it. Happier days take the stage in Chapter 4 ("From Beaux Arts to Bauhaus"), the story of how I found my footing as an architect. To learn how I wooed and wed Hermi Weil of New Orleans, you'll have to turn to Part Two's Chapter 18 — "The War Can Wait."

President Kennedy, alluding to his mute and paralyzed father, said, "Old age is a shipwreck." For me, old age is a plane crash I have survived.

Why, then, did I write? That many listeners urged me to put my stories on paper was certainly a factor. But I know it was mainly ego that drove me to stare down reams of blank pages and finally fill them with my wavering script.

"Words are forever," said Sir Winston Churchill. His are. I'll settle for a decade or less.

— Cecil Alexander, April 2012

Chapter 1

Atlanta 1918 AD - Not Yet a City Too Busy to Hate

If we falter and lose our freedoms, it will be because we destroyed ourselves.

— *Abraham Lincoln*

In 1918, the year I was born, Atlanta was a dangerous, hopeless dead-end for its black citizens. Only twelve years before a bloody race riot had swept the city, making horrifying headlines across the nation and front pages as far away as then-remote China. The residue of fear, hate, and vengeance was still heavy in the year of my birth.

It was a long time, of course, before I was old enough to be aware of the degradation of those exploited people. In 1918 my parents, both white Southerners steeped in the "Southern way of life," didn't find these conditions particularly deplorable. Such conditions, I was assured, had existed in Atlanta since before the Civil War.

My readings of accounts of the temper of those times, discussions with older blacks who were adults then, and my own observations of the city as I

1

matured give me confidence that my description of the dismal state of Atlanta's blacks at the dawn of the 1920s is basically accurate.

One City, Two Worlds

In Northern cities, most of the slums had previously been substantial, decent housing occupied by reasonably affluent whites. As the whites moved to newer neighborhoods over time, their housing was left empty and deteriorating. It was these units that became slums. While such housing was badly in need of repair, the basic structure was sound and utilities like water and electricity were restorable. Schools, offices, grocery stores, pharmacies, and doctors' and lawyers' offices that had once served the neighborhood fell vacant – but as the neighborhood repopulated, many of these services were revived.

In the South, on the other hand, the slums were often built as slums. In Atlanta, two- or three-room shacks made from scrap lumber were scattered through areas with no paved streets, no sidewalks, no street lamps, no sewers, and no police protection. A house on fire burned to the ground.

Downtown was off-limits to blacks, and those who had no choice but to go there faced an anxious trial. If a white man or woman approached a black man, the black stepped into the gutter, tipped his cap, and cast his eyes downward; black women also made their deference clear. The only black business in downtown was the Herndon Barber Shop, at 66 Peachtree Street, and its barbers cut hair growing on white heads only – no black hair ever fell on the marble floor of that exclusive emporium.

All white churches and synagogues welcomed white members and visitors, but God forbid if any blacks entered their sacred confines. The rare exceptions were funerals or weddings for employers of black servants, during which the servants, dressed in their Sunday best, sat quietly in the back pew.

At the movies blacks climbed to the "peanut gallery," the balcony just under the ceiling and far removed from the screen. At the Atlanta Crackers ballpark, blacks sat in the remote "Republican Bleachers" out in left field. (It was called so because only the GOP allowed blacks to vote in their primaries; the Democrats held all-white primaries, and the winners were shoo-ins to win the general election.) Not one of the professional or college sports teams was integrated. If a black wanted to play professional baseball, he was limited to the Black Crackers, a semi-pro club.

White restaurants and lunch counters were off-limits as well. Some stores allowed blacks to buy clothes, clothes, but they weren't permitted to try them on or return any that didn't fit.

The city's hotels – especially the upscale Henry Grady, Piedmont, Ansley, and Georgian Terrace – closed their doors to black guests. Blacks did work in these places. Some waited tables in white restaurants and worked at other menial jobs paying less than subsistence wages.

"Life, liberty, and the pursuit of happiness" were myths for these disadvantaged Americans. In 1918 this country was on the edge of a sharp cleaver, lacking only a charismatic demagogue to send it into chaos, bloody riots, or even, conceivably, civil war.

All my adult life I have been aware of the pitiful existence of Atlanta's blacks, but only as I began to write this memoir did the reality of this Southern apartheid-riven society become acutely clear to me. I'm certain that this realization has lent understanding to my discourses on race.

A Fateful Case

An ugly incident that took place in the early twentieth century saw my Uncle Harry, an attorney whose actual name was Henry A. Alexander, appeal a conviction to the Supreme Court – a foreshadowing of the stand taken by later generations of Alexanders against prejudice and discrimination.

In April 1913, Leo Frank, a young Jewish man who had moved to Atlanta from New York to help manage his uncle's Montag Pencil Company, was accused of murdering 13-year-old Mary Phagan when she came to the plant to collect her pay. It was a Saturday, and the plant was nearly deserted.

In a time when anti-Jewish feeling was rife, some Atlantans would see to it that a crime against a gentile girl by a Jew would not go to waste. Helping to whip up the fervor was Thomas E. Watson from Thomson, Ga., a populist who began his career as an attorney, not only was elected to both the U. S. House of Representatives and the Senate but wrote histories and novels. Tom Watson also changed from a liberal sympathetic to the plight of blacks to a white supremacist who, in fiery speeches and his publications *The Watsonian* and *The Jeffersonian,* railed against blacks, Catholics, and the influence of Jews on the state of Georgia.

During Frank's trial, evidence that could implicate the janitor who was present the day of the murder, including what appeared to be bloodstains on his shirt, was discarded in favor of the janitor's claims that he had helped Frank dispose of the body. The circus-like atmosphere surrounding the trial culminated in wild cheers from the crowds around the courthouse when the jury convicted Frank and sentenced him to death.

My uncle, lawyer Henry (Harry) Aaron Alexander, took the appeals to the Georgia Supreme Court and ultimately to the U.S. Supreme Court, which completely ignored the poisonous proceedings and let Frank's conviction stand. Uncle Harry and his team then sought a commutation from the governor, John M. Slaton, which spurred Tom Watson and his ilk to further escalate the public furor against both Frank and his defenders. After a lengthy and careful review, Gov. Slaton commuted Frank's death sentence to life imprisonment.

When I was in my teens, my mother told me that in the days following the commutation she was sitting on the porch of her mother-in-law's house on Forrest Avenue when a raging mob surged by on its way to the Governor's Mansion, on Peachtree Street in Buckhead. They were screaming, "To hell with Slaton and Alexander!" and "Let 'em burn in hell!" Uncle Harry had earlier rushed to the governor to stand with him when the frightening mob arrived.

"I certainly didn't want any harm to come to Harry," Mother said, "but I had just married your father, who resembles him. I was in great fear a mob would think your father was Harry and take him."

That night Gov. Slaton called out his guards, who surrounded his house with loaded rifles. In command, I've been told, was a tough, rock-like Scot. When the leaders of the scraggly mob strode toward the house, the Scot ordered the guards to raise their rifles and aim at the would-be assailants. He glared at the leaders and said, "I know all you guys, but that doesn't make one goddamn difference to me. If you take one more step toward this house, my men have orders to shoot to kill." The leaders froze, then turned around and signaled the mob to move back.

Frank had been incarcerated in a jail in the town of Milledgeville, and it was this jail a mob stormed on August 17, 1915. The men threw Frank into an automobile, raced to the town of Marietta, where Mary Phagan had lived with her mother and stepfather, and hanged him.

Echoes Through the Years

My uncle's role in this violent display of anti-Semitism made it a family-wide experience, and I was raised under its cloud. The Leo Frank case had forged a bond between the Alexander and Slaton families, but it also cast a pall over Atlanta's Jewish community, something I was well aware of as an adolescent – not least because my mother was a good friend of Frank's widow Lucille, who lived nearby.

The cloud was always there in my youth, but by the 1940s it was largely history to me. I didn't dwell on the extremely dubious conviction and brutal lynching as an immediate concern or threat.

Still, the Frank case lived on in Atlanta. In 1986 a lawyer appealed to the Georgia Board of Pardons and Parole to declare Frank innocent. Although it wasn't a complete exoneration of him as I interpreted it, Frank's good name and reputation, long after his death, was restored.

Around the same time, when I was at work in my architectural firm's office, the phone rang. "Is this Mr. Cecil Alexander?" a female voice asked.

"Yes, what can I do for you?"

"This is Mary Phagan."

I thought for a moment I was in touch with the ghost of the murdered girl. It was a real shock. When she explained that she was the niece of Mary Phagan, I relaxed.

"You were quoted in the paper," she continued, "as saying that the mob that marched out Peachtree to get the governor and your uncle was the same one that lynched Frank. I make it my business to correct any errors I see about the case. It was not the same mob."

"You're right," I said. "The paper misinterpreted me. I never said the mobs were the same, although I'm sure some of the men were active in both groups."

"OK," she said, "thank you. I'm writing a book about the case. Would you discuss it with me over lunch one day?" "Certainly." I said.

She never followed up. I never called her. The book was published, but I have not read it.

More recently, I was at a discussion of a book concerning the Frank case. At the end of the presentation a smiling lady approached me. She said, "Mr. Alexander, I am Mary Phagan – the earlier Mary Phagan's grandniece." We had a brief, pleasant conservation.

Tom Watson Brown, an Atlanta lawyer, scholar, and civic leader, was the grandson of fiery Tom Watson. Brown claimed there was no doubt that Leo

Frank murdered Mary Phagan and that his grandfather was unjustly maligned. Brown took advantage of every opportunity to speak or write in support of his convictions. We were civil when we met but avoided mentioning my Uncle Harry, Leo Frank, Mary Phagan, or Thomas E. Watson. Tom Watson Brown died in 2007.

An executive of the Atlanta History Center told me that Tad Watson Brown, the great-grandson of Tom W. Brown, could help me get my memoir published. So I met with Tad, told him it includes pages on the Frank case, and then asked him to read those pages and react. As a result of our meeting, I made some modifications.

The one point we couldn't reconcile was my reference to the Marietta men who lynched Frank as a "mob." Tad says they weren't a mob – they were among Marietta's leading citizens. I maintain that conducting the lawless and brutal lynching made them members of a mob, and their high standing in their own community only added to their lawlessness because surely they knew better.

Tad and I, who share a desire to preserve historic and beautiful buildings, have become friends. He is the president of the Watson-Brown Foundation in Thomson. Although the foundation's main goal is to provide college scholarships, it also maintains historic houses as museums, in Thomson, Thomas E. Watson's birthplace and two other homes and, in Athens, the T. R. R. Cobb House. Currently under restoration in Atlanta is the Phillip Shutze-designed Goodrum House on West Paces Ferry, which will serve as the Watson-Brown Foundation's local headquarters.

A Final Thought Before I Begin

Living a long time gives us a perspective on events that is often lacking in the young, who sometimes regard anything that took place before their birth as "ancient history." For instance, I recently I told a young woman that I was a "war baby."

"Really sir?" she replied. "Was that the Spanish American War?"

"No," I answered, "it was World War I, which ended in 1918. Thank you for not asking if it was the Civil War or even the War of 1812." How could she think I was that old, and did she have to compound the observation by addressing me as "Sir?"

It is said that if we forget history we are bound to repeat it. But if many of today's young are hazy on events long past, they tend to share the kind of all-embracing tolerance toward their fellow human beings that many in my generation, and those who came before, did not.

Chapter 2

Growing Up In Atlanta

And the white wolf-winter, hungry and frore,
Can prowl the north by a frozen door.
But here we have fed him on bacon-fat,
And he sleeps by the stove like a lazy cat.

— Stephen Vincent Benét, John Brown's Body

I lay stretched out on my back, flat against the hot curving concrete walk leading to my house. I was staring into the infinite black sky, carpeted with stars. The heat baked into the walk by the August sun was now flowing out of the walk through my shirt and was warming my back. I had a deep sense of contentment and security.

My house rose up a flight of steps at the end of the short curving walk. Light from its large windows spread in yellow elongated quadrangles across the green lawn. Our street, St. Charles Place, and the two on either side – St. Louis and St. Augustine – comprised "saintly" Atkins Park, developed soon after the end of World War I. My family moved from my paternal grandmother's house on Forrest Avenue in 1922. That street was named for Nathan

Bedford Forrest, an outstanding Confederate general in the Civil War. Forrest was known for his strategic advice for winning battles: "Git there firstist with the mostist." Unfortunately, he was also known as a founder of the Ku Klux Klan, the self-dubbed Knights of the South, who fostered violence against blacks, Jews, and Catholics.

My father was very uncomfortable living on a street named for this dangerous bigot. He insisted the correct spelling of the street's name was "Forest" with one "r," in acknowledgement of the huge forest of oaks that bordered the avenue. He had the name printed with the single "r" on his stationery. (When we first arrived in Atkins Park, there were many vacant tree-filled lots. My father took it personally when two large houses were built directly across the street from us, destroying the trees and ruining our view.)

Only 55 years separated the end of the Civil War and my birth, and war veterans who were younger than I am today were still active in Atlanta. Memories of the horrors of the war and the devastation of Reconstruction hung heavily on Atlantans and weighed down progress. In 1906, twelve years before I was born, a terrible race riot tore through the city – a disastrous event that made headlines all over the world.

Atlanta had been virtually burned to the ground In the late summer of 1864; of the 3,200 houses standing before the invasion, only about 200 remained after the mayor surrendered. Its citizens, including my great-grandparents, had been forced by Gen. William T. Sherman to evacuate their homes and seek shelter in Columbus and other Georgia towns. Almost alone among large U.S. cities, Atlanta shared the fate destined for many European and Asian cities during the twentieth centuries' two World Wars.

If Atlanta looked back in sorrow, it also looked forward with hope. Not long after the end of the war, the Atlanta Chamber of Commerce welcomed Gen. Sherman back to the city with a festive banquet. It was in this optimistic community, still burdened by its racist attitudes, that I spent my early days.

I was well aware of, and fascinated by, living on the site of a historic and bloody conflict. My father showed me the trenches that still surrounded the city. The Cyclorama, displaying a huge circular painting of the Battle of Atlanta, overwhelmed me.

Family Life on St. Charles

Looking at the world with childlike wonder, I was only dimly aware of the conflicts, if not war, that played out on a daily basis between my parents. For my mother Julia, the move to a sparkling new home on St. Charles Place was an escape from her mother-in-law, a domineering matriarch. For my father, Cecil Sr., it resulted in a slight fraying of filial bonds. Every morning on his way to his hardware store, he stopped at his mother's for a second breakfast. Every evening on his way home, he stopped in for a pre-dinner dinner. When he arrived home around eight o'clock, he just played with the meal my mother had prepared and kept warm for him on the stove. My grandmother's friends thought he was a wonderful son – and my mother's friends and her sister and brother-in-law couldn't understand how she put up with him.

I was 10 years old and accepted as completely natural the odd relationship between my paternal grandmother and her son. Looking back these many decades later, I see my family not so much dysfunctional as nonfunctional. My older sister Charlotte, always at odds with our father, was the uneasy fourth member of the family. A very important fifth member for me was my dog Snuff, a Scottish terrier.

That being said, my father was, with his regal looks and impeccable English, ready for casting as a senator, the president of Yale, or the CEO of a major corporation. He badly wanted to study law as a young man, but his older brother Henry, who went by the nickname Harry, cut him out. Harry earned his diploma at the University of Virginia and had a fine legal career. This sentenced my father, as the only other son, to work at their father's store, J. C. & J. M. Alexander Hardware. J. M. and his brother had opened the store in Atlanta after their service in the Confederate Army. (A historian recently told me it was the model used by Margaret Mitchell in *Gone With the Wind* for the Atlanta store Scarlett O'Hara opened after the Civil War.)

My father's cultured mien and imposing appearance led to a very amusing encounter in my adulthood. One evening my wife Hermi and I were having dinner at the home of Phoebe and De Franklin. Phoebe was Hermi's best friend and her husband De was our attorney. Visiting from Katona, New York was Phoebe's mother, Ruth Alice Weil Halsbad. After her husband's death from cancer, this brilliant woman went back to study at Columbia University and earned a PhD in chemistry. She later opened a groundbreaking chemistry laboratory at her Hickory Hill estate in Katona, a research facility that drew chemists and students from far and wide.

De, our host, had graduated magna cum laude from the University of Georgia and earned his degree from Harvard Law School, where he was on the Harvard Law Review. These were no trivial academic accomplishments, but his mother-in-law apparently saw them as insufficient. "De," she said, "you are not an educated man. Now look at Mr. Alexander —now *there* is an educated gentleman."

"Cecil," she said to my father, "what advanced degrees do you have?" His answer floored her. "Well, I'm afraid I don't have any degrees. I dropped out of Georgia Tech after a year and went to work at my father's hardware store." De couldn't conceal a broad smile. The remainder of the dinner went quietly.

Because my father had no real formal education, he took vicarious pride in the academic achievements of my sister and me.

My mother Julia came from the prominent Moses family in Montgomery, Ala. One of her uncles had served as mayor of the city, and four of the five Moses brothers owned the largest bank there. Judah Moses, my grandfather, didn't join his brothers in the bank and instead was a dealer in lumber. He escaped his brothers' financial collapse. When the bank went bust in the Panic of 1893, they spent the rest of their lives paying back their depositors. Judah's brothers regarded taking bankruptcy as a disgrace, a sign of a weak and unethical character. Times have changed!

Mother had an older sister, Adeline. Their mother, Charlotte Bahr, came from Frankfort, Germany. Their father, Judah Touro Moses, was born in Montgomery. I do not know how they met.

Both my mother and my aunt Adeline taught at a Montgomery public grammar school. Mother was a talented artist. Had she arrived as an adult in the mid-twentieth century, I'm sure she could have had a successful career as an artist. But the times were against her. She settled for a successful career as a teacher, one of the few careers open to women in those days. She told me often how she prepared to take her mathematics exam for her teaching license. To ensure she would pass the exam, she worked every problem in three different math books – and her grade was 100. Even today that kind of preparation astonishes me.

Mother was, I had thought, a fearful person – certainly not adventurous. Was I wrong! In a letter I found, she told a friend of the great thrill she had flying at the Montgomery Fairgrounds in 1911, only eight years after the Wright

Brothers made history at Kitty Hawk. The airplane she went aloft in must have been a fragile assembly of wood, wire, and fabric, all powered by a small, very unreliable engine.

My mother was also an avid baseball fan. It is lost, but for years I had her small, shiny brown leather scorebook. It was filled with her precisely printed details of the many Montgomery Rebels games she attended. On the inside of the back cover was pasted a photograph clipped from the Montgomery paper. It had all the quality of seeming to have been printed on fresh bread under hot water, but there is no mistaking the appeal of the tall, broad-shouldered, athletic, smiling, young ballplayer in the picture. Mother loved baseball, and I suspect she loved that handsome Montgomery outfielder, albeit unrequitedly.

To sum up, my mother was an early "airlady" and loved the game of baseball. My obsession with flying and baseball must prove there's truth to the theory of inherited characteristics.

My Sister Charlotte

My sister was the number one student by far in her class at Bass Junior High School. She later majored in mathematics and Latin at Wellesley College in Massachusetts. They were her easiest subjects! I still remember my awe when I, an indifferent student from the start, saw the title on one of the texts she brought home: "Functions of a Complex Variable." Functions of a WHAT?

In spite of our father's pride in Charlotte's academic prowess, the two of them were not friends. Charlotte smoked Camel cigarettes from the time she was 16 until her difficult, lingering death from emphysema some six decades later. Dad hated her smoking and made his feelings plain. I can still hear him: "Charlotte, there's nothing more pleasing in a father's life than to kiss his beautiful daughter. But when I kiss you, instead of a beautiful, dainty young girl, I think I'm kissing a smelly old Camel."

The only good that came from Charlotte's smoking was that I never smoked, except for a brief romance with a pipe, which I found to require far too much attention. Also, as a teenager I didn't have the guts to stand up to my father's awesome disapproval.

My own relationship with my sister wasn't without its strains. Charlotte always complained to me, "You're Daddy's favorite — he let's you do anything you want and gives you all you ask for and more." Many years later she was still accusing me, and I had had enough. "Charlotte," I said, "you're right to some extent about Dad favoring me, but that wasn't always the case. He took me out of Marist, where I was doing great, and dumped me in Boys High, where I floundered. He couldn't afford to keep you at Wellesley and me at Marist. You were the one favored, and it hurt my academic career in high school and damaged my self-confidence for years." Charlotte looked away and said nothing. She never again brought up how our father's favoritism toward me had blighted her life.

Regardless of Dad's feelings toward Charlotte, none of her suitors were good enough for him. One visit to our house by a young man, squirming under Dad's glaring disapproval, was usually enough to send even the most dauntless and ardent away for good. Charlotte lost her confidence and had a miserable social life until she went north to Wellesley. There she met a Harvard Law student, Roman Weil, from Montgomery, Ala. They pursued their courtship to the point that Roman neglected his books and, in spite of his evident intelligence, was expelled from Harvard. He later earned his law degree from the University of Alabama. Our father didn't approve of Roman – but by then, Charlotte was her own woman. She and Roman were married in 1938.

At first Roman didn't take to me, that "brat of a younger brother." I borrowed his Pontiac one Sunday and, cutting too close as I turned into our driveway, hit the curb, and scuffed one of the tires. Roman saw what I'd done and wasn't pleased. I never touched his car again.

By some turn of the wheel of chance, during World War II Roman and I were stationed together on Majuro, an atoll in the Pacific Marshall Islands. He was a decoding officer and I was a pilot. He was a lieutenant. I was a captain. So I outranked him, and pilots only tolerated ground officers. No longer was I "that brat," and we became friends.

A Look Back In Time

This is as timely a place as any to invoke my ancestry. A few years ago I was interviewed by a former managing editor of the *Washington Post,* Howard Simon, who was, at that time, the holder of a Nieman Fellowship at Harvard. I told him, mostly in jest, that I was 15 before I realized everybody had ancestors. My family's misplaced pride in our forebears made me think we were singularly blessed.

Abraham Alexander was the first Alexander to come to America, emigrating from London to Charleston, South Carolina, in 1760. There he became the reader in the Sephardic synagogue, Kahal Kadosh Beth Elohim (Beth Elohim for short), which in the early nineteenth century would become the birthplace of Reform Judaism in the U.S. (I gave his beautiful prayer book, lettered by his own hand in Hebrew, to Emory University for safekeeping, and it can be borrowed for family weddings, funerals, and Bar and Bat Mitzvahs.) Abraham became a lieutenant in the Continental Army and fought the British until they took Charleston, made his peace with them, and then later resumed the fight against King George III's forces. I suppose he wanted to be with the winners – an admirable goal, I think.

A mural painted by William Melton Halsey, depicting Abraham in uniform with a book in one hand and the American flag in the other, is on the wall at the entrance to Beth Elohim. Abraham was collector of the Port of Charleston, and with seven other Charlestonians established the Mother Council of Scottish Rite Masonry in America. I have seen his gravesite in the Cumming Street Cemetery in Charleston. His wife, an Irby and a devout converted Jew, was denied burial there; her conversion didn't satisfy the congregation of Beth Elohim, owners of the cemetery.

Abraham Alexander, Jr. came over and joined his father after the Revolution. I have a copy of his naturalization document. His descendents included Aaron Alexander, who moved to Atlanta, then called Terminus, in 1848. Aaron was against the secession of the South. His two sons, Julius and Jacob, deferring to their father's stand, didn't join the Confederate Army until Sherman drove his army into Georgia. Aaron, with his state invaded by a ruthless enemy and his home, family, and he himself gravely threatened, gave his blessing to his sons' decision to enlist.

Julius and Jacob fought Sherman's army near Savannah. After the war they returned to Atlanta and opened the J. M. and J. C. Alexander Hardware Store – which my father, Jacobs's son, finally closed in 1946 when he lost his lease and no alternative space could be found.

My knowledge of the earliest days of Moses family, my mother's family, is limited. The first of her ancestors came to America in 1651. One ancestor, Maj. Raphael Moses, was on the staff of the Confederate general James Longstreet and was engaged in the Battle of Gettysburg. Another ancestor was Isaiah Moses (I have an oil portrait of him), who had a 700-acre plantation at Goose Creek, near Charleston, which was, to my deep regret, worked by some 50 slaves.

1923: My Annus Horribilis

Enough about ancestors — they interest me but make me neither better nor worse. In recalling the year of my fifth birthday, I will borrow a lament from Queen Elizabeth, who described the year when several members of her family divorced and Windsor Castle caught fire as "our annus horribilis," or year of disaster or misfortune.

Two events hit me hard on what now seems a day I was fated to be hurt. We were at my grandmother's apartment for noon dinner. My sister and her friend locked the glass-paneled door to the porch, leaving me shut inside. Yelling and stomping brought no results, so I rammed my fist through a glass pane. There was no blood, just shards of glass scattered about.

In light of what happened when I went home, it might have been better if I had cut myself badly; then I might not have fallen from the top of a three-legged stool I was balancing on in our back yard. The fall crushed my left elbow. Screaming, I was carried into the house and put on my bed with the mangled elbow across a pillow.

Two operations and six months in a cast later, I was ready for rehabilitation. A Dickinsonian, kindly older man, Mr. Kubler, came three times a week to gradually (and painfully) straighten my arm and help it regain mobility. The candy bars he brought me helped — some.

My father saw the long ordeal as a fine opportunity. I was born left-handed, which he regarded as a deficiency surely inherited from my mother's side. He seized on the condition to turn me into a right-hander, and by the end of the year he had succeeded. No longer did I start writing with my left hand; I was now almost "normal." I still perform some of the things I had learned to do before I broke my arm with my left hand like sawing, hammering, and cutting with scissors. (I must have been hell on the furniture as a left-handed preschooler.)

Dr. Michael Hoke, an orthopedic surgeon who had a national reputation, performed a second operation on my elbow. He told my parents that the "carrying angle" on my arm was wrong and that he couldn't correct it. I would always have a crooked arm with some loss of function. Much more upsetting was his statement that the break, in three places, occurred in the growth center, and that I might mature with a withered arm.

My parents kept this diagnosis from me. And thank god I didn't know! I went on to box, wrestle, swim, play basketball, baseball, and pilot a Marine

16

plane in World War II combat, all as a right-hander. But I have no doubt I would have done better in athletics as a left-hander.

After I recovered, my father signed me up for boxing lessons at the old downtown Atlanta Athletic Club. Joe Bean, my instructor, would counter my punches while down on his knees. His boxing gloves were huge, soft pillows that inflicted no pain. If I managed to hit his face, he would pop his set of false teeth out onto the floor, much to his delight and my disgust.

The second and the most serious trauma I suffered in 1923 was in no way physical. That miserable year my name was changed, and I'll now briefly outline the history of my uncle Henry A. (Harry) Alexander and how I came to be renamed.

We were at war in Europe in 1918, the year I was born. Uncle Harry, a bachelor, was a captain in the U.S. Army and was scheduled to take his company into the trenches of France. To give him some sense of immortality should he not return from that horrible and bloody conflict, my parents named their newborn son – me – Henry Aaron Alexander in his honor. Just before he was scheduled to embark for Europe, my uncle broke his knee in a training accident. He never shipped out, but instead spent the war teaching machine-gun school in upstate New York. After the war he resumed to his practice as a highly respected attorney. A case came to him involving documents written in Russian. An ad in the paper seeking a translator brought forth a beautiful young woman – Marian Klein, a native of Lithuania who was studying dentistry in Atlanta. She did the translating and subsequently, in an ending worthy of a storybook romance, married Harry. Their marriage, however, didn't prove to be a storybook union, and I'm not sure love was involved. Years later, in her lingering Lithuanian accent, Marian lamented to me, "All Harry ever vanted from me vas sons."

She quickly produced one for him. My father said to his brother, "Harry, I'm going to change my boy Henry's name to mine – Cecil. It will be too confusing if he has your name, and your son will feel he's lost his birthright." At first Uncle Harry would have none of it – he named his firstborn Kedrin, a name of Welsh origins. Still, Dad went ahead with the change. I officially became Cecil Abraham Alexander, Jr. and Kedrin became Henry Aaron Alexander.

I was stunned. I was furious. I was beyond solace. At age 5, a kid is just beginning to know who he is, and his name is a precious part of that awareness. Now I was lost. My mother's consolation didn't help. She said, "When I married your father, I took his name because I loved him. You love your father, too, so you should be glad to have his name." If I had had the Marine vocabulary I acquired later, the air would have been wet with juicy expletives.

My cousin was called Henry, but when he sought his birth certificate to join the Marines during World War II he found he was still officially Kedrin; his father had been so busy making a fortune he had never legally changed my cousin's name to Henry. Years later I jokingly told Henry, with some truth, "I don't mind that you took my name. It's the sizeable inheritance that would've been mine I feel bad about."

Unbelievably, that horrible year had still more in store. My father, full of ambition for me, had persuaded my mother– who, as I wrote, had been a grammar school teacher– to instruct me so that age 6 I could jump ahead to the second grade in public school. And as a 5-year old, I wasn't pleased. My screams were so prodigious when I was ordered to study that Mother decided some degree of benign neglect was the best course.

In spite of my resistance I learned some basic reading, writing, and arithmetic – enough that after two weeks in the first grade I was promoted to the second grade at Highland Grammar School, much to my parents' pleasure.

It was a disaster. The second graders, none of whom I knew, resented my presence and taunted me. Having been well ahead of the first graders, I struggled to catch up with this group. The teacher expected superior performance from me, but I couldn't deliver. That terrible start to my schooling blighted my academic efforts all through grammar school – a convenient excuse, at least, for my lackluster report cards.

To sum up, in one year I badly broke my arm, was switched from left- to-right handed, lost my given name, and collapsed scholastically. Perhaps all this explains my occasional erratic behavior and my inability to spell. To reprise once more Queen Elizabeth's lament as tragedy pursued her – my fifth year was my "annus horribilis."

Atkins Park Days

Despite the travails that sometimes afflicted my childhood, Atkins Park was an ideal place to grow up. It was a neighborhood on the rise, and I'm sure that inspiration to become an architect developed as I watched houses materialize from holes in the ground to wood frames to brick exteriors topped with slate or tile roofs. I scavenged building sites for discarded 2 x 4 studs, broad planks, and nails and assembled this scrap into a small, rickety clubhouse in my backyard.

A great gift came to me once: a damaged double-hung window that couldn't be used in a new house. It was given to me by one of the contractors, and it shed both light and joy in my clubhouse. He also gave me roofing shingles that kept my friends and me more or less dry.

St. Charles Place, my street, was wide and straight. At either end, grandiose granite columns flanked of the street, proclaiming – and incised in the stone – the exclusivity of Atkins Park. A low curving wall extended from the columns, forming a semi-circular court facing Highland Avenue. On long summer nights my young friends and I sat on those walls and told each other lies while searching for answers to unanswerable questions.

Bordering the street on both sides were plots of grass about 10 feet wide. The developer had planted fast-growing but fragile Lombardy poplars in the plots, and almost every time a severe storm blew in one or more of these slim giants crashed down. Our lot wasn't spared, and Dad replaced two fallen poplars with sugar maples. Later, in an attempt to get free maple syrup, I drove a huge nail (a spike, really), into one of the tree trunks and used the claw of the hammer to pull out the spike with great difficulty. No maple syrup gushed out – not even a drip. I almost killed the tree with that spike.

Beside the grass plots was a wide sidewalk. Great for running, skating, and bicycling, the walk left every pedestrian for himself. The houses, some of them bungalows, were well built, architect-designed, had brick exteriors, and were mostly two-story. All the houses backed up to an alley shared with houses on the next street over.

Over the years the alleys became relatively soft, rounded humps as ashes from all the furnaces along the street were thrown out on what were originally level surfaces. My counselor at camp, an All-American end and track star named Vernon "Catfish" Smith, gave me a pair of his discarded track shoes. Running swiftly on the forgiving ashes in the mellow twilight, I once felt I was flying several feet above the alleyway, an unforgettable, mystical memory.

At the west end of Atkins Park's residential streets, across Highland Avenue, was a line of businesses that including two drugstores, four groceries (one was a Piggly Wiggly made famous in the movie *Driving Miss Daisy*), a shoe repair shop, a hardware store, an ice cream parlor, and a neighborhood movie theater. When I was 15, the theater manager paid me a pittance to draw pastel, larger-than -life portraits of the reigning movie stars, the likes of Clark Gable, Gary Cooper, Anna Sten, Jean Harlow, Douglas Fairbanks, Joan Crawford, and my special favorite, Claudette Colbert.

My mother regularly shopped at this strip that sat only half a block away from our house, pulling my little red wagon behind her. Once. when she visited her wealthy cousin Adeline Moses Loeb in Westchester County, N. Y., she listened in awed silence while her cousin discussed grocery shopping with friends, all of whom seemed to have a Rolls Royce, Cadillac, Lincoln, or Pierce Arrows and a chauffeur to do the lifting. My little red wagon was totally outclassed, and Mother kept silent. In later years we owned a Pierce Arrow and had a chauffeur, but the red wagon remained Mother's vehicle of choice for shopping.

An abundance of kids my age lived in Atkins Park, and four of them remain clearly in my memory. The first was a pretty young girl who was physically mature beyond her age. One afternoon, when I was about to leave after playing checkers with her on her front porch, I impulsively bent down and kissed her lips, leaped up, and ran down the street yelling, "I kissed her! I kissed her!" I'm still embarrassed.

The other three kids were boys. The scourge of the neighborhood – a boy older, tougher and meaner than the rest of us –was the proverbial preacher's kid. He lived behind me on St. Louis Place. His bullying was sophisticated. He continually formed clubs, forced us to join, and then initiated us into its secret sanctuary with brutal hazing. One trial I remember was walking off a plank 6 feet over the cinder-filled alleys behind the Atkins Place, blindfolded with my hands tied behind me. How I escaped with only cuts and bruises from that fall, I don't know.

At one point the bully's nasty attitude toward me suddenly changed. When I learned the cause I was upset and furious. My mother had given him a bicycle I'd abandoned in favor of a new one – an out and out bribe. In effect, she said to him, "I'll give you this bicycle if you'll stop harassing my son."

In spite of this new détente, the preacher's kid and I had an all-out fistfight. Thanks to my enforced boxing lessons, I did better than expected, but it was more or less a standoff. After that he left me alone. As an adult he followed a befitting profession for a sadist – that day's painful dentistry. Instead of using Novocaine to control pain, he used hypnosis. I have no idea how effective this was, since I never opened my mouth near him.

Burke Nicholson lived across the street from me. With our looks, the clothes we wore, and the equal amount of dirt on our faces, we could have been twins; even our mothers seemed confused at times. Burke's father, a former schoolteacher, was the president of a local soft drink company called Nu-Grape. Later he became president of the Coca-Cola Company, appointed by Robert Woodruff to that position.

Dad wouldn't allow a radio in our house; he thought I already had enough distractions from my homework (and he was right.) Burke's folks, however, had a powerful vacuum tube set. Listening was via earphones because there was no speaker. Our favorite program was the "narration" of Atlanta Crackers baseball games. Using the same technique Ronald "Dutch" Reagan used in his early career as a great communicator, the Atlanta announcer read from a telegraphed tape and reported the game as if he were actually there. Sound effects included crowd noise, the crack of the bat, and the ball plopping into the catcher's mitt. In our raging imaginations, Burke and I were actually at the ballpark, a long way from his living room.

One summer my dad bought me a wooden soft drink stand, which we placed close by the street in our driveway (we had no car at the time.) A block and a half away, at the corner of Highland Avenue and Ponce de Leon, a large eight-story apartment building was being erected. It was an ideal place to sell soft drinks to sweating carpenters, bricklayers, and other workmen. Unfortunately, the building was across Highland Avenue from St. Charles Place, and I wasn't allowed to cross the heavily traveled street. So I employed Burke for this adventurous mission.

One hot July day we loaded my red wagon – the same one my mother used for shopping – with all kinds of soft drinks: ginger ale, Nu-Grape, Payday (a real belly-washer), Moxie, and Coca-Cola. I dispatched Burke, with a pocketful of coins to make change, to the rising apartment building (he either had permission to cross Highland or more likely had never asked.) The thirsty workers bought him out. I neglected to tell him to bring back the empty bottles, so my profit evaporated.

Every boy should have a Bill Edwards in his life. Across the street and a few houses down lived Bill, who was several years older than I. Handsome and athletic he wasn't, but creative and intelligent he was – and to an extraordinary degree. Bill was also an organizer and a leader. Every Christmas, after the holiday day itself had passed, he asked all the kids in the neighborhood to bring their Lionel and American Flyer toy trains, engines, cars, and tracks to his house. We would then lay out an extensive rail system through every room in the one-story dwelling. As she went about her household duties, Bill's mother had to step over and around the tracks, careful not to knock over a miniature train running under her skirt. I don't know how she put up with it.

Bill led us into many other projects as well. We built crystal radio sets and were proud when we could hear music or voices through the crackling static from a station in Cincinnati. This was followed with powerful vacuum tube sets built from mail-order kits; when the atmosphere was right, we could even pick up European broadcasts. Under Bill's leadership we built a miniature town in his backyard, complete with paved streets and sidewalks, street lights, model trees, telephone poles, office buildings, stores, and houses.

Bill also invented a football game, which we played on a carpet in his house. The "ball" was a stitched-up wad of cotton. The defending "team" was made of small cardboard simulations of live "players." The flicking, thumping of boys' fingers represented the team on the offense. It was primitive compared with today's video games, but no less absorbing, much more active, and far less violent. Bill even looked after our fitness, organizing boxing and wrestling matches and long-distance runs around neighborhood streets.

Bill Edwards later studied electrical engineering at Georgia Tech, but he ended up practicing as a consulting structural engineer. His firm, Armstrong & Edwards, would consult with FABRAP, my architectural firm, on many projects. I know Edwards didn't realize his potential, since he had the makings of a Marconi, an Edison, or a president of MIT.

My Eye-Opening Trip to Chicago

Still another young man helped shaped my life, even though I spent only two weeks with him. In the summer of 1932, when I was 14, a magical curtain parted before me, and a wide, challenging vista came into view. My Dad decided to send me to the Century of Progress Fair in Chicago after learning the mother of my Savannah cousins was going to the Fair with her sons.

But it was not to be: "No," was the ungracious answer when my mother asked my aunt if I could go with them; she preferred going with only her two boys. After this stinging turndown an arrangement was made for me to go alone and stay with a Chicagoan. That "no" closed a door and opened a floodgate, turning what could have been an ordinary trip into an extraordinary learning experience.

Somehow, somebody found a graduate student studying chemistry at the University of Chicago who would be available to guide me through the Fair. The student, Ed Gruskin, lived with his widowed mother in a lakefront apartment. An extra room in their home would house me during my stay, with breakfast as part of the deal. So off I went alone, by train, to the Windy City on the shore of Lake Michigan. Gruskin met an anxious and nervous me at the station.

We went to the Fair that first afternoon. I found the garish jumble of colors on the haphazardly laid-out modern buildings unpleasing to the eye. The famous 1893 Chicago Fair, the so-called White City, with its classical buildings grouped around a large symmetrical pool and known to me only in pictures, was my conception of a fair. I was expecting a similar design 40 years later.

That all changed at night, when thousands of lights illuminated the buildings and their surrounding landscapes. The transformation from daytime ugliness to nighttime beauty was magical.

The Fair could be enjoyed on three levels. If the visitor wanted only entertainment, it was there in abundance. Sally Rand, the famous "Fan Dancer," was the number-one attraction. She moved rhythmically to catchy music around a small stage, waving several large ostrich-tail feathers formed into two fans. She adroitly manipulated these feathery semi-obstructions to give only quick, tantalizing glimpses of her allegedly naked body. Rumor had it that censors forced her to wear flesh-colored body stocking. If so, it didn't bother the huge, wide-eyed, cheering male audiences she attracted.

There was also a Midway with all of the usual gimmicks. One night Ed and I stopped to watch a clown being repeatedly knocked off a high seat into a pool of water. Every time the customer hit a small metal target with a baseball, a gong sounded and down went the clown. He would scramble back to his perch to await his next splash. Hits on the small steel plate were rare, but a crowd had gathered to watch one customer who, time after time, hit the target with a fastball. Shaking like a wet dog and hawking water out of his nose and mouth, the clown slowly climbed back to his chair, only to be dunked again.

The owner of the exhibit watched with increasing alarm. "Bud," he said to the man throwing the bullets, "that's enough. You're going to drown my man. Here's five bucks of your money back. Please go somewhere else. Say, how the hell did you get to throw like that?"

"Well," the hotshot answered, "I'm going to pitch for the Chicago Cubs. My name's Hugh Casey."

Good lord, I thought, I caught that guy on the sandlots in Atlanta. I pushed my way to him through the now laughing crowd and tapped him on the shoulder.

"Hugh," I said, "remember me? Cecil Alexander? I caught you a couple of times at Piedmont Park."

He looked at me blankly and then recovered.

"Yeah, sure. How are you?"

I knew he was wondering, "Who the hell is this guy?" We later saw him walking toward the gate, carrying an almost life-sized stuffed teddy bear. "Hey Hugh," I yelled, "Where'd you get the bear?" "Oh," he laughed, "I just knocked over a lot of wooden bottles with a baseball." Casey had a good career pitching for Chicago and Washington.

The most popular radio show in those days was *Amos and Andy*, its eponymous characters played by two white actors with exaggerated black accents. Every night of the week, the country turned on the radio, stopped household chores, and listened intently to this outrageously funny farce, featuring a collection of fake black friends and co-conspirators who hatched many failed schemes. Only one of these characters' names remains with me – the pompous and well-titled Kingfish.

On the fairgrounds were two widely spaced 700-foot tall steel towers – one called Amos, the other Andy. High-speed elevators carried customers to the viewing platforms at the top, where spectacular views of Lake Michigan and Chicago spread out below. About a fourth of the way up, six or eight double-decker gondolas hung from a thick cable, circling from tower to tower. Painted in bold letters on the side of each gondola was the name of a secondary character from the show.

Both the *Amos and Andy* radio show and the TV series that followed are considered exceedingly incorrect today, but 80 years ago the towers and gondolas attracted thousands of people waiting in long lines, eager to get to the top. And, yes, Ed and I went to the top of "Amos" and rode in a gondola with "Kingfish" painted on both sides.

If these attractions were too arduous, one could just amble along the walks, look at the flowers, or lounge on a bench while listening to the public address system play melodies like the popular song "Stormy Weather," proclaiming, "Life is bare, gloom and mis'ry everywhere, stormy weather ..." It was a most appropriate anthem for the Great Depression then sapping the nation's spirit.

An alternative was to hurry through buildings including the Hall of Science and the spectacular Transportation Building, giving a swift cursory glance at the exhibits. It gave this lazy observer a false sense that he knew all about what constituted the progress made in the last century.

Then there was the third level of experiencing the Fair, which brought a much deeper understanding of what had been accomplished before and what the future could hold. With the brilliant, about-to-be-a chemist Ed Gruskin as my tutor, I absorbed the well-executed displays of engineering and scientific principles. Chemical experiments took place before our eyes as mechanical arms behind a glass plate poured various liquids into vials, creating new chemicals. Levers, cogs, gears, and pulleys demonstrated mechanical devices and the effects of momentum, centrifugal force, and gravity. Another display was somewhat grim: vertical slices of human body parts pressed between sheets of glass, each with a detailed description.

Seeing such exhibitions was an enlightening experience for me, thanks to Ed's explanations. He changed my direction. He awakened in me unsuspected ambition and a driving curiosity. I told him I thought my grades, which had been lousy, would reflect his enthusiasm in the future. They did, but only in the courses that interested me.

With no modesty at all, but also because I had nothing to do with my genes, I recall here his appraisal of my intellect: "Cecil," he said, "Forget the bad grades. You are brilliant." Proving his assessment has been a challenge all my life, a goal I've never met.

My lessons continued outside the fairgrounds. Ed took me to the huge old Museum of Science and Industry, where we studied the exhibits in the same penetrating way we had at the Fair.

One clear night we went to Soldier's Field, Chicago's classic football stadium on Lakeshore Drive. The attraction was the projected launching of a huge hydrogen-filled balloon. It was hoped it would rise into the little-understood stratosphere. The airless fabric bag, half a football field in length, lay stretched out on the grass. Liftoff was scheduled for 11 p.m. Gas from a battery of green cylinders was just beginning to fill the balloon when we arrived. It was a slow process, and not until the early morning hours was the bag sufficiently inflated to rise many feet into the air, its shrouds still anchored to the ground.

The balloonist, Cmdr. T. G. W. ("Tex") Settle (USN), squeezed through a small porthole into a spherical aluminum ball attached to the balloon. This gondola would carry him aloft along with many instruments and life-sustaining oxygen canisters. He waved to the crowd still in the stands and closed his entrance port lid with a clang.

When the "Cast off!" order was given, members of the ground crew released the taut cables. Slowly the huge balloon rose, a gleaming white envelope caught in the beams of searchlights. At high altitudes, where the outside air pressure is greatly reduced, the hydrogen gas would expand and push the sides of the bag into a perfect sphere.

A cheer went up as the balloon was released, but suddenly all was silent. At about 3,000 feet began to drift inland over the Illinois Central railroad tracks running close by Soldier Field. A murmur rose from the crowd as we saw a large white plume of hydrogen escaping from a valve. Slowly the craft lost altitude and disappeared from view as it settled and collapsed on the tracks. The electric engines of the commuter trains were powered through an overhead heavy copper wire, and I listened anxiously for an explosion as hydrogen hit the wires. None came. The commander climbed out – uninjured.

Commander Settle (whose name was unfortunately much too appropriate that night in Chicago) later went on to a successful record ascent into the stratosphere. And I learned a valuable truth: a simple malfunction of a minor element – in this case, a release valve left open – can doom the most thoroughly planned operation.

That insight went with me when I later piloted planes. My careful inspections of my aircraft sometimes revealed conditions that, if uncorrected, could wreak havoc or worse. Perhaps I even overdid it, since one my friends dubbed me "Ole In Case Of."

At any rate, I returned home from the Chicago Century of Progress Fair as a more mature adolescent, one ready to look beyond my everyday existence into a fabulous world of discovery.

Religion, Sex, and Catholic School

I remember four other Jewish families in Atkins Park. Across the street from us were the Gordons, who had two sons. Sam and I were the same age and spent many boyhood hours together. Jack, his younger brother, was rarely invited to join us.

One street over, on St. Louis, were two very pretty Jewish girls. Elizabeth and I were in the same second grade class. When I lost interest in the droning flow from my teachers, I drifted off into the precocious sexual fantasies of a 7-year-old's imagination.

The third family was the Aaronstams, whose house was close to our own. Their son Charles and I were close friends and spent many hours together playing cards, sandlot baseball, or football when we weren't pedaling our bicycles around the neighborhood.

All of us were members of The Temple, the Jewish Reform Congregation. And all of us tried to fit in smoothly with our Christian friends. We all had Christmas trees, and Santa Claus came to our houses.

Christmas at 1111 St. Charles Place was a secular affair, and we had every Christmas traditions and trapping except Jesus. The celebration included a Christmas tree; stockings hung by the chimney with care; a visit from St. Nick (who decorated the tree, left an abundance of toys, and always consumed the milk and cookies put out for him and left a few crumbs on the rug); a huge family dinner of turkey with all the fixin's'; and joyful exchanges of "Merry Christmas" among all the family and the servants. All that was missing was a wreath on the front door and an angel atop the tree; the angel was too Christian, my folks said, and the wreath might confuse the neighbors.

On Christmas Eve a bare tree was set up in the living room, whose curtained French doors were tightly closed until Christmas morning. During the agonizing wait for my grandmother and her dear sister to arrive, my mother brought my stocking out of the living room, its contents a minor prelude, I knew, to what waited for me under the tree. Apples and oranges were always stuffed into the toe of the stocking; I ignored those and never pulled them out.

After several hours that seemed to me days, the front door bell rang – my smiling grandmother and my great-aunt, both in their crinkly black dresses, were here! Their coats and hats were carefully removed and hung with due ceremony in the closet. Now all was ready.

The doors to the living room were thrown open and I rushed in. Santa had been there! Magic! The uninspiring tree of the night before now sparkled with glass baubles, tinsel, and yards of glowing rope. Around the base lay the toys I'd asked for in my letters to Santa. From year to year they varied – electric trains, baseballs, bats, gloves, erector sets, checkers, a toy automobile I could drive, books (*Tom Swift and His Electric Rifle* was a favorite), model airplane kits, and one glorious year a shiny red bicycle. Not greeted with enthusiasm were shirts, socks, caps, and other necessities.

I believed in Santa for a few years after I should have known better – but it's no wonder I hung on. For one thing, Charlotte had been warned not to straighten me out. "We are Jewish," Dad told her. "When Santa goes, Christmas and the presents go." My sister was an eager member of the conspiracy to keep me a believer, and took her job seriously. Dad was right. Things were never the same after Santa bid us his last "Merry Christmas to all and to all a good night!"

During my extended Santa phase, one of my Baptist friends said to me, "Cecil, you're stupid to still think there's a Santa Claus. He doesn't exist. Your parents lied to you."

"Well, Jim," I said, "you believe in Jesus and I don't. I believe in Santa Claus and you don't. Let's leave it at that." My parents later told me they could hardly contain their laughter as I told them of this exchange.

Jim was hardly my only non-Jewish friend, and no anti-Semitism was directed at me when I was a child. But in high school I was turned down for membership in several fraternities because I was Jewish. It didn't bother me, though – I would have dreaded the hazing had I been I accepted.

Then there was that inevitable concern of adolescence – sex. Growing up in Atlanta I spent preadolescence with virtually no accurate knowledge on the subject. My father, a strict Victorian, never mentioned it. This innocence of a 12-year-old was shared by all of my friends. What little knowledge we had was picked up on the street corner, where we exchanged misinformation and wild rumors. One long-debated subject was determining from which passage in the mother's body a baby entered the world. It was generally accepted by us that babies came through the mother's navel.

A discussion I had with a Catholic friend almost ended our friendship when told him what I knew about the creation of babies, He recoiled in horror. "I don't believe you," he said. "That can't be. My parents are both good, God-fearing Catholics, and they would never fuck!" He was, I think, the same kid who told me that clouds were bags full of rainwater, so his ignorance wasn't limited to sex.

My first inkling of the joy of sex came in a most unromantic way. I think I was 10. I was climbing a pole in a neighborhood park, my legs wrapped tightly around it as I worked my way up with my hands. Halfway up I was suddenly overwhelmed by an excruciatingly wonderful sensation that seemed to rush from around my legs to my brain. I let go of my grip and slid down the pole. Several minutes passed before I had recovered enough from the wonder of it all to walk home. I think I knew it was something forbidden, something to do with sex. At any rate, I didn't dare tell my parents what I had experienced.

The widely accepted method of grading the extent of necking a young man was able to achieve with a "nice" girl was based on baseball terminology.

You made it to first base, a single; second base, a double; third base, a triple. And if you were adept at lying to your friends, you could claim a home run. I knew, of course, what constituted a home run, but I don't remember exactly what constituted arriving at first, second, or third base. It did involve, I recall, the extent to which the two of you had disrobed.

It's my opinion that no home runs were ever hit by any of my adolescent peers, despite some boastful claims. Getting to third base, which occasionally did happen, was a totally frustrating experience – you could see home plate, almost feel it, but were stuck at third.

I have a vivid memory of a date after I'd entered college and was home for the summer. A girl and I were in the back seat of a car on the beach at St. Simons Island, Ga., where we were attending a house party. We had been going steady for some time, but this was the first chance for some serious necking. I worked my way around the bases until we were safely at third base – home only 90 feet away. Suddenly my date jerked away and frantically adjusted her clothes.

"No, no," she said. "Stop. Please stop. I'm saving myself for my husband."

I stopped and, after adjusting my own clothes, got behind the wheel and drove her to the beach house where she was staying with her family. For the rest of the house party we made it a point to avoid each other. Our "going steady" days were at an end, terminated by my hormone-activated aggression. I hope her future husband appreciated my forbearance.

It so happened that my frustrating encounter took place on the same day in 1938 that the horrors of World War II erupted in Europe. At the time, I ranked my back-seat experience as just as earthshaking as the beginning of a war. In time I gained a more rational perspective.

Enough of sex. I thought that recalling my early initiations might shed some light on the attitude toward that fascinating subject as I approached manhood in the 1930s. But the rest of my experiences are time-honored, probably differing little from those of the caveman (though perhaps more gentle.) They certainly don't conform to those of the sexual revolution of the Sixties. If I wrote about my own experiences they would bore Generations X and Y – great for me but not newsworthy, perhaps even brushed off as coming from a dumb, naive old fart. So if you wanted to read about sex and the American male, I'm afraid you spent your money most unwisely. And it's all the more reason to take my story back to my early adolescence.

Junior High Confidential

Once I was ready for junior high, I directed my interest to baseball and model airplanes. I was in hot pursuit of a career as an ace pilot who would undoubtedly also play second base, preferably for the Philadelphia Athletics of the American League, my favorite team. When I entered the class taught by the mentor of my older sister Charlotte, the teacher expected the same performance level from her little brother. To put the best light on it, I was a terrible, uninterested, sullen student. I hated the teacher, I hated the studies, and I hated Bass Junior High. My only pleasure there was playing baseball.

From the day of my birth, my father was certain he had produced an Albert Einstein at the very least. After all, hadn't the doctor attending my mother said to him, "Congratulations, Mr. Alexander, it's a boy with a fine big head"? He didn't say what might be in that head, but my father was sure it was bulging with brains.

When my year at Bass turned into a fiasco, my father knew it had to be the fault of the school, not his genius offspring. At that time there was (and still is) an excellent Catholic educational institution in Atlanta — Marist School, then called Marist College and operated as an all-male military day school. Protestants and Jews were welcomed, and there was absolutely no effort to convert the non-Catholics. The faculty of Marist was, with one exception, made up of priests — men whom I believe were far more dedicated to teaching than to their religion.

The one lay teacher was Prof. McHuen, who taught seventh grade. His Irish brogue clearly identified him as a true son of Dublin, sprung from the old sod where he was born. My father and I met with him in his grubby, ancient, dark classroom. After a lengthy interview dominated by the professor's penetrating questions and my tentative answers, Mr. McHuen turned to my concerned father and said, "Not to worry, Mr. Alexander, if we can't teach him, we will LEARN him!"

Much to my surprise, I was put in the eighth grade instead of having to repeat the seventh. The eighth-grade teacher was Fr. Sullivan, a former major league ballplayer — a great plus for me. Sullivan's love of teaching lit up his classroom with enthusiasm and joy, and I responded well.

By the time I finished the ninth grade — this time under Fr. Emmeth — I was succeeding. With two good years behind me, I had become a scholar: I was on the Dean's List. I also wrote and drew cartoons for the school newspaper,

I'd been promoted to sergeant in the ROTC, I had won a sharp shooting medal on the rifle range. And, above all else, I was slated to be the varsity second baseman the next year.

One incident stays with me. When I was an eighth-grader at Marist, a boy who had just moved to Atlanta from New York was having a hard time: Because of some of his physical mannerisms he was taunted as being a fairy ("fairy" being an old term for "homosexual".) One day after school he was almost in tears, and he took me aside.

"Cecil, I'm having a terrible time here. The guys all kid me and keep calling me a fairy. I'm not. I like girls. Why do they call me that?"

"Francis," I said (his name didn't help), "the main reason is the way you walk. You walk almost on tiptoe and you swing your hips from side to side. It looks almost exactly like the way a girl walks."

"Yeah," he said. "Can you please help me to walk like a man?" "Sure," I said. "I'll try."

For several weeks he came almost daily to my house after school, and we worked on his gait. Finally his stride would have made John Wayne envious. We also worked on his hand gestures, and I advised him to try out for boxing. He did, and made the team as a lightweight. The taunts stopped, and he was accepted as one of the guys. He was straight, but how many of my classmates were not I will never know. (In those days, anyone who "came out of the closet" would be treated as a carrier of the Black Plague.) Nor did I suspect any of the priests; not a single one of them ever made a pass at me.

Just after those two very fine years at Marist I was hit by a devastating blow. The country was deep in the Great Depression. My father hadn't bought a suit in three years. Rather than pay for dental work, he had neglected his teeth, which were full of painful cavities. He took no vacations. His hardware store was a loser. "That store," he said, "is a bottomless hole into which I pour money." He kept the store open only to provide a living for his five old employees; otherwise they would go broke and reduced to panhandling on the street. Back then there was no such thing as unemployment insurance.

"Cecil," Dad said, "I'm distressed to say this, but I can't afford to keep you in Marist. It takes all I can muster to pay your sister's tuition and other expenses at Wellesley. You'll have to transfer to Boys High, the public school. It's a good school. You'll be fine."

My relationship with Marist resurfaced years later. I was a member of the school's lay board for twelve years. During that time I served on a committee charged with finding a suburban location for the school, which for many years had been situated downtown on Ivy Street. My firm was retained to plan the new campus and design its initial buildings. My personal contribution was the stained glass windows clerestory windows recovered from the old Marist building downtown.

During my first years on the board, Fr. Vincent Brennan was Marist's headmaster. I liked and admired him. After Fr. Brennan's retirement, Gene Asher, a friend of mine, interviewed him for a local publication called *The Jewish Georgian*. The good Father, perhaps in deference to the publication's readership, cited two Jews as Marist's "most famous graduates." One was Bert Parks, né Jacobson, a radio personality, an actor in many movies, a star on Broadway, and a fixture on television with CBS – he was best known as the long-time MC of the Miss America Pageant. The second most famous alumnus, to my amazement, was me. I'm not in Bert's league: he had millions of fans and was truly famous, and I haven't had even fifteen minutes of fame. While at Marist, Bert won all the elocution competitions. His recitation of *Spartacus to the Gladiators* stood all your hair on end, especially when he recited, "Hear your lions roaring in their dens? 'Tis ten long days since they have tasted food, but tomorrow they will feed on your flesh – and what a dainty meal ye will make!"

Now back to my school days at Boys High. Although the school was in easy walking distance of St. Charles Place, there was a still quicker way to get there. An hour before school started I would go to the corner of Highland and Ponce de Leon Avenue, where I would step onto Ponce and wield the ride-thumbing gesture made famous by Clark Gable in the comedy *It Happened One Night*. Only when Claudette Colbert raised her skirt to expose her beautiful leg did a car stop, brakes screeching. Since Claudette wasn't available, I had to rely on my thumb, which was usually sufficient.

In a few minutes a car would stop, always with a man driving, and the following conservation, with slight variations, ensued. "Hi kid, get in, where're you goin'?"

"Boys High. Please let me out where the train trestle crosses Ponce at the Ford Plant, Sears, and the ballpark."

"Sure, but wouldn't Monroe Drive be closer? "Yeah, but I walk the railroad tracks to Virginia Avenue. Boys High is nearby. It's much more interesting."

What I didn't tell him was that as I walked the tracks a slow moving freight train would often rumble up behind me. I'd step off the tracks, run along at the speed of the train, grab a steel rung of a boxcar ladder, and hoist myself up. Hanging on, I would ride to school and drop myself off. I didn't tell my parents, who would've been emphatically opposed.

The most unforgettable teacher at Boys High was a chemistry teacher named Heichew. Out of his hearing, we labeled him Dr. Sneeze. He was a zealous arm waver and vehement desk pounder, and to emphasize his point one day he smashed his fist hard against the top of his steel desk. He abruptly turned white and held up his formless right hand with his still-functioning left. "Boys, he said, I seem to have broken my hand. You're dismissed." For the next month he wore a cast. The injury didn't modify his hair-trigger temper, and his high-pitched yells were constantly heard in his classroom and echoing through the corridors.

I wish I could say that by 1936 my three years at Boys High were nothing for even Mr. Heichew to sneeze at, but they were uninspired. Here's an example of my dismal scholastic performance and the rare compassion shown by an understanding teacher:

In my junior year I was exposed to Latin. Despite two years spent studying the subject at Marist, I found Caesar's division of all Gaul into three parts beyond my comprehension. To my astonishment, my teacher, Mr. Fort, passed me with a grade of 75. After my mother had irrevocably signed my report card, I asked my amiable teacher to explain his grading. "Mr. Fort," I said, "on the two tests you gave me I made 40 on one and 35 on the other. How did I get a 75?" Mr. Fort grinned. "I added your two test grades together, and they came to 75. I forgot to divide by two. Any problem?" I had none.

Boys High was an excellent school for many students, but not for me. I never came close to the record I made a Marist. The principal, H.O. Smith, came down from the Harvard faculty, and his goal was to put Boys High on the same intellectual plane with Taft, Hotchkiss, Andover, and the other top Eastern prep schools. Any success he had in achieving his dreams certainly wasn't thanks to my presence.

I'm amazed I have degrees from Yale and Harvard. How did I get them? Yale must have thrown aside my grade transcripts from Boys High and admitted me on my very good record at Georgia Tech. Yale did, however, require me to repeat freshman year.

The Elephant in the Room

There was one huge blemish on my upbringing that I accepted without question – what in the parlance of today would be would be called "the elephant in the room." My father, his friends, the politicians, the religious institution, and most of the whites on the street believed in the patronizing, destructive assumption that the entire black race was inferior to whites in every way. I had no problem then with segregation or the concept of white supremacy – as the Southern way of life had always been, it would always be. Even the blacks found it acceptable, or so I believed.

This was the attitude I took into manhood. It was some eight years before I changed. In Chapter 9, "A Good Ol' Boy Transformed," I trace the four major encounters that changed me from a typical Southerner with a head full of racist assumptions to an active fighter for civil rights.

Chapter 3

Slouching into the World

.

Bright college years with pleasure rife,
The shortest, gladdest years of life.

—Yale college song

"No son, I won't send you to art school; artists starve. I want you to learn a profession so you can make a good living. I'm enrolling you at Georgia Tech." So declared my father. There was no appeal. I registered at the engineering school down on North Avenue in Atlanta in the mechanical engineering program, Class of 1939.

My mother had once taught grammar school in Montgomery, Ala. Of all her students, she said, one named Harold Friedman was the best – a genius, probably. By chance I was placed in his Tech class in chemistry, which was required for mechanical engineering. As brilliant as he was, Dr. Friedman couldn't penetrate my befuddled brain with the rudiments of the formula-loaded course. I looked around for an escape and realized architecture didn't require chemistry. Besides, it would put a pencil in my hand – although not to draw portraits or landscapes but plans and perspectives instead. At Tech, I was as close as I could come to attending an art school.

Sixty years later, after retiring from my firm, I ran into Dr. Friedman. "Harold," I said, "do you know you're responsible for my career as an architect? I don't know whether to thank you or kick you."

He was baffled. "How did I do that? I don't remember us ever discussing your career." I then confessed how I majored in architecture to escape from his chemistry class. "Well," he said, "since you've had a very successful career, I will gladly accept responsibility."

My year at Georgia Tech turned out well. I had top grades in all my courses, even in calculus.

Again, my father intervened.

"Cecil, you've done very well at Tech and I want you to move up to a more prestigious school." He pointed his iron index finger north toward Connecticut as he said, "I want you to transfer to Yale University. A degree from Yale will be a major achievement."

It was my record at Tech, certainly not my lackluster grades in high school, that opened the gates to the Ivy League.

A few months later a letter accepting me into the Class of 1940 arrived. My father was delighted. I was apprehensive. Even the financial warning from the Admissions Office didn't damper his enthusiasm. It stated, "Unless you have one thousand dollars ($1,000) to cover your son's room, board, and tuition annually, do not enroll him." A similar warning today would substitute just over $50,000 for the $1,000. Back then, in the depths of the depression, a Coke cost a nickel, a room at the Waldorf Astoria in New York went for $3.50, and a wool three-piece suit at Brooks Brothers was $17.00. A thousand dollars was a huge sum.

Besides my grades, my religious affiliation was a positive factor. A quota of 5 percent limited the number of Jewish students at Yale. A Southern Jew was preferred to the many applicants from New York because, I'm sure, it was believed a Jew from Atlanta would be "less Jewish" and therefore more acceptable to the 95-percent WASP student body. I wouldn't be accepted today, Jewish or not, because there would be many far more qualified students among the thousands of applicants.

My departure for college had the air of a grand sendoff. There I was at the train station in Atlanta surrounded by family, including my mother and father and my grandmother, uncle, aunt, and cousins. Dressed in their best clothes, they all looked as if they were about to attend a wedding or other formal event.

They had all made the trip to Brookwood Station, then Atlanta's suburban train depot, to see me off on the sleek Southern Crescent that would take me to Pennsylvania Station in New York City on my way to Yale. Brookwood always reminded me of the prized toy station I had when I was 10. I still remember tiny imaginary passengers stepping on board the miniature Lionel train that would transport them to far-flung locations at the other end of our living room.

The Atlanta station was sheathed in dark red brick trimmed with limestone and was topped with a blue slate roof. The main room, about the size of a gracious living room, had two ticket windows. The small waiting rooms were fitted out with long wooden benches with high, curved backs. I say rooms (plural) because, as two signs said, one was for Whites Only and the other for Colored. Today Brookwood is Atlanta's only train station, and those signs from the pre-civil rights era are long gone.

Beyond the ticket room was a short passage to a balcony overlooking the tracks. In the center of the two tracks was a long passenger platform protected by a gabled roof cantilevered from the columns running its entire length. A steep wrought iron stair descended from the balcony to the platform, but my family preferred to ride down in the huge, slow elevator that accommodated passengers' baggage. To reach the platform after descending, the intrepid elevator rider had to cross one set of tracks, which for me always held a sense of danger from a rushing train. Thankfully, I never encountered one.

We waited for the train – the transport that would to take me into the larger world outside Atlanta. I looked at my father and he gave me a smile, his eyes devouring me with a pride I felt was entirely undeserved. Dad was not only well dressed but completely Victorian in manner and attitude. I often thought he managed to look as if he'd been dispatched from central casting to play the part of a senator in some cinematic drama. My mother, quiet and reserved, stood nearby almost in my father's shadow – her usual place.

As we waited, two black "gandy dancers" drove new spikes to re-anchor the steel rails to wooden crossties on one set of tracks in a rhythmical beat. As each swung his sledgehammer from high overhead, he forced out of his lungs a deep grunt, a sound quickly followed by the ring of the steel hammer. When the spike was almost seated, one dancer took over with short taps to drive it home. The other continued tapping the rail to keep the rhythm going. The two would then move on to the next spike and repeat the performance. And a performance it truly was, one that helped move time along as we waited for the train.

All Aboard! (Preferably Clothed)

I finally heard the far-off moan of a train whistle. Coming around the curving tracks was the dark nose of the steam engine, pouring a cascade of black coal-laden smoke into the blue sky. I was 18, but my childhood fears were almost rekindled as this snorting, shrieking mass of steel ran by only a few feet from where I stood. With a clash of metal on metal, it finally ground to a halt.

I was ready to go. Kissing each member of that mob of well-wishers was an embarrassing ordeal. At last I grabbed the handrail and pulled myself on board as the conductor down the platform yelled, "Board! All aboard!"

I stepped back so the porter could put down the steel floor over the steps and close the lower half of the door in the vestibule. Then I came back to the door and stood with a forced smile as soot blew in my face, waving tentatively to my going-away party. My mother and father stood with their arms around each other. Tears made a slow passage down my mother's face. I waved a dutiful goodbye.

The train was loaded with boys and girls headed back east to college. I knew none of them but would make friends with some boys headed for Yale.

Finding my berth, I settled in across from two middle-aged matrons, both impeccably dressed. It may seem strange in a day when travel and everything else is so casual, but in my youth setting out on a trip like this was a grand affair that warranted your best clothes.

Some faint movements in the sleeping berth above caught my eye. Someone was already bedded down for the trip and wasn't greeting his traveling companions. We had just gotten underway when the train lurched into a sharp turn that made all of us clutch for a steady object. Centrifugal force took over, and the sleeper suddenly catapulted outward. In fact, he came tumbling out of the berth to land face up on the laps of the two ladies, who let out screams when they realized the figure stretched across their laps was a young man – totally naked and his gender never in doubt.

This apparition from above squirmed off the ladies' laps and struggled to his feet. He bowed with great dignity, muttered apologies, and then, with the flair of a European dandy, kissed the hand of each of his startled victims. Turning with one fluid motion, he vaulted back into his berth and wasn't seen for the rest of the trip. He too, it turned out, was bound for his first year at Yale. We later met, both of us fully clothed.

Many hours later the train rolled into Pennsylvania Station, an awe-inspiring structure designed by the renowned architects McKim, Mead & White.

The soaring vaults of the magnificent waiting and ticketing areas were inspired by the Roman baths at Caracalla. Years later the wrecking ball would break this great building into dust to make way for an uninspired Madison Square Garden, a tragic loss for New York, the nation, and the world.

Although this wasn't my first visit to New York, the city still overwhelmed me. Hailing a cab in the heavy traffic was an adventure in itself. The driver took me to Grand Central Station, where I boarded the New York, New Haven & Hartford Railroad train for New Haven.

I was nervous and apprehensive. Coming from a small Southern city where total strangers greeted each other with "How you doin'?" as they passed on the sidewalk, I didn't know what to expect in the allegedly inhospitable North. But my fears of being ignored at Yale soon disappeared. Under constant prodding from my father, I had drawn a cartoon, which several weeks before my arrival I'd mailed to the *Yale Record,* the campus humor magazine. Three or four years earlier, author Walter B. Pitkin's *Life Begins at Forty* was a bestselling book and had been made into a film starring the great humorist Will Rogers. In an act of semi-plagiarizing, I entitled my drawing, "Life Begins for Forty" – the year my class would graduate. It depicted some bulldogs wearing blankets labeled "Yale '40" standing rather aimlessly in front of the main entrance to the Old Campus.

To my surprise, my cartoon occupied a full page inside the cover of the just-published *Record,* which was distributed all over campus. It was some time before I was recognized as the cartoonist, but the publication of my drawing gave me a shot of self-confidence.

The admissions department had paired me with a roommate named Edgar Cullman, an urbane New Yorker whose old-line Jewish family had built a substantial fortune in the tobacco business. At first he didn't realize I was Jewish, something I would often encounter because of my pug nose and a surname mistakenly perceived as gentile. (Alexander the Great's benevolent attitude toward Jews led many families to adopt his name.) At the time Cullman was going out with Louise Bloomingdale, whose family owned the famous department store. When she invited me to dinner at her apartment, it proved to be a very stiff, formal affair. Butlers in swallow-tailed coats stood around the room and everyone was very reserved. I later heard that the hostess and guests thought I was what today would be called a WASP, but once they found out I was one of their own they relaxed.

Still, Edgar didn't think it was a good idea for two Jews to room together; it would, he thought, appear to his Hotchkiss prep school friends that he wanted to pull away from them and live in a self-styled ghetto. To some extent I shared his feelings. A Jewish friend of mine in Atlanta who was also going to Yale suggested we room together. I turned him down – partly for religious reasons but more because I wanted to meet boys from all over the country and not be stuck with another Atlantan in a small Southern coop.

It was soon evident that Edgar's Hotchkiss buddies (including Henry Ford II) didn't care which religion his roommate professed. They were constantly in and out of our room, either lounging on the sofa while listening to our records or just shooting the breeze. Our group also went out to eat and take in the flicks at the corner movie house. Edgar and I stayed roommates until he and Louise married in our junior year.

For more than 70 years, Edgar and I had a lifetime of friendship and the warmest of feelings for each other. His friendship was one of the most positive factors in my life.

A few years ago I was rifling though stacks of old papers and found a letter from Louise Bloomingdale written to me in 1937, my sophomore year at Yale. It read, in part:

"Personally, Mr. Alexander, Jr., I think your bark is worse than your bite. What is the good of the reading period if you hide away without giving us the benefit of your leisure time? Seriously, stop being a bear and come out of your hibernation. Love, Louise."

After seven-plus decades of hibernation, I awoke and sent the two (not quite newlyweds) the letter. Their many years together enable them to withstand the shock of Louise's ancient overtures to me – they remained married. Neither my bark nor my bite has survived the onslaught of time, so Louise and Edgar could at last relax, forever safe from my snarl and flashing incisors.

Dorm Life, Life Lessons

Although my dormitory, Bingham Hall, was relatively new, it stood in the corner of Old Campus overlooking the New Haven Green, where three old churches stood. The first night I'd gone out to get something to eat at the Taft Hotel, a venerable local establishment across the street from my dorm. When I came back, the huge gate to the campus was locked. I didn't realize I could go down the street and walk right into the quadrangle through Security. So, seeing no other way to get inside, I climbed over the gate, which must have been 12- to 15-feet high and had spikes on top.

As college dorms go, Bingham was probably not unlike many others in the Ivy League – a Gothic-style building with small windows that admitted little light. There was no elevator, which meant walking up five flights of stairs to my room (of course, when you're 18, that's not a big deal.) All the suites were laid out around a central living room with a working fireplace. Off the main room were two smaller rooms, each with a bed and a desk.

One inkling that we were men of privilege (there were no women students at the Ivies in those days) was the presence of maids. These middle-aged ladies, whom we referred to as biddies, arrived each day to clean the suite and make the beds. On my first morning in Bingham I made my own bed. Edgar later told me that bed-making was the maids' job, and I gratefully fell into letting it be done for me.

Edgar soon invited up to his family farm in Connecticut, near Stamford. I didn't have a car, although freshmen were allowed to have one if they chose to and could afford it. (At that time, our classmate Henry Ford II distinguished himself by driving a flashy new Buick, perhaps to say he was more than just the grandson of the famous automaker.) I took the train to Stamford to find a chauffeur-driven Rolls Royce waiting for me at the station. I was overwhelmed, and on the drive to the Cullman's farm my expectations ran to visions of a grand mansion. Instead I found a relaxing, rambling, and relatively modest farmhouse, and I quickly felt at ease.

During my first semester at Yale I worked hard and did well academically. As time passed and I looked around at all those prep school guys who didn't seem to be studying, I thought, "What the hell? Why am I working so hard? After all, I'm repeating freshman year." I let up, and my performance in the second semester quickly slipped.

I did, however, find a class that held my attention and pushed me to work. It was Shakespeare, taught by a professor named Paradise. A veteran of World War I, he had been gassed in the trenches and never fully recovered. His physical appearance was ghastly. With his skeletal thinness and colorless face, he looked like death to my young eyes.

Despite his appearance, Prof. Paradise was a marvelous teacher. I liked the course so much that I would get up at around 6 o'clock to prepare for it. One time I figured he was going to ask us to draw a map of England at the time of

Shakespeare; I practiced drawing it, and was the only one in class who did it accurately. We later had a test on *Romeo and Juliet*. The movie of the play had just come out and was showing in New Haven, so the whole class went to see it the night before the test. It must have been a good adaptation, because we all were given top marks.

My hard work in Prof. Paradise's class would be rewarded when I got into academic trouble later in my junior year. Remembering how well I did in Shakespeare, Paradise went to bat for me and gave me good counsel.

Dark Days

At the heart of the campus is Connecticut Hall, which goes back to Yale's founding. Outside this four-story brick building of Georgian design is a statue of Nathan Hale, hands tied behind his back as he prepared to walk to the gallows and said, "My only regret is I have but one life to give for my country." The Revolutionary War hero, who was executed as a spy by the British, had been a member of the Yale faculty.

The campus had been dropped squarely in the center of New Haven, and more than two centuries later my fellow students and I were always in danger of getting hit by a speeding car. I drew a cartoon depicting two townies driving down the street with a couple of Yalies on their fenders like dead deer. The driver says, "Let's drive down College Avenue; nine o'clock class is out." We believed the locals were out to get us, and I think they were.

As freshmen we stayed in the section called Old Campus and took our meals in an impressive structure called Memorial Hall. Part of the Bicentennial Buildings erected around the turn of the twentieth century to commemorate the 200th anniversary of the university's founding, it housed a huge open room with dark wood paneling, exposed beams, and a ceiling nearly 80 feet high.

On the walls were large portraits of former presidents – targets of irreverent freshmen who liked to flip butter up onto them.

The waiters were freshmen on scholarship and weren't very good at their job. Many Yale students had scholarships, but there was no free ride – all of them had to work. Some would become laboratory assistants or take part in other worthwhile learning experiences, but most were waiters.

While my first year at Yale was an exciting one, the following year turned bitter after a series of tragedies. That spring my grandmother, the real matriarch

Top Row: Great-great grandparents Rebecca Isaiah Moses, nee Phillips (1792-1872) and IsaiahMoses (1772-1857); Grandfather Julius Mortimer Alexander (1844-1917) with wife Rebecca Ella Solomons Alexander (1854-1938), seated, sons Henry Aaron Alexander (1874-1967) and Cecil Alexander (1877-1952), standing - **Second Row:** Me at age 5 - with a broken arm and new name - with my mother Julia Moses Alexander (1883-1938), sister Charlotte and Father Cecil Sr.; Charlotte and me with our Grandmother, Rebecca; My parents, Julia and Cecil - **Third Row:** Me "hiding" on St. Charles Ave.; Me in my sailor suit; Charlotte and me-formal portrait and laying around on the beach. Thanks to Judith Weil Shanks for several of these images.

The Yale Medal I received in 1982
Signed by A. Bartlett Giamatti, President of Yale University

The
Yale Medal

Awarded to

Cecil A. Alexander, '40

In Atlanta the name Cecil Alexander is synonymous both with service and with Yale. During his long and distinguished career as an architect and citizen of Atlanta, urban renewal, community relations, racial justice, music, and education – all have received his full and caring attention and earned him the Brotherhood Award of the National Conference of Christians and Jews.

How Cecil has made time within this staggering agenda for Yale, is a southern mystery, but the time and commitment have been total. The Yale Club of Georgia, the Alumni Board, the University Council, the School of Architecture, and several Yale presidents have been grateful recipients of his generous and wise counsel. Through his good efforts, Yale's historic ties with the colleges and universities of Georgia have been greatly strengthened.

For his service to Yale, large and small, public and private, the Association of Yale Alumni proudly confers the Yale Medal to an alumnus who exemplifies in his life the purposes of a liberal education, Cecil Alexander.

President of the University

n of the Association of Yale Alumni

College Days
Clockwise from top left: Telegram confirming my date
with a Powers model; Yale Record cover, May 12, 1938;
Illustration for Yale Record cover, 1938; Prom cartoon,
1938; Derby Day at Yale, Pierson College - I'm on the left
with my date, Marian Sulzberger (Heiskell); Party weekend,
me on left with the afore mentioned Powers model, 1939

334 Auburn Ave., N.E.
Atlanta, Georgia 30303
Telephone 522-1420

Southern Christian Leadership Conference

Martin Luther King Jr., *President*   Ralph Abernathy, *Treasurer*   Andrew J. Young, *Executive Director*

March 15, 1965

Mr. Cecil A. Alexander
70 Fairlie Street, N. W.
Atlanta, Georgia

Dear Mr. Alexander:

In the rush of events surrounding Selma in our Alabama voting project,
I neglected to express my deep gratitude for your sponsorship of the
dinner honoring me on January 26. Please accept this belated note of
appreciation.

I must confess that few events have warmed my heart as did this occasion.
It was a tribute not only to me but to the greatness of the City of Atlanta,
the South, the nation and its ability to rise above the conflict of former
generations and really experience that beloved community where all differences
are reconciled and all hearts in harmony with the principles of our great
Democracy and the tenants of our Judeo-Christian heritage.

Sincerely yours,

Martin Luther King, Jr.

Kg

46

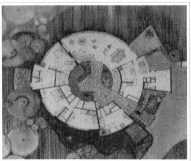

Top Row: Studying with Conrad Johnson, former Tuskegee Airman and huge influence in my life, at Harvard Graduate School of Design; my Harvard Master's Thesis
Second Row: Coca-Cola World Headquarters; First National Bank Tower; Southern Bell
Left: Plan for The Round House, now on the National Register of Historic Places
Below left: Atlanta-Fulton County Stadium, site of Hank Aaron's record-breaking home run and

five World Series, including the Atlanta Braves' World Championship of 1995
Left: With Atlanta Mayor Ivan Allen, Jr. in his office, 1966. He invited me to sit in his chair, in his place, after a particularly harrowing day, saying, "Cecil, you can *have* the damn thing!"

of the family and a woman who was very fond of me, died. A short time later my mother, who had long been ill, also died. My sister Charlotte married shortly after my mother's death, and that meant my father was left alone, something that weighed heavily upon me.

For a young man who wasn't so sure of himself or his place in the world, these events were body blows. I fought with depression and began to wonder if I was losing my mind. There was a psychiatrist on campus – but in the ethos of Yale students seeking help of this sort meant you were one step from the loony bin. I never even considered seeing the psychiatrist.

The final blow came that summer when I returned home to Atlanta. My cousin Henry and I decided to go out to watch a parade for the famed aviator Douglas "Wrong Way" Corrigan, who had crossed the Atlantic in a beat-up old single engine airplane when he supposedly had intended to fly to California. On a busy city street fronting Piedmont Park, we watched him drive by in a convertible as storm clouds gathered overhead.

In those days Piedmont Park had a golf course, and Henry and I were across the street from it. Four men had sought shelter under a tree as the rain that began to fall, when suddenly a flash of lightning struck and sent one of the men flying. His companions carried him across the street to the porch of a small house. As a qualified Senior Life Saver, I knew the primitive CPR techniques of the day and rushed over to help. The man's face had turned a deep purple and the tip of one of his shoes had been blown off.

The prescribed artificial respiration technique was the prone pressure method, which started with laying the victim on his stomach with his face to the side. After checking the mouth to be sure the tongue wasn't blocking the air passages, the rescuer straddled the victim, placed his hands on the base of the victim's rib cage, and pressed repeatedly – "out goes the bad air" (press) and "in comes the good (release.) I kept this up for what seemed an eternity until the fire department arrived. Despite my efforts and those of the firemen, the man never regained consciousness.

Looking back, it probably didn't matter what I might have done; the man would have died anyway. Yet for me it was a failure – another trauma in what had become a seemingly unending string of them.

Edgar married Louise that summer and moved off campus. I was left alone to ponder where I was going with my life and how to stay sane.

The Fairer Sex

Yale was also a time of dating and forging relationships with members of the opposite sex, successfully or not. To this day, two memorable dates stand out in my mind.

It was near the end of an eventful day – "Derby Day" at Yale, which had nothing to do with horses. Derby is the name of a small Connecticut town on the banks of the Housatonic River. Every spring the Ivy League crews raced shells on the river to the drumbeat of their coxswains.

On the banks were gathered a motley crowd of Ivy Leaguers hand-in-hand with lovelies from Smith, Wellesley, Vassar, and other institutions. Beer and more potent liquids flowed freely; the races were only an excuse for having a "go to hell" afternoon. Very few of the alleged spectators bothered to watch the laboring oarsmen as they came down the river in their gleaming wooden shells, their oars sweeping together in perfect rhythm to the coxswain's shout of "Stroke! Stroke!"

In 1939-40, my senior year, I was managing editor of the *Yale Record*, the university's would-be humor magazine. That year at the *Record* should be remembered, if for no other reason, for a member of the business staff – Henry Ford II, who later went on to a somewhat more demanding position. I like to think I gave him his start in the world of business.

In preparation for Derby Day, the *Record* hosted a mint julep party in the garden behind its small College Gothic-style headquarters. To add glamour to our staff we dressed as Roman gladiators in outfits rented from a New Haven shop. All we were missing was the ancient Roman Spartacus's warning to the gladiators (which had been introduced to me by one of my teachers back in Atlanta) – "Hear yon lions roaring in their dens? It is ten long days since they have tasted food, but tomorrow they will feed on your flesh and what a dainty meal ye'll make!"

There was plenty of roaring, but from drunks rather than lions. On a hot afternoon, mint juleps masquerading as lemonade are very potent drinks. My date for the day was the beautiful, vivacious Marian Sulzberger, whose father, Arthur Hays Sulzberger, was publisher of *The New York Times* (this flagrant name dropping is a necessary part of my story.) Knowing now what I so painfully learned in a wreck with a drunken teenager 43 years later, I would never have driven my beautiful new Buick convertible out to the Derby Day races. But we made it safely because I knew I was impaired, and as a result, I deliberately drove particularly cautiously.

Hung from the branches of a giant oak on the riverbank was a colossal Nazi flag emblazoned with the dreaded swastika. Later I learned that a Yalie touring Germany had brought back the flag; it was he and his friends who, at some physical risk, had hung the controversial banner in the tree. An enterprising photographer from the *New Haven Register*, seeing this good-looking girl and the drunken gladiator with her, had a great idea.

"Hey," he said to us "How about posing in front of that Nazi flag? It'll make a great shot."

"Sure," I said without consulting Marian. Male chauvinism was then the accepted way of life.

The deed was soon done, and the photographer thanked us and moved on. Marian and I sat down in the grass to picnic. I drank many cups of tepid coffee from a thermos to sober up for the drive back to New Haven. My efforts were successful, at least to the point that I had second thoughts about the advisability of the publication of that photograph. In fact, it hit me hard that it might not be favorably regarded if the morning paper carried a photograph of the daughter of the publisher of *The New York Times* standing in front of a Nazi flag holding hands with a none-too-sober gladiator.

I discussed my apprehensions with Marian. Male chauvinism no longer ruled, now that I was in trouble. She said, in what could only be considered a colossal understatement, that it would probably be a good idea if the picture weren't published.

So, in the dimming twilight, we drove to the offices of the *Register* in downtown New Haven. I left Marian in the car and walked in. In the past I had somehow established a good relationship with the city editor, and I was fortunate enough to find him in his office. I told him the story of the photograph but didn't mention Marian. No sane editor could fail to publish her picture with that flag if he knew who her father was. I did say, "Jim, I'm Jewish, and if you run that picture of me in front of a Nazi flag it would be very embarrassing, even dangerous, for me."

"Well," he said, "let's look at the glossies."

A few minutes later, Jim's secretary arrived with the photos in hand. As he sat looking at each image in turn, a broad grin lit his face.

"This is a great photo."

"Well," I said, "the greater it is, the more damage it will do me." Then Jim said the photo would not be published and handed me two of the prints.

Breathing again, I went back and joined Marian in the car. I showed her the prints and gave her one. She later told me later she had showed it to her father. "Oh my God!" I exploded. "What did he say?" "He thought it was funny, she answered." "Well," I said, "you can bet he wouldn't have found any humor in it if it had been in the paper."

A couple of years ago Marian was visiting her sister Ruth Sulzberger Holmberg, then publisher of the *Chattanooga Times*. Ruth had returned to her roots: Her grandfather, Adolf Ochs, had left a newspaper career in Chattanooga to buy *The New York Times* which, in short order, he made into the great paper it is today. The sisters and Ruth's husband came to Atlanta to have dinner with Helen (my second wife) and me at La Grotta, a restaurant in the Buckhead area of Atlanta.

During dinner I asked Marian if she remembered our Derby Day outing. She grinned broadly. "Of course", she said. "I still have that photograph." Thus ended a 42-year-old date – a date that made my list of two unique encounters I had with the opposite sex at Yale.

My second memorable date was totally lacking in drama. In the fall of 1939, two weeks before the Yale-Princeton football game, I realized I hadn't made a date for this tradition-loaded encounter at the Yale Bowl.

The past summer I had met a bright and beautiful student at Smith College in Northhampton, Massachusetts when she was visiting friends in Atlanta. I phoned her at Smith and asked if she could possibly, on such short notice, be my date for the Princeton game. After a very short hesitation, she said most charmingly that she was so very sorry, but she already had another commitment. Later I was told she was highly amused that I could even think she wouldn't have a date two weeks before such an important game.

Embarrassed and a little angered by her reaction, I scratched through her name in my address book. Her name? Therese (Terry) Weil. She was from New Orleans. So what? Well, Here's "what": Her sister, Hermione Weil, whom I met a year later, and I were married in 1943 and stayed married for 43 years until her death in an automobile wreck. Terry found plenty of time to be a good and supportive sister-in-law during those four eventful decades.

As the Yale-Princeton game neared, I was still without a date. Several months before, the *Yale Record* (there's that magazine again) ran an interview with John Robert Powers, the owner of the leading modeling agency in New York. I illustrated the article with a very good pen and ink caricature of Powers drawn from a photograph. In desperation, I sent a telegram to Powers, whom I hadn't met but hoped would remember my drawing It read, "Needed for the Yale-Princeton game: One Powers model." I included the original of the caricature and signed my name.

My roommate was astonished (as was I) when I received a phone call from Powers' chief associate, M. Bowles Locker. (I remember her name!) She was coming to the game and would bring, as my date, a very beautiful young model (oddly, I don't remember *her* name), whom she would chaperone. Word spread quickly that I had a date with a Powers model, and I was deluged with invitations for dances and other events that weekend.

I had a great ego-filled two days and nights escorting my beautiful trophy. I know she enjoyed all the attention. We never saw Ms. Locker, our thoughtful chaperone in absentia, except at a distance across a crowded dance floor. In my archive is a well-preserved photograph of my model and me – she in a chic hat and dress, I offering a drink to an uninterested toy Yale bulldog. Standing with us are several of my friends and their dates, none of them in the league of my beautiful charmer.

The following summer I went by the brownstone house where I thought my beautiful date lived. A rather dowdy landlady answered my ring at the door. "Does (I knew her name then) live here?" The landlady looked me over before answering. "She did, but she left. Several months ago she married and moved to Texas." That was the definitive conclusion of that date. I wonder if she, now an old lady if even alive, remembers my name? I'm sure she remembers our date, a great ego enhancer for her – and, of course, for me.

A Four-Year Detour Begins

In my years at Yale I became very close to Edgar Cullman's very approachable father, Joseph (Joe) Cullman, Jr. In fact, he became something of a surrogate father, providing the sort of easy relationship I lacked with my real dad.

Just before my graduation, I was at Joe's apartment for dinner. He took me aside and said, "Cecil, I'd like to have you come with me in the tobacco business, but I know you said you want to be an architect. Let me tell you this right up front. You should do what you feel enthusiastic about doing; but you should also understand that you aren't going to make any money as an architect. I'll give you a good job and you can move up."

Well, Joe knew about architecture, because his son-in-law, with whom I would later work with one summer, was an architect. Although he was a partner in a very successful firm, he wasn't making much money. I was flattered by Joe's offer, but I couldn't see myself as a tobacco tycoon and decided to continue along the less certain path into architecture.

On my graduation in 1940 I was faced with choosing a grad school. My thesis made the case for Yale establishing a course in industrial design, a discipline involving the designing of functional objects from locomotives to ashtrays. This field interested me, and I wanted to include it in my architectural program. At that time only MIT and Carnegie Tech (now Carnegie Mellon) offered such courses – and I settled on MIT, which, as I explain in Chapter 4, would turn out to be something of a mistake.

My first step on the path to architecture wasn't in a classroom. Instead, it was taking a pre-grad school summer job with Kahn & Jacobs Architects in New York. My boss Bob Jacobs told this long-aspiring pilot that, in view of the war that was sure to come, he should learn to fly. I recount that conversation with Bob and my days in the Civilian Pilot Training Program (the first in a long line of programs) in "Soaring with Eagles, Preparing for War," the first chapter of Part Two.

War came, all right, and graduate school was put in the back seat as I went from novice pilot to Navy Air Corps enlistee to Marine aviator – an odyssey that took me to Florida, California, Hawaii, the far-flung Marshall Islands, North Carolina, and Tennessee. The six chapters of Part Two progress from my flying lessons and enlistment to my days as a dive-bomber to my return to civilian life. The section ends with a trip my wife Hermi and I took some four decades later: a return to the tropical paradise of the Marshalls, where during the War in the Pacific I flew more than 60 missions.

Chapter 4

From Beaux Arts to Bauhaus

Less is more.

Ludwig Mies Van der Rohe

My military life, amply detailed in Part Two: *The War Years,* ended as it began — with schooling. I had been a first-year grad student at MIT as I learned to fly Civilian Patrol Training Program aircraft and commercial airliners, and in the waning days of the war I studied at the Engineering Officers School in Millington, a suburb of Memphis.

Now, in 1946, I was firmly in the civilian camp and headed with my wife Hermi to Cambridge, Mass. Despite my lackadaisical approach to my first-year of grad school at MIT back in 1941-42, the urge to earn a degree in architecture as quickly as possible motivated me to re-enter the prestigious school.

But the reality at MIT wasn't at all appealing. The two excellent professors whom I thought would be my second-year instructors had left, and the uninspired dean was still in his office. To Hermi I said, "MIT won't do. Let's go down the river and investigate Harvard. It may take two years to earn a master's, but time isn't everything. I want to get the best education I can."

It was the proximity of Harvard to MIT that led me to make a most fortunate decision. I knew little about the Harvard Graduate School of Design until my interview, but I soon learned the faculty was unmatched anywhere in the world. In 1938 Dr. Walter Gropius, who founded the Bauhaus in Weimar Germany, had come to Harvard via London to escape Hitler. He brought with him members of his excellent faculty. The star was Marcel Breuer, known for his innovative furniture design and his form-follows-function buildings.

The Bauhaus concept brought together under one roof a group of outstanding artists, industrial designers, landscape architects, city planners, and architects. These practitioners from various disciplines exchanged ideas, knowledge, and philosophies. Gropius hoped to duplicate the diversity of the Bauhaus at Harvard. Though such diversity never came to complete realization on the Harvard campus, the concept that creative designs from all disciplines could be inspired by the interchange of ideas and philosophies survived.

Breuer interviewed me, and it was he who would decide if I was Harvard material and which level of the curriculum I belonged in. After carefully examining my student design projects from both Yale and MIT, he put them aside and questioned me about my goals as an architect. My drawings and answers must have satisfied him. He said, "The architectural program at the Graduate School of Design is for two years, leading to a bachelor's degree in architecture. The master's program takes another year. You can enter the BA program at the second-year level, but if your work doesn't measure up you'll have to start over at first-year level."

Given the deferment of my education for the four years I was in the Marine Corps, I was eager to finish the program and get on with a career. "Mr. Breuer," I said, "I would prefer to enter at the second year."

"Fine," he said. "You'll be placed in the class of Mr. Hugh Stubbins."

Hermi and I moved into a gloomy, poorly designed apartment on Commonwealth Avenue – one her sister Therese (Terry) and husband Frankel Wolff, a reserve Army officer, had occupied while he was stationed in Boston. They were leaving for Mississippi. Dismal though it was, the place was warm, the plumbing worked, it wasn't far from Harvard, and finding an apartment around Boston was almost impossible after the war ended. We were relieved and delighted to have a home, even one across the Charles River.

Professors Breuer and Gropius

Of all the instructors I had at Georgia Tech, Yale, MIT, and Harvard, Marcel Breuer was by far the most inspiring and helpful. His approach encouraged the development of a creative, handsome, functional solution from the student's own concepts; he never imposed his own ideas on any of us. It was a joy to work with him. Examples of his buildings include UNESCO Headquarters in Paris and the United States Embassy in The Hague, numerous houses, and a public library in Atlanta. They enrich all who inhabit them in Europe and here in the States.

I plunged into my work, but events beyond our control couldn't be ignored. One morning I stood at ease in front of Dr. Walter Gropius, who was seated at his large, scuffed desk. On his time-lined face rested a mantle of benign authority.

"Dr. Gropius," I began, "I am here to ask for an extension on my design project. Our baby arrived six weeks early, and that has completely absorbed my time and energy. There was no chance to work on my project." (For how Hermi and I learned she was pregnant, read on.)

Mark Twain once observed, "Whenever the literary German dives into a sentence, that is the last you are going to see of him till he emerges on the other side of the Atlantic with a verb in his mouth." Gropius's reply precisely followed that structure, although it began and ended on this side of the ocean.

"You, Mr. Alexander, request an extension of time to complete your design problem, because your wife a baby prematurely delivered. Now already everything have I heard."

He gave me a searching look and a slight smile flickered across his face. Gropius was rarely seen without a cigar clamped in his lips. I had come prepared, well aware he regarded a cigar as essential to life. Before I spoke, I handed him a five-dollar cigar.

"Dr. Gropius," I said, "please accept this traditional token for celebrating the birth of a baby. I would be honored if you will."

He looked approvingly at the label, and went through the elaborate ritual required by knowledgeable cigar aficionados before drawing the first puff. Then, with great satisfaction, he looked toward the ceiling at the swirling cloud of smoke he had blown through his pursed lips.

"Mr. Alexander," he said, "your request without precedent is; however, you may a two-week extension have."

I thanked him and left his office, a space now filled with wisps of cigar smoke from my fortuitous and expensive gift.

For several years after the end of war, construction was at a standstill as the country converted to a peacetime economy. This meant that even the best architects had little or no work – and the gifted architects on the Harvard faculty were no exception. The positive result was that they concentrated entirely on teaching. At the same time, the student body was mainly comprised of veterans eager to get on with their careers; there was none of the laid back "lets have another beer" attitude found in architectural schools before the war. We were focused and serious. This confluence of fine architects who had no choice but to dedicate themselves to teaching and a group of driven, serious students is unique in the history of architectural education. It was a magical experience for those of us lucky enough to study at Harvard.

The memorable students were almost too numerous to count. One was the quiet, affable, and soon-to-be-renowned I. Ming Pei. Another was Betty Nicrosi, a Southern Belle from Montgomery. Ala; her thesis, a coliseum for her hometown, was used by her later employer as the design for an actual coliseum. Still another was a beautiful, talented South American countess whose long brown hair cascaded over her drafting table. Then there was Paul Rudolph, the future designer of the controversial Yale Art and Architecture Building. Rudolph was a graduate of Alabama Polytechnic Institute (later Auburn University); he was also a disciple of Frank Lloyd Wright and shared his mentor's antipathy for the Bauhaus, refusing to design within its tenets.

Also studying architecture at the time were a card-carrying Communist who later developed a lucrative practice with the despised capitalists; and a talented student from India whose thesis Gropius rejected because it ignored the great traditions of his native land. But the student who had the greatest impact on me, although not through his designs, was Conrad Johnson, a black man. He had been a fighter pilot in Italy with the Tuskegee Airmen, and we were the only two former combat pilots in the school. The brotherhood (and sisterhood) that bands all pilots together entirely displaced our racial differences. We became close friends. Johnson was often a guest at our apartment for dinner, and we collaborated at Harvard on the design of a major airport. His friendship was a major force in my transition from a quasi-white supremacist to an active advocate for racial justice.

My previous studies at Georgia Tech, Yale, and MIT were in the classical Beaux Arts tradition, but I adopted the Bauhaus's clean functional contemporary idiom with enthusiastic zeal. Years later, on a trip to France, I was overwhelmed by the magnificence of the cathedrals. I admitted those designers were damn good, and their integration of soaring structure, sculpture, and stained glass created a far richer and more satisfying structure then did any Bauhaus design. I still greatly admire the work of Breuer, Mies van der Rohe, Eero Saarinen, and Philip Johnson but no longer judge buildings by style; instead, I decide whether to my eye the design is excellent, good, mediocre, or bad.

Baby Makes Three

My immersion in academia didn't lessen the distractions of family life. Hermi developed a bacterial infection and became jaundiced. We called in the doctor who had served her sister. He diagnosed her infection, confined her to bed (she was pregnant, much to our delight!) and prescribed the recently approved penicillin to be administered daily with a hypodermic needle.

"You," he said to me, "will have to give her the shots. I can't come by every day. You can practice injecting an orange."

I was terrified by the thought of sticking a long needle into my wife's arm with the danger of killing her if I accidentally injected a bubble of air. But there was no alternative. Practicing by puncturing an orange did little to assuage my fears. Several agonizing days later the doctor returned.

"Good news," he said, "I have a new penicillin gel that can be administered once a month. I'll do it, so you can stop." I threw the orange in the garbage and hugged the doctor. Hermi recovered.

Still, Hermi delivered our daughter Therese, nicknamed Terri, (spelled *Terry* throughout her childhood) six weeks prematurely. And a change in the itinerary of Hermi's mother and father was a side effect of the early arrival. Their plan was to fly to New York, where we had anticipated the baby would be born. Rosetta, Hermi's mother, had two wisdom teeth pulled to be ready for the trip – terrible timing, considering Terri's birth right after Rosetta's painful oral surgery. Nevertheless, she boarded a DC-3 for Boston with husband Harold.

The weather was dark and turbulent for the entire flight. Airliners in those days couldn't climb over storms, and instead plowed right through them. The plane was approaching Boston when the rear passenger door blew open.

Landing with that door in the airstream would be very dangerous. Thankfully, a passenger who was a Marine aviator fought his way back from his front seat against the billowing aisle carpet, leaned far out the cabin, and pulled the door shut. Rosetta and Harold thought he was entitled to a Medal of Honor on his chest, which already wore one awarded for combat, and so do I.

After Hermi recovered from childbirth, Rosetta and a fine nurse from Newfoundland eased us into the exacting routine of caring for a premature baby. It was midsummer before I finished the problem Dr. Gropius had allowed me to delay, and we assembled the many items necessary to care for Terri, our own gear, and took the train to New York. Once more, my Yale roommate Edgar Cullman provided shelter. He had told us he spending the summer on his Connecticut farm, so his Fifth Avenue apartment would be vacant. "You and Hermi can have it free this summer – no rent," he said. What a friend! We moved in, looking like a bunch of Okies.

Unfortunately, our great "Newfie" nurse didn't come with us from Boston. An ad in the paper produced an acceptable response, but we weren't acceptable to the responder. She quickly discovered we weren't the permanent occupants of the luxurious apartment – we were unclean summer squatters, not the class of patrons she was accustomed to granting her service. She never put her reason in words, but her disdain was clearly evident when she announced that the position didn't suit her and she was leaving forthwith. Our reaction was basically amusement: She had quantified us exactly.

Ideas (and I) Take Flight

The summer flashed by. We didn't know it, but our drive back to Boston in our much-loved Buick was our last trip in its beautiful red leather interior.

The Commonwealth Avenue apartment was no longer available. We were homeless. For several weeks Hermi and Terri were in one hotel and I was in another – not a good arrangement, but rooms were scarce. An obscure ad tucked in the classified section of the Boston Herald seemed promising: "Available, second floor apartment, corner Linnean and Bowden Street Cambridge. Will rent only to tenant who will sell me an automobile."

Post-war automobiles were hard to find, but Hermi's uncle, a leading Houston lawyer, owned a Chrysler Agency. He offered to sell us a car at his cost. We jumped at it. It would be the key to the advertised apartment. We said to ourselves, "Any car will do."

When we saw the car roll off a freight car in Boston, we had a hard time keeping up our enthusiasm. It was an ungainly, huge black hulk apparently held together with library paste (post-war workmanship could hardly be called workmanship – "slipshodship" is a better description.) In contrast, our sleek little Buick – even with its odometer registering over 150,000 miles, including those driven in four safaris across the scorching American desert – was in excellent shape.

Should we sell the beautiful Buick or the ugly Chrysler? Emotionally, there was no question: We wanted to keep the Buick. But our unwanted decision came to us in a rainstorm as we sat under the convertible's tattered, leaking roof. No roof replacements were available because manufacturers couldn't meet the demand. Reluctantly, we offered to sell our Buick to the apartment owner. Even with its leaking roof, he accepted.

It was a tearfully wrenching decision for us. The car was a part of our lives, our home on wheels. We were hugging each other in it under a full moon at the base of Atlanta's Stone Mountain when Hermi whispered "yes" to my proposal. It had been our faithful transport as the Marines ordered me around the country from Jacksonville to Memphis and seven cities or towns in between. We took four days to drive from Atlanta to Boston after the war. I still feel sorrow over giving up that car. Hell, we could have put up umbrellas inside when it rained.

Our new Cambridge apartment, unlike the one on Commonwealth Ave, was filled with light and cooling breezes. The exception was the kitchen, which was only a little larger than a utility closet; Hermi could stand in the middle and reach all the appliances.

In today's crime-ridden cities, I wince to recall how Hermi and I exposed Terri to possible danger. During the winter, Hermi encased her in layers of clothing, bumped her in her carriage down the steps to the sidewalk, kissed her, left her there, and hurried back to the warm indoors. Having lived through the kidnapping of the Lindbergh baby and the concern over security that resulted, I'm baffled that we didn't consider leaving our baby unattended to be stupid. Thankfully, our stupidity was never tested.

The Harvard campus was just a few blocks away from our apartment. "Alex [as I was nicknamed then], why don't you come home for lunch? It would be fun to be together. Cooking a little more for you is no problem, and it will take only a few minutes for you to get here from the campus."

"Great," I said. "I'll see you tomorrow at 12:30."

For a week I came home for lunch. After five days of cooking in the stifling miniature kitchen, Hermi was exhausted. "This isn't working," she said. "I think you'd better eat lunch in Cambridge."

There was little free time at Harvard, and 12-hour days were routine. As the due date for a design problem loomed, 24-hour days became the norm. Procrastination was a common vice: We hoped a flash of creativity would light up our brains and a great design would flow from pencil to paper. So, after we'd stared into space for days on end, it took all-night sessions to compete a full submission with plans, sections, elevations, perspectives, and models. If I was lucky enough to be hit by that creative flash, a thrill just short of an orgasm coursed through my body.

There was one extracurricular activity I made sure to fit into my schedule: flying with the Marine Reserve Squadron at the Squantum Naval Air Station. There were two reasons – my love of flying and the pay. Our planes were the beautiful but demanding Corsair F-4U fighters that had devastated the Japanese during the War in the Pacific.

Before our first flight in those high-powered, touchy aircraft we were shown a film titled "How to Land a Corsair." In the Pacific we landed slowly and settled on the front wheels with the tail wheel inches off the runway; the tail wheel quickly touched down, brakes were engaged, and the plane rolled to a stop having used only half the runway. The Squantum film advised a different technique. It correctly stated that if the Corsair approached too slowly it could easily stall, flip over and crash. The solution in the film was to land fast on the wheels using the full runway to stop the plane.

OK, I thought, if that's what they want, I'll do it.

On my first flight I lined up the single-seat airplane with the narrow, short runway. It had been over two years since I had flown. The Corsair was not a forgiving aircraft. I was tense.

In accordance with the film's instructions, I came in fast, touched the two front wheels to the tarmac with the tail high, and rushed down the short runway. The end of the runway, with Dorchester Bay just beyond, was coming at me and I was about to catapult into the water. My only recourse for stopping the headlong dash was to stomp hard on the left brake and spin the plane around in a tight arc – a "ground loop."

I hit the brake and the Corsair started to turn – but instead of staying flat, it rose vertically. The wind shook the plane so hard I thought I might go over. I made a stupid move unbuckling my straps in anticipation of dropping from the cockpit 15 feet above the ground. A fire truck, siren at full blast, caught my eye. It was headed my way, so I didn't jump. Two firemen stood on the roof of the truck and reached up to help me down. I was unhurt physically and so was the Corsair, but my ego was in tatters.

The squadron commander called me to his office so I could tell him what happened. "Sir," I said, "overseas we landed slowly tail-down, just above stalling speed. The plane stopped halfway down the runway, and we never had any problems. When I landed here, I followed the film's instructions. I came in fast and was running out of runway. I tried to ground loop but ended up on the nose. That 5,000-foot runway is too short for that technique."

"You're right," he said. "You were the first pilot to follow the film's instructions. No more. I'm junking that film."

From that experience I took back one lesson: In architecture, as in flying, if you're told to do something untried, *don't*. Let someone else be the hero.

On my desk is a prized memento, yellow with age. It is the framed note from Dr. Walter Gropius promoting me to the thesis. For some time I had thought about what I would design for this final crucial project. I settled on an aircraft laboratory. There were two reasons — one, it was in a field in which I was very knowledgeable — aviation; and two (not a lofty reason), it was unlikely that any of the jurors judging my project would know anything about aircraft laboratories.

My thesis proposal emphasized my interest in aviation and said nothing about the second, less acceptable reason for choosing it. Approval was granted without question.

Jaunts to Buffalo and Hartford

I traveled to two laboratories to research the requirements for my thesis. In Buffalo, N.Y., was the recently completed Curtiss-Wright Laboratory, which the firm had just given to Cornell University to be used for teaching and research. The second was a United Aircraft lab in Hartford, Conn.

When I arrived by train in Buffalo, a howling blizzard greeted me. A snowy blast snatched the hat off my head and sent it flying away in a swirling white cloud, lost forever. I found a snow-encased taxi outside the station, and after a sliding, skidding drive of several miles I was deposited at the laboratory, barely visible through the storm. Lab director C. A. Furniss greeted me in a disheveled office piled with folders and directed me to a wobbly chair in front of his desk.

"Yes, young man, what can we do for you?"

When I told him the reason for my visit, he responded enthusiastically and asked, "So what do you want to know?"

"Everything," I said.

"Oh," he laughed. "I'll give you overall information, and then we'll talk to some of the engineers and look around at our equipment. We have a subsonic wind tunnel large enough to test full-size fighters; its walls are steel plates welded together. An inspector reported that a lot of the welds were faulty, and if they were subjected to high pressure, they would collapse." The original engineer and the firm who welded the plates said the consultant was dead wrong. The tunnel is safe – ready to go." He paused, then said, "So who do I believe? Re-welding will cost a fortune, and Curtiss-Wright says it's not their problem." I don't know how the supposed crisis was resolved, but the tunnel did not collapse.

Mr. Furniss led the way into a large open room with several rows of desks, all lit by the cold light of fluorescent tubes. At a few of the desks, engineers were working with their slide rules; this was, after all, almost half a century before computers made slide rules obsolete.

Most of the men – no women – were standing around a coffee pot, steaming cups in hand, deep in animated conversation. Furniss pointed at the group and said, "Most of the creative ideas come from these coffee pot discussions. You can't measure productivity by the time our engineers spend at their desk – we pay them for creative thinking, not desk time. The guys at the desks over there are probably recording what came out of one of those get-togethers. A chance meeting on a stair landing could produce an idea or a solution worth a year's salary."

I knew then that the lab of my thesis would have many spots for such informal meetings. My trip to Buffalo was well worth losing my hat.

The Hartford laboratory I visited was operated by the major military supplier, United Aircraft. When the director of research, Mr. F. W. Caldwell, heard the reason for my mission, he welcomed me and said, "I'll be glad to show you around."

He took me outside to the laboratory's wind tunnel. There was no danger of this one collapsing; it was made of a 2½-foot-thick shell of reinforced concrete. "Our main tunnel can sustain airspeeds just under the speed of sound and can handle full size fighters," Caldwell said. "You see that?" he asked, pointing toward a large stainless steel sphere. "That's a supersonic wind tunnel 'liberated' from Germany. The air in it can be evacuated, leaving nearly a complete vacuum. Come on in the lab I'll show you how it operates."

Once we came to the sphere, he pointed to small nozzle on it. "After the vacuum is created, that valve is opened and for a fraction of a second air moves through that nozzle at supersonic speeds," Caldwell explained. "A very small wing section mounted in the airstream reacts to the air blast, and its perform- ance is recorded and interpreted."

The sphere was being evacuated as we stood there. The sound of the pumps was an ear-mangling scream pitching higher and higher; I was sure there would be an explosion. The pumps suddenly stopped. A valve opened, and with a piercing screech, air was sucked into the sphere.

The director suggested I write Eggers & Higgins – a New York architec- tural firm that had adapted the supersonic sphere for use in the States – and request a set of plans to use on my thesis. This I did, and the firm sent me complete set of drawings and specifications.

My two field trips and long hours reading articles and books supplied me the information I needed to design my aeronautical laboratory.

Missions Accomplished

At Christmas, Hermi went home to New Orleans to be with her family. While she was gone, an epidemic of dysentery began to kill children in Cambridge. My age didn't protect me, and I've never been sicker. It was an agonizing effort to struggle to the toilet – a trip I made often. One night, as I lay awake staring into the dark room, the ghostly, glowing figure of a man appeared. He walked slowly across the room and sat on my bed, looking at me. I didn't feel threatened. It was, I'm sure, a hallucination brought on by my lack of sleep and high fever, but at the time he was very real – and still is. After a few minutes he faded away.

I gradually healed and was able to go back to my drafting table. From sev- eral preliminary plans I chose the one I thought had the most promise. Then came the arduous part – making a large model, plus twenty sheets of drawings showing plans, sections, elevations, and perspectives.

Hermi worked with me. One feature of the wind tunnel was the two large cooling towers on either side. Using cardboard, Hermi made small replicas of the towers. Only after she had built them did she realize they weren't identical. She sobbed and fled the room. After calming down, she came back and rebuilt the off-size tower so it mirrored the other one.

Another mission she undertook was finding a toy ball of the right size – a ball to represent the spherical wind tunnel. Template in hand, she went to a Cambridge toy store. The clerk thought she was a nut when, after measuring several balls with the template, she said, "None of these will do. Sorry."

Woolworth's selection was no better. At Kress's, a red plastic ball slipped neatly into the template. She brought it home in triumph. I painted it silver. It made a fine supersonic sphere.

The term "niggering" has deservedly gone the way of unacceptable racial slurs. It referred to a practice followed in all architectural schools. As a senior student neared the completion of a project, students from the lower grades would help finish the drawings and the models. As my presentation evolved, many students became fascinated with the project and helped out for hours and hours. Toward the end, sixteen students were working with me (it would be many years before I had that many employees in my office.)

There was one more interruption in my work – a very brief one. It was June, and Harvard's commencement exercises were in progress in Harvard Yard. Robinson Hall, where the architectural school was located, was close to the Yard. Through the open window I could hear the band and unintelligible speeches. I would graduate when I finished my thesis, probably in September. But there would be no commencement ceremony. This, then, would be as close as I could come to a formal graduation.

"Hey guys," I said. "I'm going out and hear the speeches. Anybody want to come?"

They had no interest. The main speaker, Gen. George Marshall, was being introduced as I entered the Yard. Security in these post-war times was very sparse, and I stood just a dozen feet from speaker's platform and the general. He announced the Marshall Plan that would in time save Europe from riots, civil war, and communism, and change the world. But I wasn't impressed.

"What did the general say?" I was asked when I returned to my desk. "Aw, not much. Just a bunch of platitudes and clichés – if Europeans will help themselves we'll help them come back."

I can only excuse my lack of perception by reminding myself that many people in high places thought the same way. The Marshall Plan succeeded only because the Europeans rushed to accept the challenges and the money.

When I finished my thesis, I reported to Dr. Gropius. I would now present my laboratory plan to a jury of faculty and several outsiders, and Dr. Gropius would select the jury.

"Mr. Alexander," he said, "I will assemble a jury and we will have your presentation in about two weeks. The date I will confirm. It occurs to me that an aeronautical engineer would make a knowledgeable member of the jury. What do you think?"

Oh man, I thought, there goes my scheme to have a jury totally ignorant of the requirements of an aeronautical lab.

"Doctor," I said, "I don't think that's a good idea. An aeronautical engineer would judge my project strictly from an engineering viewpoint. He wouldn't care about the architecture. I'm afraid his views, limited as they are solely to function, could overcome the architectural solution. While I've done considerable research including visits to two labs, my thesis isn't an engineering solution. It is architecture. I would prefer you not include an aeronautical engineer on the jury."

In a few seconds, Gropius nodded and said in his roundabout way, "Your concern I understand. An aeronautical engineer I will not include on the jury."

"Thank you," I said, greatly relieved.

The presentation went well. The many detailed sheets of drawings and the beautifully built model were very impressive. All the jurors complimented me. I silently thanked my many assistants, including one classmate who had helped build the intricately detailed model of the wind tunnel flanked by the perfectly matched cooling towers made by my wife.

The thesis produced three job offers. A faculty member who served on the jury made an offer immediately after my presentation. Eggers & Higgins, the firm that sent me drawings for the supersonic sphere, wanted to retain me after they saw a copy of my thesis. Another jury member, a Boston architect, later tendered an offer. My dream would have been to go with Marcel Breuer, and, had he asked me, I would have enthusiastically accepted . But he did not. I decided to look beyond the three offers.

My formal architectural education was over. It had taught me the decided differences between classical Beaux Arts training and the contemporary dictums of the Bauhaus – "form follows function" and "less is more." There were no similarities in the two approaches. Gropius said, "The successful architect is first a handyman around the house." Accurate dimensions and clearly delineated drawings, not beautiful plans and perspectives, were the goal.

Creativity of the secretive sort was required in the Beaux Arts programs. Students even surrounded themselves with plywood screens and covered their drawings when they left, shielding their designs from fellow students. The Bauhaus, on the other hand, encouraged sharing ideas. The idea wasn't seen as the vital element (no idea was really original) – it was the *development* of the idea into a distinguished but functional building that defined the value a project. Some of the students didn't go along with Bauhaus-style sharing and resented anyone who copied their design.

Another major difference: When the Beaux Art student finished his preliminary design, complete with three-dimensional perspectives, he was graded. No matter how poorly his initial design was judged, he was stuck with it; the finished project couldn't deviate at all from the preliminary one (a rule not likely to produce enthusiastic efforts.) The Bauhaus student, however, was graded only on the final submission, and changes could be made right up to the last minute.

Perhaps the most important difference was the approach to structural and mechanical designs. Beaux Arts ignored engineering completely. In real practice, graduates usually designed the building architecturally and then called in the engineers and said, "Make this stand up, heat it, and light it." The Bauhaus approach called in the engineers from the inception of design. Their requirements were totally incorporated in the building plan and often exerted great influence on the final solution.

Still another difference: Beaux Art designs were closely derived, even copied, from Classical, Renaissance, and Romanesque examples. Bauhaus designers, while acknowledging the early designs of Corbusier, Gropius, and Mies van der Rohe, tried to stand out on their own, using untried materials and exotic structures in the effort to become true form-givers.

These were the incompatible approaches to architecture I had learned by the time I left Harvard. But the Bauhaus was my guiding principle. I had only distain for the classical copyist, though after a visit to Europe and its grand cathedrals my arrogance faded.

After a year at Georgia Tech, four years at Yale, one year at MIT, four years in the Marine Air Corps, two years at Harvard, and with a wife and baby in tow, I was ready – more than ready – to get on with my career.

I now had an unequaled architectural education. On a more personal level, my friendship with fellow Harvard student Conrad Johnson had changed my attitudes toward race forever.

Chapter 5

Back To Atlanta

This was his Georgia
This his share
Of pine and river and sleepy air

— *Steve Vincent Benet, John Brown's Body*

After graduating from Harvard Graduate School of Design, I moved my wife and our new baby to a farmhouse near Stamford, Conn. so I could commute to my job in New York. One Friday could have been spelled "Fry-day" it was so hot, and it was then that the New York, New Haven & Hartford train's sweltering, standing-up-all-the way commute convinced me I had had it with the Big Apple.

There was another factor, too: I didn't enjoy my work or my boss's strictness. Coming back from an office errand one Thursday, I stopped at an Orange Julius stand to get one lousy cold drink. My boss (who shall remain nameless) walked by and saw me, stopped, and gave me a going-over for taking a break on company time. As I remember it, my salary was all of $70 a week. He also turned down my request to cut fifteen minutes out of my lunch hour and leave fifteen minutes early to catch the 6:15 train. His refusal meant that I had to run all the way to Grand Central Station, leaving the office at exactly 6:00; if I missed the 6:15, the next train left an hour or more later.

Hermi was delighted on that hot night when I said, "Let's go home!" She had wanted to leave but thought I felt a New York job would be important for my career. So we left New York and Connecticut (where our contacts were only with whites (except for a few friends' servants), and waded into what would soon become the bitter civil rights struggle in Atlanta and the South.

All my life I had been embarrassed and inhibited by the way my father bragged about me to his friends, and even to strangers. My father's lack of a Phi Beta Kappa key or any other scholastic trophies from a formal education led him to metaphorically dangle my sister and me from his gold watch chain as his surrogate academic achievements – a habit that bothered us both.

If I was going to have a comfortable life in Atlanta, this had to stop. So I took on the tough assignment of having it out with him.

Rather than writing what could have been perceived as a "Dear John" letter, I called him.

"Hi, Dad. I have something important to discuss with you. Are you available for a conversation now?"

"Yes son. What is it?"

"Hermi and I have had it with my commuting and New York, and I'm not enthusiastic about my job. We've decided to leave. Our first choice is Atlanta. But I have a problem. You've always bragged about me to your friends. I appreciate your support, but there's a negative side. I'm embarrassed by it and react by being overly modest, self-effacing, and reluctant to assert myself. If I'm to succeed professionally, I'll have to display more self-confidence. Dad, if we come to Atlanta, will you not brag about me so I can be myself?"

I don't recall his exact words in response. He was badly hurt, and in a subdued voice he said he would stop. He then added, "I want you, Hermi, and Terri to live with me as long as you wish. 1111 St. Charles Place is your home. It will be my joy to have you."

Home Sweet Home?

We moved in, but my father's welcome had its prices. To care for Terri, still an infant, we employed a young African-American woman from New York. She wasn't attuned to the inferior status of blacks that had long been fundamental to Atlanta's way of life. And my father certainly wasn't ready to accept a black woman who didn't "know her place." The issue went from a hissing fissure to a volcanic geyser when he found her using his bathroom.

This problem and lesser conflicts made Dad's promise of "This is your house" far from real. Hermi wanted out – and now! She spent many of her days house-hunting. I was now working at Henry Toombs's architectural firm, so I could help Hermi with the search only on weekends.

"Oh, Alex, I found it!" was Hermi's greeting one Friday evening. "I've found a cute little house with three bedrooms, and it's in a new subdivision."

"Great," I said. "I work until noon Saturday; we'll look at it tomorrow. "

After a long, wandering drive, Hermi pointed to an unpaved red clay road dotted with miniature white-stucco bungalows. "There it is!" There wasn't so much as a tree or streetlight, and the road was completely isolated – no sign of human activity in any direction except for those cabins.

I made my feelings clear: "Hermi, this won't do! It's inaccessible There are no stores within miles, no buses, and these are little cookie-cutter shacks. We can do better – a whole lot better."

"You won't even look in one, " she said. "I have a key."

"It's no use, dear. Even if the interior was great, this location is just miserable. Let's keep looking."

After several more abortive missions, Hermi found a very acceptable house for rent. It was on Zimmer Drive in an established neighborhood, and only a block from convenience stores and a streetcar line. The exterior was red brick; the interior was freshly painted and well furnished. The house also had a large back yard. We leased it for a year with an option for two more.

My father was hurt by our departure. "Why do you want to leave? The house on St. Charles is yours; you can live here without paying any attention to me. Please don't go."

"Dad," I said, "we are truly grateful to you for taking us in, but this house is yours and can never be ours. Hermi needs a place of her own."

So, heavy with a fine mixture of relief and guilt, we began the move to our new house, just a few miles away. To celebrate our freedom we arranged a 75th birthday party for my Uncle Harry. The day before, a freezing rain had hit Atlanta and coated the streets with a slick sheet of ice. To prepare food for the party, Hermi had to borrow kitchen equipment from Dad. Getting a car up or down his steep driveway was impossible, so I carried pots, pans, dishes, tablecloths, napkins, towels, and the like, slipping and sliding down the steep front yard to the sidewalk. Hermi then took hold of the loot and put it in our car for the treacherous ride back.

By the next day a wave of warm air had melted the ice, and the party could go on. Late in the afternoon my uncle and some twenty of his friends showed up. Hermi had arranged an inviting spread of hors d'oeuvres around a large birthday cake. I had whipped up a large bowl of Chatham Artillery Punch, named for Savannah's famous county; I don't remember the ingredients, but its powerful wallop of alcohol is completely disguised with fruit juices. It's possible to down several large glasses without effect – then Bam! You're reeling drunk.

My uncle and his guests, drinking what tasted like non-alcoholic punch, downed glass after glass. After an hour of gentlemanly behavior, the artillery fired. The room was rocking with shouting, backslapping, singing senior citizens led by my uncle. The party was a success. I ordered a half-dozen taxis. The guests who were still too drunk to drive climbed in to be distributed to their homes and wondering wives; they came back the next day, well hung over, to pick up their cars. If I ever serve Chatham Artillery Punch again (I haven't), a large sign next to the bowl will read, "Chatham Artillery Punch. Extremely potent. One to a customer."

Life on Zimmer Drive was pleasant. Terri made friends with the little girl next door, who came to our back door every day and called out, "Mrs. Alexander, can Terri come out and play?"

Four minor mishaps interrupted our uneventful lives on Zimmer Drive. Hermi left our car, out of gear and without the brake set, teetering at the top of the steep driveway. Something – a gust of wind, a passing truck, a gremlin? – set it in motion, and the car raced down the drive and crashed into the garage door in our backyard. Fortunately, no one was in the way, but replacing the door and repairing a badly bent fender was expensive.

I was responsible for a potentially marriage-denting occurrence. I usually took a streetcar to my office, but one day I needed our car to carry a building model to a client. At the end of the day, my mission accomplished, I forgot the car and took the Highland streetcar home. Hermi was at the door when I walked in.

"Cecil (she didn't call me Alex when I was in disfavor) where is our car?!"

"Oh my God! it's at the office. I forgot I had it."

"Well, we have tickets to the symphony tonight. How are we going to get there without our car?"

"I'll call a cab," I said, and we'll pick up the car after the concert."

They say "music hath charms to soothe the savage breast," but Beethoven's charms didn't soothe Hermi. It was a lost evening.

A second mishap of sorts had to do with a birthday party. Hermi wanted to carpet the area with grass and ordered a truckload of fertilizer (let's call it manure), which was spread across the yard. Her timing was bad. The next day a dozen or so pretty little girls in their party best arrived with their mothers for Terri's birthday. They looked in dismay at the smelly, gooey substance spread out below balloons, Happy Birthday signs, and colorful strips of crepe paper hung from tree limbs. They then gathered up their skirts and tiptoed to folding chairs scattered around a table covered with presents. The birthday cake was duly sliced, but little was eaten; the environment just wasn't conducive to consuming food – not even birthday cake.

The fourth occurred when Terri accidentally locked herself into a bathroom – a minor but memorable scare. I had to climb a rickety ladder, force open the second-story window, and scramble over a tub to reach the locked door and free my frightened daughter.

Our Move to Peachtree Road

On June 6, 1949, Hermi and I welcomed another daughter: Judith Marian, but Judy to us from the start. We fully expected this child to be a boy and had chosen no name for a girl. She was known as BGA (Baby Girl Alexander) until we arrived at a consensus. Shortly before her birth our lease on the Zimmer Drive house was expiring, so I approached my Uncle Harry about renting a small, two-story timber house at the front of his property on Peachtree Road. He was glad to have us.

Before moving in we wanted to do some renovating. I found a carpenter who was better at tearing down walls than he was at carpentry. Under his sledgehammer, two walls on the ground floor became dust. This opened up an unobstructed living and dining area. A large window at the rear of this space (with a nice view of the woods), two new mantelpieces, and new kitchen equipment completed the transformation.

The results reflected my Bauhaus studies at Harvard. Architectural magazines could find few houses in those post-war years that showed any signs of contemporary design, and I'm sure only this severe shortage led *House Beautiful* to give over four illustrious pages to extolling the remodeling of that old house on Peachtree Road. We had modernized only indoors, and I figure the magazine must have eventually recalled and destroyed those issues showcasing a nondescript house fronted by a septic tank and a field.

A few months after we moved in, the field went boggy and we had to have it dug up. For several weeks our front yard was a muddy, gray, smelly swamp. It was in no condition to greet visitors – most particularly, one couple who came. The wife of Dick Dominick, the Marine squadron mate whom I mention in Chapter 17 (Part Two), had a close friend who had recently married an Atlanta lawyer and moved there; their names were Phoebe and De Franklin. Dick was a member of the wealthy family that owned Dominick & Dominick, prominent New York stockbrokers, and Phoebe just assumed that friends of Dick's would live in a stately mansion on a high-toned boulevard. When she saw our front yard, she was shocked.

"De, this dump can't be where Dick's friends live," Phoebe told her husband. "It must be the wrong address."

Of course, it was the right "wrong address." In spite of this terrible introduction, Phoebe and Hermi became the best of friends and shared many rewarding hours together.

Uncle Harry, who had a deep appreciation for beautiful women (Phoebe was well qualified), often came to check on his house when Phoebe was visiting. How he knew when she was there I don't know. ESP?

Our two little girls filled our lives with wonder, joy, sweat, tears, and love. Judy went to sleep every night with the comfort of a Go Gulf sign flashing in her window (Uncle Harry had built and rented a Gulf gas station way out on the curb of his Peachtree Road property to a man he held in high regard.) She also had a large well of childhood terrors. One we couldn't put to rest was her fear that "the stars are going to come in the window and get me." A more realistic one was her reluctance to walk on the long path through the woods to my uncle's house. "Those woods are full of snakes and teenagers." She was right about the snakes, and at times the teenagers were there too. Each spring Uncle Harry offered a bounty to several boys for every copperhead and moccasin they caught. So, yes, there were teenagers.

Both girls took ballet lessons ballet, and Judy in particular loved to dance. Her first toe shoes were symbolic for her – her badge of another step on the road to being a grown-up. One Christmas, Judy and Terri were enthralled by the way their new green tutus shimmered under a recessed light in the ceiling. Terri became an impressive gymnast, effortlessly tumbling and doing back-bends, her waist-length hair, normally worn in Pippi Longstocking-style braids, tied up in a bun.

"Don't see me" became an all-purpose family watchword. Terri, when she was a toddler, coined it as she sat in a bureau drawer, her face smeared with chocolate from the box she had opened, when her mother walked into the room. Terri had an invisible playmate she called Figgy. When we became concerned that Figgy was taking the place of real playmates, we played a rather naughty trick on her.

"Terri," I said, "we would like to meet Figgy's folks. Would you take us to his house?"

She looked a little uncertain but said "Yes." The three of us cruised slowly down Peachtree Road. As we passed each house or apartment, Hermi pointed to it and asked, "Is that Figgy's home?" After a series of "no's", Terri pointed at an apartment building and said "Figgy lives there." We parked the car, went inside, and, following Terri's instructions, took the elevator to the third floor. We then walked down the hall to a unit where Terri stropped and said. "This is it."

Hermi rang the bell, and a pleasant lady opened the door. Hermi said, "Our daughter, Terri, is looking for her friend Figgy. She thinks he lives here."

"Oh no, we don't have any children. The people across the hall have two boys, and maybe one of them is Figgy."

"Thanks, " I said, "but Terri was sure he lived here. We don't need to bother your neighbor."

That was the end of Figgy. He was soon replaced with real-life friends.

Later, we had a short visit from *my* imaginary friend. While still in New England, Hermi and I saw the Broadway play *Harvey,* starring Jimmy Stewart. Harvey was a 6-foot-tall rabbit and existed only in Stewart's imagination. One night Hermi and I were sitting on the sofa in the living room when the front door creaked open. We had been discussing our reactions to the play.

"Why, Joe," I said, "looking at the door. "Come right in."

"Who are you talking to?" said a baffled Hermi. "It's Joe McSpivak, my 6-foot Scottish terrier from Miami. "Come in, Joe, and have a seat with us on the couch."

"Don't you come in." declared Hermi. "Leave now."

"Come on, Hermi, that's no way to treat my old friend. Sit here, Joe, next to Hermi."

Hermi slid away to the far end of the couch. After a few minutes, while I asked Joe about his health and what fire plugs he had found recently, I said, "Hermi, I have to go to the drugstore. I'll leave Joe here with you."

"No you will not! Take that damn thing with you!"

So Joe and I left the house together. When I came back home alone, Hermi refused to open the door until I convinced her that Joe was was off to see Figgy – and possibly Jimmy Stewart's friend Harvey.

Next door to us lived Phillip Trammell Shutze, the architect I worked for after my year at Georgia Tech. Phil didn't drive. Whenever I saw him waiting for the streetcar I would pick him up and drop him off at his office on the way to mine. Shutze, an unreconstructed classicist, recognized only classic design as architecture. In spite of my Bauhaus training, which he couldn't stand or understand, we had many hours of interesting talk on those long rides.

Living near my uncle also exposed us to a series of unusual events. The large underground storage tank serving the Gulf gas station was leaking and needed replacing. The city refused to issue a permit for the job. To get around this bureaucratic roadblock, my uncle had the new tank installed while the city was asleep. When the Building Department found out, he was arrested for breaking the law. A fine was levied, but the tank remained and the station was back in business. "No one can call himself a citizen of the United States unless he has been arrested at least once" became Uncle Harry's watchword.

His second encounter with the law involved a full-size outdoor advertising sign he erected within a few feet of Peachtree Road, even though a city ordinance forbade signs in such a location. My uncle took his case to court. The sign bore the message "Reelect Ike and Dick." As a loyal Republican, he was endorsing Eisenhower and Nixon for president and vice president. Without fear of contradiction he said, "That sign is a political message. Demanding its removal infringes on my freedom of speech, guaranteed in the Bill of Rights. The city ordinance is not applicable – the sign must remain."

"Case Dismissed" announced the judge, citing the First Amendment. But the judge's blessing didn't protect the sign from the hand of a prankster. One night, after three strokes of a paintbrush, the sign suddenly read, "Re-erect Ike's Dick." Uncle Harry was livid. A painter came out the next day and restored the original message. Harry posted his aged, dim-witted night watchman by the sign with a shotgun. "Uncle Harry," I said, "I'm not coming to visit you as long as Mr. Shirley is in your driveway with a shotgun. He's half blind and has no judgment. He may even shoot you." My uncle smiled and said, "Don't worry. The gun isn't loaded."

A member of Nixon's campaign saw the restored sign and photographed it for presentation to the vice president. Somewhere is a letter from Nixon thanking Henry A. Alexander for his support.

One morning our stay in the Peachtree Road house came close to tragedy. I was in the living room when I heard a sharp thud from the kitchen. Close inspection revealed a .22 caliber bullet embedded in the door of one of the soft redwood cabinets. I also found two small ones in the front door that opened to the living room, the other in the screen door that fronted it. I inserted a pencil through the two holes and sighted out across Peachtree to a dormer window in the house opposite ours. In the other direction, the pencil pointed to the bullet lodged in the kitchen cabinet. The slug had passed above the stair landing near the bottom of the stairs – a passage in constant use. It was almost a miracle no one was there when the bullet whizzed through.

My call to the Police Department produced a detective whose intelligence level made Inspector Clouseau, the detective in Blake Edwards's *Pink Panther* films, look brilliant. "No one fired at your house deliberately," he said. "It had to be a random shot from a hunter." I responded, "Look at this," indicating the pencil still in the door. "It points directly to that dormer window across the street. That's where the shot came from. Please check it out."

The culprit turned out to be a teenage boy who had been aiming at our doorknocker. I showed him how his bullet could have killed one of us and let him off with a lecture. His parents confiscated his rifle and paid for our repairs.

Mismatched Memberships

My uncle Henry Alexander did more than rent us a house on his Peachtree Road property. When we returned to Atlanta he enrolled me in two very different organizations. The first was his American Legion, a group that was proud it had voted against the bonus for veterans of World War I. I attended two meetings – my induction, and later with my friend, Ham Douglas, who asked me to go with him.

The national president of the Legion, a survivor of the Malmédy Massacre, where over a hundred American prisoners were murdered during the invasion of Europe, welcomed all the recruits with a wide smile and a beefy handshake as he moved among us bellowing, "It is always a privilege to shake the hand of a fellow Legionnaire!" Any misgivings I had about the Legion were reinforced by his theatrics.

My attendance record was dismal. The second of the two meetings I went to had one plus: I won the door prize (I don't recall what it was.) Douglas later reported to me that the reaction from the members as I walked to the podium was "Who the hell is that guy?"

One good thing came from my membership. Whenever I was introduced to an audience hostile to my stand on civil rights, I made sure my introduction included "Member of the American Legion," which invariably calmed the audience down at least somewhat.

The second organization was the Atlanta Historical Society. My uncle Harry and Walter McElreath were the two principal founders. Its purpose was to preserve the history of Atlanta through collecting and preserving documents, photographs, and artifacts.

My induction into the Society was quiet – no one stated it was "a privilege to shake the hand of a fellow member." I went to many interesting meetings, with the most memorable one held at Margaret Mitchell's stately home on Peachtree Street. It was the only time I had a conversation with her (in truth, I mainly listened.)

She was almost trembling with disgust when she related her opinion of Atlanta's public schools:

"Our schools are worthless," she growled. "They don't teach the kids the basics an educated person must know. It's all fluff and social graces. The worst of it is the 'Career Book' farce. All the high school seniors are told to choose a career they will pursue as adults. They will interview adults practicing those careers – doctor, lawyer, banker, truck driver, or garbage collector – and assemble a Career Book with those interviews, clippings, and other material to be turned in at year's end. The ones too stupid to select a career are told, 'You can be a writer like Margaret Mitchell.'

"One afternoon a golden-haired young girl appeared at my door. 'Yes, honey – what can I do for you?' She said, 'Mrs. Mitchell, I want to interview you for my Career Book.' I answered, 'Well dear, please don't take this personally, you're only doing what's required –but I want you to go back and tell your teacher that I said, 'Those Career Books are a lot of goddamn nonsense!' Hugging her book and her curls flying, she turned and fled down my walk."

Margaret Mitchell's reputation as a feisty lady was well deserved.

Hermi and I, and later Helen and I, attended many enlightening meetings at what later became the Atlanta History Center (AHC.) It moved from a single large house on Peachtree to a complex of several buildings surrounded by gardens on West Paces Ferry. Louise Allen, the wife of my good friend (and former mayor) Ivan Allen, was a strong proponent of its expansion. For a number of years I served on the AHC Board. Helen and I were interviewed about our World War II experiences – hers in the USO and mine in the Marines. I have also given the AHC archives a number of my files.

An AHC staff member, Michael Rose, has been most helpful in advising me on publishing my memoir. Another member of the staff whom I have fond memories of is Franklin Garrett, the unofficial historian of Atlanta. There was nothing he didn't know about the city's history. Over the years we became close friends. The Center was then under the industrious and creative guidance of Salvatore Cilella, the now-retired president and CEO. I think of the Atlanta History Center as the embodiment of the city's spirit.

Dad died while we lived on Peachtree. In spite of his tendency to brag on me to others, he had been an ever-present part of my life, always cheering me on, telling me I could do anything I set my mind to. It was a comforting feeling knowing he was behind me. They say a son is never old enough to lose his father – he is never ready to take his place. I still wish he were around. My inheritance allowed Hermi and me to seriously consider a home of our own. And once more it was time to move on.

Before I get to the design and construction of our beloved Round House, however, Chapter 6 will detour to my career in architecture and civic service in my fast-changing hometown.

Chapter 6

Two Careers - Architecture and Community

Doing well by doing good ...

— Anonymous

It wasn't long after we returned to Atlanta that a call came for me. "Cecil, this is Frank Neely."

The voice on the telephone snapped me to attention. Neely was CEO of Rich's (Atlanta's top department store), a member of the Atomic Energy Commission, and one of Atlanta's most prominent civic leaders. He also happened to be the husband of a cousin of mine, Rae Schlesinger.

"Your dad told me you've just been awarded your master's degree in architecture at Harvard," he continued," and you and Hermi are back in Atlanta. He also said you're looking for a job in an architectural firm."

"Yes, sir."

"I'd like to introduce you to Henry Toombs," Neely said. "He's a fine architect and he's now designing our Rich's Store for Homes. You probably remember that he designed our house out on the farm in Norcross. If you'd like to work for him, I'll ask him to interview you. He has a medium-size office and a wide range of commissions. You'll like him and you'll learn a lot. Are you interested?"

"You bet I am," I answered. "Thank you so much. I'll call Mr. Toombs for an appointment."

This wasn't the only promising lead to come my way. When I was in New York I visited the firm of Ketchum, Gina & Sharp, probably the number-one designer of retail facilities. Mr. Ketchum offered me a job. I told him I hated to turn him down, but that my wife and I had decided we would be happier living in our hometown of Atlanta.

"Well," Ketchum said, "in that case you should check out our Atlanta office. It's the in-house architect for Davison's. The locals' job is to remodel the large flag-ship store in downtown Atlanta and design a number of smaller stores throughout the state." Davison's department stores were Rich's main competitors.

"Fine," I said. "I would certainly like to look into your suggestion. Ketchum responded by saying he would call the Atlanta office manager and tell him I'd be there. And I was, before I saw Henry Toombs. The Ketchum office – a long, narrow, well-lit, big-windowed space – was on the third floor of the Davison's building. The senior architect greeted me warmly and led me down the drafting tables on either side of the room to introduce me to all the architects and draftsmen. One of them was Joe Amisano, who would later become Toombs's partner in the firm Toombs, Amisano & Wells.

"Is it OK if I call you Cecil?" he asked.

"Sure, just don't call me Captain. I'm through with the Marines."

"Good, come on in my office," he said. I sat down in front of his desk, totally unprepared for his next offer.

"Cecil, I want you to be the manager of our drafting room."

It took me a full minute to grasp that he was offering me a senior position. "Wow," I said, "but I'm not prepared to take over your drafting room. I just got my master's in architecture and the only experience I've had is working in offices during the summers."

Apparently the senior architect knew about all of this in advance of our meeting, which made me wonder about his judgment. "All right," he said. "I'll be glad to take you on as a senior designer."

"Thanks," I said, "I'll let you know next week."

The next day I walked up the narrow stairs to the second floor office of Toombs & Creighton Architects. Toombs met me at the receptionist's desk and led me to his office. After telling me about the scope of their work, he introduced me to his partner, Bill Creighton. The two architects once worked together in New York and had been partners in Atlanta for several years. Toombs was a short, wiry, grey-haired man – pleasant but direct, with no small talk. Creighton was tall and a little heavy, had an affable smile, and was ready to chat about anything at all.

After a short conversation, they offered me a job in their drafting room. The salary? Seventy dollars a week – $3,640 a year, or $1.20 an hour! Ditch diggers did much better, even in 1947. So much for the earning power of degrees from Harvard and Yale! I said I would come back in a day or so with an answer. I needed to think this over.

Ketchum, Gina & Sharp offered me twice the salary, but there was no variety of work in their Atlanta office; all commissions dealt with retail stores. Toombs & Creighton's workload included several large houses, a bank, the remodeling of the Atlanta Federal Reserve Building, and the large Store for Homes addition to Rich's department store. Furthermore, I didn't think it would be wise to walk away from a job sponsored by Frank Neely, a. k. a. "Mr. Atlanta." So I said "No, thank you" to Ketchum and "Yes, thank you" to Toombs & Creighton. My father thought the salary was mean and offensive. Hermi kept her peace.

Lessons from H. Toombs

Henry Toombs was an excellent draftsman. In fact, his drawings were works of art. But he made clear to all his employees that he had no need of beautiful drawings. "Your drawings," he repeated many times, "are contract documents, not artworks. Clear delineations and accurate dimensions are what I want – only what a contractor needs to build the building. Drawings are just a means of getting a building built, and otherwise have no intrinsic value."

To make this point, when he came to an architect's table to look at his drawings, he sometimes set a wet Coke bottle down on a carefully drawn sheet, wrinkling the paper and smearing the lines. Even more destructive were the live coals he knocked from his pipe, scattering burning embers across the paper.

During my first year, every job I was assigned was never finished, and for many different reasons. One I well remember was an addition to Frank Neely's farmhouse. Toombs had designed a roomy, sunlit brick house for the Neelys before the war, and now they wanted to add a master bedroom suite. Toombs called me in, handed me the drawings for the original house, told me in detail what the Neelys wanted, and said, "Go to it." I met with the Neelys to hear from them firsthand and walked with them through the house and the gardens. Over the next several weeks I finished the plans and several renderings.

When the couple met with Toombs and me, they looked over my drawings, then went to the next room to confer. Once they emerged Frank said, "You've done a good job. It's exactly what we want."

I beamed.

"Henry," he asked Toombs, "how much will this cost?"

"Our contractor, Van Winkle Construction, gave me an estimate of 16 thousand," said Toombs.

"What?!," cried Neely. "The whole damn house didn't cost me that much five years ago!"

"Come on, Frank," said Toombs. "You know there's been a war since then. It's a good price."

"Not for me, it isn't," came the reply. "Forget it. Thanks, Cecil."

We slinked away grumbling.

At times Toombs' behavior was peculiar. One day when I returned from lunch, I walked by the conference room and heard the dull thudding sound of a hammer. I looked into the room to see Toombs swinging a hammer at the plaster model of Rich's Store for Homes. When he saw me he lost his concentration – and the hammer slipped from his grasp and went crashing through a window. It landed in the street below.

He calmly said, "Cecil, would you mind fetching that hammer for me?" I found the hammer in the middle of the street, surrounded by shattered glass. After I picked it up and returned it to Toombs, he continued his assault on the plaster model until it was reduced to a pile of white dust.

A second revealing incident occurred around noon one day. Toombs and I were walking out of the office at the same time and passed the receptionist; he turned his head toward her to her to say, "Jane, I won't be back after lunch. I'm getting married this afternoon. See you tomorrow." The marriage turned out well.

One of Toombs's designs was the hospital at Warm Springs, Ga, for polio victims. George Haas, a friend of mine and the brother-in-law of my future business partner Rocky Rothschild, was paralyzed by polio in his mid-thirties. He was taken to Warm Springs and put in an iron lung, a steel cylinder respirator in which the patient lay with only his head protruding. On a visit, I found Haas in a private room, confined in the lung. He gave me a big smile in greeting. I brought him news from Atlanta, but we soon ran out of topics of conversation and I left.

Many children were confined in similar devices. Although iron lungs sustained life, they brought torture chambers to mind. The humane aspect of what could have appeared to be a "house of horrors" was Toombs's gracefully designed buildings – low structures encircling a landscaped court and adorned with classical columns and details. For the immobilized patients, the architecture provided a modicum of relief from a sterile life in an iron lung.

Toombs also designed President Franklin D. Roosevelt's Little White House at Warm Springs. Polio-stricken FDR spent many days floating in the warm water, soaking his paralyzed legs. I'm not sure how the president and Toombs met, but they were certainly compatible. While rifling through a drawer at the Toombs & Creighton office, I lifted some old blueprints and saw Henry's drawings for the Little White House, drawings signed with "Franklin D. Roosevelt, Architect." Roosevelt wasn't a licensed architect – and whether he signed the design in jest or not, his self-designation as an architect raised heated objections among many licensed practitioners.

I suggested to Toombs that the drawings should be in a museum instead of lying around in his file, advice I believe was ignored. I have no idea where the drawings are today.

Soon after joining Toombs & Creighton I visited my in-laws in New Orleans. We went to Yom Kippur services at their temple. As was my wont at services, my mind shut out the boring litany and went in search of a more entertaining subject. Toombs had been given the prestigious commission to design the memorial for the Rhone American Cemetery and Memorial in Draguignan, France, and I passed the time by mulling over my own concept for the memorial. I sketched out a design on a blank page in the temple services program – a long, granite-walled hall, some 20 feet wide and 12 feet high, set below ground level. At either end was a broad flight of steps down to the floor. Over the hall was a 6-foot-thick slab suspended by cables from a soaring parabolic arch across the slab's center; a large, circular opening that would afford a dramatic view of the arch. The dark, dimly lit granite walls were engraved with the names of the servicemen buried in the cemetery.

On my return to Atlanta I drew up my design and showed it to Bill Creighton and Henry Toombs. They looked at it silently and reacted with only a couple of nods. No way was their $70-a-week draftsman going to design this important memorial, I realized. I had hoped my design might influence Toombs's solution, but his restrained, classical jewel showed no evidence that he ever even glanced at my drawings.

A few months later, a drawing of Eero Saarinen's steel arch soaring over the banks of the Mississippi in St. Louis was published in a leading architectural magazine, and it bore a strong resemblance to my design. Creighton came to my desk and opened the magazine. "Look, Cecil," he said. "You were there ahead of Saarinen with your arch. We should have given your design more consideration."

"Thanks," I said. Without classical columns, my design never had a chance.

Many years later the famous Vietnam Memorial appeared with its two long walls covered with the names of the men who died in that misbegotten war. This riveting feature was also part of the below ground-level walls of my design for the memorial in Draguignan. So much for being ahead of one's time. There's no reward for being first if your idea dies at birth and later comes to fruition through another designer.

Alexander & Rothschild Opens for Business

Bernard "Rocky" Rothschild was a Naval officer stationed in Atlanta during World War II. He met and married Barbara Haas, a member of Atlanta's oldest Jewish families (Barbara is the sister of George Haas, the polio patient I visited at Warm Springs.) Rocky was an architect from Philadelphia, a graduate of the University of Pennsylvania. His father was a architect before him.

My phone rang one day in 1946. It was Rocky.

"Cecil, let's have lunch. I want to run an idea by you."

"Sure, how about next Tuesday, at Herren's?"

Even before we ordered lunch Rocky said, "You know, I've been A.K. Adams's in-house architect since I left the Navy. It's been interesting and educational, but limiting. Adams builds only factories and warehouses, and I'm ready to find a broader practice. What would you think of you and I forming a partnership?"

I had anticipated his question. "Rocky," I said, "I think it's a great idea, but the timing isn't good. Toombs recently made me job captain for the Federal Reserve Bank he is designing in Jacksonville. Running that job is the first decent assignment I've had, and I'll learn a lot from it. Let's talk again after I finish the documents."

"OK, I understand," said Rothschild. "We'll keep in touch."

Two days later I was finishing a sheet covered with my detailed drawings for the bank — it was drawn in ink on a linen sheet tacked down at the four corners. Toombs came to my desk and pushed me aside. He then grabbed the sheet of drawings, tore it at four thumbtack corners, and crumbled the center into a mass of wrinkles. "Put this in the file drawer," he said. "We're stopping work on the project. The client won't let me set the building back far enough for decent landscaping in front. We're not going to work until he changes his mind." I looked down, astonished at my rumpled sheet, and mustered only an aggrieved "OK."

Two actions followed. I took the sheet home and ironed it flat so it could be finished at some future date; then, the next day, I put it in the file. Of greater consequence was my call to Rothschild. After telling him what Toombs had done, I said, "This is it — one more job in the file. I'm ready. Let's go. Alexander and Rothschild — or is it Rothschild and Alexander? — is launched!" We decided that my name should be first so it would be near the front of the listings in the phonebook.

Rocky and I met with Henry Toombs to tell him I was leaving. He not only tried to keep me but also to hire Rocky. "You know, boys, you'll get only minor jobs for years; with us, you'll be involved in major work. You'll learn a lot." We told him we knew he was right, but we wanted to try.

When I told Bill Creighton goodbye, he understood. "I don't blame you Cecil – all you've had to work on here never materialized into a finished building. You've been currying dead horses."

Rocky's in-laws, the Haases, lived in a barn of a house in the old Inman Park suburb, Atlanta's first. They offered us a large upstairs bedroom gratis to use as our office. What it lacked in a business atmosphere was more than made up in free space. Also, two large glass windows overlooking a small park let in natural light. We were grateful, and soon moved in with our drafting boards, files, a few chairs, and a sofa.

As I embarked on a new phase in my life, my father was doing the opposite. He had lost his lease on his hardware store and, in the tight post-war market, was unable to find a new location. He was forced to close the store and sold his stock to a friendly competitor, King Hardware.

After breakfast one morning, he opened his checkbook on the table. Slowly he wrote out a check for $10,000, payable to Alexander & Rothschild Architects. It was a share of the money he made selling the stock of J.M. and J.C. Alexander & Co. He slowly tore the check from the book and held it out to me.

"Son," he said, "this will help you and Rocky get started. I wish you all the best in your new business."

His head dropped down, and he was enveloped in wrenching sobs. It was the death rite for a store his father and uncle had started just after the Civil War. He had struggled to keep it open during the Great Depression, and now the only remnant of his years of struggling was the yellow check he had just given me. He believed he had failed. I put my arm around his shoulders and his sobs finally stopped. He smiled and patted me on the arm. "The store is in good hands, son." he said.

Alexander & Rothschild's first commission came as a surprise. Lee Meyers, a liquor dealer, wanted to build a house. He never would say why he called us, a new, inexperienced firm working in a bedroom. All architectural designs are compromised, but if the building is successful, compromises are kept to a minimum. The Meyers house was totally compromised, with good design secondary to what Meyers demanded. Lee Meyers also has the distinction of being the most difficult client I had during my many years of practice.

I was eager to use the new techniques I had learned at Harvard, and one of these was a method of heating a house. Copper coils channeling very hot water were buried in the concrete floor slab, and the heat radiating from the slab warmed the house. Meyers agreed to this innovation, and the copper coils were installed. Meyers also had a demand of his own: a flush-valve toilet, the kind used in commercial installations. There is no tank, and water is run under pressure directly to the toilet; then, when the handle is pressed, the bowl is emptied in a turbulent surge.

The morning after the Meyers family had spent their first night in the house, my office phone rang. "Alexander & Rothschild Architects," I said. A voice charged with anger shot into my ear. "Is this Alexander?" I recognized his voice. "Yes, Lee. What's up?"

"Goddamn it, Alexander, when I flushed my toilet this morning, I scalded my balls! Why was the water so damn hot? What are you going to do about it?!"

"Lee," I said, "I think the water line to your toilet must be in contact with the very hot copper coils in the living room floor slab."

"For Christ's sake! What are you going to do to fix it?"

"There are two solutions," I said. The first one is expensive and messy. We can dig up the slab and find where the toilet line is in contact with the heating coils and move it."

"What's the other one?," he hissed. Is it expensive? Will it make a mess?

"No, there's no mess and no expense."

"Well? Go on! Go on!"

"Lee, just stand up when you flush."

He slammed the phone down. I heard no more about it. Subsequently, I had a number of complaints from my clients, but Lee Meyers's was unique.

I have regretted the destruction of several of my buildings, but when the Meyer's house was knocked down I rejoiced. Still, I learned a valuable lesson from the Meyers job: Atlanta's weather is ill suited for coil-heated slabs. Chilly early morning temperatures on spring and fall mornings followed by afternoons that warm up into the 80s are a surefire recipe for discomfort in coil-heated houses.

Another early commission came from my sister Charlotte and her husband Roman Weil, who wanted me to design a home for them on Thomas Avenue in Montgomery, Ala. At the time they had three children, so it would be a large house. Unfortunately, they weren't comfortable with contemporary design. The house was a compromise, airy and open but with a traditional shingle roof.

I made a design error that turned out to be disastrous. Between two of the downstairs rooms was a large glass sliding door. The glass wasn't shatterproof, and nothing alerted you that it obstructed your passage. Ken, the younger son, ran full-force into the door. It shattered, and a shard sliced Ken's leg; I think he walked with a slight limp for years afterward. Whatever the effect, it didn't interfere with his successful career as a lawyer. Ken and his wife, Pam Wilcut, live in Seattle. Ken's older brother, Roman Weil Jr., is an economist who had a brilliant career on the business school faculties at Georgia Tech, the University of Chicago, Stanford, and Princeton.

Like Roman Jr. the Weils' two daughters survived the house unscathed. Judith (this is the second "Judith" mentioned thus far in this book; It's a popular name in my family) has long been married to Hershel Shanks, founder of *Moment,* a magazine devoted to the culture and concerns of Reform Jews;

Judith herself, after many years as research editor and then administrative editor for Time-Life Books, retired and now devotes her energy to assembling historic family documents and artifacts. Carol Weil has lived in New York for some 35 years with her companion, Jerry Maltz, an architect. She was a reference librarian at Time Inc. in New York. Jerry, in addition to his successful architectural practice, is an environmental psychologist and an Interior design educator.

The offspring of the Weil children have made their own mark. Roman Jr.'s marriage to Cherie Buresh produced three children before the couple divorced. Charles (Sandy) Weil, is an energy analyst, statistician, and data architecture data designer; his wife, Anne Parker Weil, is a commercial real estate asset manager and blogs (flaxandtwine.com) about creative projects and life (with beautiful photography) with Sandy and her three children. They have recently relocated from Boulder, Colorado to Baltimore where Sandy has taken a job with the Baltimore Ravens as their director of football analytics. Alexis (Lexie) Weil Laesh is a Seattle physician and is married to Brad Laesch, a chemistry professor. Ken Weil, as mentioned before, is now an attorney living in Seattle with his wife Pam, and is the father of Rachel Bigby and Caitlin Weil Smith, who married Jed Alexander Smith, founder of Drugstore.com.

A "how to have children" publication of some sort must have circulated in the Weil family, considering it has produced twelve great-grandchildren. As far as I know, the house in Montgomery still stands.

My Push for Urban Renewal

Charles Massell was one of my close boyhood friends. After graduating from the University of Virginia he went to work as the contractor for his uncle, Ben Massell, called by Mayor William B. Hartsfield "Atlanta's one-man boom." After World War II, Ben built dozens of one-story speculative office buildings with affordable rents. So, when firms or professionals were unable to find offices in any other Southern cities, Atlanta was ready with plenty of space renting at $2.50 a square foot. It was Ben Massell's foresight that put Atlanta on the road to becoming a world-class city.

In 1947 Ben was ready to build a major office building for the federal government. I had told Charles about the excellent education in architecture I'd received at Harvard, and in a good bit of detail. Armed with this information,

Charles said to his uncle, "Ben, I think we should use Cecil Alexander's firm, Alexander & Rothschild, to design the federal building. He just got his master's at Harvard and is well-versed in the latest building techniques and cost-saving approaches."

Ben made quick decisions: "All right, Charles, bring him in."

Working in a free upstairs bedroom and our experience limited to a single house, Rocky and I were commissioned to design the first major post-war office building in the South. The Feds wanted large, uninterrupted floors. Massell wanted a cheap building. In response to these two directives I designed an eight-story, U-shaped reinforced concrete building with very large floors and wide column spacing. The elevators were placed in an external tower adjacent to the floor slabs. On the south elevation were concrete "eyebrows" over the rows of windows, which shaded them from the summer sun. The exterior was faced with cream-colored brick. Built for $5.24 a square foot, the building was rented by Massell to the government for $1.43 per. It is now a successful condominium, and the new owners have applied to have it placed on the National Register of Historic Places.

Ben Massell later had us design a government office building at the corner of Peachtree and Baker streets, on the northern edge of downtown. It was clad in an all-metal window wall, and Massell approved this then-innovative exterior because its thin sheet allowed for more rentable area than a building with a conventional brick façade. Just before the building was ready for occupancy, it was hit by torrential rain driven by 30-mph winds. Water went through joints in the wall like thousands of miniature Niagara Falls.

What could be done immediately to seal the joints? We found a solution: caulking with Thiokol, invented during World War II as a liner for aircraft fuel tanks. If a tank were pierced by a bullet, the Thiokol expanded and sealed the hole. This magic product protected the fuel in my dive-bomber tanks and saved me during World War II. It kept the water out of the Peachtree-Baker building and saved my career as an architect. I owe a lot to Thiokol.

My first foray into the civic arena was as president of the Atlanta chapter of the American Institute of Architects (AIA.) My last address to the members as president changed my life. "Architects," I said, "are failing to recognize our need to eliminate slums. If we don't recognize this as an obligation for our profession we will end up designing shoddy buildings at the end of mean streets." The *Atlanta Constitution* published my remarks. Alvin Ferst, an old friend of mine and an adviser to Mayor Hartsfield, clipped the article and saved it.

The federal urban renewal program in Atlanta was stalled. Mayor Hartsfield didn't want the city in the "real estate business." A requirement of the federal government for funding urban renewal was the appointment by the city of a citizens' committee to act as a catalyst for the program. Atlanta's business community supported urban renewal as a means of phasing out slums and converting the cleared land for profitable development. Under pressure from these "Big Mules," Hartsfield reluctantly agreed to appoint a Citizens Advisory Committee for Urban Renewal. My friend Alvin Ferst showed the mayor the article stating my views on slums and suggested he appoint me as chairman. I'm convinced that Hartsfield accepted Ferst's suggestion only because he thought I would be ineffective and the program would flounder. I was a young, unknown architect with no standing in the community, and I had no experience whatsoever in politics. He appointed six additional people to the committee – two white women, two black men, and two white men. Only Ivan Allen, Jr., a wealthy businessman (and future mayor), had any clout.

I recall several occurrences during my chairmanship that were critical to the future of the committee. The Atlanta newspapers, the *Journal* and the *Constitution*, had given very little space to the urban renewal program. Allen arranged a meeting with the editors of both papers and our committee. We told them, "Without media coverage, our efforts to promote the program are futile." Ralph McGill, the courageous and progressive editor of the *Constitution* responded: "We've only been nitpicking urban renewal. We need to really cover it. We don't promise not to question your actions, but we'll be involved."

Turning to Jack Spalding, editor of the *Journal*, he asked, "Jack, do you agree?" Spalding said, "Yes."

McGill then appointed Gene Patterson, the executive editor of both papers, to implement their effort. He assigned reporter Alex Coffin and another newsman to cover all our meetings and any significant developments.

A second encounter with the mayor almost terminated the committee. We asked Hartsfield to come to lunch at the AIA building, which had one of the very few restaurants where our bi-racial group would be served.

Ivan Allen led off the confrontation. "Mr. Mayor, you won't support this committee's efforts to advance urban renewal. If you don't want us to function, we're here to tender our resignations." Infuriated, Hartsfield pounded the table and yelled at Allen. The meeting was in tatters, and urban renewal was about to fall into a bottomless hole.

All of a sudden several waiters, one holding a large candle-lit birthday cake, trooped in singing the happy birthday song to the mayor. All anger drained from his face as he relaxed, smiled, and thanked us all. The meeting was saved. The mayor said he favored urban renewal and welcomed the committee's efforts.

The cake was my idea. Someone had told me our lunch with Hartsfield was scheduled on his birthday, so I ordered the cake, never dreaming it would save the program. It could've been called the most influential seven layers of white-iced confection in Atlanta's history.

It wasn't long before my new role took me to Pittsburgh. During the war I had flown over the city many times, day and night, but never saw it – the dirty smoke belching out from the steel mills shrouded it in a rolling mass of smoky clouds. At night the fiery red glare from the mills reflected on the clouds, assuring me that Pittsburgh was down there; in daylight only the radio beacon gave assurance that we were over a large, thriving metropolis. Then, in 1944, Pittsburgh leaders realized their city needed to clean up or it would perish.

Richard King Mellon led the mission to coordinate and implement the clean up. He and other members of the Mellon family formed the Allegheny Conference, whose membership included the metropolitan area's most influential residents. The steel mills were gradually shut down, the grime was cleaned off the buildings and streets, and comprehensive downtown development was underway. A new Pittsburgh sparkled in the sun.

I chose to visit the city now because I thought it could be an invaluable source of information for use in Atlanta's urban renewal program. I arranged a visit with the director of the Allegheny Conference, an intelligent, outgoing young man. Under his guidance I became thoroughly familiar with the particulars of Pittsburgh's renaissance.

Toward the end of my visit I met with legendary Mr. Mellon himself. When he heard I headed a commission with only seven members, he shook his head. "A committee that small will have no impact." he said. "You need across-the-board leaders from all segments of the city. And they must agree to be personally involved. They mustn't delegate someone to act for them."

Mellon, I knew, was a friend of Robert Woodruff, CEO of Coca-Cola. "Mr. Mellon, I'm sure Mr. Woodruff would welcome your visiting Atlanta to discuss how Atlanta could emulate Pittsburgh's renewal. "No," he said, "I'm not sure you need another city's direction."

When I met with Mayor Hartsfield on my return to Atlanta, I told him Mr. Mellon had said Atlanta needed a larger committee, one composed of civic leaders from all corners. Hartsfield didn't wait an instant before he said, "No, no way. Atlanta's business leaders won't join. Urban renewal is awash with racial problems, and the Big Mules won't touch it."

Big Mules and Brick Walls

I lost the battle, but I had just begun to fight. Malcolm Jones, a retired Army colonel, headed the city's Urban Renewal Department. He was a tough, determined administrator dedicated to the program's success. He also was in total accord with the need to enlarge the committee.

The chairman of the City Council's Urban Renewal Committee was Hamilton Douglas. Ham was smart, honest, and motivated. He was quoted saying, "Jones and Alexander are two of the most persistent people I know." The statement came a year after Jones and I nagged the mayor until he finally spat out, "All right! All right! Write a letter! I'll sign the damned thing. Send it to anybody you want, but no one – no one – will join your committee. Urban renewal is too controversial. Too much race!!"

We mailed out eighty-seven letters to black and white men and women who were influential in the city's life. Much to the mayor's surprise (and, I suspect, dismay), eighty-six accepted. Two-thirds of the respondents were white and one third black – then the ratio of the races in Atlanta. The majority were men. At a time when the mayor and the so-called white power structure ran the city, my committee had become a powerful force. Someone said, "If Alexander's Committee wanted to move the state capital to Macon, it would be done."

I appointed an executive committee, which I chaired. There were also committees dealing with developers, lending agencies, public relations, and zoning, among others. Zoning was the most crucial and controversial matter, and designating land for the resettlement of African-Americans who had to relocate when their slums were cleared was bitterly fought by the neighborhoods where such housing was proposed. Most of the available land had to be rezoned. It was at the zoning hearings in City Hall that the most intense battles were fought.

One of these confrontations led furious whites to pack the Council chambers and almost tear the city apart. The Atlanta Housing Authority – chaired by

John O. Childs, the city's leading realtor – assumed the responsibility of providing the required units as public housing. At that time it was accepted practice to designate housing by race. For Atlanta to qualify for federal funds 1,000 relocation units had to be built. Two sites were selected: the Field Road area west of downtown for 650 units, and 350 units for the abandoned Egleston Children's Hospital, located in a decidedly white part of town. To build at either site, the land had to be rezoned for multi-family occupancy – and it was the public outcry against rezoning Egleston that became an epic battle.

The first step was the presentation of the Planning Commission's recommendation for the use of the Egleston site to the Aldermanic Zoning Committee. We thought it would easily pass. To the proponents' surprise, the committee voted four "yes" and four "no." Hartsfield's supporting vote was necessary to pass the ordinance, and when the bill was presented to the full aldermanic board it was soundly defeated.

Responding to both the anger of the black leaders and our fears that the urban renewal program would be lost, the Advisory Committee arranged another meeting with the aldermen held at the excusive Capital City Club, over my objections. (Although Jacob "Cooch" Alexander, my great uncle, had been a member of the club, when the wives of members joined the ladies turned a civic club into a society enclave that excluded Jews; I assume my great uncle resigned.) To present our case, I attended the meeting. One of the few aldermen who went was Douglas Wood, who had opposed the zoning but now felt he was wrong and that the bill should be passed. He said he would reopen the case and introduce an ordinance to rezone Egleston. The rezoning of the Field Road site would be presented at the same time.

The battle lines were drawn. Leading the opposition was the Rev. Lewis Newton, pastor of the large Druid Hills Baptist Church and a board member of the Georgia Baptist Hospital – both institutions near the Egleston Hospital site. Early on Newton had secured pledges of support from a majority of the aldermen. To reinforce his position, he brought the church choir to sing hymns at City Hall.

A second leader of the opposition was Pete Latimer, who was not only the president of the Atlanta School Board but was retained by the board members as their paid attorney. He stirred up fierce anger among parents whose children attended nearby all-white Grady High School. Objections to Latimer as an elected city official who opposed the rezoning were raised, but accusations of blatant conflict of interest didn't stop him.

Powerfully arrayed in support of the rezonings were the Citizens' Advisory Committee, the Atlanta Chamber of Commerce, the AFL-CIO, the Urban League, the League of Women Voters, the Black community's Empire Real Estate Board, the Atlanta newspapers, and Atlanta's small business and civic leaders. So once again there would be a vote by the full board. The first step in our strategy was for members who might have influence with the aldermen to contact them. Then, at the hearing, the less heavily opposed Field Road site would be brought up first. The theory was that aldermen who opposed the Field Road rezoning would retaliate against the aldermen who supported it by voting to rezone Egleston.

Mayor Hartsfield, a good headcounter, thought he had the votes in the bag – one of the opposing aldermen was recovering from an operation and it was thought he couldn't make the trip to City Hall, and one of the original "yes" voters assured the mayor he would now oppose the bill. When the hour for the hearing arrived, there wasn't an unoccupied square inch in the spectators' area of the chambers or the hall outside. The crowd was restless and angry. No speeches were allowed, but the mob made their feelings known with shouts and foot-stomping.

As lawyer for the Atlanta Housing Authority, Jack Izard of the prestigious law firm King & Spalding, made our initial presentation. I followed with an impassioned address; later, when I heard a recording of my remarks, I was startled by my emotional delivery. The CEOs of Atlanta's large department stores – Dick Rich of Rich's and Charles Jagels of Davison's, fierce business competitors, – joined the voices in support. One angry Rich's customer tore up his credit card and threw it in Dick's face. The only presentation in opposition I recall was that of Pete Latimer. For me, it was unforgettable. He spewed lies about my activities and denounced my character. I never again spoke to him, and I was delighted when he wasn't re-elected to the School Board.

The approval of the six hundred fifty Field units was addressed first. It easily passed. Then came the tense re-vote on Egleston. The sick alderman, looking pale and weak, came in just long enough to vote a quavering "no." The alderman who assured the mayor he would support the zoning flipped back and voted "no." None of the Field Road aldermen voted for Egleston. So our strategy didn't work. The vote was tied. This left it to Lee Evans, the president of the board, to cast the deciding vote. After reading a long defense of his decision he said, "I am voting against the rezoning of the Egleston site." I was devastated. It was, I felt, the end of the urban renewal program and of the coalition of blacks, the white business structure, and Mayor Hartsfield, who had kept Atlanta on a progressive course.

Fortunately, I was wrong. The six hundred fifty Field Road units convinced the federal government that Atlanta could build the additional three hundred fifty units. In a few months another site was zoned, bringing the total to the required one thousand units. Although the black/white coalition was initially stressed by concerns that the mayor and the white community had failed to deliver, the coalition would ultimately hold together and elect Ivan Allen as mayor for two terms.

As I left the room, I saw my fifth-grade teacher, Mrs. Richardson, sitting among the Baptist opponents. She looked at me with sorrow and shook her head. "Cecil, I don't know what has happened to you. You were such a nice little boy." Our pictures were on the front page of the *Constitution* the next morning, but not together.

The Citizens Advisory Committee was the catalyst for five urban renewal projects and the acquisition of 5,000 housing units for families relocated from the slums. When I retired years later, there was a long editorial in the *Constitution*, complimentary of both the accomplishments of the committee and my leadership.

Chairing the committee was time-consuming. Although I neglected my profession, I knew the contacts I made would eventually lead to architectural commissions. Rothschild, my partner, didn't see it that way. At one point in a stretch when I was frequently absent from the office, a disgruntled Rocky said, "Cecil, you're not contributing to our practice. If you won't resign from that committee, you'd better find yourself another partner."

"Rocky, the contacts I'm making will eventually generate business for us," I replied. "Right now nobody is building. Even if I spent all my time in the office it wouldn't generate any commissions for us. Aw, come on, let's not break up our partnership. Here's another solution: I hear Bill Finch's firm, Finch and Barnes, has a lot of work and is understaffed. Let's approach him with a proposal to merge."

Rocky agreed, and I set up a meeting with Finch and his partner, Miller Barnes. Bill and I had known each other since we were both at Tech. Both of us had also been Marines, an even stronger bond. Finch and Barnes liked the idea of merging, but they had an unexpected requirement, An employee of their firm, Caraker Paschal, had just been offered a partnership, so would have to be a principal. Although I had some reluctance at being outnumbered in the proposed set-up, Rocky and I agreed. A coin flip decided the order of the names in the firm. Finch won the first toss, putting his name first. I don't remember how the other names were determined, but we became Finch, Alexander, Barnes, Rothschild & Paschal Architects. It wasn't too long before we were called FABRAP, since our official name was too long to write, speak, or remember. I never liked FABRAP. To me it sounded too much like a contraction of "fabulous wrapping paper."

After an extensive search, we found office space on the second floor of an old five-story office building at 70 Fairlie Street in downtown Atlanta. It had three distinguishing features: It was a walk-up; the cooking odor from a greasy spoon on the ground floor came curling up the stairs and sent the essence of hamburgers and hot dogs wafting through our office; and it had a view across Fairlie Street to the rear of the fine old post office, which housed a number of federal courtrooms. Almost every morning a car would park at that building and marshals would pull a manacled prisoner out of the back seat and push the pathetic, shuffling captive down the sidewalk. This wasn't a cheerful scene as I approached my drafting board. But we stayed at 70 Fairlie Street, smells and all, for years.

Our premises were fitted out with a row of offices for the partners, a meeting room, and a large area for draftsmen. Mrs. Virginia Barber, who served as a receptionist and typist, oversaw the area. We had the space and we had a staff, but one vital component was missing – architectural commissions.

The Georgia Power Project

Charles Massell unexpectedly called me one morning. "Ben Massell wants to see you at 2:00 this afternoon at his office. Can you make it? I'll be there." So would we.

Without even a "hello," Ben Massel told us, "I'm bidding on a new building for the Georgia Power Company. Would you like to draw the preliminary plans including a perspective? I'll pay you if I get the job."

FABRAP had one job in the pipeline – the addition of a screened-in porch to my cousin's house. We were in no position to reject any possible commission with or without assured compensation. "Yes," I said. "What's the program?" Massell shoved a page across the table to me. On it was a minimum of information – the total area of the building, the required foot-candles of light at desk height, and the site. The site was on the block where I had already designed the Peachtree-Baker office building for Massell, so our plan would incorporate the existing building in the layout.

To enhance Massell's proposal, I decided our design should reflect the specific requirements of the company itself. At the time, Georgia Power occupied an old office building in the central business district, and I asked Jack McDonough, the company's president, if I could inspect the offices and interview department heads to learn what they wanted in the new building. He agreed, and had his secretary show me around and introduce me to the interviewees. The specifics culled from my investigation enabled me to have a complete report on my drafting table in three days. But Ben Massell didn't get the job. Henry C. Beck, a developer from Texas, was the winner.

We were just adjusting to our defeat when a call came from Joe Hutchison, the Atlanta partner of the Beck Company. "Jack McDonough wants us to use you as architects," he said. "He says you know the power company's requirements and he would be comfortable with you handling the job."

I was elated. My research had paid off. Furthermore, Beck would pay us upfront and at standard rates, neither of which would have been forthcoming from Massell. Working with McDonough was great, but working with Hutchison was only semi-great; Hutchison ignored our specifications whenever he found he could buy inferior materials more cheaply.

Several features of the project set it apart from Atlanta's other office buildings. We called in Abe Feder, a lighting consultant, to light up the exterior; his experience included lighting Rockefeller Center and the stage lighting for the musical *My Fair Lady*. Feder surrounded the new building with powerful beams that bathed the white marble in dazzling light. Our concern that migrating birds attracted by the light would crash into the building proved to be wrong.

A second feature was the large fountain in front of the entrance – a reflection of the company's use of hydroelectricity. (In recent years, the Cooper Cary architectural firm was employed to remodel the building, and I would've preferred demolition of the building to their decision to bulldoze the fountain and destroy the façades.) A third innovation we made was using the building's ceiling lights to heat the building.

For once, the announced Grand Opening *was* grand. Abe Feder, acting as Master of Ceremonies, called in the Atlanta Symphony Orchestra and the Atlanta Ballet. He then directed a truly beautiful program with dancers whirling around the building's columns to the magnificent sounds of the symphony. To my knowledge, no building had ever been dedicated with such an extravaganza. (I wasn't around when the coliseum in Rome was dedicated, so it might have been grander.)

Across Peachtree Street from the construction site for Georgia Power headquarters was a cafeteria where I often ate lunch. I had just finished a meal when a glance up at the nearly-completed office tower shocked me to the bone. The gleaming white Georgia marble exterior was randomly marked with large black rectangles. A closer look revealed that some marble slabs had fallen out, revealing the black waterproofing fabric beneath. From my limited view of the front and one side, I could see that at least twenty slabs had fallen to the ground or to a low roof at the base of the tower. Although alone, I shouted, "What in the hell happened?!"

It was several weeks before our engineers and a testing laboratory figured out the cause. Ollie Reeves, Atlanta's most trusted masonry contractor, had tried a new material for setting the thin marble slabs. Slivers of wood, which can contract under pressure, were traditionally used to set stones – a method that probably went back to the ancient Greeks and the Romans. I'm sure Reeves himself had used wood until he experimented with the Georgia Power building.

On our building, Reeves used Plexiglas on all four sides of each slab. When the material was tested in the lab after the failure, it hadn't contracted an iota under pressure. So when the hot sun caused the marble slabs to expand, they hit the Plexiglas spreaders and there was no give. Instead, the slabs bent, cracked, and fell, exposing those dark black rectangles.

Replacing the slabs was tedious. First, all the joints (even those not directly affected) had to be cut out with a skill saw by a workman dangerously balanced on a board hung from the roof. Then all the joints were sealed with Thiokol, the same product we used on the window wall. A concealed fastener on every slab ensured that all of them were secure. The cost, including laboratory investigation, was $ 16,000 – in today's dollars, at least half a million. We agreed to pay $5,333, as did the general contractor and Georgia Power.

At the time we didn't know that Jack McDonough, president of Georgia Power, was mightily impressed that we picked up a third of the cost. When he retired, I approached him with an offer he could certainly have refused – a job at my firm at minimum pay. His perks would be a private office, a secretary, and a free parking space.

"Cecil," he said, "because I admire FABRAP assuming responsibility for the marble collapse, as well as your design of our building, I would be proud to work with you. What will I be doing?"

"Great, great!" I said. "We want you to help us get commissions and advise us on management."

"That's fine. One other thing: If I come, you have to move out of that dilapidated office over that smelly restaurant!"

Moving on Up

In 1960, FABRAP moved to the eight-story Grant Building, an old but solid and well-kept office building near downtown Atlanta's Five Points, next door to the Commerce Club.

McDonough turned out to be a good provider. Among the buildings he secured for us were four at Georgia Tech – the Student Center, the Chemistry Building, the Ceramics and Chemical Engineering Building, and a large multi-use sports facility for non-varsity athletes. His advising on management wasn't as successful. Our 30-person architectural firm and the hundreds of employees McDonough managed at Georgia Power had little in common; supplying electrical power from a monopoly to customers who must have your product was a long way from supplying architectural services in a fiercely competitive market. Nevertheless, Jack's smiling optimism boosted our morale. It was during his tenure that FABRAP secured all of the major commissions we had in Atlanta.

Jack didn't cultivate Jewish relationships, except in one instance. Once a month he had lunch with Boolie Maier and Frank Ferst at the Commerce Club; the three men had been together at Georgia Tech back in the Twenties, and that old tie overcame any religious differences.

Hermi and I invited McDonough and his wife for dinner several times, but they never reciprocated. However, a headline in June 1967 made McDonough one with us. The morning the Israelis won the Six Day War, I was walking by his office. Jack was sitting at his desk, the morning paper spread out in front of him with its headlines screaming of Israel's overpowering triumph. A huge grin lit his face. "Boy oh boy! Man oh man," he yelled. "Did *we* [the operative word] ever beat their asses!" He did not convert, however.

I had been right a few years before – my contacts with Atlanta's business leaders and their approval of my handling of the Urban Renewal Committee led FABRAP to a series of major architectural commissions. I did well by doing good.

Meanwhile, Mayor Hartsfield decided to divorce his wife of many years to marry an attractive young woman who had taken his heart and every other part of his anatomy. And he knew this would finish him politically. Love conquers all, they say, but it doesn't conquer politics. Hartsfield announced he wouldn't run again and carried out his matrimonial plans.

The mayor's decision also had implications for me. His timing was such that the impending availability of his office would take me into the political arena, if only tentatively.

Chapter 7

The Round House and Beyond

"Those who construct their own shelter duplicate themselves.

— *Jack McLaughlin, Jefferson and Monticello*

In 1953 my old friend Alvin Ferst asked me to help him choose a lot for his house. He also told me I would be the designer. (It was Alvin who, a decade later, would recommend to Mayor William B. Hartsfield that I assume chairmanship of the Citizens Advisory Committee for Urban Renewal.) "Fine, Alvin," I said, "I'd really enjoy working with you. There's a lot on Mt. Paran with great possibilities. Let's go look at it."

For whatever reason, Alvin didn't like the lot. He ultimately bought a house in Golf View Terrace designed by my future partner Bill Finch. But I *did* like the lot, and I took Hermi to look at it as a site for our own house.

"It's beautiful, but it's too far out," she said.

"You're thinking about the compact living patterns in New Orleans," I explained. "Atlanta isn't confined by a river. In a few years this will be considered close in."

She was still dubious, but agreed to accept my recommendation. We paid $10,000 for six acres, a reasonable price in those days. Hermi and I wrote a program for the design of the house, and with this as my guide I started drawing a preliminary plan. I went through numerous schemes – an L shape, an open U, a rectangle, a square. Hermi's reaction to each was "That's great. Let's build it!" My inevitable response: "Well, I want to work on some other approaches. Let me try again."

The square scheme, set on a knoll some 200 feet from the street, had good possibilities. However, I kept remembering the easy beauty of the Pantheon in Rome, a circular structure covered by a dome with a round oculus in the center that allows sunlight to light the interior. "Why not," I thought, "try a circular plan?" It all fell into place. Hermi said once more "Let's build it!" This time I said yes.

It took six months of hard work at the office for two architects and me to prepare the construction plans and specifications for the contractor. Nothing came "off the shelf." Because of the curves and angles, every feature required detailed drawings; the kitchen alone took several sheets. In one row of the cabinets a small, triangular space was left at one end. It would have required a 3-inch-wide cabinet door to access the space, which would have tapered to a point, creating a triangular space only 12" x 12" x 3". When Hermi saw the space was enclosed she said, "I don't want to lose that space. Please put a door to it." She backed off when I pointed out the miniscule space we lost and I told her there were 90 cabinet doors in the kitchen.

An unusual feature of what we would call the Round House was the reinforced concrete columns supporting the main floor and the roof. To preserve a huge old oak tree in the center, I surrounded it with a circle of rooms opening to a central court, where the great tree stood.

We visited the site day and night. The finished plans were nearly complete when Hermi and I went for a last look. As we ventured into the site, I was surprised to see what the light from a full moon revealed at the crown of the hill. "Good Lord, Hermi, look at that!" The huge old oak lay flat on the ground, its trunk split by lightning. I was free to cover the court now that nature had relieved me of saving the tree.

Back at the drafting board, I designed a folded plate roof – a series of triangular gables around the court with glass windows and in the center a large, circular, plastic-covered skylight. (Thanks to the Pantheon.) The court would be paved with stone and flanked by two gardens.

Bids were taken. The low price was $120,000, twice our budget. (Today the 5,000-square-foot, five-bedroom, five-bath house would cost at least two million dollars.) Our dream house became a nightmare. The contractor said, "The price is high because we haven't had any experience with reinforced concrete." I tried to explain how a single wood form for pouring the concrete could be used over and over around the circle. He shook his head, unconvinced. So, out with concrete and in with wood and steel. The second time around, the low bid from the firm of Adams & Willis was $93,000, still a third over our budget.

"Hermi," I said, "we can't do it. I'll have to start over with a more conventional plan."

Just after the bids came in, we went to New Orleans to visit Hermi's parents. Our lawyer, De Franklin, and his wife Phoebe were there at the same time. We met for lunch one day at Commander's Palace, one of the city's many fine restaurants, and I told De the sad story of the high bids.

"Cecil," he said, "Build it! You can afford it; it's an investment in your family and your future."

It was the best advice he ever gave me. I took it – and Adams & Willis went to work. Bowie Adams was in charge of the job for his firm. He soon found out that the foreman who was laying out the house didn't know how to measure anything but right angles. He put him on another job and took over the day-to-day supervision himself. Under Bowie's control, the workmanship in all phases of construction was outstanding.

A rumor circulated that we intended to cover the living/dining room oak floor with wall-to-wall carpet. Because of the curving area, laying the wood was difficult, but it was done beautifully. The foreman came to Hermi and said, "Mrs. Alexander, we hear you intend to cover the floor. We worked hard on it and we think it's an excellent job. The men are very proud of it. They asked me to plead with you to leave it uncovered."

"Oh, no," said Hermi, "we wouldn't think of covering this floor; it's beautiful!" In all my years as an architect, this was the one time I was asked not to cover up work. Workmen were usually delighted to have their sometimes-sloppy jobs hidden.

Perfection takes time. A year dragged by. The final task was building the folded plate roof over the court. A wooden frame was erected to support the segments of the roof as it was built. Only when it was completed would the ceiling be self-supporting.

"Cecil," Bowie said one day, "the roof is finished." We're taking the support out today. Do you want to watch?"

"I'll be there," I replied.

The structural engineer who worked with me to design the roof was Jim Polychrone, a member of the Georgia Tech faculty. I called him and said, "Jim, they're taking the scaffolding out from under the roof today. Come on out and stand with me under the roof while it's done."

"No way," he said. "I'll wait until I'm sure that roof will stay up there without the scaffolding." To me his reluctance showed a serious lack of confidence in his own design. We remained friends, but I never used him again.

I stood under the roof as the scaffolding came down. There wasn't a creak or the slightest movement – the design was successful. The roof still stands some 60 years later.

At the end, Hermi and I had some animated disagreements about details, so we decided we needed an arbitrator. We called in Florence May, an accomplished interior architect. Hermi and I agreed that if any arguments arose we would go with whichever side Florence endorsed.

Florence didn't accept either of our positions – she firmly stated her own. One decision where she prevailed is a singular feature of the house. The flat roof surrounding the circular court was supported by small, round columns, the kind usually used in basements. I asked her what she thought of enclosing the columns with wood trim.

"Don't touch them," she said. "Leave them bare."

We did. If you look closely you can see the word "Bethlehem," (the steel company, not "O little town of") embossed on each of the columns.

Mickey Steinberg, who later became one of John Portman's top architects, gave me an epilogue to the roof story. He told me, "At the time your roof was being designed I was working for Jim Polychrone. He turned the project over to me. I designed your folded-plate roof, not Jim." Soon after, "You can move in. Here's your final bill" was Bowie Adams's good-bad announcement that he was finished.

Hermi and I hadn't been able to agree on some of the major furniture – in particular, a sofa around the freestanding circular fireplace in the living room. So, with only our old pieces of furniture in place, the house seemed bare. At night, the large windows in the rear of the house became large black squares. There were no lights out there; only dark forest. This frightened our younger child Judy, who had been comforted by that friendly "Go Gulf" sign lighting up her window in the Peachtree Road house. With tears on her cheeks she cried, "Daddy, why did you have to put so much glass in this house?" With this dubious endorsement rankling me, we settled in for our first night in a totally different environment. I don't recall sleeping that night.

On a Sunday, not long after we settled in, the doorbell rang. It was Luther Randall and his wife. He owned Randall Brothers Inc., the firm that made the laminated rail curving down the stairs to the lower floor.

"Come right in, we're glad to see you," I said.

"Cecil, I want to show my wife where our vacation went."

"Sure, but I'm not sure what you mean."

"It's that laminated handrail on the stairs to the lower floor. Our shop thought it was a simple curve. After the rail was built, we realized the curve was compounded and had to bend both horizontally and vertically to conform to the stairs. So we built a new and much more complicated one, which allowed for no time off." He then led his wife to the curving stairs with pride and showed her the perfectly matched laminated rail. "And there," he said, "is our vacation. Beautiful, isn't it?"

The house afforded some unique vistas. Stepping out from our bedroom after waking up, we had a beautiful view of the sunrise through the glass wall of windows enclosing the living/dining room. Through those same windows we had a mural that changed colors as the forest of trees blazed with reds and golds in the fall or the fresh green hues of spring. Wildlife, too. I caught on film a brightly colored pileated woodpecker flying through a white snow shower.

Hugh Stubbins, an architect and one of my Harvard instructors, said about the house, "This is like a treehouse; you're looking at the treetops through these windows. It's beautiful and exciting." I saw a photo of a building he designed after his visit, and its roof was identical to my folded plate design. I considered it a sincere compliment.

1958's Shattering Event

Just one year after we moved into our new house, a traumatic event ripped through our lives. The Temple – the most dominant symbol of the Jews as a valued and welcomed segment of Atlanta's population – was bombed. Our girls were ready to go to Sunday School when Hermi called our friend Helen Eisemann Harris, whose children were also ready to leave, and told her what we knew, which at the time wasn't a lot. We told the kids that a boiler had exploded, although we sensed it was something much more sinister, and kept them home.

Headlines in the paper confirmed that some time before daylight a bomb had been detonated against the west wall of Friendship Hall, the assembly hall adjoining the schoolrooms behind the main sanctuary, destroying that end of the building.

A photograph of Mayor William B Hartsfield and Rabbi Jacob Rothschild kneeling in the rubble appeared on the front page of the *Atlanta Constitution*. Editor-Publisher Ralph McGill wrote a powerful column asserting that the bombing was the terrible result of years of hate and prejudice throughout the South. The photo and McGill's column also made it into newspapers across the country.

FABRAP was commissioned to inspect the building and the sanctuary for structural damage. Beyond the demolished area, we found no problems. The stained glass windows in the west wall of the sanctuary had been blown out, but no other serious damage was found. We were, however, concerned about the sanctuary's large chandelier, which was suspended by a chain from the top of the central dome. Andy Gravino, our daring engineer, was raised up to inspect the condition of the support of the heavy crystal lighting fixture. He found no damage.

At the following Friday night service, every seat was taken except those beneath the chandelier. As was our custom, Hermi and I arrived late. I saw the empty seats under the dome and said, "Come on honey, let's sit there. Our engineer said it's absolutely safe." Every eye was on us as we slid into our seats. A murmur of disbelief filled the auditorium and heads were shaking at our stupidity. We survived.

I recall only one statement by Rabbi Rothschild as he looked out over the packed congregation: "So it takes a bombing to bring you here." Donations poured in. The one I remember best was a torn, dirty dollar bill with a note reading, "No one should bomb the Lord's house where our friends the Hebrews worship." The shaky handwriting was that of an elderly woman from South Georgia. The wave of support reassured us that the Jews of Atlanta were totally accepted as members of the community. Before the bombing we weren't so sure.

Voices from smaller Southeastern cities complained that we Jews who supported civil rights were exposing them to physical and financial threats. "You in Atlanta are in a safe community. You're not threatened, and you have no right to expose us." The bombing clearly showed that we in Atlanta were also at risk but felt morally driven to take a stand. We heard no more, and no one else was bombed. Another voice was that of my brother-in-law Roman Weil, who headed the fund drive for his Temple in Montgomery. He was having difficulty raising funds, and when heard how money had rolled into Atlanta he asked, "How did you do it?" My reply? "Easy. All it takes is for someone to bomb your temple."

The group of thugs who allegedly set off the bomb was brought to trial twice. The first trial ended in no verdict; the prosecutor had demanded the death penalty, and since no one was injured or killed the jury thought death was too harsh a punishment. A second trial also failed to convict the bombers. The jury foreman, a friend of mine, told me afterwards, "The jury was certain the defendants were guilty but the prosecutor did a poor job and didn't prove his case. Legally, we couldn't render a verdict of guilty."

Years later the story of the bombing engaged the talents of a gifted Atlanta writer, Melissa Fay Greene. Her book *The Temple Bombing* vividly recreated that devastating event. (An extraordinary human being, Melissa has also used her writing to call the world's attention to an under-the-radar problem: the plight of Ethiopian orphans whose parents have died of AIDS. She and her husband, attorney Don Samuel, adopted four Ethiopian children and one Bulgarian child and have raised all of them as their own. They also have four biological children – nine kids in all! Her most recent book, *No Biking In the House Without a Helmet* [2011] is a delightful account of life with her family. If Melissa writes a how-to book for emulating her many accomplishments, it should be an instant bestseller. Melissa and my daughter Judy are great friends [Judy photographed Melissa for her 2011 book and was an early manuscript reader] and Melissa's second son Lee and my grandson Jed were best friends growing up.)

Over the years, we had many visitors, and some of them qualified as VIPs. These included Leonard Cohen, the poet laureate of Canada, songwriter, and singer – the first cousin of my late cousins Henry, Rebecca, Esther, and Judith Alexander. As a teenager, Leonard dressed in a preppy coat, tie, and saddle shoes; as an adult he became a monk for a time and changed his dress to a flowing robe. Today he continues to perform before adoring audiences around the world.

A chance meeting at the house had an effect on the politics of Georgia and Tennessee. Nashville's Mayor Ben West was in Atlanta for a meeting and had dinner with us. I mentioned the effort of Mayor Hartsfield to break Georgia's county-unit voting system, which made an Atlanta citizen's vote a fraction of that of a rural voter. Morris Abram was handling the mayor's suit against the state, and my former employer Henry Toombs was his client.

When West heard this, he lit up. "Get Hartsfield and Morris Abram over here. I have a similar suit in Tennessee. I want to discuss it with them." They shared with West the strategies in their legal approach, and he filled a notebook with their advice. Several months later I had an excited phone call from West. "I couldn't reach Hartsfield or Abram, but I had to share this news," he said. "We won our suit against Tennessee, and our legal arguments were based on what I learned from Abram and Hartsfield. You should put a plaque commemorating that meeting on your wall." I congratulated him and said the Atlanta suit was still pending; it was eventually won. One of the old friends who got in touch with me to express approval of the outcome was McGeorge Bundy, my Yale classmate and one of President Kennedy's "best and brightest."

From time to time, violinists, pianists, singers, a harpist, a flutist or a glee club (specifically Clark Atlanta University's Huff 'n' Puffs, former members of Yale's famous Whiffenpoofs) filled the atrium of the Round House with sparkling music. A most memorable "concert" occurred in the court just after a Georgia Tech-Alabama football game, when my brother-in-law Roman arrived with a bunch of Alabama fans. One of them, a tall, gangly, sloppy, semi-drunk young man, positioned himself on the raised walk around the court. Without any prelude, he raised his gravelly voice in a wretched version of *Without a Song*. It echoed from the walls and windows, bringing silence from every other source. After several choruses, the off-key solo died. The "singer" smiled, wiped his mouth with his sleeve, and said to me, "I knew the acoustics in this room were great. I just had to test them. They're wonderful."

He was right about the acoustics. Every artist who performed in the room spoke of their excellence. But it was an accident. When designing the atrium I took many factors into consideration, but acoustics wasn't one of them. One joyful byproduct of the acoustics was the singing of our canary, Holly-Joe. Every day of the week Atlanta's classical music station filled the room with sound, and Holly-Joe joined in. If, by chance, the music was popular or jazz, he remained silent.

All in the Family

After Hermi's father Harold died, she no longer made monthly trips to New Orleans. One day she said, "Let's have a baby. This time it'll be a boy." So, ten years after his sister Judy was born, our son Doug arrived. Dr. Abraham Velkoff had scheduled a golf game on the day Hermi went into labor. To save his tee time, Velkoff gave her drops to speed the delivery. But Doug would have none of it — it was ten o'clock that night before he appeared.

When I designed our house, I didn't have an active little boy in the program. Doug soon made it clear this had been a grievous oversight. Mounted on his tricycle, he peddled at high speed from the kitchen, through the entrance hall, around the atrium, and then full tilt across the dining room, directly at the large glass doors. Only at the last second did he cut his wheel toward the kitchen, missing the sheet of glass by inches.

We discussed putting up some sort of barrier in front of the doors, but I hit on a less obtrusive means of saving his life.

"Doug," I said, "when pilots come in to land, they circle airports to the left. You're making right turns on your bike. You've said you want to be a pilot, so why don't you circle through the house the other way? It'll be good practice for landing an airplane."

"Sure," he replied. "I'll go the other way. Thanks. Dad."

No more was Doug headed pell-mell at the glass doors. I'm still proud of my solution, and sometimes wonder if I should have written a book about how to trick your kid.

At dusk one evening, Hermi and I were looking at our three children sitting together around the dining room table. Terri was about to begin to empty our nest. She would leave in the fall for Wheaton College in Massachusetts. Softly, I said to Hermi as I nodded toward the three, "Time is a terrible thief. They'll soon be gone."

The most memorable event at 2322 Mt. Paran Road was daughter Terri's marriage to architect Herb Millkey. He was a Roman Catholic, though a very casual one. Our rabbi refused to marry a mixed couple, and it took a while for me to revive our friendship. Herb's priest was not only willing to participate in the ceremony but he also gave the couple a Hannukah menorah as a wedding gift. Hermi's mother prevailed upon another rabbi, Louis Binstock, originally from New Orleans and a close family friend, to come down from his present congregation in Chicago to perform the service. The house was filled with orchids from the greenhouse of our neighbors, Helen and Bud Mantler. I escorted Terri down the brick walkway and across the flagstone court to join the rabbi, the priest, the groom, his best man, and the bridesmaids, all arrayed in front of the glass wall framing the woods beyond. Mayor Ivan Allen and his wife Louise were among the honored guests.

Hermi considered herself the official house mother for every young couple coming to Atlanta. Among her "children" was Hava Rothschild, an Israeli who taught Bill Rothschild the son of our rabbi, in Tel Aviv. Their relationship evolved from student-pupil to husband-wife. Bill and Hava were about to move to Cincinnati, where Bill would finish his studies at Hebrew Union College. Hava's wardrobe was much too tropical for Ohio, and Hermi not only insisted that she borrow her fur coat but also gave her sweaters, scarves, gloves, and wool dresses.

Three years after Terri left for college, Judy left for Boston University. Her experience in an urban university at a time of political upheaval was far from the experiences Hermi and I and Terri had at Smith and Yale and Wheaton. She did, however, get to study with some notable professors, including Howard Zinn, the renowned historian and political activist.

Between her sophomore and junior year, Judy and her roommate took a year off to travel through Europe, to St. Petersburg (then Leningrad), and to Morocco. It was a journey of discovery – not only for reasons of the history and culture of the places they visited but also because these young people were off on an adventure of their own for the first time. Some stories Judy told me years later made me glad I hadn't known about them at the time. But I was pleased that she spent many hours in the great museums and galleries of the world. During her month in Paris she went daily to an atelier in Montparnasse, on the Left Bank of the River Seine, to study life drawing and became quite good at it. In later years she and I would take life drawing classes together – an enjoyable activity to share.

The Story of the Japanese Bell

One morning in 1961, after my departure from the romantic ambiance of the Round House and the arrival at my much less romantic office desk, my secretary Mrs. Barber called from the outer office. "Mr. Alexander," said the ever-attentive Ms. Barber, "Mayor Hartsfield is on the phone." (I had given up asking her to call me Cecil — we are still Ms. Barber and Mr. Alexander some 50 years later.)

The mayor, as was his wont, wasted no words on a greeting. "Cecil, after the war, the Navy gave Atlanta a Japanese bell. It's in storage at Piedmont Park. I want you to design a tower for it. I'll put it in Hurt Park. I'll have a policeman pick you up and take you to the warehouse. When can you go?"

"Any time," I said.

The Navy apparently gave our city only one bell, even though there were two ships named USS *Atlanta*. The first was destroyed off Guadalcanal and sank in what is called Iron Bottom Bay; its replacement of the same name survived the war. I had expected the bell to be from a battleship or some other Japanese naval vessel. It was not. I recognized it as a temple bell. The dark bronze cylinder stood about 4 feet tall and was covered with Japanese characters. It rang when a round plate cast on the bell was struck with one of the small logs suspended from chains at either end.

I called Hartsfield back and said, "Mr. Mayor, that bell isn't a spoil of war. Ir was taken from a temple — it's a religious relic. We're trying to lure Japanese business to Georgia, and displaying the bell in downtown would offend any Japanese who saw it."

"All right, forget it," he grumbled.

A year later, Hermi, our friends Phoebe and De Franklin, and I were planning to go on an architectural tour of Japan. I called Mayor Hartsfield and told him where I was going and wondered if he'd like me to find the origin of the bell. He said, "Fine. I'll send the Japanese wife of one of our policemen out to translate its inscription." (The cop had married her when he was with the U.S. Army stationed in Japan.) In a later call, Hartsfield said the woman was unable to read the characters, so I made a rubbing of all the inscriptions to take with me.

By some happy chance in Tokyo, I met a young Japanese-American who was attached to our embassy. I told him about the bell and my rubbings.

"Would you," I asked, "see if you can have the rubbings translated and try to find the temple the bell came from?" He was pleased with the assignment. "I'll get on it right away," he said. Several weeks later I received a letter from him. The inscription on the bell was cast in classical Japanese, which explained why the policeman's wife couldn't interpret it. A Japanese language historian read the characters and found the bell had hung in a temple in Yokosuka, a city on Tokyo Bay.

My embassy friend warned me that the temple might not want to receive the bell because it could be considered defiled – but a second letter said the temple would be very glad to recover it. I told all this to Mayor Hartsfield, and then took it upon myself to assure him the Japanese would certainly give Atlanta a relic in return.

An international meeting of the Rotary Club was to be held in Japan. I called Marshall Weaver, a friend who was the president of the downtown club, and told him about the bell and its history, and that the Navy had already agreed to take it back to Japan. Would he and Rotary Club delegates escort the bell back to the temple in Yokosuka? He thought it was a great idea.

After two voyages across the Pacific and the 6,000-mile round trip by land from San Francisco to Atlanta and back, the bell was returned to the Jodoji Temple. Weaver reported that on the day the Atlanta Rotarians delivered it, the street in front of the temple was covered with a red carpet. Crowds of cheering Japanese lined both sides of the street. Standing in front of the adults were hundreds of school children waving miniature Japanese and American flags in both hands. I've always regretted I wasn't there. It would have been a rewarding and unique experience.

A year later, two gentlemen from Yokosuka came to Atlanta on a business trip, and Mayor Hartsfield received them at City Hall. A photographer for the *Atlanta Constitution* caught the mayor and the two Japanese visitors bowing deeply to one another. Thanks were all the two gentlemen brought with them – there was no gift from Yokosuka. So much for my assurances to the mayor that protocol would require the Japanese to return a favor in kind! To his credit, the mayor never called me on it. Today a similar bell is displayed in Atlanta's Carter Center, one presented to Jimmy Carter by the Japanese. There's no connection between it and the Yokosuka-Atlanta bell as far as I know, and the U.S. Navy certainly didn't liberate it.

Either consciously or subconsciously, my quest to return the bell to Yokosuka was inspired by John Hersey's Pulitzer Prize-winning novel *A Bell for Adano*. I don't know if it was based on an actual happening. Hersey wrote about a church bell being replaced in the Italian town of Adano after World War II. At the end of his life, Hersey was Master of Yale's Pierson College, the residential college where I lived while at Yale. I composed a letter to him to tell how he had inspired "A Bell for Yokosuka." Friends suggested changes to the draft of the letter, and it lay unfinished on my desk for months. Then Hersey died. Damn!

Close Friends, Chance Meetings

Hermi's sister Terry was very involved with Democratic politics in Maryland. During the Carter-Mondale campaign she put her vast energy and political smarts to work for Vice President Walter Mondale. Her reward was an invitation to his post-inaugural reception. Hermi, who had worked hard for Jimmy Carter, was delighted when Therese invited us to come with her. A possible ancestral link came to light while we were at the reception. In the middle of the large reception hall, I saw Terry talking to a tall man with Negroid features but with the pale, white skin of an albino. I walked over to them. Terry introduced us. We were both Alexanders. From the moment he heard my name, his attention was riveted on me. Up and down, up and down, from my face to my shoes, his piercing eyes took me in.

When Terry paused in her monologue, the gentleman said to me, "Where is your family from, Mr. Alexander?"

"Charleston, South Carolina," I answered.

"Well, cousin," he said with no flicker of a smile, "so is my family. Someday I'm going down there and find out who the hell I am."

As we walked away from this unsettling encounter, Hermi suggested, "Why don't you send him a copy of Uncle Harry's history of your family?"

"No way," I said. "There's a will reproduced in there where one of my ancestors left her slaves divided among her children and an account of a sea captain who sailed from Charleston to and from the West Indies. He was surely a part of that famous triangle of slaves, rum, and molasses."

My rising status as an architect and an active citizen brought me in contact with some interesting people. Rudyard Kipling wrote: "Or walk with kings – nor lose the common touch."

I haven't walked with kings (unless I include Martin Luther King, Jr and his kin) but I have taken a few steps with a prince: HRH Charles, the Prince of Wales. If his mother, Queen Elizabeth, who recently celebrated her 80th birthday, ever steps aside or dies, Charles should become king. Of course, he may have to contest it with one of his sons. If he does ascend the throne, then I can say, at least a future king met me. In that event, I hope I will not lose the common touch.

Prince Charles of Great Britain came to Atlanta on some obscure royal mission long before he became a subject for the *National Enquirer*. A reception was held at the Governor's Mansion – and since the British consul general and his delightfully undiplomatic wife had become our friends, Hermi and I were invited. I was standing alone in one of the large, brightly lit and blandly furnished rooms trying to appear at ease. "Hi Cecil," said the consul (he pronounced it "Cessil," of course.) "Look over in the corner. Some bloke has the prince literally backed into that corner and is jabbering his ears off, and I need you to break it up."

We walked over to the corner. "Excuse me, Your Majesty," said the consul, "May I introduce a prominent Atlanta architect?" He did not mention my name. The prince smiled and, looking directly at me, said, "Oh yes, Mr. Portman, I've heard a great deal about you." John Portman is an internationally known Atlanta architect-developer. The consul rushed in with, "Oh, I'm sorry Your Majesty, this isn't Mr. Portman, it is Cecil Alexander, another highly respected Atlanta architect." The prince and I were amused, the consul was mildly embarrassed, and life went on.

The prince had just won his wings in the RAF, and we talked about our common interest in flying. In fact, I gave him a one-liner he used the next day in a talk he gave in Charleston, South Carolina, to laughter and applause. "You know," I said, "Great Britain and the South have something very much in common. We both lost a war to the United States of America. Or, if we include the War of 1812, you lost two." This line was printed in the *London Times,* which gave full credit to Prince Charles as the originator. Neither Mr. Portman nor I earned a mention. So much for my fifteen minutes of fame!

Portman is still famous, and so is the prince. Now, many years later, my memory of the Prince Charles's physical appearance includes three elements: his large ears, a wide smile, and black velvet loafers with the prince's seal emblazoned on the toe of each slipper. We haven't been in touch recently.

For years my mother-in-law, Rosetta Hirsch Weil, a fine violinist herself and the first female soloist in the Houston Symphony, had invited visiting symphony soloists to stay at her home on Audubon Place in New Orleans. Yehudi Menuhin and his sister Hephzibah, who was often his accompanist, had stayed there many times. A strong friendship had developed between the Menuhins and all the members of the Weil family, including my wife Hermi.

In the 1960s we were visiting the Weils at the same time Yehudi and his sister were. The day of their concert we drove them to the symphony hall so they could rehearse with the New Orleans Civic Symphony. After the rehearsal, the Weils were taking us to lunch. Handing me his two violins, Menuhin said, "Cecil, will you please take my fiddles back to the house?" I said I would, but I wasn't at all comfortable with this task. One was a Stradivarius and the other of equal quality – both worth millions and irreplaceable. When I carried fine instruments into the Audubon Place house and gently put them on the front hall table, I was profoundly relieved. Then I went down to the French Quarter to meet Yehudi, Hephzibah, my wife, and her family for lunch at Antoine's, a fine French restaurant. It was a delicious lunch at noon and a beautiful performance that evening.

My first contact with Menuhin wasn't so pleasant. He was a 14-year-old prodigy playing in Atlanta at its dismal barn of an auditorium. At the rear of the auditorium was Taft Hall, where the Georgia National Guard drilled, and they were there in force on the night Menuhin played. Accompanying his violin during the first part of the concert were shouted commands and rifle butts pounding the wooden floor (not a melodious sound.) At intermission Menuhin's manager came on stage and announced, "Unless that infernal noise is terminated, Master Menuhin will not continue." Minutes later, shouts of glee came from Taft Hall as the guardsmen were dismissed early. The concert continued.

I was about the same age as Menuhin and desperately struggled to extract music from my violin (not a Strad!) No prodigy, I. That most difficult instrument requires an exquisite, acute ear; unlike a guitar, it has no fingerboard frets to tell the player where to press; it's all up to the violinist's musicianship to produce the proper note. While I loved the mechanics of playing the instrument, I had great difficulty distinguishing a sharp from a flat.

With his beautiful playing, Yehudi Menuhin made it very clear that I wasn't up a blind alley: I was up a tone-deaf one. Frankly, as a teenager I hated him for showing me up so with so little effort. But years later, when Hermi and I entertained Menuhin in Atlanta, we became close friends. There was no pretense, no ego, and no demand to be treated as a star. To paraphrase Ralph Waldo Emerson, Menuhin was "first a man" – a man who also played the violin and would later be knighted.

One memorable lunch at our home in Atlanta almost ended in tragedy. Yehudi and his eldest son Krov had been estranged for years. He asked if we would invite his boy to the lunch so they could begin to repair their relationship. At the time, Krov was undergoing Army underwater demolition training at Ft. Bragg, hardly a desk job. Lunch went well in the sunlit dining room. Father and son were making great progress toward mending their schism, but all pleasantries stopped when Krov choked on a piece of rare beef. His cheeks grew red and his eyes wide as he lurched from the table and tried to breathe. I ran after him and pounded on his back. The meat was dislodged, and he sucked in air in great gulps. This took place long before the Heimlich maneuver was introduced, and this athletic young soldier was near death, saved only by my clumsy pounding.

Whenever we could, we met with Menuhin and his British second wife Diana (formerly Diana Gould), a former ballet dancer, each time they came to Atlanta. Hermi and I had lunch with Diana in London during a trip there. She was deeply involved in helping the poverty-stricken of London and lived in the slums to more closely identify with their needs – truly an inspiring and dedicated human being.

In early 1986, some three years after Hermi's death, I sponsored a concert with Menuhin conducting the Atlanta Symphony Orchestra. Hermi was a gifted violinist with perfect pitch, and I asked Yehudi to play the Bruch Concerto, her favorite piece. Conducting had exhausted him, so he couldn't do it. But his warm and loving statement about Hermi in the concert program was ample reward for my sponsorship.

On a later trip to Atlanta, Menuhin was the guest of honor at a family lunch at the home of my daughter and son-in-law, Judith and Ed Augustine. My second wife Helen and Yehudi immediately liked and understood each other. After lunch, Helen took him shopping to buy red shoes for his wife Diana. He walked through Lenox Mall totally unrecognized, carrying the shoes in a bag dangling from the skillful hand that held his bow in concerts. Yes, Menuhin was a celebrity. But to me he was much more – a most valued friend.

I also had the pleasure of becoming acquainted with a talented author, the result of a phone call from Jim Townsend, the founding editor of *Atlanta* magazine. Jim said the wanted me to meet Pat Conroy. "Pat is writing a book about a Marine aviator," he explained, "and wants to meet and talk to a Marine pilot to get background." I said, "Sure. When and where?"

About a week later I met Conroy for lunch at the Commerce Club. After greeting me, he said, "My father was a Marine aviator." I asked, "Then why aren't you talking to him?" Pat laughed and said, "If I ever write the book and you read it, you'll know why!"

He did write the book: *The Great Santini,* about a father who raised his children in the hell of a homegrown Marine boot camp. At first the book didn't sell well, but after the film of the same name, starring Robert Duvall as the iron-fisted father Bull Meechum, was released it became a bestseller. The book is presented as fiction, but its "resemblance to persons living or dead" is so clear there's no question it is autobiographical. Bull's fictional son is the very nonfictional Pat Conroy and Bull is certainly Pat's father. Pat wrote on the flyleaf of my copy, "To Cecil Alexander, the inspiration for Col. Hedgepath." Thankfully, Col. Virgil Hedgepath was the only decent Marine in the book.

Atlantans on a French Canal

A trip we took in early 1983 was in sharp contrast to the one that took Hermi and me to the island of Majuro, a nostalgic journey covered in Part Two, Chapter 23. This time we crossed the Atlantic, not the Pacific, and we floated in luxury on a quiet canal through the picturesque French countryside rather than bouncing along the rutted roads on an atoll.

I don't remember whose idea it was, but it was a good one. Our traveling companions were our close friend Phoebe Franklin Lundeen (Phoebe and her husband De had divorced a few years before) and her husband John Lundeen (a real estate mogul) and John's sister Bess Lundeen Finch and husband Bill Finch, my good friend and partner at FABRAP.

Waiting for us on the Canal de Bourgogne (Burgundy) was a converted barge, *Le Papillon* ("The Butterfly".) We and our more-than-ample luggage were welcomed aboard by the crew – the captain, a rather sour American; the first mate, a joyous young Frenchman; the female chef, an attractive graduate of the Cordon Bleu School of Cooking; and the housekeeper, also a Cordon Bleu chef.

The barge had originally hauled coal through France's network of canals. A couple from Connecticut spent some $300,000 converting it to the luxurious yacht it became. There were three cabins. Phoebe was in pain from cancer in her hips, so we agreed she and John should have the largest and most comfortable cabin. The Finches and Alexanders flipped a coin for the next one. We lost, leaving Hermi and me with a long narrow space with two single beds on either side of a small chest of drawers, plus a row of hooks on the steel wall – the only place to hang clothes. Access to the toilet required climbing through a small opening in the bulkhead at the end of the room. We lost big time!

Except for our meals and sleeping, most of our trip was spent lounging on cushioned benches on the open forward deck. It was a wonderfully relaxed way to enjoy the French countryside as green fields, rows of trees, rolling hills, and quaint villages blended into the ever-changing Burgundy landscape. Every day the barge stopped at a village, which our chef and the housekeeper would bike into to buy food and wine. The wine taught me the difference between screwtop Manischewitz wine and fine French wines — an expensive discovery, considering that ever since I've bought only the best.

At regular intervals we stopped at canal locks, which make it possible for boats to climb or descend hills. At each lock is a cottage that's home to the lock keepers (often a married couple), who operated the gates. John Lundeen leaped off the *Le Papillon* at each one and helped the lock keepers as they turned the stile that slowly opened and closed the gates. He was always most welcome.

Entering a lock was announced by bangs and heavy jolts as the craft hit the lock's stone sides. The gates behind the barge closed, water rushed in, and the barge slowly rose to the upstream level. Then the gates at the front opened and *Le Papillon* continued its way. We went through 90 locks on the trip, and the banging and jostling wasn't what I would call pleasant. When you've seen one lock, you've seen them all — 90 was 89 too many.

One evening when we were tied up by a lock, a woman debarked from a much larger barge behind us it and joined Finch on the bank. "Sir," she said, that's a beautiful barge you're in. How many passengers are there?" Finch said, "Just three couples. We're old friends." She cried, "Only three couples! Six people! On that thing back there are 25 people, and they're all bastards!" This made us feel all the better about our choice of boats.

Aside from the locks was another deviation from our bucolic drifting: a tunnel. Said our captain, "See that pinpoint of light? That's the end of the tunnel. It's long." The gasoline engine had to be shut down and the barge's engine run by overhead high-tension power lines only inches above our heads. The arching stone tunnel reflected on the water, making it seem *Le Papillion* was floating in a tube — a unique but claustrophobic sensation.

Later we went from deep in a tunnel to high in the sky. "You have to go up in my friend's hot air balloon." came the exciting order from our first mate. "It's the only way to really see France." A balloon was one of the few airborne crafts I hadn't flown in, so I was quicker to agree to the hot air experience than my fellow travelers were.

The first mate drove us to the launch site. When the balloon was inflated, we six and the pilot tumbled into the wicker basket. The ground crew let go of the ropes and we rose up in an unreal escape from the earth. Our drift across the green landscape held all the magic of the Oscar-winning movie *Around the World In Eighty Days.* At one point the wind died and the balloon hovered over a large chicken farm. When the balloonist lit up the burner to gain altitude the roar panicked the hens, and the farmer ran out waving a pitchfork at us. The burner muffled his curses, but his rage ascended to us in full force.

Full burners failed to elevate the balloon as it drifted toward a hill covered with tall trees. "Get down, Hermi," I yelled. "We're going to hit the trees." And we did. Then, with our help the balloonist we bent, broke, and twisted limbs that had caught the balloon's ropes until they came free. A grinning Hermi was caught in a photo holding one of the branches.

As we continued our flight we approached a row of towers strung with high-tension power lines. On her recent birthday, Phoebe's children had given her a balloon ride, and long after takeoff the balloon stalled low over power lines and ended up landing with a thump in the middle of a busy expressway. Phoebe didn't want a repeat performance. She reached across the crowded basket and tapped the balloonist on the shoulder and said, "Lets go down. I don't want to drift over those power lines." The balloon-ist nodded but kept on firing hot air into the bag to keep it aloft. Phoebe turned to him, put her nose in his face, and screamed. "Didn't you hear me? Take this thing down now! NOW!" He got the message. As we descended he ordered us to bend our knees to absorb the landing shock. We hit the ground hard. The balloon bounced over a fence, and as the air escaped it flattened out across the field.

Five or six cars filled with boisterous Frenchmen had followed us into the field, knowing the balloonist would break out wine for his passengers, and for them as well – a well established custom. Our balloonist gave a case to one of the followers and handed a bottle to each of us. But there was a difference: Our wine was fine French wine. Theirs was cheap wine from who-knew-where.

One thing I took away from our balloon flight: "Done that. No need to ever do it again."

Our cruise ended at Beaune. We toured that ancient town and were charmed by its handsome buildings and narrow streets. We then flew home. In spite of noisy locks, a too-tight-for comfort tunnel, and a cut-short balloon ride, it was an enchanting trip.

Hermi's Refuge and its Revival

We had all been concerned about Phoebe's life-threatening cancer, but it was Hermi who was killed in a car crash soon after we returned home – a tragedy that is the subject of Chapter 12, "My World Ripped Apart." Phoebe succumbed two years later, in 1985; after telling her family goodbye, she herself cut her life support and drifted off. When I remember Phoebe and all she did for humanity, a line from a poem by Stephen Spender echoes: "I think continually of those who were truly great."

One evening Hermi and I were stretched out on the stone court surrounded by the circling glass wall of the Round House, and a full moon cast light through the trees and into the court. From the stereo came a flow of the poignant Civil War songs – "The Battle Hymn of the Republic," "Dixie," "When Johnnie Comes Marching Home", "Just Before the Battle, Mother," and many others. When the Union troops marched into Atlanta, they camped one night on our hill. Were their ghosts still here, listening to those tunes of glory? The music and that thought made the hair on my neck bristle.

Hermi had been a healthy, athletic, ready-for-anything person in her youth, but in her fifties she was beset with a series of what she mockingly called "dread diseases," including breast cancer, a heart attack, and diabetes. So much for keeping her teenager's figure and not smoking. When asked by anyone why she, not I, had the heart attack, I replied, "Easy. I'm married to her and she's married to me."

While the toll on her health sapped her energy, it never slowed Hermi's involvement with her family, her friends, the racial issues consuming Atlanta, and life itself. Standing with me in the court, she looked around at the indoor plants and out the windows to the trees. "They are," she said, "going to have to carry me out of here feet first." I'll never leave this magical place while I live."

I think often of the night we lay under the large skylight in the court and looked up at the heavens. "We are on spaceship Earth," I said, "traveling beneath those stars in our big round house."

I moved from the Round House in the mid-1980s, and there is postscript to its story. Ted and Susan Pound bought it some ten years ago from Gerry Hull, who bought it from me in 1985. Both families understood the value of preserving the house, but the Pounds grew determined to restore it. To make sure the original ambiance was retained, they asked if they and their architect could consult with me, and I of course agreed to their request.

In one corner of the court is what Ted Pound referred to in a June 2007 *New York Times* article on the restoration of the house as "the Cecil Alexander Shrine," with several framed articles and photographs from the past – embarrassing to me, but only, I confess, a little. The Pounds pursued (and reached) their goal with vigor, and in 2010 the Round House was listed in the National Register of Historic Places.

Chapter 8

Politics – A Few Strange Bedfellows

These are the times that try men's souls.

— Thomas Paine, The American Crisis

"If you'll run for mayor, I'll go all out to support you." That's what I heard from some friends in 1961. I put extra weight on the prodding from our neighbor Dr. Joe Wilbur, an outstanding and caring physician involved in the city's health services for the poor. I wasn't exactly being drafted – there were no rallies of thousands of young women leaping up and down, waving signs, and screaming, "We Want Alex!!!" There were just a few borderline supporters proclaiming in soft whispers, "Alexander might make a somewhat decent mayor." I did, however, have potential support from an interesting source: the more progressive members of the Young Republicans.

When I came home to Atlanta in 1948, the "good ole boy" Democrats in Georgia stood politically well to the right of even the most conservative Republicans. This was especially the case when it came to the treatment of blacks. The Democrats ran all-white primaries, excluding all blacks from the political process. Moreover, the Democratic Party's voter registration process made it difficult, even dangerous, for a black to register to vote.

When Franklin D. Roosevelt had run for his third term in 1940, he was vigorously opposed not only by the Republicans but also by members of his own party. Among his goals were swapping 50 World War I destroyers with Great Britain for access to American bases in Bermuda and the West Indies and pushing through legislation authorizing the draft. His Republican opponent – Wendell Willkie, "the barefoot boy from Wall Street" – was a successful utilities businessman but a total novice in politics. His nomination followed a long, bitter battle with Sen. Robert Taft of Ohio ("Mr. Republican") and the 38-year-old "diaper" candidate, Tom Dewey, who'd risen from a crime-busting attorney general of New York to governor. Taft was a staunch isolationist who opposed any help Roosevelt had given (or wanted to give) Great Britain. He was opposed to the draft and pledged to keep American boys out of another European bloodbath. Dewey was thought to share Taft's platform, but he kept quiet.

If Taft or Dewey had been nominated, Roosevelt possibly wouldn't have supported Great Britain and prepared the U.S. for war by instituting the draft. But Willkie, until recently a Democrat, believed as FDR did – and deeply. In his 2006 book *Five Days in Philadelphia*, award-winning journalist Charles Peters credits Willkie's support for Roosevelt's pro-British policies with saving western civilization from Adolf Hitler. Willkie was far more liberal than the veteran Republicans who dominated his party, but he was easily able to pack the convention with supporters screaming, "We Want Willkie!" Author Peters also sees the then-recent fall of France to the Nazis as a factor. The United States seemed very vulnerable, with only the British Empire fighting Hitler and Benito Mussolini, Italy's fascist dictator.

Willkie was nominated on the sixth ballot, overcoming several favorite sons as well as Taft, Dewey, and even former president Herbert Hoover, who had hoped to be drafted. Willkie ran a wildly aggressive campaign, and his roaring speeches reduced his voice to a grating croak. He directed his attacks primarily against FDR, whom he called "the third term candidate." The race was close, but the country rallied behind Roosevelt, a proven leader.

Although Wilkie lost, he was a magnificent loser. Roosevelt admired him so much he sent him as an envoy to Winston Churchill and King George VI to reassure them of his continuing support in their lonely fight. Roosevelt also asked Willkie to deliver to Churchill a copy of Longfellow's patriotic poem *O Ship of State*:

> *Thou too sail on, O Ship of State!*
> *Sail on, O Union strong and great.*
> *Humanity with all its fears,*
> *With all its hopes for future years,*
> *Is hanging breathless on thy fate.*

Churchill responded with a broadcast message rather than a private letter: "Give us the tools," he said, "and we will finish the job."

Why (Not) Me?

The 1940 election was the first I was eligible to vote in, having passed overnight from naïve childhood at age 20 to responsible manhood at 21. Willkie had my enthusiastic support. He lost, but I became an ardent Willkie Republican – so it didn't require a change in my party loyalties to listen intently to the Young Republicans urging me to run for mayor of Atlanta some three decades later. Randy Thrower, who would become an outstanding Atlanta attorney, led the group. President Nixon eventually appointed him as commissioner of the Internal Revenue Service, and Thrower showed his rock-hard integrity by resigning when asked by Nixon to turn over tax returns from people on the president's enemies list.

Another push for me to run came from Marilyn Grayboff, an activist Democrat, when she held a political gathering at her house. She had recently moved from New York with her husband Ira, an architect who joined our FABRAP firm as a senior designer. Hermi and I, with some 30 other die-hard Democrats, were sprawled around the Grayboff living room discussing the upcoming city elections.

I was sitting with Vernon Jordan on a short flight of steps into the living room. Vernon – tall, handsome, and ebony-hued – was known in the elite circle of Atlanta society ladies as the Black Prince; with his regal bearing, a princely crown would have fit him well. During a momentary lull in a discussion about mayoral candidates, one of the guests suddenly jumped to his feet and jabbed his finger toward Jordan and me. "Hey, there's our ticket: Alexander for mayor and Jordan for vice mayor!"

"Oh sure," I thought. "A Jew and a black running together – not exactly a shoo-in." Besides, Hermi had already declared me ineligible. I grinned, shook my head "no," and waved my hands dismissively. "Thanks," I said, "but no way. No way at all." Vernon said nothing, and the moment passed.

Vernon later considered a political career but decided he would be more effective supporting black institutions. Ultimately he served as president of the United Negro College Fund and the National Urban League. He now has an excellent legal practice in Washington and was known as President Bill Clinton's "first friend."

I should explain why I was being approached to run for mayor. As the chairman of the Citizens Advisory Committee for Urban Renewal (CAC), I had led a powerful biracial group of 86 Atlanta leaders (one-third black, two-thirds white – then the city's racial ratio) in the successful execution of the city's five renewal projects and the relocation of some 5,000 families displaced by slum clearance.

During a CAC meeting at the Atlanta Journal-Constitution office building, a powwow attended by Ralph McGill, editor and publisher of the *Constitution*, Jack Spalding, editor of the *Journal*, Gene Patterson, executive editor of both papers, and others, McGill turned to Patterson and said, "Gene, I want you to head up our effort." From that point on we were well covered by the papers, and in the news and editorial sections alike. Some editorials commented favorably on my efforts. (I later heard that Ralph McGill had said I would make a good mayor.) We also had a good amount of coverage in neighborhood papers and *Atlanta* magazine. I was interviewed on television and radio by informed and – for the most part, friendly – reporters and commentators. Our public relations were so successful that all candidates running for all offices in the next Atlanta election told the League of Women Voters they supported urban renewal. Even Lester Maddox, the avowed racist, said he was in favor.

My efforts carried me to all sections of the city. Poor whites and blacks knew me and regarded me as a proponent of decent, inexpensive, and safe housing for all Atlantans. Business leaders approved of my actions as well. Of course, I also had my enemies (if only a few), who resented my efforts on behalf of blacks.

It was, therefore, wide exposure of my successful handling of a dangerous program that made supporters urge me to run. They thought I could win. I was flattered. I was tempted. But two obstacles stood in my way. The first was my wife Hermi's adamant opposition; she knew if I were mayor I would rarely be home. The second was that it seemed very likely that Ivan Allen would run. My high regard for Ivan convinced me he would make an outstanding mayor, and I didn't want to get in his way. So I shut down that window of opportunity in spite of its appealing view.

Ivan Allen's Run for Mayor

It was Mills B. Lane, Jr., a wonderfully eccentric Atlantan and CEO of Citizens Southern Bank, who launched Ivan Allen's campaign for mayor. Lane was known for his freewheeling loans based not on collateral but rather on his judgment of the borrower's character. When my late partner Rocky Rothschild and I were starting our architectural firm, we met with Lane to establish our credit and float a loan. I handed him a page detailing our financial status. He glanced at it and threw it aside. "There's no way I can lend you boys a thing on that. How much do you need?" He not only gave us the loan but also two neckties embellished with the upbeat slogan "It's a Wonderful World!"

Without telling Allen, Lane mailed out 80,000 cards to Atlantans to gauge their reaction to a run. The returns were 60 percent positive. When Allen saw the results, he decided he could be elected and announced his candidacy. Some old rats in the political barn were appalled that a banker launched Allen's campaign, but Mills Lane wasn't your ordinary banker. He was one of the good ol' boys who just happened to be a banker and a Yale graduate.

I wanted to take an active part in the campaign, and to ensure I could do a thorough job I took two months leave from FABRAP. I worked sixteen-hour days and seven-day weeks for Ivan Allen. It was exciting. It was rewarding. It was exhausting.

My long association with Ivan on the urban renewal committee led me to believe he was uniquely qualified to lead our city into a new era of racial harmony and well-planned growth. His program as president of the Atlanta Chamber of Commerce had laid out in detail a practical agenda for getting Atlanta up and running, and the goals he set at the Chamber became the basis for his mayoral platform.

Ivan's first move was to enlist Helen Bullard, an advertising executive and brilliant political strategist, as his campaign manager. It was a hard sell because Milton M. "Muggsy" Smith, one of Ivan's major opponents, had consulted Helen in all of his past races. Helen liked and admired Smith, and I never knew why she came over to Allen.

Helen Bullard's brilliant, incisive mind rested in a head attached to a short, very round, indifferently clad body. Before answering a question on political strategy she would look for long minutes off into space, weighing the effect of the proposal on every district of the city – on the whites, the blacks, the rich, the poor, the young, the middle aged, and the old. Only then would she reply. Her answer would either support the suggestion with some caveats or cut it dead.

Helen and I worked well together, with one exception. One Sunday during the campaign, near noon, I called her at home to discuss an idea. She was furious. "Cecil, Sunday is the only day I can rest, and you wake me at 12 o'clock!" She slammed down the phone. It was my turn to be furious – to me, twelve noon didn't seem unreasonable time to call. I avoided Helen until the tension eased.

Helen had her concerns about Ivan Allen. Four years before, in 1957, he had tested running for governor of Georgia. This meant voicing the obligatory, though muted, remarks in support of segregation. Allen soon realized, however, that a wealthy, well-dressed Atlanta businessman couldn't be packaged as a viable candidate for governor of a state run by rural politicians and their redneck supporters. He withdrew.

Still, this history troubled Helen. In the midst of the '61 campaign she and I were having a lunch break at the Dinkler Hotel when she said, "Cecil, are we selling a candidate who doesn't exist? Does Ivan really believe segregation is poison for Atlanta? If he doesn't, that worries me."

"Helen," I said, "Ivan is a totally believing convert. I have no misgivings. He is now, I am certain, the man we are selling – a liberal on race. Daddy King said so about Ivan when he told me, 'Give me a converted segregationist every time. He knows what he believes because he had to work hard to get there. You can trust him all the way!'"

Helen never again raised the issue. And it occurred to me that my evolution from a genteel racist to a civil rights advocate put me in the same category Daddy King so simply but vividly defined.

Allen's campaign headquarters were in the center of downtown Atlanta in a store vacated by Ivan Allen & Company, his office supply business. It was a long, narrow space on two levels with openings at either end – one to

Peachtree Street, the other Broad Street near Five Points. Allen's offices were on an upstairs balcony. Like the other volunteers, I was on the ground floor and was equipped a desk, a phone, and a pile of files. Stacks of campaign posters and brochures stood against a wall, and several TV sets were placed about the space.

Helen was known for her exceptionally reliable polls and had compiled a very selective list of about 200 voters from different segments of the city. Several weeks into the campaign her polls showed Ivan with 70 percent of the vote. When Allen saw the figures he told her, "This is a shoo-in. Let's cut way back on our expenses; there's no use wasting money."

"Now Ivan," Helen said, "the people don't know you. What will they think when they *do* get to know you?" Ivan grew doubtful about Helen's polls, which tended to survey the same 200 people over and over again, and shifted any polling to Joe Heyman, an Atlanta banker and erstwhile statistician. (Joe happened to be a cousin of my wife Hermi.) When the people got to know Ivan, his poll rating slipped to below 50 percent, bearing out Helen's prediction. We heard no more about cost cutting.

As chairman of the CAC, I had made friends with black leaders in the West End community, and I was assigned to focus on them during the campaign. The West End, a largely white, lower middle class neighborhood on the edge of the city, was ignored by the Atlanta business and political establishment, so I put several West End leaders on the urban renewal committee and listened attentively to their needs. I became their conduit to the power structure of Atlanta.

Because I worked closely with black leaders, they trusted me. My endorsement of Allen convinced most of them that he was the right choice for mayor. A white labor leader (and Allen supporter) told me, "You have a call on 30,000 votes in this election." Maybe I did. Ivan had four opponents in the race: Jim Aldredge (a county commissioner); Charlie Brown (who had held numerous local offices); Milton "Muggsy" Smith (a state legislator who was liberal on race); and Lester Maddox (a vehement opponent of what he called "race mixing" and owner of the soon-to-be notorious Pickrick Restaurant.)

One strong political leader in the black community, attorney Don Hollowell, was reported to be wearing a large Muggsy Smith button. Ivan grabbed me by the arm one day and said, "Cecil, go down to Hollowell's office and get him to take off that Muggsy badge." I thought, "Oh, sure" But I went.

Hollowell agreed to see me, and my whole pitch was what an excellent, caring mayor Ivan Allen would be. Hollowell heard me out without comment.

After a short while he indicated the meeting was at an end and showed me to the door, the Muggsy Smith badge still gleaming on his chest. Later, Q. V. Williams, a prominent black realtor, called me. Hollowell had asked him whether I was well connected to the white power structure. "I told him, you can bet on it," Williams said. Hollowell soon went to Ivan's office to pledge his support.

The Race Heats Up

Despite his standing with the black community, Allen's addresses to audiences of any color tended to fall flat. One night Helen Bullard and I sat in a back pew listening to the mayoral candidates speak at a black church on Hunter Street (now Martin Luther King Boulevard) — a church whose congregation consisted mainly of poorer blacks. Muggsy Smith went to the core of their concerns. "When I'm mayor, my door will always be open for you at City Hall," he thundered, "and there ain't nobody gonna call you 'boy!'" At the end of his speech the congregation stood and cheered.

In contrast, Ivan's speech dwelled on highways, stadiums, auditoriums, and and the like, and he made no mention of the congregation's needs. When he finished, the clapping was muted. Helen leaned over to me and whispered, "When will Ivan ever learn you can't sell footballs to paraplegics?"

It was true that Ivan presented what Helen called "electronic speeches." The warm, caring personality he projected to a small group or face-to-face was lost in front of a large audience. I decided to try to help. We were having lunch when I said, "Ivan, in a small group you present yourself beautifully as a warm and caring man — but you address a large audience as one mass, not as a group of individuals. Try picking out two or three people and talking directly to them."

Ivan blew up. He leaned across the table and shouted, "That's the same stuff Helen Bullard has been hitting me with! I am what I am. You two are destroying my confidence. You'll ruin me!" We finished our lunch in silence.

Things changed (and dramatically) at a Kiwanis Club luncheon in West End, where all five mayoral spoke. Ivan went last. The four previous speakers, including Maddox, had given bland outlines of their platforms and made no mention of their opponents. When Ivan took the podium, he first rolled up his sleeves to hide his expensive cuff links. He then tore into Maddox and his supporters, saying that bigoted, dirty gutter-dwellers represented the worst elements of the city. Maddox's face went white; he was in shock.

A photo opportunity after the luncheon revealed Allen's growing political smarts. He waited until the other candidates were lined up, then walked in front and stood in the middle, a broad grin lighting his face. In contrast, his competitors' expressions barely concealed their annoyance.

From that West End confrontation on, it was a two-man race – Allen vs. Maddox. The other three candidates, with the possible exception of Smith, were mere also-rans. Helen's grand strategy had been to convince Allen to put himself front and center and show the fire in his belly – a brilliant stroke. A talented artist who painted with oils, Helen declared running a campaign to be "like developing a painting. You first block in the whole canvas with neutral colors and then fill in the blocks with color. You never veer from the layout, though you vary the colors and intensity. In other words, you change the emphasis, not the strategy." Helen's strategy for Allen was to *connect,* and he began to charm even his largest audiences.

Muggsy Smith did two decisive things in his campaign – the first brilliant, the second devastating. The first was to place a full-page ad in the *Constitution.* At the top was a pencil sketch of a Tom Sawyer look-alike wearing a slightly askew baseball cap. The line underneath read, "Why do they call him Muggsy? The ad went on to say that as a kid, Smith had been a fan of Muggsy McGraw, the legendary manager of the Baltimore Orioles and the New York Giants. It then painted Smith as an all-American boy who had pulled himself to success through hard work and sterling character. The ad worried us.

Then, in the middle of the campaign, Smith took off for a two-week vacation in Paris. The hardworking all-American boy image went up in the fragrance of French perfume. So long Muggsy – bon voyage! Decades later, President George W. Bush would suffer similarly as he bicycled at his ranch while Hurricane Katrina wreaked havoc on the Gulf Coast.

Another dagger in Smith's back was also of his own making. The theory of nullification (not in the U.S. Constitution, I believe) postulates that if federal laws are damaging to the citizens of a state, the state government can nullify said law. When the civil rights laws came down from Washington, the Georgia legislature – including member Muggsy Smith – voted for nullification, an action that in no way pleased black citizens. Smith also voted to impeach all members of the United States Supreme Court.

Morris Abram, an Atlanta attorney I knew well, came to headquarters to ask Ivan to endorse his application for membership in the Commerce Club. I told Morris it would further his cause with Ivan if he went to the capitol and copied the nullification resolution and impeachment proposal; Muggsy's name was on both. Abram did as I advised and eventually was admitted to the Commerce Club. I simply took Abram's copies to Helen Bullard, telling her we should distribute a flyer in black neighborhoods showing that Smith voted against black interests. Helen's latent regard for Smith came out, and she didn't want to be involved. So I sought the support of Ivan's father. He bought in enthusiastically and said, "I'll pay whatever it costs."

The flyers were distributed a few days later – and overnight, most of the Smith signs on the lawns in black neighborhoods disappeared. Was this dirty politics worthy of Karl Rove? I choose not to regard it that way. We only published the facts; it was Smith who created them.

The campaign was nearing its end, and a political rally was to be held at a prominent black church. Allen learned that Muggsy Smith planned to have a large contingent of supporters present to convince voters citywide he was winning. To counter this move, Allen arranged to host a huge pre-rally dinner at the Waluhaje Hotel, owned by Walter H. "Chief" Aiken, a black homebuilder and long-time friend of Ivan's. Notices announcing the dinner were posted in stores, plants, and on telephone poles. Ultimately, it took 40 buses, all festooned with Allen banners, to take the crowd from the dinner to the political rally at the church.

Muggsy and his entourage were still on the sidewalk when Ivan's army arrived. His face paled as the hordes spilled off the buses carrying "Ivan Allen for Mayor" signs. This mighty wave turned the meeting into a tsunami of Allen support. Ivan couldn't (or probably didn't want to) conceal his joyful reaction to his triumph, although he told me he couldn't help feeling sorry for Muggsy.

The night of the election, Ivan's headquarters were packed with black and white supporters. One of the assistants, wearing headphones, listened to the radio station broadcasting election returns and recorded them on a large blackboard. Knowledgeable politicians predicted the outcome from the various wards, and it was clear Ivan and Maddox were in a close race.

As the North Atlanta vote came in, we hoped those votes would put Allen over the 50 percent needed to avoid a runoff. But he fell short. So there would be another all-out campaign – a true fight to the finish. I had promised Hermi that after the election we would take off for a long weekend on our sailboat at

Lake Lanier – but it was not to be. Helen Bullard called an all-day meeting that Saturday to map out the strategy for the runoff. Hermi was not happy.

Campaigning resumed, and late one night I had a phone call from Gene Patterson of the *Constitution*. He said, "Cecil, I shouldn't be telling you this, but the night of the election Maddox hired that gadfly photographer who makes his living taking questionable shots. At Ivan's headquarters he took several photos of black and white supporters shaking hands, even embracing. Maddox is running one of the photos in an ad in tomorrow's paper, and we can't legally or ethically turn it down. I wanted to alert Ivan. OK?" I thanked Gene and told him I would call Ivan.

When Ivan heard the story, he thanked me and immediately arranged several TV spots for the next day. Looking directly into the camera, he said, "We sure did have a mixed crowd at headquarters. They're my supporters, and I was glad to have all of them – white and black." Instead of having any impact, the Maddox ad became both a widespread joke and a deadly miscalculation.

One evening all the candidates held forth in the auditorium of an insurance company. As we left the meeting a newsboy was at the door hawking the next morning's *Constitution,* whose front page trumpeted an endorsement for Ivan Allen. Muggsy Smith's son-in-law grabbed a copy and read the headline, his face contorted in anger. He saw me and snarled, "How can you support that anti-Semite Ivan Allen? He detests you people." I didn't answer. There was nothing in my years of friendship with Ivan to support this accusation, which I wrote off to frustration.

I often spoke in support of Allen at black gatherings, many times with Daddy King sitting on the platform with me. If I made a point he liked he would say, loud enough for all in the hall to hear, "Make it plain, make it plain." These words from a great preacher were enough to make me feel I must be quite an orator. He was an inspiring cheerleader.

When I had worked as an architect for Henry Toombs years before, he required all of his employees to take the Dale Carnegie course "How to Win Friends and Influence People." At meetings, each student was expected to make a two-minute speech – one of the few parts of the course that didn't strike me as bull. Those speeches turned me from a nervous, bombastic speaker into a smooth-talking ham. I loved to orate then, and I still do.

Helen Bullard heard me one night at a meeting and decided to put me on TV. I wrote what I intended to say and gave it to Helen for approval, then read it from a teleprompter. One point I made was that Ivan's office door at Ivan

Allen & Company was always open; you could just walk in. I said that his door in City Hall would likewise always be open.

Celebration and Grief

When it was certain Ivan had won on the night of the runoff (he carried 64 percent of the vote), he, Helen Bullard, his family, and some volunteers (including me), went to the *Constitution* newsroom. Aubrey Morris, a fine radio reporter, interviewed Allen. His questions were routine, but the happy mayor-elect answered them with great enthusiasm. Toward the end of the interview Morris went up to Louise, Allen's wife, with his microphone. "Mrs. Allen," he said, "you know that First Lady Jackie Kennedy is setting the style for young women across the country. As the first lady of Atlanta, will you be the fashion leader for the city?" Louise looked at Aubrey in amazement and said, "Oh Aubrey – come off it!" She wasn't about to take seriously her new position as first lady. In fact, she never considered herself as anything but herself, and that was formidable enough.

I walked behind Ivan and Helen Bullard to campaign headquarters. Ivan had his arm as far as it could reach around Bullard's wide, sloping shoulders. These two almost looked as if they were different species – Allen tall, slim, and impeccably dressed; Bullard short, obese, and stuffed into her nondescript outfit. But their mutual joy at the success of the long campaign made them seem a loving couple able to bridge all differences.

Ivan's open door was the hallmark of his administration. Not long after he moved into City Hall, Mayor Allen invited Dick Lee, the mayor of New Haven, Connecticut, to Atlanta. Ivan did indeed keep his door open, as promised, and anyone could walk in unannounced. Mayor Lee was dumbfounded. "Anybody who wants to see me has to work his way through my receptionist and two secretaries before coming in my office." Lee later met with members of the Atlanta's City Council. Afterwards he told me, "I like to get out to other cities like Atlanta. It can be very helpful – a great learning experience." I thought he meant that he himself learned from such visits. Wrong! "Yes, I believe your Council members learned a lot from me." If it takes a strong ego to be a successful politician, Mayor Lee was exceedingly well endowed.

If Ivan was now where he wanted to be, I was let down. From being a vital member of his entourage I seemed to be on the outs, hearing nothing from him for weeks on end. Deciding to do something about it, I called Ann Moses, Ivan's good-looking young secretary. "Ann," I said, "you know there was a small group of us volunteers who worked our tails off for Ivan during the campaign. Since he moved into City Hall we've heard nothing from him. How about a lunch where he brings us up to date on the city and his plans?" Ann was very protective of the mayor, and I didn't know how she would react. To my relief she said, "I'll see when we can set it up to fit Ivan's schedule."

Some days later we met at the Commerce Club. Ivan thanked us profusely and went over his plans and dreams. I felt better; I was still an insider – well, sort of. In time I would again be an active part of Allen's administration, as I recount in Chapter 9. Years later, after Ivan had served two terms, I was pleased that he credited me as one of the people who made him mayor. On the flyleaf of his book, *Mayor: Notes on the Sixties* (1971) he inscribed "To Cecil Alexander, who was my close associate and excellent advisor and who had a better understanding of the civil rights problem than anyone else that I knew. With great appreciation, Ivan Allen." So I feel rewarded for the time and effort I put into his campaign. It was a high point in my life, a time of excitement and tension, of plotting and executing, of striving and winning. All my experience, all my knowledge of Atlanta, and all my love for the city were called upon. Adrenalin surged through me every day of the campaign and kept surging for weeks thereafter.

Over the years I tried to get Helen Bullard to sit for a television interview recalling her life in politics. She never would. What a loss! The last time I saw her was in the early days of Jimmy Carter's campaign for president. I wasn't alone in thinking Carter was running a losing race. When I told this to Helen she gave me one of her long, penetrating looks. "Cecil, I'm going to pray for you, dear boy." She walked away and left me speechless. I miss her still.

About six months after Allen took office, he and all of Atlanta received some shocking news. An Air France plane bound from Paris's Orly Airport to Atlanta had crashed on takeoff, killing all on board except two stewardesses sitting in the tail section. A hundred and six of the passengers were from Atlanta – an outstanding group of citizens interested in bringing the highest level of art and cultural attractions to the city. They were inspecting museums and concert halls in Europe.

I'll never forget the moment I heard the news. On the clear Sunday morning of June 2, 1962, I was driving through Atlanta's verdant suburbs with the top down on my convertible. The flow of Mozart from the car radio was interrupted by the terse announcement of the crash. Among the dead was the beautiful and talented artist Helen Seydel, who had capably served two years as my assistant when I chaired the Citizens Advisory Committee for Urban Renewal. I was devastated by her death. A line from an Edgar Allen Poe poem recited to Helen by a city councilman who had fallen hard for her kept repeating in my head: "Helen, thy beauty is to me as those Nicéan barks of yore," usually followed with "Your bark is worse than your bite!" Many other friends, though none as close as Helen, died that day.

Ivan Allen immediately flew to Paris and took on the courageous, gruesome task of identifying the victims. He would then speak with their next of kin via trans-Atlantic phone to tell them what he knew of the crash and try to comfort them. Many of the dead were lifelong friends of Allen's.

The French government received Allen as an honored guest. Our sterling mayor never condemned Air France, and he represented Atlanta flawlessly. As a gesture to Atlanta, France presented the Woodruff Center with a bronze statue by Auguste Rodin. (Arthur Harris, Helen Eisemann's first husband and the French Honorary Consul for Atlanta, arranged for the gift.) The male figure's head is bowed in grief, the shoulders bent forward. The statue stands today outside the High Museum of Art, one finger polished to a shining gold from the rubbing by countless visitors.

The Air France crash reverberated for years in the community, but life went on in the fast-growing Sun Belt. In the early 1960s an overall planning unit for Greater Atlanta was created, called the Atlanta Region Metropolitan Planning Commission (ARMPC.)

Ivan appointed me to substitute for him at ARMPC meetings. He never came. I reported to him on the meetings, though he usually seemed uninterested. This concerned me, since I thought he should be directly involved. A couple of years later I became vice-chairman of ARMPC. It was time, the commission decided, to begin the process of providing rapid transit, which was included in Mayor Allen's platform for Atlanta.

After many meetings we developed a basic scheme and chose a large national transportation-engineering firm, Parsons Brinckerhoff, to plan the routes and develop a budget for a new light rail network — the Metropolitan Atlanta Rapid Transit Authority (MARTA.) The explanation of what it took to bring MARTA to fruition is convoluted, so suffice it to say that after a 1968 public referendum to fund the rapid rail system failed, a second referendum, in 1971, passed — and MARTA was on the road to revolutionizing public transportation in Atlanta.

In the mid 1970s my firm, in a joint venture with George Heery's firm, designed the huge Five Points MARTA station at the intersection of the east-west and north-south tracks. It was a challenging commission. The structure is no Grand Central Station, but I think it is handsome and functional.

The Stadium and Other Political Arenas

One of six plans in Ivan Allen's campaign platform had called for the building of a major league baseball stadium. Now that he was mayor, his first job was to find a team that could be lured to Atlanta. Furman Bisher, sports editor of the *Atlanta Journal,* told Allen that Charlie Finley, the eccentric owner of the Kansas City Athletics, was coming to Atlanta to look at possible stadium sites. Allen and Bisher showed Finley three sites but Finley rejected them. Then it hit Allen that the Washington-Rawson area was an ideal spot: It was at the southern edge of downtown Atlanta at the interchange of three Interstates and had been cleared by urban renewal. After touring the site Finley said, "This is the greatest site for a stadium I've ever seen. If you build it, I'll bring the Athletics here as soon as it's finished." But the American League refused to let Finley leave Kansas City. The agreement was dead.

Trying again, Ivan enlisted Arthur Montgomery, president of the Coca-Cola Bottling Company, to search for a team. Montgomery met with a group of wealthy young Chicagoans including Potter Palmer, a member of the family who built Chicago's famous Palmer House Hotel and who held all the shares in the Milwaukee Braves. Attendance at Braves games had fallen below a million for each of the past three years, and the owners were ready to move the team. Several meetings later, an agreement was struck: The Braves would come to Atlanta in 1965, and a new stadium would be ready. Allen had enlisted the ebullient banker Mills Lane, who agreed to retain architects at his own expense to design the facility. Allen asked him to hire my firm, FABRAP.

Arthur Montgomery, now head of the Stadium Authority, wanted the firm of Heery & Heery – so at the end of a shotgun we formed a joint venture.

In spite of partner Bill Finch's problem with the audacious George Heery (Finch being the "F" in FABRAP), the venture stayed together for eighteen years under the name of Finch-Heery Architects. We designed some 70 athletic facilities, including the Cincinnati Riverfront Stadium, the Buffalo Bills Stadium in New York State, and the Carrier Dome at the University of Syracuse.

A handsome multiuse stadium for the riverfront in Detroit was blocked when the bonds were declared invalid. Henry Ford II and Bill Ford led the opposition; Bill wanted the new stadium to be built in the Michigan town of Pontiac. I wrote to Henry II, my Yale classmate, seeking his support for our design. He wrote me back a "Dear Cecil" letter saying, in so many words, "Blood is thicker than water." His brother Bill would have his support.

We had only a year and a half to design and build the Atlanta stadium, when a project that size usually took three to four years. I got busy doing on-site research at the Mets Stadium on Long Island, Yankee Stadium in the Bronx, the St. Louis Cardinals Stadium, and the Washington Senators Stadium.

A week before I visited Washington, a riot between students of a black high school and a white high school broke out at the Senator's stadium following a game, then spread to the surrounding neighborhoods. It was knowledge of this bloody riot that led me later, as president of the Atlanta Chapter of the American Jewish Committee, to discourage members' attendance at the March on Washington – the one where King, on the steps of the Lincoln Memorial, gave his immortal "I Have a Dream" oration. There was no violence. I now regret writing the letter, but I believed at the time I was protecting my members from possible harm.

When I returned to Atlanta I passed my notes, sketches, and photographs to Bill Finch, who would head up the design of the stadium. Within six months the architectural and engineering documents were finished and had been approved by the Braves. The stadium, which could accommodate not only baseball but also football and soccer, was a handsome round structure supported by large steel bents painted white.

To ensure construction would be finished on time, a $600,000 bonus was paid to the contractor. The stadium was finished one week short of the year-long schedule, at a cost of $13,000,000; the entire project, including roads, parking areas, a pedestrian tunnel, and fees, came in at $16,000,000. Today, when stadium construction runs to hundreds of millions of dollars, our stadium seems like an incredible bargain.(Current-day are much more elaborate, of course, but not enough to justify the sky-high cost.)

The Atlanta Stadium was ready, but the Braves were blocked from coming to the city by a Milwaukee lawsuit – so the sparkling new facility was used for the season by the Atlanta Crackers, the city's minor league team. The following year the lawsuit was settled and the Braves came south. On opening night, nearly 60,000 fans showed up. Mayor Allen threw out the first pitch, hitting the catcher's mitt dead center. It was, he said, the thrill of a lifetime. I felt the same. As a kid I'd dreamed that one day Atlanta would have a major league team, and here were the Braves in the stadium my firm had designed!

Today my choice as designer would have evoked critical headlines – "Mayor's Crony's Firm Chosen as Architects for New Stadium." But in the 1960s such so-called cronyism was accepted as standard practice. Our performance, I believe, entirely justified our hiring.

In 1996, following the use of the field in the Olympics, the giant structure – which had been renamed Atlanta-Fulton County Stadium in 1975 – was imploded to clear parking space for the new Turner Field. It was a terrible waste. Parking decks could have accommodated the parking at about the same cost as implosion; the structure could have been used for a world center for female athletes, or for soccer, or as a museum; or it could have provided space for neighborhood facilities, including adult education and a police precinct. The grin on the face of Mayor Bill Campbell when he pressed the button setting off the demolition is still one of my most distasteful mental images. And it wasn't the only mistake Mayor Campbell made – he went to prison from 2006 to 2009.

Ivan tried to give FABRAP the architectural commission to design the Atlanta Civic Center. His friend Jack Adair headed the effort to produce the facility on the Butler Street urban renewal site. It would consist of a 5,000-seat auditorium and a large exhibition hall. Allen told Adair he wanted my firm as architects, and I thought it was a done deal.

Robert & Company, then Atlanta's largest architectural engineering firm, had done all of the City of Atlanta-commissioned designs while Hartsfield was mayor. They made an end run around Ivan and Adair to work on the City Council. As a result, we were asked to form a joint venture. (That again!) In my innocence I approached Jesse Shelton, who was running Robert & Company, with a proposal. FABRAP would do the architectural phase and Robert & Company would be the engineer. He yelled, "No way! No way! We're going to be the major architectural designers. Take it or leave it!"

We left it.

Allen chastised me for not seeking the support of the members of the City Council. I wished he'd told me I should, since I thought he and Jack Adair would make the decision themselves. Ed Moulthrop, a fine architect, was the Robert & Company designer of the Civic Center, but it isn't one of his best efforts. Shortly afterwards, Moulthrop gave up architecture to concentrate on crafting wooden bowls, which are now displayed in the Metropolitan Museum of Art, the Museum of Modern Art, and other world-famous institutions. To honor my second wife, Helen Eisemann Alexander, I commissioned a Moulthrop bowl that has been displayed in the lobby of Atlanta's Woodruff Arts Center.

Callaway vs. Lewis vs. Bond

"Politics makes strange bedfellows" is an old saw. Certainly Abraham Lincoln bore this out when he slept in the same bed with some of his male cohorts. I never got in bed with Howard "Bo" Callaway, but I looked into his bedroom. Callaway, a West Point graduate, was a respected right-wing Republican from Columbus, Georgia. His family had grown wealthy in the textile manufacturing business. On a large piece of land near Columbus and Roosevelt's Little White House, in Warm Springs, the Callaways developed a resort – Callaway Gardens, originally intended as a vacation spot for blue-collar whites. Tennis, horseback riding, golf, an ersatz beach, dining, housing, a small chapel, bicylcle paths and beautiful gardens covered the rolling acres. Over the years it evolved into an undeniably upscale resort with Jaguars, Cadillacs, and Porsches scattered throughout the parking lots.

I need to explain why I, a liberal Democrat, would work in 1996 for the election of this wealthy conservative scion to the governor's chair in Georgia's State Capitol. The one and only reason? His opponent was the race-baiting former restaurateur Lester Maddox. Bo might be a right-winger, but compared to Maddox he was my kind of right-winger.

I met with Callaway's campaign manager. "If Bo wants the Atlanta black vote," I told him, "I think I can help." The manager welcomed me, but it was soon clear that Callaway's approach to the blacks across the state would be very muted. He was in terror of offending his base – the good-ol'-boy bubbas.

Bo Callaway listened to my entreaties that he publicly move to a moderate stand on race, but he never acted on them. A meeting of Bo and some dozen black leaders had been set up at Paschal's, a black-owned restaurant on Hunter Street (now Martin Luther King Boulevard) where black politicians hung out and made their deals. At the last minute Bo and his advisors decided to bow out. They must have wondered, "What if this meeting became known?"

A respected white attorney named Jack Izlar and I were sent to fill in for the candidate. When we arrived, disbelief and anger greeted our explanation that Callaway had sent us in his place. I had fought many wars for racial justice with these men; they knew me and, I think, trusted me. But I wasn't Callaway. Izlar and I never sat down – we quickly said goodbye and walked out. It was the end of my selling of Bo Callaway to black voters.

With the election imminent, Bo's manager called me. "I know, Cecil, you've been terribly frustrated by Bo's reluctance to move to a moderate stand," he said. "But in tomorrow's paper you'll see a statement by Bo that will be deeply gratifying for you." On the front page of the Sunday paper was Callaway's announcement that he didn't consider Dwight Eisenhower a traitor, as the red baiting Senator Joe McCarthy had alleged. That was a bombshell? Not even a respectable pop. Even if Callaway had made a statement worthy of Martin Luther King, Jr. it would have been much, much too late, coming as it did one day before the election.

On election night I went to Callaway's headquarters in an office building on West Peachtree. As a graduate of West Point, Bo leaned toward rigid military protocol in his attitudes and administrative practices. Different-colored cards were issued to all who entered based on their role in the campaign. Gold cards admitted the exalted holder to any area, including the candidate's inner sanctum. Silver cards were much more restrictive. I was handed one. When I understood its implication I was just plain outraged – not because of my demotion to second-class but because of the whole silly, elitist business. I shoved the card back across the desk at the clerk, saluted smartly, did a military about-face with clicked heels, and marched out of the office, leaving a puzzled worker behind. Some citadel of democracy!

The election returns favored Callaway by only 3,000 votes over Maddox. Ellis Arnall, a former governor, ran a write-in campaign after being beaten by Maddox in the Democratic primary and won 50,000 votes. I had written Arnall and urged him to withdraw. "You will," I wrote, "take votes away from Callaway, which will open the way for Maddox to win." He answered with a very cordial letter that completely ignored my appeal. Arnall's votes would certainly have gone to Callaway.

Because neither Callaway nor Maddox had a majority, it was up to the Georgia House of Representatives to select the governor. Since the House was 100 percent Democratic (or close to it), the result was never in doubt. Lester Maddox, a Democrat who just two-and-a-half years earlier had used a pistol to drive away two black men trying to eat at his restaurant, was now the governor of Georgia. It seemed to be the finish of the glorious motto on Georgia's Great Seal: "Wisdom, Justice, Moderation."

Maddox, with some exceptions, proved to be only a figurehead; he neither advanced nor hindered the state. Looking back, I think we weathered his term better than we would have the savvy, intelligent Callaway's conservative agenda. I don't know what I learned from my dalliance with Howard "Bo" Callaway, but I certainly didn't come away with anything of value.

My next political venture was of the greatest value. One evening in 1985 I sat on the sofa in the living room of my daughter Judy and her husband Ed Augustine. Across from us, in an easy chair, sat John Lewis. Some two decades earlier, this heroic associate of Martin Luther King, Jr. had been badly beaten by police while crossing the Edmund Pettus Bridge in Selma, Ala.

John and I had been long-time friends, having served as co-chairmen of Atlanta's Black-Jewish Coalition. As such, we stood with Coretta King at a press conference in City Hall condemning Louis Farrakhan for his anti-Semitic stand. We also headed an effort to persuade all Georgia senators and congressmen to support the Voting Rights Act of 1965. Another goal was to heal the fissure between Jews and blacks caused by Jewish reluctance to support affirmative action, which Jews saw as a way of establishing quotas that limited Jewish access – something that had been universal in this country. As I wrote in Chapter 3, when I went to Yale the quota for Jews was 5 percent, and the fewer from New York City, the better. Blacks saw affirmative action as a way to gain admission to college, secure meaningful jobs, and advance economically.

Lewis hunched forward in his chair. "I'm going to run for Congress. Cecil, I want you to be my campaign co-chairman. Will you do it?" I couldn't think of turning him down. "Yes," I replied.

My involvement in Lewis's campaign wasn't as consuming as my role with Allen, but I devoted a great deal of time and effort. The paid campaign manager was C. T. Martin, later a long-time Atlanta city councilman. Lewis's opponent was Julian Bond, a smooth, intelligent, light-skinned black. Well financed by the elite, he presented himself as a certain winner, a cut well above his somewhat inarticulate, self-educated, indifferently dressed opponent.

Lewis's speech became slurred after he took a billy-club blow to the head during the march on Selma. Some years before, I was asked to speak at the prestigious Downtown Rotary Club by Charlie Yates, a revered champion golfer. When I remembered I would be graded on my speech and realized

Charlie would be judged by my grade, I became anxious. A speech therapist, Sandy Linver, founder of a company named Speakeasy, had pitched her lessons to a group of Atlanta professionals (including me), and I arranged for several sessions with her before to my Rotary Club engagement. She didn't try to change my delivery; she merely tried to improve it. I recall her repeated demands to "Breathe, Cecil, breathe!" Ms. Linder did an excellent job. The club's jury gave me the highest mark, and I could look Charlie Yates in the eye without blinking.

It was easy to think that Sandy could help John Lewis, and when I proposed coaching from Speakeasy he readily agreed. He kept his training quiet and went weekly to Sandy's office. The improvement in his presentation was immediate and remarkable.

Lewis' headquarters were in a nondescript two-story brick building at the corner of Peachtree Street and Ralph McGill Boulevard. But our weekly campaign strategy meetings as the months progressed in 1986 were held in the boardroom of a lawyer's office overlooking downtown. They were chaired by the daughter of Harlee Branch, past CEO of the Georgia Power Company.

Bond was the clear frontrunner. As the race heated up, rumors were openly aired that Bond frequently used illegal drugs. Lewis never directly accused him, but proposed that both he and Bond submit to drug tests. Bond declined, saying such a test would infringe on his right to privacy. Whatever the truth, Bond's failure to accept testing raised suspicions but put barely a dent in his high polling numbers.

The night of the election, fifteen or so of Lewis's loyal but pessimistic supporters came to the headquarters. My wife Helen and I were there ready to stay to the end. As the tallies came in from around the city, the numbers were posted on a large board. In the beginning Bond was well ahead, but Lewis slowly closed the gap. When the count was down to the last few precincts, the final votes swung to Lewis. He had won! The excitement and joy in that little office suite burst into loud cheering, hand-shaking, backslapping, kissing, and hugging. Helen and I joined a circle of hand-holding dancers.

At Bond's headquarters the gloom and disbelief were overpowering. My stepson Art Harris, a TV reporter for CNN, was there. He told me it was as though Bond and his acolytes had been punched in the face by a heavy, soaking-wet boxing glove. Dozens of bottles of expensive French champagne sat forlornly in tubs of melting ice. The large crowd quickly dissolved with hardly a word spoken, leaving the room strewn with torn posters, campaign brochures, crushed coffee cups, crumpled lists, and darkened TV sets. It was a desolate, tragic place – a place that only shortly before had radiated supreme confidence in what would surely be a resounding victory for Julian Bond.

Several weeks later, Helen and I were at a Yale function in New Haven. A lunch was held at the Peabody Museum, where dinosaur skeletons filled a great hall. Tables were arranged around the displays, and I found myself looking up at the open jaws filled with the razor sharp teeth of a Tyrannosaurus Rex leaning menacingly over our table – an uneasy setting for enjoying a nice dinner of filet mignon.

Seated at the round table was a tall, handsome, fashionably dressed black lawyer from Chicago. We introduced ourselves and said we lived in Atlanta. The lawyer became animated. "The wrong man won that race between Julian Bond and John Lewis," he said. "It should have been Bond." I paused as asked, "Why do you say that?"

"Julian Bond would make a much better representative for us," he said. "He's is intelligent, articulate, handsome, and dresses impeccably."

"Well," I said, "you're right; Julian Bond would have done well for the blacks, but only the blacks. As you see, I'm white. I wanted a congressman who would represent me equally with members of his own race. Lewis, I know, will do just that. I felt so strongly about his abilities, his character, and attitudes that I co-chaired his campaign. He and I are old friends."

The lawyer went back to his steak. I winked at Helen and shot a baleful look at that huge skull with the long teeth looming over my head.

One aspect of the meeting pleased Helen. Just after our marriage in 1985, we had gone to another Yale gathering, where Helen's "Hello, My Name Is" ID tag listed her not as Helen Alexander but only as "Guest of Cecil Alexander." She wasn't at all pleased. (Now, decades later, she jokes about it.) In the hall of the dinosaurs, Helen came into her own. Her badge proclaimed for all to see that she was Helen Eisemann Alexander, a full-blown person in her own right. The dinosaurs were impressed.

My last foray into politics was a command performance. In 1993 my son Doug announced he was running for an at-large seat on the Atlanta City Council, one of three such citywide positions in the government. I believe my good standing with the black community was a factor in his first victory. But he and I were equally proud when he won a second term solely on his record, with whites and blacks alike voting him into office.

Chapter 9

A Good Ol' Boy Transformed

.

The only thing necessary for evil to triumph
Is for good men to do nothing.

— Edmund Burke (attributed)

In the introduction to this book I recounted how Mayor Ivan Allen dispatched his political advisor Helen Bullard and me to the June 1967 uprising at the Dixie Hills housing development, where a policeman had shot and killed a black man and wounded a black boy. Our purpose was to determine whether the mayor should go and become involved. On our return we advised the mayor to stay away, but he did not. Now, as I begin this chapter on my awakening to civil rights cause, I continue the story of what happened that hot summer day.

Neither Helen nor I had ever been to Dixie Hills, a neighborhood filled with rundown houses and empty lots. When we arrived it wasn't long before we heard angry cries – the parking lot in front of the shopping center was fast filling with screaming black men. Helen and I looked at each other, shook our heads, and agreed this was no place for the mayor, who could be the target of violence. We hurried back to City Hall and told Allen he should leave the matter to the police. His response? "I'm going."

With a mixture of concern and exasperation, I asked "Why did you ask us to check things out if your mind was already made up?" He just grinned and said, "Cecil, you're going with me." The mayor didn't ask – he told me. A police captain then picked us up in his squad car for the drive to Dixie Hills. I was glad to have an armed officer with us, but it also concerned me: Who was more the focus of black anger than the police?

We drove with no flashing blue lights and no sirens, and the car's interior was equally quiet– no discussion of a strategy for the coming encounter. Several times I almost asked the mayor what he wanted me to do, but since he hadn't spoken of his own intentions I thought it best for me to stay mum.

The mayor had found himself in a similar situation the previous September at a clash in the Summerhill community – a riot led by Stokely Carmichael, president of the Student Nonviolent Coordinating Committee (under his leadership the "non" should have been dropped from the name.) One of a rising tide of angry young black leaders, Carmichael didn't believe in Martin Luther King, Jr's passive approach. If violence seemed the best and quickest way to win, Carmichael thought, then bring it on! Later he would become the "honorary prime minister" of the Black Panther Party.

When the mayor arrived in Summerhill that day in the fall of '66, Atlanta Police Chief Herbert Jenkins, along with his security officer Lt. George Royal, were already there. Grabbing a bullhorn, Mayor Allen climbed onto the hood of a car and began to urge the crowd to disperse. Eight or ten men surged toward the car and shook it until Allen fell off; fortunately, Redding and Royal caught him. An armored car loaded with more police soon showed up, and the situation grew increasingly tense as armed officers filled the streets. The angry crowd seemed to ebb and flow but showed no signs of retreating.

The mayor's secretary had previously enlisted a large group of black ministers who had agreed to help quell any riots, and they walked through the crowd of brick- and bottle-throwing and shouted for them to go home. Gov. Carl Sanders had also deployed the National Guard, but it had mainly been he mayor's courageous action that deflated the riot. Stokely Carmichael left and the crowd moved on. The mayor had won.

When I compared the Summerhill confrontation with what was about to face us that night in Dixie Hills, it hit me like a sledgehammer: On our way to the disturbance we were three men were alone – no armored cars, no police, no preachers, and no National Guardsmen in sight. The evening was oppressively hot, and a single bead of sweat ran down my forehead. I was taken back to the night before my first mission as a Marine dive-bomber pilot, when my fear was two-pronged – first, fear of Japanese anti-aircraft fire; second, the dread of failing to live up to the historic heroism of the Marines. Now, in Atlanta, those same fears mingled in my brain: I was afraid of being harmed by the mob and of letting the mayor down. In the Pacific I had carried out my mission and hit the target (a gun emplacement) with my bomb, and came safely home – so I convinced myself I would again find courage and survive.

When we got to the street in front of the Dixie Hills mall parking lot, the mob was still very in evidence, screaming more loudly by the minute. The car was still rolling when the mayor pushed open his door and hit the pavement running. Capt. Jenkins and I soon joined him.

Mayor Allen's handling of an unruly, angry crowd was one for the books. As we plunged in, he stopped, introduced himself and shook hands with man after man, looking each in the eye as he said, "I am the mayor of Atlanta and am here to find out from each of you what happened." A small circle cleared around us as Allen addressed a teenager. I clenched my jaw and narrowed my eyes as I swept my head around looking for danger.

No one attacked us, and I've often wondered why. The captain's pistol, ready at his side, was certainly a deterrent. Also, no one could be sure that Allen and I weren't armed. It must have been the sheer audacity of the mayor that awed the rioters. For more than two hours he shook hands and greeted men in the lot while the captain and I tried to shield him. And it worked: He turned a large, dangerous mob into people with whom he now had a direct line of communication.

Mayor Allen took the police captain's bullhorn and then, in a conciliatory tone, announced, "We're going into the office here. We'll meet with you three at a time until every one of you has had his say. If it takes until daylight or noon tomorrow, we'll be here."

The mayor asked me to take notes. Not surprisingly, as the meetings progressed it turned out that almost everyone had the same grievances – police brutality, poverty, bad schools, poor jobs, segregation, and white paternalism. We listened attentively to the heated complaints until the sun rose. The mayor assured each group that after consideration of their concerns and developing a plan to allay them, he would take immediate action. When we went outside, the parking lot was empty.

As I recall, it was determined that the policeman who sparked the Dixie Hills unrest had killed the man and wounded the boy with no real provocation; he was heavily disciplined. Never again during Mayor Allen's two terms did an Atlanta policeman wantonly kill a black citizen.

Mayor Allen had been as good as his word. For me, the Dixie Hills near-riot was my first step on a long road first glimpsed more than three decades earlier, when I had gingerly formed my first friendships with blacks.

The Passenger, the Motorcyclist, the Chauffeur

It was my twelfth birthday – March 14, 1930. A short walk from my home was the Highland Avenue streetcar, which ran on two steel rails embedded in the street on its way to downtown Atlanta. I was riding it to meet my father at his hardware store so he could take me to lunch at Herren's, the best of the few decent restaurants in the city, to celebrate the day.

After a short wait I saw the boxy dark green streetcar, about 50 feet long, approaching. The motorman was visible behind the large windows. He swung the lever to stop the flow of electricity from big overhead copper wire that brought power to the trolley car's motor.

The motorman applied the brakes to the steel wheels, and the car screeched to a stop. The long cars had an aisle down the middle flanked by wooden seats for two passengers on either side. Leather straps hung from a horizontal rod, also on either side, in the front and back of the car for standees to grab. When the car reached the end of the line, the motorman got out and reversed the trolley, came back on board, flipped the hinged seatbacks so that the new passengers would face what was now the front of the car, and took up his station at the new front; both ends had identical controls for the motor-man. A switch took the car to the parallel set of rails, and it was on its way in the opposite direction. (An aside: Years later, Bill Finch, a partner in my archi-tectural firm, was a Marine colonel stationed during the Korean War in the capital city of Seoul. He was startled on his arrival in the city to see an Atlanta streetcar approaching to pick him up. Displayed on a roller sign in front was the destination "Ponce de Leon Ballpark." Seoul had bought Atlanta's streetcars when our city replaced them with buses – so when Bill felt homesick, he could go out and wait for transportation to "Emory University," "Five Points," "Little Five Points," or many other Atlanta "stops.".)

As I boarded the streetcar that day, I had no doubt about how the races would be seated or standing; I had been well educated in the inviolate relationship between blacks and whites in the South – to wit, the whites were supreme. So the blacks would be in the back of the streetcar, the whites in front. If the rear seats were all taken, any additional black passengers stood in the aisle at the back, even if there were empty seats farther up.

I paid my ten-cent fare and looked out at the seats, all of which were taken except for one. On a bench halfway back sat a well-dressed woman, her face hidden by a large hat. I sat down beside her. Seconds later she turned her head toward me, and I was shocked to see I was sitting next to a "colored lady." She was light-skinned, but there was no mistaking her race. It still haunts me that I sprang from my seat and walked quickly to the front of the streetcar, where I stood holding a pole behind the motorman for the rest of the trip. This was the automatic reaction of a well-taught product of the Old South. I hadn't been taught to hate, as in the song from the musical *South Pacific,* but I was an A student in "gentlemanly" white Southern behavior.

The South I grew up in ran the gamut of white racial attitudes and actions. They went from the extreme violence and hatred exemplified by the Ku Klux Klan extremists to polite patronizing by educated whites. My father was certainly one of the latter. He would never think of referring to our servants or to the man who for years was the janitor at his hardware store as "nigger" – the proper word was "colored." He and most of his peers were raised by black nurses, as were their children. This included me. It was impossible to hate a woman who could be closer to you than your own mother. The relationship was one of love, and race wasn't a factor. I believe that this childhood relationship, as a clear memory in the minds of most of Atlanta's white leaders, accounts to a large extent for the more or less peaceful changes in race relations in the Sixties. Yes, it was paternalism, but the childhood love was real.

I thought of two black men I knew as friends in my early years. On the street where I grew up, St. Charles Place, was a unique residential pattern. Behind the houses were servant's quarters attached to the garage, and they were rented out to blacks. But the tenants were rarely servants who worked in the owner's house; they didn't want to be on call all day and all night.

One tenant in our servant's quarters, Alonzo, was a deliveryman for the neighborhood grocery store. He had a magnificent Harley-Davidson motorcycle. Often, when he wasn't working, he would knock at the back door and call out, "Hi, buddy! Want to go for a ride on the Harley?" Unless I was reluctantly doing homework or practicing the violin with my semi tone-deaf ear, I would shout, "You bet! Let's go!" As Alonzo cranked up the powerful engine with one foot, I would climb on the back of the seat and grab him around his waist. The thrill of careening down the short, steep driveway and then leaning hard into the turn down the street was powerful. I fell totally in love with motorcycles, and the feeling toward my friend was almost as strong.

Years later, when I was able to grab the bars of a cycle myself, a tragic death cured me of my obsession. Georgia was home to Young Stribling, a real contender for the World Heavyweight boxing title. The clean-cut Stribling loved to move fast – in the ring, in his airplane (*King of the Canebreaks,* the boxer's nickname), and especially on his Harley-Davidson. It was this last hobby that killed him. Driving fast on a narrow, two-lane country road, he was hit by a truck trying to pass. Stribling was thrown in a violent arc against the pavement. He survived a few days, but died in a nearby hospital. His death made national headlines and put an abrupt end to my motorcycle dreams.

The second black man I became friends with, Lone, worked for my family as a chauffeur. He wasn't well paid. During the depression in the South, everyone was poor. The upstairs maid was poor at $7.00 a week. The downstairs maid was poor at $7.50 a week. The cook was poor at $8.00 a week. The laundress was poor at $1.25 a day, the butler was poor at $10.00 a week, the yardman was poor at $9.00 a week, and the chauffeur was poor at $11.00 a week.

People burdened with their own financial problems struggled to keep their servants; invariably, some servants were let go when their employers neared bankruptcy. Since there was no safety net, these unemployed men and women would have to move into crowded shacks in the slums with their relatives or friends and go house to house in better neighborhoods, begging for food. I sharply remember the knocks at the door by a hungry person, often with children. One man had a haunted grey face that terrified me. I hated to see him peering through the filmy curtain at our front door.

Lone, our chauffeur, kept his job. He drove our magnificent dark green Pierce Arrow four-door sedan, distinguished by headlights projecting gracefully from the front fenders. My father bought this top-of-the-line-car in 1928, only months before October 24, 1929 – the "Black Thursday" when the bottom fell out of the stock market. We kept that automobile for ten years or more, and I still remember the sound of the six cylinders beating away in its massive engine.

As a young man, Lone had played first base for the Atlanta Crackers. This was years before the gutsy Jackie Robinson went through his agonizing years of integrating major league baseball. So who better for me to play catch with in the backyard?

A former owner of our house, an actress from New York named Betsy Lee, had beautifully planted the backyard when she lived at 1111 St. Charles Place. She had hired Atlanta's leading florist, Wakendorf, to perform an overnight miracle complete with a fountain and beds of blooming flowers and plants. She'd wanted to create a lavish setting for entertaining the great tenor Enrico Caruso, her friend, due in Atlanta with the Metropolitan Opera's annual visit. Miss Lee was amply rewarded for her efforts when the front page in the next morning's paper showed a large photograph of Caruso cavorting in the fountain created just for him.

The florist warned Lee that the plants and flowers he set out wouldn't survive, but they did – that is, until my boyhood activities turned a once beautiful yard into a dustbin. And it was in that dusty backyard that Lone and I played catch. He never threw the ball directly at me. To teach me how to catch wild throws, he threw over my head and far to my left and right. Hard grounders came at me over the rough ground, bouncing wildly. My chest and often my face, not my glove, stopped these throws.

Most cities of any size had a black baseball team; Birmingham, for example, fielded the Black Barons. Some of these players were great, such as Josh Gibson, a catcher, and Satchel Paige, a Hall of Fame pitcher, who lived long enough to pitch in the formerly all-white major leagues. (As an aside, Paige also lived long enough to pitch to me at Atlanta Braves Spring Training.) Again, color be damned. I was a boy working out with a living, breathing professional baseball player – my friend Lone.

Mixed Attitudes

In spite of my friendships with Lone and Alonzo and my grandmother's loving cook Frances, I grew up completely at ease with the distorted race relations of the time. This was the way it was, and it was totally accepted (or so we thought) by our black brethren.

We were appalled by the lynchings, but we accepted the Klan as a political fact of life. Cliff Walker, a governor of Georgia in the 1920s who was a friend of my father and wrote movingly about him after Dad's death, was a member of the Klan. He had to be to get elected. The liberal U .S. Supreme Court Justice Hugo Black, from Alabama, had to outlive his past as a member of the Klan when he worked for racial justice on the court.

Years after my boyhood, I berated a black minister for not having let whites know forcefully that the Klan, lynching, bad schools, being called boy, being patronized at best and (at worst), being called a nigger, was unacceptable. His answer was indirect but powerful: "When I was a teenager I hid in the woods and watched a white mob lynch my uncle." I could feel my face flush as I said, "Please forgive me for that stupid remark." He had told me in one short sentence why the blacks kept silent for so long – mortal fear.

It was this mixed attitude toward race that I carried into my late teens, then my twenties in college and the Marine Air Corps. Because my encounter with the only black student at Yale is so revealing of my father and his white peers' attitudes, I will recount it here.

Early one fall morning I was walking across the Old Campus at Yale, where all freshmen lived in dormitories surrounding the green quadrangle, shaded by ancient elms. I walked near a tall, good looking young black man holding a football. He called to me, "Hey, want to play some catch?" I answered, "Sure." He said, "OK, go out for a long pass." He threw me a perfect spiral.

For an hour or so we passed the ball back and forth to each other. Reluctantly he said, "I have to get to class. I'm a graduate student in the Art School." I thanked him and said, "Let's do it again," as he jogged away, holding his football gripped in one large hand.

In my next letter home, I related my chance meeting with the black art student and how I had enjoyed the time I spent with him. Back by special delivery (or was it telegram?) came my father's agitated reply: "You must discontinue that association with that colored boy. Such a relationship is not acceptable in the South." This admonition was added to those he gave me just before I left for Yale. "Do not gamble; money has wings. Do not drink." The subject of sex was never mentioned.

All my life I had desperately tried to please my father. I was in awe of his massive anger when I displeased him. The miles separating me now from his commanding presence were not enough to liberate me from his domination. I never met with the black art student again.

It was this deeply impressed attitude toward race that infected my thinking through my year at Georgia Tech, my three years at Yale, my year at MIT, and my four years in the Marine Air Corps during World War II. None of these ancient institutions allowed black members in their elite white enclaves; only black servants were permissible.

My first real encounter with race confronted me as a Marine second lieutenant in 1942. With a group of black soldiers and white Marines, I stood waiting for a bus to take me back to the Marine Air Corps Station at Ewa, where I was stationed. Several Marines, and as many soldiers, were loaded with beer. They started shoving – blacks vs. whites. Just as the animosities were about to escalate into an all out brawl, the bus rolled up. The two groups, still shoving, boarded the bus. They reached the seats and left the aisles full of standees, including me. As the bus pulled away, the shouting, cursing, and hard shoves accelerated. I looked to see who on board was the senior officer. It was, I realized, one Second Lieutenant Alexander – me.

Not only was I senior, I was the *only* officer. By now we were out of the city and moving through fields of pineapples. I ordered the driver to pull over and stop, hiding my uncertainty by using my commanding, deep voice. I ordered an Army sergeant and a Marine sergeant to take charge of their men. "Separate them, all soldiers in the front, all Marines in the back" (a reversal of Southern space allocation.) The sergeants managed to execute my orders, although it took some strong profanity to get results.

Then I said, "All right, men, you will remain in your area until we get to Ewa. If there's any more fighting or cursing, the driver will stop the bus and all the soldiers will get off. Five miles down the road the Marines will get off. It's a long walk to Ewa. You two sergeants will be held responsible for maintaining order. I want your names and serial numbers."

My ploy worked. The remainder of the journey was tense but peaceful. We finally came to the gate at the station. The soldiers were in the guard unit at Ewa and lived in tents just outside the fence, and they were still grumbling as they left the bus. Then the guard at the gate waved us in. The bus stopped and Marines piled out. I thanked the bus driver. He thanked me as I swung to the ground with shaky knees.

I debated reporting the incident but decided not to pursue it. One of my fellow pilots berated me for not doing so; he was a Yankee from New York, and I thought his total lack of racial experience gave him a "by the book" attitude. Reporting the near-riot would have only increased the ill will between the two groups.

Four Big Steps

There were four factors that changed my racial attitudes from those of a boy and a young man brought up in a completely segregated, white supremacist South to a World War II combat veteran actively involved in civil rights.

The first was my realization that black veterans would come home to a vastly different country than the one I would re-enter. My opportunities would be limited only by my education, skills, intelligence, and contacts. The black veteran, no matter how well he had served his country or how skilled he was, would face barriers erected against his race. His opportunity for financial success, career, advancement, and social acceptance was greatly limited. I believed that until this inequity was corrected, we were not a democracy, we were a hypocrisy. We were certainly not equally equipped for our pursuit of happiness, as promised in the Declaration of Independence.

The second factor was a fortuitous meeting I had with a fellow student at the Harvard Graduate School of Design. Conrad Johnson was a former Tuskegee Airman who had flown combat missions in Italy. He and I were the only former combat pilots in the architecture program at Harvard. The mysterious brotherhood of combat pilots, in fact of all pilots — men or women — overcame any separation we might have felt because of race.

The Tuskegee Airmen were an invention of President Franklin D. Roosevelt. The NAACP was pounding the White House with demands that the Army Air Corps, the Navy, and the Marine Air Corps admit blacks into their pilot training programs. The 1940 presidential election was coming up, so the black segregated unit was created at Tuskegee, Alabama. This gave the NAACP its pilots without the vote-costing integration of existing programs, which would have unleashed a torrent of angry white voters. In spite of horrendous experiences in the small towns of the South, on military bases, and even from their own white officers, the Tuskegee Airmen compiled an outstanding record in combat.

Conrad Johnson and I became close friends, and he often came for dinner at my apartment. We collaborated on a student project — the design of a major airport. Our friendship lasted for his lifetime. Never once after meeting this highly intelligent, talented, courteous-to-a-fault black man did I patronize a black person or feel superior.

The third factor was my wife, Hermi. Hermoine Weil was born in New Orleans, a city very similar to Atlanta in its attitudes toward race. Her father and mine were identical in their patronizing relationships with their black employees, plus any inadvertent contacts they had across racial lines. But Hermi left New Orleans when she was 17 to follow her sister, Therese, to Smith College in Northampton, Mass. They both majored in social work, and they both came back to the south entirely open to accepting people as they found them, regardless of race. She and my present wife, Helen, shared these views, and we three worked together for racial justice in Atlanta.

The fourth factor was the time and the place. Atlanta was a pivotal point in the civil rights movement in the decades following World War II, and it was impossible to ignore this powerful force. It was also impossible not to take sides. Thanks to the four factors I have noted above, I made my decision to join the movement.

It's one thing to be interested in race relations and it's another to be effectively involved. When I retired as president of the North Georgia Chapter of the American Institute of Architects and gave my final address, I tore into architects for living next to slums and ignoring them. The publication of my remarks attracted attention and led to my appointment to head of the Citizens Advisory Committee for Urban Renewal, which would be deeply involved in matters of race. (I discuss the appointment fully in Chapter 6: "Two Careers – Architecture and Community.")

In my pursuit of racial harmony, I had some upsetting encounters. Late one afternoon, I received a phone call from a stranger. "Is this Cecil Alexander?" he asked. "Yes," I replied.

"Are you on the tube now urging the niggers to move out here?"

"I'm not watching TV, but I probably am."

"Well my name is [let's call him Joe Redneck]. I'm a former FBI agent [he gave his address, which was close to mine] and I'm telling you – you are a traitor to the United States of America."

I shot back, "I'm a decorated, retired Marine lieutenant colonel. I served in combat in World War II. I resent and deny what you called me." I hung up.

At that point none of my hate callers had identified themselves, so they didn't seem all that threatening. This one, though, was different. I bought a 38-caliber revolver and kept it under my bed.

I found having the gun very disturbing; it somehow made me feel even more vulnerable. Overseas I had worn a pistol in a shoulder holster for many months – so when I came home, taking the weapon off left me feeling naked. But that was six years past, and I'd long since not missed that piece of hardware on my chest.

I heard nothing more from my accuser. Perhaps my war service baffled him. If it had come to a "High Noon" shoot-out between us, he probably would've been quicker on the draw.

The UN Comes to Town

Not all incidents were threatening. One event I became involved in when Ivan Allen was mayor was merely nerve-wracking. Here's how it began:

Former Atlantan Morris Abram, a brilliant lawyer born in the small town of Fitzgerald, Ga., and later President of Brandeis University, was appointed by President Lyndon B. Johnson as U. S. representative to the United Nations Commission on Human Rights. He called Mayor Allen and told him he wanted the commissioners to visit Atlanta and observe civil rights in action.

"Fine," said the mayor, "we will welcome them."

My first knowledge of the pending visit came as I sat in the mayor's office after Allen summoned me there. "Cecil," he said, "the UN Commission on Human Rights is coming to Atlanta with Morris Abram. You will be the official host. You will plan the two days here and accompany them wherever they go." I was in disbelief. "Ivan," I said, "Atlanta is in turmoil. The black activists are on the street and the Klan is in silk robes all over the city. It's a bad time – a dangerous time – to host the UN."

"Yes, I know all that," he replied, "but Atlanta is an open city. I'll not deny access to the UN or anyone else. You'll take the assignment, right?"

I answered, "Give me a couple of hours. If I can find someone to work with me, I'll do it."

I called Jack Allen, a highly effective businessman who had joined me in various civic efforts after he and his family had moved to Atlanta. We had somehow met and struck up a friendship.

One evening Hermi and I had dinner at Jack's home with his wife Debbie and an unusual guest – a government official from West Africa. He was tall, very dark, and carried an intricately carved cane that he never put down, not even during dinner. Nor did he ever remove his dark glasses, which made his face inscrutable.

I found starting a conversation with this gentleman was impossible. It was a strange evening, but it told me that Allen had no hang-up with race or foreigners. I called him and laid out the proposition that he help me host the UN delegates. He accepted.

Though the weekend was tense, Jack Allen and I did a masterful job in routing the delegation around the silk-robed Ku Klux Klan and the black student protesters. We started by meeting the visitors at the airport only to find the terminal filled with young whites carrying protest signs which, to my relief, turned out to be railing against something other than the UN or the delegates' racially oriented visit.

After the delegates settled in at their hotel, the first stop on our tour was Collier Heights, a beautiful and predominantly black neighborhood in Southwest Atlanta. It matches many of the all-white enclaves in North Atlanta in the quality of the homes and landscaping.

Before the visit, we arranged with one woman who lived there in a roomy two-story house to serve refreshments to the delegation when we toured the neighborhood. The buses stopped and fifteen delegates climbed out and walked to the open door, where our hostess stood smiling and ready to welcome all. Cokes, coffee, and pastry were consumed in her well-appointed dining room. Then it was back to the buses.

We later learned the Russian delegates thought it was all a setup. They were certain the neighborhood was white and the black hostess was brought in for the occasion. This notion was reinforced by the absence of anybody on the sidewalks or in the yards. Since then, I've found this absence of people in the morning in any middle or upper-class neighborhood is more or less the norm. Why leave the comfort of a well-heated or air-conditioned home to work or walk in the sun, the rain, and breathe the polluted air?

Our most intense visit was to the campus of the predominantly black Atlanta University Center, made up of Morehouse College, Spelman College, Clark Atlanta University, and Morris Brown College. Here we met presidents of the Center's four schools, including iconic Morehouse president Dr. Benjamin Mays, an outstanding educator and man. After a rather short presentation by the presidents on the role of the Center, questions poured in from the delegation:

"What is the real racial situation in Atlanta?"

"Do your graduates get jobs with white employers?"

"Why is Atlanta University Center all black?"

The residents answered these and many more incisive queries in a positive vein. But the content of the meeting wasn't on my mind. Word was out that Dick Gregory was headed for the campus and would lie down in front of the buses. Gregory was once a very funny stand-up black comedian who held forth at the Hungry I nightclub in San Francisco. He focused on race, but not in a nasty way. One of Gregory's statements on the slow pace of civil rights involved Atlanta. Back in the Sixties he predicted that in the year 2000, a forward-looking white politician would stand in the center of Atlanta and, in a whisper, validate the Emancipation Proclamation.

But Gregory was no longer a comedian. He was now a feared civil rights activist with a strong following. It was this made-over Gregory who was on his way to disrupt our efforts. I ground my teeth at the slowness of the meeting, wanting be long gone when Gregory arrived. At last, the questions stopped and the delegation walked onto the grassy campus. Before them was a large circle of demonstrating students who were holding hands, swaying in unison, and singing "We Shall Overcome" and other freedom songs. The Russian delegates, with big grins on faces, walked to the circle, broke in, and joined hands with the students. I couldn't tell whether they knew the songs, but they were very good at swaying and hand-holding.

A friend, George Goodwin, a public relations professional involved with boosting the city's image, had arranged for the buses and told the drivers to start their engines. We herded the non-demonstrating delegates into the buses, then waited and waited and waited for the singing to cease. Word came that Gregory was on his way, and Goodwin and I were frantic.

For no particular reason, the singing stopped at last. The Russians slowly made their way around the circle, shaking hands and bowing. With a last wave, they turned and ambled onto the buses. Without waiting for the Russians to sit down, we left in a fast start, chasing up clouds of dust (the drivers were aware of the problem.) Whether Gregory ever made good on this threat and arrived, I don't know.

To my great surprise, I recently saw Dick Gregory being interviewed on television. He looked gaunt and frail, wearing a long, scraggly beard. He was giving the United States a scathing going-over as a racist nation without equal. Time had not calmed him down. To this day I'm thankful he didn't show up at the UN gathering at the Atlanta University Center.

I consider the UN delegates' visit a borderline success. We avoided the black slums, the black student demonstrators, and the Klan. They would have given an entirely different view of Atlanta had we run into any of them. Instead, the image the delegates were left with was of a well-educated, prosperous, black population who felt reasonably comfortable with the progress of racial relations – not exactly accurate, but there was more than a grain of truth in it.

At any rate, Mayor Allen complimented me on my effort. My own assessment of my effort was "We survived."

Downs and Ups

There was another minor incident involving Ivan and me, this one with no threat of violence. Early in our work with the Citizens Advisory Committee for Urban Renewal, we met with five or so black leaders. Our aim was to reassure them that their concerns regarding slum violence, housing, and jobs would be addressed. Among them were Daddy King (Martin Luther King Jr.'s father) and the Rev. G. Holmes Borders, a revered power in the black community. Allen had much to learn. At one point I shrank away thinking "Oh no!" as Ivan answered the concerns raised by Borders. He said, "Don't worry. We'll take care of you people."

Borders strode over to where Allen sat with one hand swung over the back of his chair. He reached down and vigorously rubbed the back of his hand on the Mayor's hand. "See," he said, eyes flashing, "It won't rub off!" I still think the gesture was a non sequitur that failed to make his point that the blacks could take care of themselves and needed no help from condescending white men. But there was no doubt we were no longer welcome. We left.

Times changed. Some years later, Rev. Borders was called on to pray before a predominately white crowd of some 60,000 at Georgia Tech's Bobby Dodd Stadium. The occasion was the annual football game between Georgia Tech and the University of Georgia. The feeling between the two institutions was well illuminated by the title of a book about their rivalry: *Good Old-Fashioned Hate*.

Rev. Borders's long, long, prayer was inspired. He blessed everything God and man had created, and finally implored, "Lord, dear Lord, take care of these boys today on this field of friendly strife. Help them play at the top of their abilities, to play cleanly, according to the rules, as true sportsmen, and guard them from injury. And, Oh Lord, I know you must be even-handed, but if you will lean just a little bit – just a little bit – Oh Lord, dear Lord, please lean toward the Techs."

The people in the stands rose as one, the Tech fans screaming approval and shouting, "Amen!" and the Georgia fans booing. Mayor Allen, a Tech graduate, was there, and I like to think he looked at his hand to see if it was all white or if some brown had rubbed off. At any rate, it was a long time before another prayer was offered before a Tech-Georgia game.

Atlanta's black leaders felt at times that the liberal whites were impeding progress in an effort to keep the peace. Once I invited Rev. Samuel Williams to address the congregation at The Temple, the original Reform Jewish Congregation in Atlanta. When questions were asked at the conclusion of his highly intellectual presentation, I made a mistake. "Rev. Williams, what can a progressive white person of good will do to help your cause?" Rev. Williams, with whom I had worked often and thought I knew well (I was mistaken), stared at me for a long minute, then put me away with a biting answer: "Get out of the way. Just get out of the way." In spite of this, we stayed friends and I did not have to retire to a cave.

Rev. Williams taught philosophy at Morehouse, Martin Luther King, Jr.'s alma mater, and was pastor of the highly regarded Friendship Baptist Church. I'm not sure when, but at some point he divorced his wife of many years and married Billye, an attractive student of his. In spite of this rather unorthodox course of action for a professor and a minister, Rev. Williams was so highly regarded that he kept his position at Morehouse and remained pastor of the Friendship Baptist Church for life.

Billye and her new husband soon adopted a baby girl who had one black parent and one white parent. Much to my pleasant surprise (I thought Billye didn't approve of me), the new parents asked me if I would be the baby's godfather, representing her white birth father. (They asked a black woman to represent her birth mother.) They named their new daughter Diedra Cecile — her middle name after me. The irony of a white lay Jew in the South being the godfather of a black Baptist minister's child has always delighted me.

Sadly, with his career again ascending and a beautiful wife and daughter to love, Rev. Williams suddenly died from an embolism following an operation at the Hughes Spalding Pavilion, then a private hospital for blacks. There can be no assurance of the cause of the embolism; however, the story was that two very young nurses' assistants told Rev. Williams after his operation that he must get up and walk. Weak and hurting, he angrily ordered them out of the room. Whether or not they reported his refusal to get up to higher-ups is not a known part of the story. All that is known is that an embolism caused his death.

I was honored to be a pallbearer at his funeral. Billye, having been married to an intellectual giant, later married Hank Aaron, an athletic giant, who adopted Ceci. I am often asked, "If you are godfather to Hank Aaron's daughter, what is your relation to him?" My answer: "I am his god-fan." Ceci is a beautiful blend of the two parents who gave her life. She is now a professor of Spanish at Morehouse College and the mother of two delightful children, Emily and Victor Haydel.

I found myself in many other situations of lesser significance. Hermi and I had weekly meetings of a small bi-racial group at the Round House. A range of issues was intensely discussed – not only racial problems but schools, police, mortgages, religion, zoning, and so on. I have only one vivid memory. A white psychiatrist, a man who was very sure of himself, insisted on using the old white, gentlemanly Southern pronunciation of Negro – "Niggra." After hearing this a few times, I took him aside. "Leo," I said, "the way you use 'Niggra' in speaking of Negroes will offend our black members."

"No it won't," he answered. "They know I'm a friend and supporter, no matter what I say. I don't feel comfortable with the word 'Negro,' and I've never used it." I countered, "OK, but you're wrong. You and I are good friends, but if you referred to Hebrews as 'Hebes,' I'd sure as hell set you straight in a split second."

At our next meeting we were gathered around the fire in our conical copper fireplace. A young, attractive black woman was sitting on the sofa next to the doctor with the pronunciation problem. He was discussing, at length, the city's racial problems. In the course of his talk, he continuously referred to "the Niggras." I could see the woman next to him was disturbed and very uncomfortable. She edged away from the doctor, almost falling off the end of the sofa. Finally, taking advantage of the psychiatrist's sudden coughing spell, she seized the floor. She announced loud and clear, "I am very uncomfortable. The word is Negro. Neegrow!'" Then she spelled it out: "N-E-G-R-O! Not Niggra. I am leaving." The doctor followed her to the front door, trying to calm her with the line he had given me. She would have none of it. She jerked the door open and slammed it behind her.

One very embarrassed white man rejoined the group. "Sorry, very sorry," he said. It was the end of that meeting. I don't remember whether we ever met again, and I don't know whether the psychiatrist ever changed his pronunciation or just avoided having to say the word.

One sector of Atlanta's population that has never been given the credit they so bravely earned is the women. They spoke out loudly for racial justice and went boldly into the middle of the warring factions seeking peace and justice. Many of these "ladies in white gloves and high heels," as they called themselves, were from the wealthy families of Atlanta's North Side. Their husbands held positions of power, but were reluctant to speak out and be branded by their peers as mavericks or worse, no matter their true feelings. Having worked with most of this female "power structure," I'm convinced that while the women were motivated by pragmatic economic concerns, some felt deeply that the white South's treatment of its black citizens was morally wrong – and those in the latter group formed an action group called Partners for Progress.

My first wife Hermi and her good friends Phoebe Franklin and Nan Pendergast were among the founders of Partners for Progress. Helen Eisemann, now my second wife, joined soon after group was organized. I much admired the Partners' response to the enactment of the Public Accommodations Law: In their shiny high heels, silk stockings, and neatly coiffed hair, they trooped around to Atlanta restaurants and assured the owners of each that if the restaurant were integrated they would become steadfast customers. They took the same tack with hoteliers, saying they would encourage their visiting friends to stay at hotels that complied with the law. I know for a fact that the women of Partners for Progress stiffened the spines of some of the city's weaker proprietors and pushed them to accept integration.

The women and I also faced a real test of our resolve. As one of the active members of the racial mediating committee born of the M. A. Ferst strike (described in Chapter 10), I was asked by Mayor Allen if Hermi and I and Bob Wood (the other active member of the committee) would call a strategy meeting at the Round House to set the stage for peaceful integration of public facilities. We assembled groups as diverse as restaurant and hotel owners, the media, educators, politicians, and lawyers. We urged them to place ads in the newspapers, ads not saying whether or not they approved of integration, but simply stating they would comply with – and support – this new law of the land. Predictably, the restaurant owners were the most reluctant to run such an ad. Ironically, the second group most reluctant was the lawyers!

The president of the Atlanta Restaurant Owners Association was Ed Negri, owner of Atlanta's most popular restaurant, Herren's, located in central Atlanta. Negri called a meeting of the restaurant owners at Herren's following the gathering at my house. In the Sixties, there were very few restaurants in the city, so one large table accommodated all the owners. Ed Negri invited me to attend as the only non-proprietor.

For long hours the restaurateurs argued vigorously about the thrust and wording of an ad supporting the law. At last a draft acceptable to all but one owner was composed. Then this young, very agitated fellow said, "Wait a minute. Why should we run that ad? Why should we risk our businesses, and even our lives? I say drop the whole thing. Lester Maddox will have the Klan out picketing our restaurants, no one will come in, and we'll be ruined."

Negri's face flushed and he pounded the table. "I've had it! No more discussion! We are going to run the ad. We're going to do what's right, Maddox and the Klan be damned!" The meeting adjourned and the ad was published in the next morning's *Constitution*. The Klan responded in force. Every restaurant that signed the ad was picketed by Klansmen in full colorful silk hoods and gowns – none more heavily than Herren's.

Partners for Progress was seeing their first real challenge, and they met it. Groups of these women and their husbands went for dinner that night, walking past the sneering Klansmen. Hermi and I and ten other couples threaded our way through the Klansmen into Herren's and were seated at a table close to a large window where we could be seen by the angry bigots as we ordered and ate a full meal. It was a tense experience, and probably not very good for our digestion – but we kept our cool. After dessert we walked past the pickets to our cars and drove off with a feeling of satisfaction. Ed Negri told me that the first year of integration cost him a loss of $30,000. He is, I know, an unsung Atlanta hero.

Helen was, like Hermi and me, heavily involved in civil rights. And both of my dear wives concentrated their efforts on individuals more than broad issues. An outstanding example was Helen's approach to garner assistance for the daughter of her chauffer, who was aphasiac. Following is Helen's own account of her efforts, taken from her autobiography:

Needing something to occupy my time, I began doing volunteer work. There was an African-American man who worked with us named James Williams. Well educated, he had been in the military, but couldn't get any job other than working in white households. We had long talks about the situation in the South and the discrimination that African-Americans faced on a daily basis.

He and his wife had a daughter named Linda who was aphasiac – a partial or total loss of the ability to articulate ideas or comprehend spoken or written language that resulted from damage to the brain caused by injury or disease. To function in society, sufferers require intense individual training.

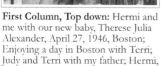

First Column, Top down: Hermi and me with our new baby, Therese Julia Alexander, April 27, 1946, Boston; Enjoying a day in Boston with Terri; Judy and Terri with my father; Hermi, the girls, and me with Hermi's parents, Rosetta and Harold Weil of New Orleans, on our front porch on Peachtree Road. **Second Column, Top down:** Cruising a Norwegian fjord with my cousin Henry (left) and Hermi; our young family in New Orleans at 18 Audubon Place, Hermi's childhood home; Hermi and me; Hermi in high spirits; our 1957 holiday card, shortly after we moved to Mt. Paran Road; with close family friends over four generations, Cecile and Gene Usdin, at the Blue Room at the Roosevelt Hotel, New Orleans

Left, Top to bottom: with Doug around 1960; with Doug around 1963; with Doug, fellow Braves fan; me in the circle of sunlight of the Round House atrium **Middle, Top:** with Judy in 1971, after her year abroad **Middle, Bottom:** the Round House, looking across the atrium to the copper fireplace. **Right, Top to bottom:** walking Terri down the "aisle" for her marriage to Herb Millkey, 1968; with Hermi, being escorted by Doug, following Terri and Herb's wedding; the five of us together at Deborah Wolf Adler's 1970 wedding to Arthur Alan Adler, Jr., Baltimore, Maryland; at Myrtle Beach, South Carolina with Herb, Judy, Hermi, and Terri.

Left column, top to bottom: with Hermi and Judy, Estes Rocky Mountain Park, Colorado; Lake Lanier with Terri, Alex, Rachael, Doug and Hermi on our sailboat, Hermes; Atlanta Braves Spring Training, Palm Beach, Florida; sailing trip to the Virgin Islands
Left: displaying one of my hidden talents -- napkin folding; Hermi and me just prior to sailing on the QEII to England
Below, clockwise: sailing at Lake Lanier wearing my Yale '40 hat; Hermi in the Balenciaga gown I gave her; with Judy on the SS Canberra, 1973, Voyage to Darkness -- a total solar eclipse off the coast of Senegal; with Hermi, Terri and Herb, shortly after their marriage, just before they set off to drive across the country to make their home in California.

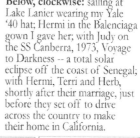

Famous People ~~Who Have Met Me~~ Who I Have Met

Top left: Congressman John Lewis, my old friend and hero, visited me at home in August, 2012 **Bottom left:** Robert Woodruff, President of The Coca-Cola Company from 1923 - 1954 and a major philanthropist, otherwise known as Mr. Anonymous, becomes an honorary AIA member, 1976 **Top right:** Hermi and I meet with A. Whitney Griswold, legendary president of Yale University from 1950 to 1963 **Second right:** With Hank Aaron, the Homerun King and father of my goddaughter, Ceci, at Hermi's and my 40th anniversary party, 1983 **Third right:** Judy and I enjoyed a Braves game with former Braves star, Dale Murphy, and his son. 1993 **Bottom right:** Helen, Judy and I have an audience with the actor Robert Redford at the home of our friends Phoebe and John Lundeen, 1984

I called the Junior League Speech School about accepting Linda but they turned her down because she was black! It made me very angry that a person so in need could be treated this way simply because of the color of her skin. I said to my friend Phoebe Franklin, "we've got to do something about this."

That was the beginning of a ten-year relationship that helped make this training available to the black community in Atlanta. We raised money to train an African-American teacher, Irene Asbury, who could work with these students. She had to go to Washington University in St. Louis, Missouri to receive training, because there were no schools in Georgia that could accept her. However, the state Board of Regents paid part of the two-year expense under its "separate but equal" doctrine.

When Irene came back, we started the first speech clinic for black children in the city. The Junior League sent their doctors over occasionally to help us, but they were still not off the hook in my mind.

Spelman College and Clark Atlanta University alternatively provided us with a small house for the clinic. As the program grew we enrolled about 50 students who were deaf and needed retraining of some sort. Getting students into the program was not always easy. At times their parents were afraid to send them to us because they weren't sure about placing the children under the care of these strange white folks. That changed as they got to know us and realized we truly were dedicated to helping their children.

Over the course of building this program we were joined by many people who pitched in to help us in ways too numerous to mention. Among those who gave of their time and personal resources were Hermi Alexander, Eleanor Massell, Jane Abram and many others.

After 10 years the program had grown too large for us to do justice to the students. At a meeting with Ira Jarrell, then superintendent of the Atlanta Public Schools, we turned the clinic over to the Department of Education of the City of Atlanta. Our program became the first special education program in the state. Eventually the walls of racial discrimination slowly began to crumble and programs like this one became available in other parts of the state.

Ralph McGill, the progressive editor of the Atlanta Constitution, wrote of the clinic, "It's an investment in humanity."

A large plaque honoring the founders of the Speech and Hearing Clinic is on permanent display at the Loudermilk Center for the Regional Community. A smaller reproduction of the plaque hangs proudly in our front hall, complete with a moving photograph of Helen bending down to put her arm around a young girl who was a student at the clinic.

A poignant letter is reproduced in *Reporting World War II*, a book compiled by many writers and radio personalities who covered the war. The letter, written by Corp. Rupert Trimmngham to *Yank* magazine, the soldier's mouth-piece, is not in the professional writer's category. It was written by a black G.I. who pours out his anguish. His friends told him it wouldn't be published. He thought it would be, and he was right.

In his letter, Corporal Trimmingham wonders why he is fighting. He was changing trains in a small Southern town at lunchtime, he writes, but none of the restaurants in the town would serve him or his black buddies. The soldiers went back to the restaurant in the train station. Yes, they would allow them to eat, but only in the kitchen. After eating an unappetizing meal elsewhere, they walked back to the station where they saw two armed guards escorting German war prisoners into the restaurant. They were seated at tables, and waiters served them.

Trimmingham was very angry, and with just cause. How can it be that he, a soldier in uniform, whose life could be lost in battle defending his country, be denied food in a restaurant that welcomes the sworn enemies of the United States of America?

I first read this compelling letter as I finished this chapter, and it annihilated any uncertainties I had about my efforts to bring justice and fairness to our black citizens. Similar occurrences, I am sure, could still happen in small Southern towns (and yes, in other regions of this country), but they will not happen in Atlanta without immediate and severe repercussions.

A Footnote

An additional note on the vicissitudes of my involvement in the civil rights movement is in order, so here it is.

One day a City Hall gadfly named Dave Walker leaned over from behind me at a City Council Committee meeting and hissed, "Racist" in my ear. I had just finished speaking in support of preserving the imposing Atlanta-Fulton County Stadium, which my partner Bill Finch and I had designed. It was to be destroyed to make way for a parking area for the new stadium. At no point had I mentioned anything remotely racist.

Walker, who is black, took the floor after me. He called me that "old guy," and filled his rambling discourse with nasty comments. I was furious. When he left the podium, I intercepted him, demanding that he hear me out. When he failed to stop, I reached out and touched him with one finger. He shouted that I had assaulted him. My son Doug, then a member of City Council, came between us and held me back; he could see I was ready to slug Walker with the hard right I still had from my boxing days. (My attorney told me that, legally, my light touch did constitute an assault.)

On his way out, a reporter from the *Constitution* interviewed Walker and wrote an article without speaking with me. Among other statements she quoted were his threats to sue me for assaulting him and the probability I had been a member of lynch mobs.

I called the editor of the paper and complained that the article failed to cover my side of the encounter. The paper's response was an editorial with my photograph headed, "Old Guy a Racist?" It was followed by a detailed account of all I had done for racial harmony and the statement that I was in no way a racist. The last sentence advised Walker to do some historical research on my support for civil rights.

Walker was the publisher of a newsletter. Several weeks after our encounter, he printed an apology, saying that as a relative newcomer to Atlanta, arriving with only a few cents in his pocket, he had no knowledge of my activities. I wrote him to acknowledge his apology. Now, when we see each other, we exchange nods and smiles. He still hangs out at City Hall and dreams of someday becoming mayor.

Chapter 10

Honoring King Amidst The Politics of Race

We are caught in an inescapable network of mutuality, tied in a single garment of destiny.Whatever affects one directly, affects all indirectly.

-The Rev. Martin Luther King, Letter from Birmingham Jail

At the dawn of 1965 the "Big Mules," Atlanta's most influential business leaders, assembled at the Piedmont Driving Club, that social bastion of the city's white elite. J. Paul Austin, CEO of Coca-Cola, had invited them, though perhaps "ordered them there" would be more accurate. When they were seated, all with a cold bottle of Coke at hand, Austin addressed the group. The following is a paraphrase what was I was told just after the meeting by a person who was present.

"Gentleman, your failure to support the dinner honoring Martin Luther King for winning the 1964 Nobel Peace Prize will be on the front page of every major newspaper and played on every television station on this earth. It will destroy Atlanta's hard-earned reputation as a city of good will between the races. Coca-Cola is an international enterprise. It cannot – it will not – keep its headquarters in a city where its leaders, through prejudice, won't honor its most acclaimed citizen. The Coca-Cola Company can and will leave Atlanta if, because of your neglect, the King dinner fails. Coca-Cola does not need Atlanta. It's up to you gentlemen to decide whether Atlanta needs Coca-Cola."

The air bristled with energy even as these captains of industry sat in stunned silence.

Mayor Ivan Allen addressed the group after Austin and also let them have it: "I'll be glad when you gentlemen have bought enough tickets to make the King dinner a success. But I doubt if any of you will be there yourselves. Don't worry – your mayor will be there."

At the time, few leading businesspeople and professionals had bought tickets for the King dinner. Early the next day I had a jubilant call from Helen Bullard, Mayor Allen's long-time political adviser. She, along with Archbishop Paul J. Hallinan, several other Christian ministers, and Rabbi Jacob Rothschild of The Temple had planned the dinner and promoted ticket sales.

"Cecil," Helen said with unconcealed glee, "Jim Robinson at the First National Bank ordered 50 tickets to the dinner!" By the end of the day, the CEOs who had heard Paul Austin none too gently fling down the gauntlet, had purchased hundreds more.

The Big Night

Mayor Allen was right about who would actually show up. The only CEO who came, as I recall, was the head of the Atlanta Transit Company, Bob Sommerville – a Londoner who had come to Atlanta some ten years before and had vigorously done his part to achieve racial justice ever since.

At one point Bob and I served together on the board of the Atlanta Chamber of Commerce. During a meeting, the issue of admitting blacks came before the board. As the motion fell short of passage, Sommerville's already ruddy face turned a furious bright red and he jumped to his feet shouting, "Wrong! Wrong! Wrong! Shame on this board!" Fearing Sommerville would have a heart attack, the chairman quickly adjourned the meeting.

On the night of the dinner, Sommerville walked from table to table before the speeches began and introduced himself and shook with everyone. He was showing that at least one of the Big Mules was attending.

At the long head table, elevated several feet above the floor, sat many distinguished attendees: Hobart Taylor, Jr. representing President Lyndon B. Johnson; Mayor Allen (as promised); Chief Herbert T. Jenkins of the Atlanta Police Department; some members of City Council; the ministers and rabbi who had organized the dinner; Ralph McGill, the courageous editor of the *Atlanta Constitution;* and the entire King family.

Only a week before the dinner, Janice Rothschild, the rabbi's wife, approached Steuben, crafters of fine glass bowls and sculpture. "Could Steuben," she asked, "make a large crystal bowl commemorating King's Peace award, suitably inscribed?" As almost an afterthought, she said the dinner was only a week away. Her friends had said, "No way! There's not enough time!" They were wrong. Steuben produced a magnificent bowl bearing King's name and describing the occasion. To the rabbi's delight, a large photograph of the Rothschilds presenting the bowl to King appeared in *Life Magazine,* fulfilling the rabbi's dream of appearing in a national magazine. And I'm sure Steuben got its money's worth in free publicity.

The dinner was held in the main meeting room of the Dinkler Plaza Hotel (formerly the Ansley), in downtown Atlanta. My firm had designed a large addition to the hotel as our first major project, and I knew the meeting room had a maximum capacity of 1,200 people. Now some 1,900 sat at round, white cloth-covered tables. The fire marshal stayed quiet but alert.

The dinner went off smoothly, but not without tension. Whispers spread from table to table that Klansmen were gathering outside. The rumor was false but it circulated throughout the evening.

Only two things marred the proceedings, and both were non-events: the absence of Atlanta's white business leaders (who sent their underlings just as the mayor had predicted) and Ralph McGill's failure to speak. Jack Tarver, president of the company that owned the *Journal* and *Constitution,* had been very supportive of McGill in the past, but it was said that he ordered him to remain silent. Fortunately, these two lapses didn't ruin the dinner, which was deemed a success. The speeches, though filled with clichés, were sincere.

The proceedings seemed to please and excite Dr. King and his family. A satisfied but apprehensive crowd moved out through the revolving doors to Forsyth Street, where they were greeted not by the Klan but by a ring of smiling Atlanta police officers and a few loud but harmless picketers who opposed the dinner.

This letter from Dr. King, now in my safe deposit box, exaggerates my contribution to the dinner (though I did sell a number of tickets to friends who sat at my table and several adjoining ones):

March 15, 1965

Dear Mr. Alexander,
In the rush of events surrounding Selma in our Alabama voting project, I neglected to express my deep gratitude for your sponsorship of the dinner honoring me on January 26. Please accept this belated note of appreciation.
I must confess that few events have warmed my heart, as did this occasion. It was a tribute not only to me but to the greatness of the city of Atlanta, the South, the nation and its ability to rise above the conflict of former generations and really experience that beloved community where all differences are reconciled and all hearts are in harmony with the principles of our great Democracy and the tenants of our Judeo Christian heritage.
Sincerely yours,
(signed)
Martin Luther King, Jr.

There was a small gathering at my house after the dinner, and it included some of those at the head table. One was Hobart Taylor, Jr., a black lawyer from Texas who occupied an office in the White House as Counsel to President Johnson. Some time later I used this contact with Taylor to propose a national committee with the mission of promoting the acceptance of civil rights legislation nationwide. A national committee was formed, and I was invited to the initial meeting in Washington as a Georgia representative.

When I saw Taylor I asked him, "Is this the committee I wrote you about?"
"You're here aren't you?" he answered.

I was disappointed that I wasn't given a leadership position, since the committee was my creation. I thought I should have been involved in making it function.

The chairman was a prominent businessman who was otherwise heavily occupied in matters unrelated to the committee's duties. At that first meeting, certain goals for the various states were discussed but no assignments were made. There was never another meeting as far as I know. The committee was, I think, a failure. Almost half a century later, many of the efforts I recommended, including featuring African Americans in advertisements, are commonplace. But this is thanks to the black community's burgeoning buying power, not the committee. As Rev. William H. Borders, a mighty political force in the black community, said in a late 1950s interview for the *Wall Street Journal*, "Atlanta has white folks. Atlanta has black folks. But the money is all green."

Atlanta must have had something more. The money was just as green in Montgomery, Birmingham, Selma, Little Rock, Memphis, and other Southern cities, but only Atlanta moved through the racial upheaval with a generally positive mood of goodwill.

My First Meeting with Dr. King

Despite the failure of the national committee, the Dinkler Plaza Hotel dinner had two great oucomes: Nobel Prize-winning Martin Luther King, Jr. was duly honored by his hometown and the Coca-Cola Company remained in Atlanta.

Dr. King often left the city to extend the reach of his struggle for civil rights. He was, for instance, heavily involved in Birmingham, where he was jailed on dubious charges. While in prison he wrote the compelling "letter from a Birmingham jail" (now in book form.) His absence suited older black leaders in Atlanta, who resented this young minister's rise to the pinnacle of the non-violence movement. King returned to Atlanta when he felt he could be useful.

One occasion was the strike of black workers at M.A. Ferst Ltd. Ferst manufactured pencil lead, which was actually compressed graphite. The black graphite dust lay over everything and floated in the air, polluting the lungs of the workers. The dark, humid plant, with grimy leather belts powering the machines that ground the graphite, had the look and feel of a nineteenth-century sweatshop.

In spite of the nasty working conditions, M. A. Ferst paid employees a reasonable wage. The company also gave a few black employees positions of authority, a labor relations initiative rarely seen in similar firms. There could have been several reasons for the strike: wages, working conditions, sick pay, insurance, or all of the above. I don't recall the "why," but the strike shut down the factory, and there was no light at the end of the sewer.

In an unusual role for Dr. King, both because the plant was in Atlanta and he had yet to take on a labor problem, he joined the picket line outside the dark-red brick Ferst building.

Mayor Allen had formed a mediation committee to resolve racial issues. Except for one black educator who was chosen by accident, the ten-man committee was white. Restraints put on most of the members by their employers or the members' positions in the city kept all but two of them from operating effectively. I was one of the two. (Although my partners had misgivings about my race-related activity, after an early confrontation they never again tried to restrain my efforts, as controversial as those efforts often were.) The other member was Robert M. Wood, the head Legal Counsel at Sears.

Bob and I were well turned out: He had won a white Rolls Royce as a prize in an Atlanta Symphony function, and in this magnificent machine we arrived in glory at many controversial meetings. We called ourselves the "Gold Dust Twins" (only when in each other's company, of course), after a cleanser that featured cute twin black boys on its cardboard box. Sometimes we were able to bring the two sides together in an uneasy compromise, frequently because there were no other alternatives.

My office phone rang one Monday. "Hi, Cecil, this is Bob – Bob Ferst." Bob's family owned the pencil-lead plant, along the very successful Scripto Pencil Company. We had known each other since we were five, and my first schoolyard fight in the second grade was with Bob. We swung away at each other with our large brown paper lunch bags firmly grasped in our fists. Years later, we boxed each other at Yale, though no lunch bags were allowed.

"Cecil," he said, "You're on the mayor's mediation committee, aren't you?"

"Yes. What can we do for you? Is it the strike?"

"Yes, that's it. Would you go alone to meet Dr. King and urge him to withdraw his support for the strikers?"

"I'll try, Bob," I said – not because Bob was my friend but because the mayor had commissioned me to intervene in such situations. "I can't make any promises, though."

I picked up the phone and called Dr. King at his home on Auburn Avenue. To my surprise, he answered. "Dr. King," I said, "you may know I'm on Mayor Allen's mediation committee. May I come talk with you about the M.A. Ferst strike situation?"

"Sure," he said. "Would two o'clock this afternoon suit you?"

"I'll be there at two. Thanks."

King met me at the door of his gray, two-story wooden house with a wide porch facing Auburn Avenue. "Come in," he said. "Glad to see you, Cecil." Rev. King sat down in a huge old leather chair and seemed to almost disappear into its battered surroundings. I perched on a stiff-backed chair a few feet from him, looking down at his slumping figure. His body was relaxed but his eyes were fully alert.

"Dr. King, M.A. Ferst wants to negotiate a settlement to the strike, but they think your participation takes a regular labor management negotiation to another level. Your involvement is national news – it becomes a part of the civil rights movement. The stakes now go far beyond a simple labor dispute, and a settlement becomes very difficult."

King gave a noncommittal nod and said, "Thank you. I appreciate your coming to see me."

He struggled out of his chair and went to the door. I followed, stepped out on the porch, shook his hand, and left.

I reported to Bob Ferst that I'd made no visible impression. Eventually the strike was settled, and I remain uncertain of both King's role and mine. That first contact was probably unproductive, but I was to have other more definitive associations with Dr. King.

A Knock on Lovett's Door

This next episode, this one having to do with integration, involved a highly respected Atlanta prep school: Lovett School, a private institution originally housed in a rambling one-story wooden structure on a narrow road in the leafy suburbs of Atlanta.

Eva Edwards Lovett, a queenly presence, was founder and principal. Under her leadership the school was characterized by a friendly, relaxed atmosphere in which the students enjoyed learning and the enforcement of discipline was rarely required.

I was a public school advocate, but Hermi, who in New Orleans had attended only private schools, held out for sending our two daughters to Lovett. It was the right decision – they both prospered there.

Mrs. Lovett was aging and wanted to retire, so she sought a buyer. The Episcopal Cathedral made her an offer, and she accepted.

The cathedral purchased a large tract of land at the intersection of Paces Ferry Road and the Chattahoochee River. Dick Aeck, a prominent Atlanta architect, planned the campus and designed the initial buildings. As a member of the building committee, I was able to persuade the school to accept a contemporary design over a Georgian standard-issue. To make my case I secured letters from the presidents of Yale and Harvard justifying the recent contemporary buildings on their historic campuses as an honest reflection of the times.

The curriculum, extracurricular programs, and atmosphere of the new Lovett was in sharp contrast to the old school, which would have been at home in a small New England town. "Laid back" was out, and driving hard for top grades was in. Athletics, a minor factor at the old school, was now emphasized. Lovett was on its way to competing with Westminster School, Atlanta's leading prep school. A vastly expanded budget meant higher tuition, and heavy fundraising was a fact of life.

It was this radically changed institution that asked me to serve on its board. The school's future now seemed secure. Yet hidden just below the surface was a serious challenge – integration.

Lovett was hardly alone in its dilemma: how to integrate a private school without losing most of its white supporters, then risking bankruptcy when parents withdraw their children and ignore fund drives. In no way do any of the attitudes then in force apply to today's Lovett and its private counterparts, but telling the story of those times is required if one is to understand the tremendous upheaval that brought about changes throughout the South. Following, in detail, are my activities at Lovett School in regard to the King family, activities that almost lost FABRAP the First National Bank commission.

Early one Sunday afternoon in November, I had a phone call from the chairman of the Lovett admissions committee, a highly respected banker active in many civic causes. "Cecil," he said with some agitation, "our committee is faced with a crisis. Please meet me at the school at four o'clock." Full of questions I kept to myself, I said, "Sure." The crisis was that Dr. Martin Luther King and his wife, Coretta Scott King, had sent a telegram to the school seeking admittance for their son Marty. There were only a few days left before admissions for the spring term would close.

By chance, Mrs. King had recently sat next to a maverick Episcopal priest, Rev. John Burnett Morris, on a flight from Atlanta to New York. She told him of the King family's difficulty in finding an excellent school for their son. The

Rev. Morris told her the Episcopal Church had decreed that all its institutions must be integrated forthwith. Therefore, she should try Lovett School. It was that meeting that induced the Kings submit an application for their son.

Addressing his committee soon after, the admissions chairman said, "Lovett must tackle this now. The Episcopal leadership has ordered all Episcopal institutions to integrate. As you know, our shield says 'An Episcopal Day School' and shows the Episcopal cross. Attendance at daily chapel and use of the Book of Common Prayer is required of all students, including non-Episcopalians. Our headmaster is an Episcopalian priest, who will have to resign if we don't integrate. The school's bylaws state that two-thirds of the board must be Episcopalian and the Dean of the Cathedral must be the board chairman.

"Our problem is made much more difficult because the candidate for admission is the son of Dr. and Mrs. Martin Luther King, and we will be caught in a powerful spotlight. Our decision will be in articles across the country, and black and white Atlantans will be analyzing our every move."

A long discussion finally came to an end around seven o'clock. A compromise would be offered to the full board, and it included the following points:

– Lovett would not admit Marty King now but at mid-year.

– Lovett would have a plan for integration in place for the next fall term.

– We would work hard to inform parents, alumni, and students of the need to integrate the school, then urge their acceptance.

Our proposal set off a firestorm. Calls and letters flooded in: "You'll ruin the school!" "You'll not get another cent from me!" "I will take my two children out!" "Funding will dry up and Lovett will have to close." "You are spineless!" And so on.

Lovett School called parents to a meeting one evening. The school auditorium was packed well beyond the capacity allowed by the fire code. On and on the impassioned accusations went. One parent, the tall, handsome Dr. Robert Bunnen, clutched the microphone. "Please hear me!," he said. "My family controls the well-financed Norman Fund, and we pledge to make up any deficit caused by integrating Lovett." (In fact, the fund was controlled by the family of Dr. Bunnen's wife, Lucinda. Lucinda Bunnen and her sister, our good friend Phoebe Weil Franklin, had moved to Atlanta from New York after World War II. What they found in the South appalled them, so they and their Norman Fund actively supported racial justice.)

Dr. Bunnen's pledge briefly silenced the crowd, but soon the heated objections resumed. A few parents who were only concerned about funding stayed quiet, but the majority wasn't mollified. Sheer exhaustion finally ended the meeting. The board sent a letter to all parents to assure them that Lovett School would never integrate.

Helen Eisemann, my future wife, was outraged by the assumption that all the parents (she in particular) opposed integration. She wrote a flaming letter to the board, a prelude to the withdrawal of her three children at the end of the school year.

A meeting of the full board was called to discuss the crisis in the intimidating, dark-paneled boardroom of the Trust Company of Georgia. To my dismay, the chairman of the Lovett admissions committee didn't show, and a local attorney took charge. A long, feverish argument ensued before the vote on the admissions committee's recommendation.

At one point the cathedral's dean pounded on the heavy mahogany table with both fists. "Talk all you want about morality, fairness, brotherhood. That's not the issue. It's dough, it's the dough, it's the dough!" He ended his diatribe by slamming his open palms on the table with a room-filling slap.

The vote was called at last. I raised my hand. "Yes, Cecil?," asked the ad hoc chairman. "Given the absence of the chairman of the admissions committee," I said, "I move to table the motion until he can be present." There was one positive vote – mine. Then, a motion not to integrate the school in accordance with the admission committee's recommendation was unanimous with one exception – again, mine.

Because Lovett had no direct funding from the Episcopal Church, the board took the position that it wasn't bound by the church's order to integrate. I was the only Jew on the board and, as such, felt unqualified to argue with a board dominated by Episcopalians. I resigned with a conciliatory letter. My action was leaked to the paper, giving me publicity I certainly didn't want. I totally rejected the idea, urged by a local Jewish organization, of making it a national issue.

Years later, a man who served on the board said to me, "I should have voted with you." His company, a leading general contracting firm, had worked with my architectural firm on major projects. I appreciated his regrets and, in a rather strange way, felt sorry for him.

Today Lovett is a highly diversified institution. It ranks high scholastically, and it graduates are sought by top colleges. The past is now past.

Years after this incident, my wife and I went on an Aegean cruise with the lawyer who chaired the board meeting that ended with integration rejected. As we and his wife sipped drinks at happy hour one afternoon, he said to my surprise, "Cecil, I made a mistake about integrating Lovett. We shouldn't have accepted the admissions committee's recommendation." I thanked him and felt no need to say more.

Dr. King's Death

When, on April 4, 1968, Mayor Ivan Allen received word that Dr. Martin Luther King, Jr. had been shot by a sniper at a Memphis motel, Allen rushed to his home to be with Mrs. King and assist her. She wanted to go immediately to Memphis, so Allen made her flight reservation, took her to the airport, and stayed with her until she was told her husband had died. She cancelled her flight, and Allen drove her home to be with her children.

The mayor's actions, typical of his innate grasp of what was right, set the stage for King's funeral. Robert Woodruff, the chairman of Coca-Cola, called the mayor. He said, "Tomorrow, Atlanta will be the center of the universe. The city's handling of King's funeral will make world news. Do whatever you think necessary to protect the crowds and discourage anything negative. Don't worry about the cost to the city – send the bill to me."

Those may not be Woodruff's exact words, but they're close to what Allen relayed to me. Woodruff was more than an outstanding businessman - he was Atlanta's guardian angel.

Ebenezer Baptist Church, the Kings' sanctuary, was filled to the thresholds for the funeral service. Many political leaders from Washington and across the country were present, and watchful police surrounded the church. Everyone who entered had to assure the guards at the door they were invited. The service went off without interruption and did great honor to King's life and his contribution to his country.

In the procession, the casket was placed on an old wooden wagon drawn by two mules. Close behind the wagon came Coretta Scott King and the King children, followed in turn by the prominent people in attendance. Behind them was a huge throng of mourners, I among them. Hermi had wanted to go, but I was afraid that violence would erupt and refused to take her. She never forgave me.

The great throng was mostly black, but a substantial number of whites were evident. Dress ran from bib overalls to suits for the men, and most of the women wore black dresses. The day was clear, and bright sun shone down on the procession.

Four events remain strong in my memory. The Central Presbyterian Church was on the route, not far from Ebenezer. This white congregation opened its doors to all visitors who came to town for the funeral and provided cots in an assembly hall. Standing in front of the church was the gently smiling minister, surrounded on either side by members of the church. Church members took the hands of scores of black visitors, escorted them inside, and gave them food and drink before they rejoined the flood of mourners.

Immediately across the street from Ebenzer is the State Capitol, occupied that day by our infamous racist governor, Lester Maddox. Maddox had won the office by exploiting his racist views verbally, in writing, and physically – the last by waving an ax handle at two black men who sought to enter his Pickrick Restaurant. Now, at Maddox's order, state police armed with tommy guns surrounded the capitol. Around the corner, draped in black, was the Atlanta City Hall. The contrast – the church and the city in deep mourning versus the governor ready to kill any demonstrators whom he thought threatening – was a vivid example of the yawning chasm of opinion regarding the activities of Dr. Martin Luther King. Jr.

The cortege wound through downtown and then up the long hill to the campus of Morehouse College, King's alma mater. The streets were lined not with police but with firemen in their blue uniforms, another brilliant stroke by Mayor Allen. Benign firefighters rather than militant police represented the City of Atlanta. Order was "maintained," not "enforced." Along the way I saw one of my commercial clients standing at the curb. I called to him, "Come on! Join us!" He smiled but shook his head "no."

As we approached the crest of the hill, I looked back toward the city. The broad street was filled with mourners, and the wide column disappeared into the tall buildings at the city's center. This undulating mass of people was like a colorful river moving slowly along.

As I turned back, I saw a tall muscular black man in front of me raise his arms high over his head. Then, in a rich and powerful baritone, he sang the first line of "We Are Climbing Jacob's Ladder." All around him, voices joined in singing this stirring old spiritual. For me it was the highlight of the day. The beautiful, swelling music seemed to carry us along on a bright rolling wave.

Only one other time has music so deeply moved me. During the Vietnam War, the Atlanta Symphony Orchestra presented Benjamin Britten's "War Requiem." At a dramatic point in the soaring work, the Atlanta Boy Choir (whose brothers and fathers might have been dying in Vietnam), dressed in long capes, marched in from the rear of the hall and mounted the stage. Their high young voices blended with the orchestra in a stunning, glorious crescendo. It took this performance, overarching in its drama, to match the emotion of the sound of the Jacob's Ladder spiritual.

A final service for King was held on the Morehouse campus at the top of the hill. Some years later, King was buried at the completed King Center on Auburn Avenue next to his church. His tomb was inscribed, "Free at Last. Free at Last, Thank God Almighty, I'm Free At Last."

The King Center

J. Max Bond, Jr., a distinguished black architect based in New York City, designed the King Center, now called The King Center for Nonviolent Social Change. I had been asked to serve on the Center's board and was assigned to the Building Committee. We had many meetings to discuss the program, then the design, and finally we monitored the construction phase.

As the only architect on the committee, I was often called upon to resolve differences. When the original design was released for negotiations with a contractor, the high price he submitted was far over budget – a shock. Daddy King was furious. He pounded the table, strode menacingly around the room, and demanded that something be done to bring down the cost.

This put me front and center. I met with the architects to discuss ways to reduce costs. A major problem, I thought, was the architectural drawing showing how the contractor should build the forms for a series of concrete vaults. This was at odds with what I had always practiced: never tell the contractor *how* to build; show only the plans and specifications you *want* for the finished product and let the contractor do his job. An architect who dictates how the building should be built scares the contractor, who in turn increases his price to cover extra expenses.

The drawings were re-issued, some expensive items were eliminated, and the instructions on how to build the vaults were removed from the drawings. The revised documents went back to the contractor, and this time the price was within budget – and Daddy King was smiling.

There were two members of the committee that left unusual imprints on the proceedings. Coretta Scott King and Jesse Hill.

As committed to the cause as she was, Mrs. King came to every meeting at least an hour late. This required restating all that had transpired before she appeared, adding time to already over-long sessions.

Mrs. King once scheduled a meeting with me at my office for a Tuesday at 10:00 a.m. She arrived the day before at 11 a.m. I didn't know if I should say (to myself) that she was an hour late on the wrong day or 23 hours early. In any event, we had a productive meeting no matter her time of arrival.

Jesse Hill was CEO of Atlanta Life Insurance, the region's leading black insurance company. Behind the scenes, Hill acted as an outstanding and effective mediator as social upheavals hit Atlanta. A street in downtown Atlanta now bears his name.

Hill always dashed into meetings late, sat for a few minutes squirming in his seat, rapidly (in a strong voice) made his views known, grabbed his felt hat, and ran out. At one meeting he jumped up saying, "I've got to fly to New York. Goodbye." I called after him, "Jesse, are you taking off on your own from here, or are you going to get on a plane at the airport?" He joined in the laughter as he ran for the door. Hill later became the first black president of the Atlanta Chamber of Commerce. He is a fine citizen.

Coretta Scott King died in a Mexican hospital of uncertain standing in 2006. The cascade of articles and editorials and television programs extolling this lady was phenomenal. Yes, she was the steely presence behind her husband, but she was also a powerful advocate for racial justice in her own right.

The King Center is deep in debt and requires many millions of dollars' worth of repairs. The King children seem to be at odds over whether to sell the facility or to struggle to hold onto it. I hope these problems will be, in the words of the best-known freedom song of the civil rights era, "overcome some day." Martin and Coretta King's legacy deserves an active and unsullied shrine.

Chapter 11

Fine Stables for the "Big Mules" And Other Venues

Slow mules creaking a lazy load ...

— *Stephen Vincent Benet, John Brown's Body*

If I often rubbed shoulders with Atlanta's "Big Mules" (the city's power elite), it was sometimes because they were hiring or firing me. Whether I was designing a headquarters or a house, these movers and shakers often displayed the stubborn streak that earned them their nickname. In this chapter I continue writing about resuming my work as an architect once my work on Ivan Allen's 1961 campaign for mayor was complete.

Although Allen's campaign took me away from my job with FABRAP, it led the firm to some Mayor's Office commissions, including the Atlanta-Fulton County Stadium. It wasn't long after our merger with Bill Finch that I got a call from the Atlanta partner of Henry C. Beck, Joe Hutchison. "Cecil," he said, "you and Finch need to come over to my office. Jim Robinson [CEO of First National Bank] asked me to interview architects." We went, and Joe told us our conversation was top secret and if we leaked any information we'd be dropped from consideration. In a whisper, he said "The First National Bank wants to build a 40-story, million-square-foot office building in partnership with H. C. Beck. I assume you're interested?"

"You can bet on it," I said.

We had several more clandestine meetings, so secretive the CIA would have approved. A week after the last one, Hutchison called again. "Cecil, FABRAP will be the architects for the First National Tower. Meet me here at 8:00 in the morning and we'll discuss an agreement." It didn't take us long to sign a contract and return it, but a serious obstacle sprang up.

When we were closing the agreement with First National I was involved with the effort to admit Martin Luther King, Jr.'s son Marty to Lovett School. My actions at Lovett (described in Chapter 10) almost resulted in a heavy blow to my firm. A nearby neighbor of ours, Lou Oliver, CEO of Sears for the southeastern region and a member of the bank's board, told me about a meeting that was a near disaster for us. The chairman of the board was a powerful citizen of Atlanta, Jim Robinson of First National. He told the board he had decided against retaining FABRAP, and for two reasons. "I don't like what Alexander is doing out at Lovett on the integration issue, and I don't think we should employ two Jewish firms." The ownership of the other architectural firm, Emory Roth & Sons in New York, was entirely in Jewish hands. But Finch, Alexander, Barnes, Rothschild & Paschal (FABRAP) was not. In fact, only Rothschild and I were Jewish. When Robinson finished, my supporter Lou Oliver took him on.

"Jim," he said, "you picked Alexander's firm because you know they'll do the best job, didn't you?"

"Yes, I did." "Well, then, what does what Alexander is doing at Lovett out of strongly held convictions have to do with his firm's architectural abilities? Also, to address your second reason, three of the five members of FABRAP are Christians, so I don't think the firm qualifies as Jewish. And if it did, why would that disqualify it?" Oliver carried the day. It would have been devastating to us if we'd lost that job. What a friend!

Henry C. Beck and the First National Bank were equal partners in ownership of the project, and this put us in an untenable relationship with Beck. If we were critical of Hutchison's choice of materials or his construction methods, he took off his contactor's hardhat and put on his owner's fedora. He convinced Robinson that our representative whose job was to observe construction was a pipsqueak who'd failed as a contractor and "didn't know shit." Problems did indeed pop up. The exterior window wall wasn't as we'd specified and leaked, the heating and air conditioning weren't up to speed, and one of the 40-story steel columns was four inches off-center. But we got everything back on track.

I had many meetings with Jim Robinson as the design and construction of the building progressed, and his negative attitude toward me gradually evaporated. At the outset he made it very clear that he wanted a wide range of design choices. "When I go to my tailor,' he said, "I don't want him to say 'this gray pin-stripe cloth will make you a beautiful suit.' I have him lay out five or six different patterns and then pick the one I want. That's how I'll make decisions on this building. You bring me several alternatives, and I'll choose."

I made a habit of presenting Robinson with at least two alternatives, but when the building was 90 percent complete I took a stand. The item at issue (not exactly a D-Day decision) was the paper-towel dispensers in the restrooms. I put a model of the one I'd chosen on his desk and said, "Jim, this is the towel dispenser we'll use." He looked at the metal box, pushed it aside, and once more launched into his tailor analogy of multiple choices. When he finished I said, "Jim, I'm not your tailor. I studied architecture four years at Yale, one year at MIT, and I have a master's degree from Harvard. I think in this rather minor matter, you could take my recommendation." He looked at me, laughed, shoved the dispenser to me across his desk, and said, "OK. You're not my tailor."

The tension between Jim Robinson and Mills Lane, CEO of Citizen's and Southern Bank, was on par with the tension between Hitler and Churchill. Their enmity slowed Atlanta business leaders' promotion of issues they deemed necessary for the city to progress. It was decided that a lunch honoring both CEOs might ease the strain. After lunch, as a gesture of friendship, Robinson invited Lane to tour the new building, then nearing completion. The two men were alone on an elevator to the roof when it stopped between floors. It took over an hour of frantic effort to free them. The discussion between two big shots trapped against their will was the subject of amused speculation. When asked to comment, Lane limited his remarks to, "Let Robinson put his money in balky elevators. I'll use mine to finance the city's future."

The First National Bank Tower is an example of International Style. Its floors have no interior columns, so the space is very flexible. Vertical transportation via a fleet of elevators and escalators is excellent. The tall lobby is finished in fine materials. Hutchison had said, "Give a building more elevators than the minimum, with fine cabs and a rich-looking lobby and you don't have to worry about anything else." It had its share of problems, but the building still stands. The Woodruff Foundation bought it from a German group, who had purchased it from the original owners and gave it to the State of Georgia for offices.

The great increase in rent in the Grant Building, where FABRAP was housed, energized my efforts to find clients. In this pursuit, I attended a civic lunch at the Piedmont Dining Club. As I left the building, I caught up with Ed Forio, a Coca-Cola executive. Several weeks before it had been announced that Coke was preparing to build an office building for their U.S. Division. Atlanta-based Robert & Company had been the architect for all of Coke's recent structures, so I assumed they had they had a lock on the project.

"How's the Robert firm coming with your new building?" I asked Forio. "They don't have it," he answered. "Twenty-one firms are under considera- tion." "Can you make it twenty-two?" I asked.

"OK, but you have to have your proposal in by next Tuesday, and that's only four days away." I responded, "We will!"

I ran to my car and raced to the office. Working 16-hour days, we assembled a state-of-the-art proposal. It included a letter recounting my family's long rela- tionship with Coca-Cola and how shares of its stock had paid for my education at Yale during the Depression. I also mentioned my chairmanship of the Citizens Advisory Committee for Urban Renewal in the days I had worked with Coke.

A few days later, Coke's project manager called with the miraculous news that FABRAP would be their architects for the Coca-Cola USA building. It was a successful venture, and the construction went smoothly all the way through its completion in 1968. The letter from Paul Austin (transcribed below) is one of my most treasured relics.

December 26, 1968

Dear Cecil,

John and I have just completed a tour of the new construction. We walked through the machine shop, the garage, and ended up in the new building.
I did not want a moment to pass before congratulating you on rendering for us a top-notch building. It is exactly what we wanted. It is pleasing in its aspect without

being overdone in any way at all. I am particularly impressed with the entrance foyer and the second floor balcony area, which, as you know, leads out toward the cafeteria. If the right atmosphere is conducive to better morale, then I believe that the Coca-Cola personnel will have the best esprit de corps *of any group in Atlanta. Kindest personal regards,*

Sincerely,
(signed)
Paul

cc: Mr. J.C. Staton

Jim Robinson lived in what is called "The Pink Palace," a pink stucco mansion on West Paces Ferry with dual rows of pink dogwoods lining a long straight driveway from the street. Not long after he allowed me to choose the towel dispensers for the First National Bank Tower, Robinson asked me to come to his home.

I arrived around five o'clock one afternoon, to be greeted at the door by both Jim and his wife. "Come on in, Cecil," he said. "We want you to remodel our kitchen."

The kitchen, a large room with dark wood cabinets and wall panels, was built in the 1920s, and very little had been changed since then. Mrs. Robinson took charge. "We want to do it over completely." She told me in detail what she envisioned – in essence, a kitchen with the same character as the rest of the house – and I said, "I understand. I'll be here tomorrow to measure the space and take some photos. I'll want to talk with you often as I develop the design."

Ten days later I finished the drawings, and the Robinsons signed off on them. A contractor was retained at a price that probably matched the initial cost of the entire house. The Robinsons were pleased with the finished kitchen, and I was relieved.

Whenever I reported to Hermi that I'd landed a big job, she wanted to celebrate. She couldn't fathom why I didn't share her enthusiasm. There were two reasons: Yes, we had a great new project, but now we had to design the thing and get it built, hardly a trouble-free triumph. The second downer was my realization that I had to find the next job. The one in hand would all too soon cease to generate a cash flow.

"The Real Thing" at Coke

A few days after the Robinson's new kitchen had been used and found serviceable, Jim invited me for breakfast. When I walked in, I was surprised to see Paul Austin, the CEO of Coca-Cola. I knew Coke was planning a new headquarters, and FABRAP was eager for the company to award us this second, much larger job. It became evident as we sat down that Robinson, who had given me the similarly scaled First National Bank Tower job, had brought us together so Austin could decide whether FABRAP was the best bet.

Between bites of grilled bacon and eggs, Austin gave me a grilling on FABRAP's capabilities and my philosophy of design – much to my surprise, since he was so happy with our previous work for Coke. In any event, some time later Austin gave us the job, so I must have told him what he wanted to hear. Arranging that breakfast brought any negative feelings I had toward Jim Robinson to an end. I was grateful for his help back then, and still am.

When I told Bill Finch we had the Coca-Cola job, his reaction was "Shit!" It was what I had come to expect from him. I think if I'd brought in the commission to design a new capitol for the United States of America it would've been the same. Bill had a very low opinion of big business and government, except for the Marine Corps, which he considered sacrosanct.

As the principal-in-charge I was the prime contact with the Coca-Cola Company. The objective of my initial meeting, held in Paul Austin's office, was for me to be introduced to Charles Adams, who would represent Coke. Charlie had an easy manner and a ready grin. He had just returned from rescuing Coke's Japanese operation, which was in serious trouble. Adams left it running smoothly and profitably.

FABRAP designated the young and talented Tom Pardue as our principal designer. We also picked a project manager, and working with Adams we developed a detailed program for Coke's headquarters. After the approval of various department heads and Austin's blessing, we were ready to execute the design. The floor plan was unique. In most office towers the elevator core is parallel to the exterior walls. We ran two cores up "catty-corner," bisecting the office space into two equal triangles. Two exterior columns, each holding elevator shafts and fire stairs, projected from the two corners of the square tower.

Adams told me that if any salesmen approached me wanting to furnish materials or anything else, I should refer them to him. So, when an executive with Atlanta Life, the leading black insurance company, asked me if his firm could write insurance for the building, I sent him to Adams. Several days later, an agitated Adams summoned me. "Why in hell did you send that insurance jerk to see me?" he demanded. Before I could answer he shouted, "You do that again and you'll have a red-hot poker rammed up your ass, and you'll know whose hand is on the other end." I was too astonished to say anything. I turned and stomped out.

The next morning I went back to Adams's office, knowing that what I had to say could get FABRAP fired. "Charlie, you really offended me yesterday. You seem to have forgotten you told me to send any salesmen to you. That's all I did."

"Have you ever read *The Virginian,* by Owen Wister?" he asked. "No? Well, there's a famous exchange in that book. Somebody calls the Virginian a son of a bitch. The Virginian, with his hand on his revolver, looks hard at the guy and says, 'When you say that, smile.'"

"Charlie, were you smiling when you railed at me yesterday?" I asked. A broad grin broke on Adams's face as he replied, "Yes, I was smiling." I left his office, my dignity intact and FABRAP still employed as Coke's architect.

As time went on I felt I was being isolated from Austin. I went to him and suggested that we meet once a week. "Paul," I said, "I don't think you're getting a realistic concept of your building. People tell you what they think you want to hear. I want to be able to tell you exactly what's going on." He considered what I said for a minute (I wondered if he was going to tell me to get the hell out of his office.) "All right, that's a good idea," he said. "We'll meet once a week." There was only one meeting.

On a positive note, there were perks working for Coke, one being the three trips I took in corporate jets. The first flight was to present FABRAP's finished preliminary design to the executives, a not-unusual time saver.

By the time I finished the appraisal we were approaching New York. As the plane came in to land, the executives looked at Austin, who signaled his approval, and then all of them bobbed their heads in concurrence. I was as nervous as I was on my first dive bombing attack in the Pacific. And even though the only thing they had in common was that I was airborne, the relief I felt was the same. Also, never in my college days could I have imagined I'd be making a presentation of a design for Coke's headquarters in a plane 30,000 feet above ground!

The outcome of the second trip wasn't successful. I asked Charlie Adams to come with me to Washington to look at the marble on the exterior of I.M.

Pei's addition to the Mellon Art Museum, which was the same marble we wanted to use on Coke's building. Charlie liked what he saw and agreed we should use the marble.

When I called the supplier to give him the news, he said, "I'm sorry. I've just been told there's no more of that marble in the quarry." Charlie wasn't pleased when I told him. He asked, "Why didn't you find this out before we flew to Washington?" – a milder rebuke than I expected.

I don't recall why I made the third flight, but I won't forget the only fellow passenger, an older man in a well-tailored black suit. He came down the aisle, sat across from me at a small table, and surprised me with, "Hello, Cecil. How are your wife Hermi, and Terri and Judy?"

He then introduced himself as Jim Farley, and I was no longer surprised he ticked off the names of my wife and daughters. Farley, who had been the political genius guiding FDR's first two presidential campaigns and was appointed postmaster general by the president, was known for his phenomenal memory. And, if he hadn't yet met someone, as in my case, he found out all about the person before the first meeting. Laptops hadn't been conceived of at that time, but Farley wouldn't have needed one even if they were available. His brain would out-compute them.

We were just airborne when Farley, then president of Coca-Cola International, launched into a diatribe against President Roosevelt, interrupting his stream of invectives only for an occasional swallow from the Coke brought to him by the flight attendant. Roosevelt had promised he wouldn't run for a third term and that he would actively back Farley as his successor. FDR lied to him again and again, he said, knowing full well he intended to "accept a draft" he himself was orchestrating. On and on Jim Farley ranted, using every expletive known to a Marine.

My reaction? I just sat and listened, wishing I had a hidden recorder.

The rant ended only when the plane's door opened at La Guardia Airport. "Goodbye, Mr. Farley," I said. This and "Hello, Mr. Farley," were the only statements I made on the entire trip. Maybe it's a stretch to say that Farley, a bona fide celebrity, met me; I was just a receptacle for his ample supply of bitterness. I never saw him again, but I'm sure he would've greeted me as Cecil and asked after my wife and two kids by name. By then he might have even mentioned our Scottish terrier, Shorty McSnorter.

Since then, my only air travel has been on commercial airliners. For a time I flew my own Stearman biplane, but I sold it when I became too deaf to hear the traffic controllers.

After the approval of our preliminary design, there was still a great deal to do before we were ready with the final drawings, models, and cost estimates we would show Adams. His reaction was disheartening. "The building is too big," he said. "We don't need that much space, and it's way over budget."

I said, "Charlie, every time we've done a headquarters the firm needed more space within five years of moving in. You will too. Why not rent an extra floor to someone close to Coke? We'll take a floor, and I'm sure there are others. The contractors are hurting right now, and you'll never build any cheaper." "Well," he answered, "I'll discuss it and let you know." The next day he said, "We have to reduce the floor sizes and take off six floors. You better get to it." I assumed he had talked to Paul Austin, so there was no recourse. We did as we were told.

Larry Gellerstedt's construction firm, one of Atlanta's most professional, was employed to build the headquarters. This included the office tower, the laboratory (called the technology building), and a garage. On the roof of the garage was a helicopter-landing pad. Above the first floor, which had columns only at the corners, were 16-foot-high steel trusses running from corner to corner. The trusses supported the floors above, a design feature I didn't favor. Word came that the four trusses had been built and were being shipped from Pittsburgh. They didn't arrive – the railroad had lost them! A desperate search located them on flatcars resting on a side track somewhere in North Georgia. Once the trusses arrived, the tower took shape quickly.

I was bemused when I learned the operator of the construction elevator I took every day was a former member of the Ku Klux Klan. We had many pleasant conversations as he took me up and down – none referring to cross-burning or other wicked Klan practices.

While construction of the Coke Headquarters was in process, the fabled Robert Woodruff invited me for lunch with my boyhood friend Burke Nicholson. Burke had recently returned to Atlanta after retiring as head of Coca-Cola's European Operations. After we finished lunch and the table was cleared, Woodruff, known as "The Cigar," reached into his thermidor, removed one of his delights, rolled it in his fingers, clipped off one end, put it in his mouth, fired it up, and blew a large smoke ring toward the ceiling.

I waited until this performance was over and then said, "Mr. Woodruff, I taught Burke all he needed to know for his distinguished career with Coca-Cola!" I then told the story I've related in Chapter 2 – how as my soft drink stand assistant in Atkins Park, Burke failed to bring back the profit-making empties after he sold Cokes to a group of construction workers across North Highland Avenue. (My parents wouldn't allow me to cross the busy street.) "I told him, 'Burke, always bring back the empties' – and that was what launched him." Woodruff chuckled softly. "We'll include that directive in our executive training program from now on. 'Bring back the empties.'"

Paul Austin asked me to meet him at his large home on Blackland Road. I did, and he and Mrs. Austin told me she wanted to widen the already ample living room. I said, "That's going to be very expensive. The front walls on both floors will have to be taken down and rebuilt, and big steel beams will have to be installed to hold up the second floor." I suggested it would be much less expensive to lengthen the room to gain additional space, but my reasoning didn't sway Mrs. Austin. She wanted the room widened. There were other changes to be made, but none as expensive as this one.

Ed Van Winkle, who had built many of Atlanta's fine houses, was chosen as the contractor. Work was well underway when I had a visit from Van Winkle. "Cecil," he said, "we've lost control of the job. Mrs. Austin makes change after change. She doesn't ask you to alter the drawings – it's all by voice and finger-pointing. Costs are running wild." I said, "OK, I'll tell Paul." His reaction was to call a meeting of the contractor's staff, FABRAP, Jeane Austin (his wife), and himself. Austin had Van Winkle repeat his concerns, and what followed was unique in my years as an architect. "Gentlemen," he said while pointing at his wife, "when I give orders at the office, they're obeyed. Let me know directly of any changes she wants; it's my money she's spending." We were all dumbfounded and embarrassed, but no more changes were requested.

The office tower was about 80 percent complete when Austin called me to his office. He was steaming. "I've just been told the tower has a smaller floor area and six floors have been eliminated," he said. "How did that happen?"

"Charlie Adams ordered it," I replied. "He said the company didn't need that much space, and costs were over budget. I thought he'd cleared it with you. We certainly argued against cutting back."

Austin buzzed his secretary and told her to send Adams to his office immediately. "Charlie," he demanded, "why did you cut down the tower? I never said there was a cap on spending. I'm furious – you're off the job. Alexander, I'll talk to you later." When I met with Austin I told him how I'd offered to rent a floor for FABRAP if Coke couldn't use the space immediately. I also said that we had lost $300,000 in fees when the building's size was reduced. Those points, I think, made the case. He didn't fire FABRAP. He would also retract the dismissal of Adams, although I still don't know whether Adams had ever cleared the change with Austin.

Later we were informed that Austin was in the early stages of dementia. As the disease progressed, the CEO's wife became more involved. Austin told his staff that any directions coming from her should be regarded as coming from him.

The executive offices in the new headquarters were on the top three floors. Our design called for an open, three-story-high atrium with a walkway around each floor. The design didn't conform to a strict interpretation of the code, but we worked with the city's cooperative building inspector to come up with a solution – the installation of sprinklers that delivered a high-volume deluge of water into the atrium and a number of powerful exhaust fans. A fire would activate both these systems and allow for a safe escape.

The Fizz-Out

When Austin was stationed in New York, he and his wife retained an interior designer for their apartment. Mrs. Austin brought him to Atlanta to advise on interior finishes, furniture, and furnishings in the executive area. Ferry, Hayes & Allen Design, a highly regarded interior design firm in Atlanta, was the designer of record, but Jeane Austin discarded their plans.

Word got to Charlie Adams that Mrs. Austin was taking over the furnishings for the executive offices. He told me, "She can do anything she damn well pleases with Paul's office, but if she goes beyond that I want you to tell me and I'll stop her."

Later I old Adams she had run Ferry off the job and that she and the New York designer were taking over. "Thanks," he said, "I'll stop her."

Mrs. Austin rolled over Charlie like a tsunami. She included in her decorating the selection of paintings for the executives' area. After they were hung, some brave critic, after hours, stuck Post-it notes on each painting, with grades. Most of them were given an F, with a C-minus the highest grade. But history rendered the final verdict. Jeane Austin is credited with the elegant furnishings and artistic flourishes of Coca-Cola Plaza, and Coke bigwigs and seasoned decorators deemed them a great success. Far be it from me to detract from what is one of the Austin family's proud legacies.

Another fine character in the ongoing Coke drama was Sam Ayoub, the company's financial officer; he and his wife became good friends with Hermi and me. Sam had introduced Coke to the lucrative business of dealing in foreign exchange, and he was untouchable.

After word got out how angry Austin was that the building had been downsized, I became a nonperson. People avoided me unless they had to pass on vital information. Someone who had seen Ayoub having lunch with me warned him he'd better break off our friendship. Sam was warned, "Alexander is a pariah. You'll hurt yourself if you're friendly with him." Sam told him, "Cecil and I are friends, and our wives are too. You can ram your opinion."

Sam, a Coptic Egyptian from the ancient Christian sect, was furious with the Carter administration for stopping the Israelis every time they were about to wipe out an Arab army.

As a young man he was employed to escort millions of pieces of paper money printed in England to Haile Selassie in Ethiopia. He took passage on a rusty old cargo ship with every available space stacked with crates filled with negotiable Ethiopian bills. On the ship were a gang of toughs who were ready to kill the ship's captain, kill Sam, take over the ship, and spirit those crates away to a safe port; they would've become rich as Croesus overnight. Sensing the danger, Sam took the top tough aside and told him, "Until Haile Selassie signs each of those bills, they're worthless. Those crates are full of just so much paper." Sam's not-so-little trick saved his life, the ship, and millions of dollars of Ethiopia's wealth.

Selassie was so taken with Sam he asked him to set up Ethiopia's banking system and the national airline. After accomplishing these two vital tasks, Sam decided to go back to Egypt. But Nasser was in power at the time, and Sam couldn't stand him – so he left. I'm not sure how he made contact with the Coca-Cola Company or when, but Sam's work with Coke ended his wanderings and rewarded him with an outstanding career.

As a young man Sam tried to swim the English Channel. He was within sight of people standing on the French coast when the wind turned against him. For four hours he swam against the tide and wind, but he couldn't gain an inch. He passed out, and sailors on the boat accompanying him pulled his limp body into the boat. He was in his seventies when he told me this story. I could tell he wanted to go back and conquer the Channel – age be damned!

Several years before Sam's death, Egyptians who regarded him as a national icon invited him and his wife to come home to be awarded a government honor. He invited Hermi and me to go, and we accepted enthusiastically. But it was not to be, Hermi contracted one of the dread diseases (she used this term lightly) and we stayed home. What a trip that would have been! It's ironic that my best friend at the Coca-Cola Company was an Egyptian. Sam was a true and valiant supporter. He died in 1997, and I miss him.

After years of an excellent relationship with Paul Austin, I found myself held off at a great distance. Looking back, I believe it was the onset of dementia that caused this rift. Whatever it was, old times were long forgotten. We were (there's no other word for it) *fired*.

As principal in charge, the ultimate blame is mine, but the immediate cause rests with our project manager, whom I'll call Craig. We were under contract to design the visitors' center. Craig refused to touch it until Coke gave us a program detailing their requirements. It was never forthcoming. I should have insisted that we submit our own program for Coke's reaction. I tried, but Craig refused to move. I should have taken him off the job. This lapse opened the way for a new player to inject himself. Mrs. Austin, aware that her husband was losing control and probably seeking some guidance, installed the interior decorator she had brought from New York as her project manager. He would now be our client and control us. He told us we had to prove ourselves to him before we could proceed with the visitors' center. A meeting was called. I said that because Craig and I were no longer acceptable, Bill Finch and another project manager could take over. There was no reaction, and we were left in limbo.

Austin had emphasized that the building was to be surrounded by wrought-iron security fencing and there would be no parking lot out front. I was out of town when Craig met with Austin to show our drawings for vehicle access to the building and the surrounding landscape. When Austin saw no security fence and parking area was planned for the front, he was furious. He adjourned the meeting and stalked from the room with his building crew following behind. "Get rid of them!" he growled. Our hope of getting the visitors' center or any future work with Coca-Cola was now gone.

Losing the Coca-Cola Company job was a severe blow. I still feel it to this day. Work was turned over to George Heery, who got the message. A tall wrought-iron fence topped with spikes surrounds the building. An elaborate visitor's center sits next to the tower and a high-rise office building stands on the other side. Heery's visitors' center is a good design, but the black glass office tower is totally unrelated to the buildings we had designed, and destroys the sense of unity.

Messrs. Nasher and Wright

Our relationship with Coca-Cola definitely had its ups and downs, but a few of our other commissions never even got off the ground. In the late 1960s Sherman Drawdy, president of Georgia Railroad Bank & Trust, retained FABRAP to find a developer for a large tract of land the bank owned – land across the street from the Georgia State Capitol. I interested Ray Nasher, a leading Dallas developer, in the site, and he retained my firm in a joint venture with Skidmore Owings & Merrill (SOM) to build a multi-use project. Nasher later became disenchanted with SOM and had FABRAP work alone. High interest rates and a skeptical and vicious real estate reporter killed the project. While I was managing the project for FABRAP, Georgia Railroad Bank & Trust acquired the Peoples Bank in Atlanta, and Drawdy asked me to serve on the board. My only knowledge of banking came from designing several banks, coupled with an ability to write checks – not very good qualifications for a board member. But I couldn't say "no" to a client. The chairman of the board was the former governor Carl Sanders, and a fellow member was Bobby Dodd, the revered former Georgia Tech football coach. An article on the financial page of the *Constitution* said my board membership was a great asset. No way! Sanders conducted all the bank's business, and the board never raised any questions. This made me uncomfortable. I felt exposed to being sued. When Drawdy died, I turned in my resignation within a week. My wife Helen's association with Georgia Railroad Bank & Trust, which I write about in Chapter 15, was far happier than mine.

It was around this time that I had an encounter at Tech with an architect of some note. "Your name is Alexander?" he said, his face inches from mine. "That's a difficult name to live up to. See that you do!" This admonition came from Frank Lloyd Wright, America's supreme architect of the twentieth century. Wright was a visiting lecturer at Georgia Tech, speaking to the students and faculty. Having thus instructed me, he turned away abruptly, his empty coat sleeves flapping, and stalked off.

Had he known that I had studied architecture under Walter Gropius and Marcel Breuer, who had brought the ideas of the Bauhaus from Germany to Harvard in 1938, he would, I am sure, have demanded that I change my name to Brutus or Benedict Arnold. The Bauhaus concept that "form follows function" and that "less is more" was anathema to him. As far as Wright was concerned, the only form that mattered was what he created – function be damned – and as he weaved his intricate patterns he dismissed "less is more" as a bankrupt approach to architecture. Egotism was his strong point.

Yes, he was a fine architect, but his personal relations were questionable. It was years after his death before the people of Madison, Wisconsin, where he lived at Taliesin East, put aside their abhorrence of Wright's attitude and built a conference center he designed for the lakefront. As far as my being guided by Alexander the Great (whom I assume Wright had in mind), I've never found any lack of worlds to conquer, which history tells us the young warrior bemoaned at the height of his conquests.

A Call from Southern Bell

I no longer remember how we were originally considered as architects for Southern Bell headquarters around 1973, but two representatives of the company, Roy Steel and Dan Vess, interviewed us. In addition to questions about our experience, staff, adherence to budgets, and knowledge of building codes was a great deal of emphasis on how we related to clients. "Roy, Dan" I said, "we consider clients' requirements, both the physical structure and the atmosphere, as the basis for our design. We work closely with them throughout the project. Some of the best ideas have come from our clients". I showed them the letter from Paul Austin, reproduced earlier in this chapter. They liked what they heard, and we were chosen.

I later heard that Portman was their first choice – that is, until he said, "Give me your requirements. I'll take them to my office and design your building." There would be no ongoing interaction between Portman and Soutwestern Bell, so Steel and Vess dropped him from consideration. Our joy at getting the commission was lessened when we were told, "We want you to work with us to choose an experienced New York architect for a joint venture with FABRAP." Our plea that we were fully qualified to do the job all by ourselves was rejected.

Kahn & Jacobs Architects should have been high on the list for consideration. The firm had designed Bell's offices in Birmingham, and Southern Bell president Ed Rast was well satisfied with the building. Bob Jacobs, who had promoted my career, was the Jacobs of Kahn & Jacobs. I would've been very comfortable working with him. But Rast had strong reservations. He told me, "Bob is too old. He might not be around to finish the job." He never asked for my assessment of the firm. He knew its work well and liked it, but nothing could overcome Jacobs's age. "These discussions, Cecil, are strictly between us," Rast said. "Next week we'll go to New York and interview Pei and Skidmore, Owings & Merrill."

Two days later I got an agitated call from Jacobs. "I hear you and Ed Rast are coming to New York to interview architects and we're not on the list. Why not?" I told him he had better talk to Ed. The next day I was leaving our office and just about to step into an elevator when our receptionist ran after me. "Mr. Rast is on the phone," she said, "and he sounds very upset."

I rushed back and picked up the phone. "Yes, Ed. Cecil here." With no preamble, he blistered my ear. "I thought you understood that our discussion about New York architects was private! Bob Jacobs just called me. He was very upset that Kahn & Jacobs wasn't being interviewed. How did he know? Have you talked to him?"

"Yes," I answered, "Bob called me. I've known him since 1936, he encouraged my career, and I had a summer job at Kahn & Jacobs. There was no way I couldn't take his call. He already knew we were coming to New York and that his firm wouldn't be interviewed. When he started interrogating me about their being omitted I said, 'Bob, you had better talk to Ed' and said goodbye. Ed, I have no idea where he got his information, but it wasn't from me." To my vast relief, Rast chuckled and said, "Well ok. That's Bob Jacobs. Don't you worry about it." Years later I found out that Rast's secretary had told Jacobs about his exclusion.

Bob never accepted my statement that I had nothing to do with his failure to be interviewed. I was at a meeting in New York of the World Wildlife Fund, and so was Bob. He refused my handshake and looked past me as we entered the hall. At the end of the program, I followed him to the elevator. "Bob," I said, "what's the matter?" As he stepped into the elevator, still not looking at me, he said, "You stabbed a knife in my back."

The doors closed, and that was the last time I saw him. I later met with his son, Bob Jr., who believed his father's version of events. Actually, the decision was entirely Rast's and was based on his belief that Bob was too old to attempt a job that would last for several years.

I still don't know if Bob Jr. believed me. I do know that I'm still sad about his father's reaction. Ironically, Jacobs's call to Rast could have lost FABRAP the commission.

I was hoping Southern Bell would choose I. M. Pei, a fellow student at both MIT and Harvard and a solid, creative designer. Unlike most star architects, he wasn't concerned with his own ego. Unfortunately, his firm's recently completed John Hancock Tower in Boston was in a structural crisis at the time. When high winds struck the building it twisted, apparently the reason many large glass windows popped out and fell to the ground. I don't know the final analysis. Rast said, "The windows falling out doesn't stop me, but I'm afraid Pei will be distracted by legal actions. Let's go to Skidmore."

Skidmore, Owings & Merrill (SOM) were recognized as the leading architectural firm in the country. We met with Roy Allen, who would be SOM's principal-in-charge, as I was with FABRAP. Paul Pippin would be their managing architect and young Manuel Fernandez their designer. It took Rast only a few minutes after meeting this team to say, "We want you as equal partners with FABRAP for our headquarters."

It was a good decision, and we made a good team. Paul Pippin was unforgettable. He insisted that the architects fly first class on trips between New York and Atlanta. This put me in an embarrassing position on one trip to New York. I was settled in my first class seat as the plane finished boarding, and in walked Roy Steel and Dan Vess, who nodded to me on their way to the cheap seats in coach. After takeoff I went back to find a seat with my clients, but there were no vacancies. Roy laughed and waved for me to go back up front. Once on the ground and in a taxi to SOM's office, I rode on the jump seat while Roy and Dan sat in comfort in the back seat, equalizing to some extent the trip's seating arrangements.

Another Pippin demand was for an onsite office for the architects during construction, which would be housed in one of the trailers (we'd initially been assigned a single desk.) Paul recorded every event, and by end of the project he had filled a 10-foot-long shelf with notebooks. So impressed was I with Paul that I arranged for him to address the Atlanta AIA and our officers. I persuaded the dean at Yale to have him lecture in the architectural management program. In 2007 I wrote an enthusiastic letter recommending him for a fellowship in the American Institute of Architects College of Fellows. He was accepted.

I'm not sure when Roy Steel told me where Southern Bell tower was to be erected – on the site of Fox Theatre, and Peachtree Street and Ponce de Leon. I was shocked. The 5,000-seat Fox is a magnificent example of the golden age of movie theaters, and its stage rivals that of Radio City Music Hall in New York. A sky full of winking stars and wispy clouds arches across the ceiling. Onion domes mount its exterior turrets, and the Moorish style is reflected in every detail of the interior. It is a beloved, historic hall of entertainment.

"Roy," I said, "you're riding a tiger when you announce you're destroying the Fox. There will be a huge outcry against it." Roy replied, "Well, don't worry. We'll just go out there early one morning with a headache ball and knock it down." The headache ball never swung. As I predicted, there was an uprising not matched since the Civil War. The Fox, in all its glory, was saved.

As an alternate site Southern Bell chose the lot immediately behind of the Fox, facing West Peachtree. For some unfathomable reason, Mayor Maynard Jackson refused to issue a building permit, but he backed down in a hurry when Rast said, "All right, we'll build it in Marietta."

It was a difficult site. The MARTA station being built in front severely reduced the size of the tower site, and construction noise would disturb Fox Theatre patrons. The ultimate solution was to slant the tower's ground-floor columns in at the base. As for the noise, Bell agreed to suspend any major procedures when the Fox was in use. Location aside, the building's design makes it very energy efficient. The walls are some 30 inches thick, and the windows are set into the interior face of the wall, shielding them from the sun.

Ever since Hermi saw the film *The Fountainhead,* based on the novel by Ayn Rand and centered on a right-wing architect name Howard Roark (played by Gary Cooper), she wanted to reenact the climactic scene. Cooper is standing at the top of his mile-high skyscraper, a fierce wind ruffling his hair. He stares down at his lover, who is riding up alone in the open construction elevator. At the top she steps off into his arms, they share a passionate kiss, and the film ends. Hermi's chance came when Larry Gellerstedt, the general contractor, agreed to a reenactment at the 50-story Bell building. Larry and I waited at the top, the not-so-fierce wind blowing our hair, while Hermi rode up in the construction elevator. She stepped out and threw herself in my arms. We kissed and then sat down to a romantic lunch in the sky, provided by Larry. The building isn't a mile high and I'm not Gary Cooper, but Hermi's wish was fulfilled.

Several disagreements arose during the design and construction phases. For one, the walls of the ground floor lobby are covered with glass tiles. I wanted Bell Telephone blue. Southern Bell president Ed Rast wanted red. The tiles are red. For another, FABRAP and SOM designers had specified costly decorative hinges for the doors in the executive suite. When Roy Steel saw them he said, "Oh no, we can't use those. The regulator will give us a hard time for wasting money." I shot back, "Come on Roy, the main lobby is 35 feet tall when it could be only ten. You think when the regulator sees that soaring space he's going to be concerned about the hinges?" I won that one. Another design detail I sold was the bronze caps over the ends of the cables at the top of the lobby. At first Ed Rast didn't want to emphasize them, but I prevailed.

A third memorable dispute: SOM wanted to plant Japanese magnolias, beautiful trees with sculptural limbs, in the huge plaza fronting the tower. Roy, Dan, and I flew to New York (all in coach) to see the specimens planted in front of the Frick Collection, one of the renowned art museums on Fifth Avenue. We took photographs of the trees to show Rast, and he liked what he saw. Then he asked, "How much?" I answered that planting and shipping would cost $5,000 per tree. "Good Lord!" Rast cried. "If it got out that we paid $5,000 for one magnolia, Japanese or not, I'd lose my job! How about dogwoods?" I lost that one.

And a fourth: The same plaza was meant to be centered with a large sculpture, and I thought Henry Moore's figures were beautifully suited to the purpose. I showed Rast photos of some of Moore's larger work and told him about his standing as perhaps the finest sculptor of the century. Again he asked, "How much?" I replied, "Probably $500,000." Rast's emphatic "no" was followed by "Every tour bus will stop in front of our building, and the guide will say, 'See that bronze thing on the plaza? It cost a half a million dollars, and that's why your phone bill is so high.'" All these years later, the plaza still needs a sculpture.

A few years ago I had lunch with Ed. "Cecil," he said, "I was wrong, The lobby tile should have been blue, we should have planted those Japanese magnolias, which I saw later at the Frick, and above all, I should have bought a Henry Moore for the plaza."

"Blame me, Ed," I said. "I should have been a better salesman." (Whenever I pass the Southern Bell building I ache when I see the empty space where a Henry Moore could be.) Ed's final admission left me upset. "You were right," he said. "We didn't need Skidmore. FABRAP could have done the job alone. Since Pippin insisted on approving everything done in your office, the material had to go to New York to be checked and then sent back to Atlanta. The job would have moved much faster without Skidmore."

Good Days, Bad Days

It's too bad there was only one Jack Warner. In the late 1960s I was lucky to have him as my client. When he was CEO of Gulf States Paper Corporation in Tuscaloosa, Ala., he retained FABRAP to design the its headquarters. His energy, intelligence, enthusiasm, optimism, and unfailing good humor made working with him a joyful experience.

Unlike most clients, Warner came to us, though why he decided to I've never known. As the co-designer and principal-in-charge, I met with him often. His only requirement, beyond adequate space for his operation, was that the design be Asian. "None of that bare, modern stuff!" he said. Fortunately, I was just back from a two-week architectural tour of Japan. (In Tokyo, I was surrounded by a covey of giggling Japanese young women who thought I was Marlon Brando.) An additional qualification for FABRAP was our Chinese-American designer Jimmy Chow, who had the appropriate name and appearance. His knowledge of Asian architecture, however, all came from books. He arrived in Atlanta from Hong Kong at age two and studied architecture at Georgia Tech.

Warner and I flew in his firm's plane to inspect several company headquarters. One stop was Kalamazoo, Michigan, where bad weather delayed our flight back to Atlanta. When I called Hermi to inform her, she thought I was kidding when I said I was in Kalamazoo; she knew the name only from Glenn Miller's comic song "I've Got a Gal in Kalamazoo" and didn't think the city was real.

The Gulf States Paper plan evolved into a large Japanese garden surrounded by mainly one-story buildings with soaring tile roofs. (The garden was designed by David Engel, an American who had lived and studied in Japan.) Clay roof tiles are made in Japanese factories that have been in business for a century or more, but Warner turned down my recommendation that we order tiles from Japan; I think he thought the cost would be too great. He did approve copper cladding, a fine roofing material that certainly isn't cheap.

After six months of intensive designing we were ready to show our drawings and the model to Warner and his operations officer. The meeting was held in our office. On the conference table we placed the large model of the central building. Sections of the model lacked walls and roof so the interior laminated wooden beams were visible.

For four hours we discussed space allocations and the interaction of the various departments with the operations officer. Warner sat back in a corner saying nothing. When we finished I said, "Jack, you haven't commented. Is everything all right with you?" Pointing at the model, he gave his only criticism: "The corners of the roof should curve up more." I don't know whether he heard any of the hours-long discussion or if he didn't really care – but we curved the corners as ordered.

After writing down these memories of the Gulf States Paper project, I sent Jack Warner a copy. He differed with me about his role in the long meeting and made other comments as well. Rather than alter my recollections, I'm letting him speak for himself in the following letter (transcribed below) — and he may be right.

Dear Cecil,

Thanks for sharing your memoir draft with me. I did review it and, you know me, I do have a few corrections and statements! On page two in the fifth paragraph, I would like to take out the statement, "Warner sat back in a corner saying nothing." I think it should state the following:

For four hours the operations officer and we discussed space allocations and the relations of the various departments. The model itself had been built at the direct request of Warner. He insisted that we build a model so he could review what was being done and made the following suggestions. After a quick inspection of the model, Jack noted that the walls of the office cubicles and elevator went all the way to the ceilings, thereby blocking the magnificent sweep of the sloping ceiling. He ordered that the top of the wood to the ceiling be made of plexiglass. Jack also went up to New Hope, Pennsylvania and ordered sets of George Nakashima furniture as at that time it was made by ol' George himself from his worshipped wood panels.

Jack also got David Engle to build the interior Japanese garden and pond so as not to obstruct the breathtaking vista view. Engle had lived in a Japanese monastery and learned how to design from the Japanese. He had even been employed by Japanese individuals to design their gardens. Mr. Warner also bought Nakashima furniture from Pennsylvania for the office, boardrooms and main office building. Though Warner did make some suggestions for the building designed by Alexander, he had fewer suggestions for Alexander's architectural firm than any other architects of an oriental nature. This resulted in a building that was one of the best examples of Oriental architecture anywhere.

Usually when Warner and architects meet there is a falling out before completion, but Cecil Alexander was a survivor and did a damn good job in his own right. Cecil was unusual in that regard.

Sincerely,
(Signed)
Jack W. Warner

When the building was finished, Warner adorned the interior walls with handsome oil paintings from his fine collection of American Indians and landscapes. George Nakashima, a premiere woodworker and furniture maker, designed furnishings. The reception desk is a slab of wood with natural rough edges — truly a unique design. In 1970, when the building was completed, costs were low; back then, the price of only a few cents over $26 per square foot was unusual. Today the building, boasting unconventional construction, balconies around the pool, details that aren't off the shelf, and a copper roof, would probably cost $200 or more per square foot. This focal point of the Gulf States Paper complex opened with a great deal of fanfare. As I remember it, the governor of Alabama and a Nixon administration cabinet secretary addressed the crowd.

Some years ago the complex was sold to the Rock-Tenn Company. Jack Warner went into the lumber business and now owns thousands of acres of timberland. On this land, at the North River Yacht Club, dramatic life-size bronze sculptures of wild animals by the English sculptor Terry Matthews stand tall, as does the fine Yellowhammer Inn, where Helen and I recently had the pleasure of staying.

Even more remarkable is the Westervelt-Warner Museum of American Art, Warner's wonderful collection of early American arts and crafts. The collection is showcased in Tom Armstrong's *An America Odyssey — The Warner Collection of American Fine and Decorative Arts* (2002.) Armstrong interviewed me when he was writing the book, and I cherish Jack Warner's inscription on the title page:

To Cecil Alexander — The greatest architect who designed the office building in 1960. The older it gets the better it looks! Oriental architecture, don't you see? Your friend, Jack Warner

In Chapter 8 of this memoir I discussed FABRAP's partnership with George Heery and how, as Finch-Heery, we designed Atlanta-Fulton County Stadium, the Five Points MARTA station, and a number of other facilities. In the early 1970s Finch-Heery was chosen to design the Georgia World Congress Center. Before we were cleared to proceed as developer, real estate developer Jim Cushman convinced the state that he could produce the center, including financing, at a bargain price while still using us as the architects. After a year of false starts, Cushman gave up. He told the State, "I can't get the money."

To make up for the lost year, the state decided to use the "design-build" approach rather than the usual construction method. In design-build, the client chooses a contractor in the beginning, who in turn selects an architect. The contractor controls the design, reducing the architect's role as a creator. It speeds the building process, but at the expense of the architect's role as a separate entity. The contractor chosen for the center was Hardin Construction, headed by Ira Hardin. Bill Finch of Finch-Heery was principal-in-charge and head of design.

Soon after, Ira Hardin asked me to meet him at his office. "Cecil," he said, "I don't want to work with Bill Finch. Can't you get rid of him?" "No way," I said, "we've worked on this project together for a year. I can't do that." Hardin appeared to accept this, and I left. From that time on I had little to do with the project. It came as an unpleasant surprise that Finch and Hardin came close to blows. The cause was the unfair contract Hardin wanted us to sign and Finch's refusal to accept Hardin as the client.

When the state heard of the differences, a meeting was called at the capitol. Hardin, Finch, and I were there, but Heery was out of town. Also present was the state representative in charge of building programs. I considered him a friend. I was wrong. A heated, hour-long discussion did nothing to resolve our differences, so the state took over. "Mr. Hardin," the state rep asked, "can you work with Finch-Heery?" With only very brief hesitation, Ira said "No, I can't." The representative broke into a broad grin and clapped his hands (so much for my thinking he was a friend.) We were fired. The replacement architect was given a contract with the terms we had demanded. Hardin had no intention of getting along with Finch, and he used the lousy contract to get rid of us.

Games, Fairs, and Malls

While Jimmy Carter was president, the 1980 Olympic Games were held in Moscow. To express disapproval of the Soviet invasion of Afghanistan, (how ironic!), Carter withdrew U.S. participation. Two former events had already cast serious doubt on the continuation of the Olympics. The first was the assassination of the Israeli athletes at the 1972 Olympics in Munich; the second was the financial debacle at the 1976 games in Montreal. In light of this situation, I suggested to Finch-Heery that Bob Eskew, Heery's job promoter and director of sports facilities, join me in investigating the possibility of locating the games permanently in Greece. I was told, "Go ahead." Of course, we hoped our sponsorship of the concept would lead to a planning and architectural commission.

Dr. John Skandalakis, a prominent Atlanta physician, had strong ties with the Greek government. He wrote a glowing letter of introduction to the top officials in Athens, telling them the nature of the mission and urging their cooperation. His letter gave us access to —- and the enthusiastic support of — Prime Minister Konstantinos Karamanlis.

Several sites were considered, but the coast of the Ionian Sea, close by the original Olympic games, had the most appeal. Its one major drawback was its distance from Athens, which is on the other side of the peninsula. Bob and I were driven there by our guide, a taciturn immigrant from Sweden who blew up when I declared, "The United States supports Turkey in our own interest. It shouldn't be considered a position against Greece." He was about to let me have it when he must have been restrained by his knowledge that I was a guest of the prime minister.

We went first to Olympia, where archeologists were carefully excavating the site and restoring the broken buildings; there was enough in place to give some sense of the various buildings and the layout. We then drove a few miles to the coast. A broad, sandy beach lay in a gentle curve against the sparkling waters. The guide (now calm) told us the water just offshore was deep enough to accommodate large ships. It was a magnificent site. I could envision the Olympic Village, all the athletic venues, hotels, and year-round spas stretched out along the pristine beach.

When I described my concept to Prime Minister Karamanlis, he very much liked the idea and believed a new highway, high-speed rail line, airport near the site wouldn't be obstacles. He said he would push the concept to the International Olympic Committee at the upcoming Winter Games in Lake Placid, New York.

Bob Eskew and I met with the Greeks at Lake Placid and waited as they presented to the other countries the concept of a permanent Olympics location in Greece. It was flatly rejected. Despite the problems in recent host cities, every one of the nations wanted the Games.

The next Games were held in Los Angeles and were a huge financial success. And that was the end of my dream.

Back on home ground, FABRAP won a national competition to design the Federal Building at the 1982 Knoxville World's Fair. Energy conservation was the fair's theme. As designed, our building — using wind, solar, and gasified wood pulp — would have generated enough power to provide Knoxville with a substantial amount. The fair's commissioner said our design wasn't commercially viable and ordered us to use only solar collectors. That was a mistake. Fairs should demonstrate the "*new* new thing" and then let entrepreneurs make it marketable. At the end of the fair, the building was sold for a dollar (I would have paid five) and later demolished. With its open, airy display areas and its IMAX Theater, it would have made a great science museum.

Some two decades earlier FABRAP had designed another building for a fair – the General Cigar Pavilion at the 1964 New York World's Fair. The most attention-getting aspect of the design was the series of huge smoke rings shot upward from the building; the force was so strong that planes landing and taking off from nearby La Guardia were routed well clear of the smoke. A New York reporter interviewed me and asked, "How did a firm down in Atlanta get the commission to design General Cigar's building?" "Well," I said, "we're experienced, prize-winning designers and world-class architects – and, oh yes, I roomed at Yale with Edgar Cullman, the company's CEO." My full statement was published. I doubt the pavilion sold many cigars.

Building for fairs had its challenges, but shopping centers are the most exasperating clients an architect encounters. Every store in a mall demands to be in the most visible and accessible location. Atlanta's Phipps Plaza was no exception. Our client was the developer Joel Cowan. Only after he brought in a tough, experienced builder of malls did a workable program evolve.

Uncle Harry Alexander owned the site fronting on Peachtree Road, but a small portion of the land belonged to my sister Charlotte and me. Cowan swapped us ownership in a co-op on Sutton Place, on the East River in Manhattan, for our land. The value of the apartment dropped precipitously as the escalation of rents slowed, and the family agreed that on my uncle's death we would sell the New York property. But no buyers were around. Fortunately, I made contact with the president of Equitable Real Estate, which bought the building – but at a price far below the estimated value Cowan had set for the swap. Making matters worse, an article on the *Atlanta Journal* real estate page quoted Cowan as saying he'd gotten the better of the Alexanders. The Phipps Plaza site had greatly increased in value while that of the New York property dropped like a stone. Cowan apologized when I told him his interview had caused my uncle's family to give me hell for making the deal.

Academic buildings are as exasperating to design as malls, and the Rollins Science Laboratory at Emory University is an example. Its handsome, orderly exterior doesn't reveal the infighting among the different departments over floor space and location.

Our Pitch to a President

I've described how most of our projects had problems – but none more than our attempt to secure the commission to design the Carter Center. Hermi and I were enthusiastic supporters of Jimmy Carter, and we were present when he announced he would run for president; I still have one of the faux straw hats distributed that evening. Later, Hermi became active in the Democratic women's organization called Fifty-Three, which took its name from the percentage of women voters. The leader of the group was an attractive young woman with the unusual name of Luketerfeder (I don't vouch for the spelling.) I felt Hermi, one smart lady, was mainly used as a gopher (as in "Hermi, will you *go for* some coffee".) Hermi didn't seem to mind this waste of her talents, but it annoyed me.

At the end of Carter's term he announced he would build his presidential library. I asked my friend Bob Lipshutz, a member of Carter's inner circle, if he would throw FABRAP's hat into the ring of potential architects. He said yes, and he did. We were on a list with three other firms invited to compete for the commission – Jova/Daniels/Busbee, Heery & Heery, and John Portman & Associates. The terms of the competition didn't meet those required by American Institute of Architects (AIA), but because of the historic significance of the project all four firms decided to ignore the AIA's requirements – a big mistake. In my files is a letter from Carter, saying he would choose one of the Georgia architects.

I visited presidential libraries, including the Kennedy Library, the Eisenhower Library, the Truman Library, the Johnson Library, and the (Franklin D.) Roosevelt Library. I talked with their staffs, gathered brochures, and took photographs. They had many things in common as far as content, but the designs varied widely. I thought the Kennedy Library in Massachusetts was outstanding. I thought the Johnson Library in Austin, Texas, was a pretentious mausoleum befitting a monarch, not a president of the United States.

When I returned to Atlanta I arranged a meeting with the Carters at their home in Plains. Two subjects were paramount. Carter, an expert woodworker, wished he had a shop so he could make furniture for the library. The second subject was mine, and I broached it reluctantly: Did they, I asked, want to be buried at the library? Rosalyn said no, they wanted to be buried "out there," pointing to their backyard.

After the interview I prepared a program to guide our architects. Marvin Housworth was the lead designer. One feature of the design was a bell tower in a shallow pool, next to the crisp, modern library. I urged Housworth to turn the tower into three separate shafts, all bound together at intervals. It would represent our three government entities – Judicial, Executive and Legislative, all separate but bound by the Constitution. My idea was rejected. The tower stayed a single shaft and had no symbolic impact.

After spending some $80,000, we submitted our entry to Carter's office in the Russell Federal Building. Heery said his entry cost about the same; Portman said he spent $130,000 – in all, $370,000 of gratis designs. Word came to us that the president favored our design and his wife favored Portman's. Weeks went by and we heard only the sounds of silence.

During that time Carter went to a meeting in Hawaii. There he met a developer named Chris Hemmeter, who had come to Honolulu a few years before with less than a hundred dollars in his wallet. Now he controlled millions of dollars of Hawaiian real estate. He was a Republican, but he and Carter hit it off. Chris put Carter up free in the presidential suite of one of his hotels, where the men discussed the library. Carter told him the budget was $25 million. Chris told Carter, "That's much too low. It ought to be at least 50 million, and I'll raise it for you."

When Carter returned home he called Chris, and said he wanted his help in choosing the most appropriate design. After his arrival in Plains, Chris was shown the four submissions. As he considered each one, he asked the Carters which features they liked best and why. Chris was an able draftsman and, I'm told, immediately sketched out a scheme incorporating all of the aspects the Carters favored. The Carters were enthusiastic. Chris said he would tell his architect to meet him at his condo in Vail, Colorado and then tackle the finished preliminary drawings.

Later, I got a call from Carter's young assistant. "Cecil," he said, "I know this has been a long time coming, but come to our office Tuesday at nine. I know you'll be pleased." I asked, "May I bring the other members of FABRAP with me?" He said, "No, come alone."

My partners agreed with me that we had the job. When I walked into the Carter suite I saw Carter, his long-time advisor Charles Kirbo, and the assistant who invited me. What baffled me were ten or twelve easels bearing drawings labeled "Carter Library," signed by a Honolulu architect and featuring circular buildings.

Carter and Kirbo told me about the role of Chris Hemmeter and his architect. I was stunned. "Would you," Carter asked, "be agreeable to forming a joint venture with Chris's architect?" I answered, "Mr. President, I can't make that decision alone. I have to talk to my partners." Bewildered and fuming, I went back to my office. After a hot discussion ("heated" isn't strong enough), we decided if the design wasn't set and we could influence the final design, we would enter into a joint venture.

At a second meeting it became clear that the design wouldn't be changed. Sensing our displeasure, Carter fired us.

Jova/Daniels/Busbee accepted Carter's terms and became the associate architects. It was a good decision. They designed several additional buildings at the site, along with the handsome entrance walk. President Jimmy Carter can still say he used a Georgia architect.

After FABRAP was cast out, Hermi and I took a long delayed trip to Hawaii. Chris Hemmeter knew we were coming. When I tried to pay the bill at the hotel (one of his), the cashier said, "There's no charge. Mr. Hemmeter picked it up." Much to Hermi's annoyance, I refused the gift. I didn't want to allow him the satisfaction of feeling he had atoned for our loss of the Carter Center. Regrettably, I won't be around to design Obama's library.

All Things Considered ...

To borrow the gist of baseball player Chico Escuela's statement, "Baseball has been very, very good to me," I can say architecture has been *somewhat* good to me. We had an interesting practice designing for many outstanding clients, but financially I could have done better selling insurance.

In the main, architects are interesting professionals. We meet a wide variety of people and encounter a great range of problems that make for interesting stories. Most of us chose architecture because we wanted to become fine designers. Then, when we started our own firms (as many of us have), we found the act of designing to be crowded out by rent payments, payroll demands, nasty clients, faulty building products, dishonest or incapable contractors, and conflicts among employees. I had my share of such problems, but now and then I found the time to concentrate on design.

Besides design, my contribution to FABRAP was finding clients and solving problems, and this had its rewards. The biggest disappointment was the collapse of FABRAP after we turned management over to the next generation. To avoid bankruptcy we sold out to Rosser White Engineers. Rosser paid the firm's debts, but nothing was left for the partners' pensions.

Legally, Rosser can claim any buildings we designed before the buy-out as theirs, and they have done so. Yes, it's legal, but I don't feel it is fair. I've told Rosser what I think, but nothing has changed.

A curse I live with: when looking at a building I designed, I see only the mistakes (my Round House being the exception.) I answer the question, "If you could live your life over again, would you want to be an architect?" with "Maybe." Other careers that appealed to me were newspaper publishing (not so good these days), teaching, cartooning, commercial art, inventing, and flying for a commercial airline. Except for newspaper publishing, I did some moonlighting in all of these fields – and for that reason was exposed to plenty of diversity.

I am certain I will pass this way but once. And this time around I'll just settle for life as an architect who has plenty of other interests.

Chapter 12

My World Ripped Apart

Never give in ... never, never, never give in.

— *Sir Winston Churchill*

On that quiet night in October 1983 the sky was completely overcast. Still, ambient light from the sprawling city of Atlanta spread a pink glow on the clouds. Hermi and I were almost home.

I turned our Buick onto Mt. Paran Road, the narrow, twisting street where we built the Round House some 30 years earlier. Slowing to make the abrupt turn into the driveway, I suddenly saw two headlights piercing the darkness and headed directly toward us.

Several months before, a similar apparition held no danger. In that instance, the car was in a curve in the road on the left. It, too, seemed to be coming head on, but as the driver followed the curve the car swung away and passed. So, for an instant, I thought the car now bearing down on us would speed on by. It did not. I frantically tried to pull the car to the right to get out of the way, but a steep bank at the roadside blocked our escape. All I could do was jam my foot on the brake and clutch the steering wheel.

When the hurtling car crashed into the left front corner of the Buick, I heard my car crumple like a huge can in the grip of some gigantic hand.

What had brought my wife of 40 years, still beautiful, trim, and active, to this spot at that deadly moment?

It was a social obligation. I had recently been induced to head the Yale fund drive in the Southeast, and the young woman who represented Yale, a Ms. Robinson, was coming to Atlanta with her husband to meet me. Hermi wasn't at all enthusiastic about my role in the fund drive; she thought I should be spending my free time with the family. So, when the Yale representative hadn't called me by 7:00 that evening, Hermi was annoyed.

When I finally located the Robinsons, they were at the home of Bob Ferst (another Yale alumnus) and his wife Jeanne. We decided we'd all go out to dinner and discuss the campaign. After a quiet meal at a restaurant in Buckhead, I volunteered to take the Robinsons back to their downtown hotel.

"Hermi," I said, "why don't you let the Fersts take you home? There's no need for you to go with me."

"No," she said. "I want to stay with you." And it was on the way home that we met disaster.

How many times have I agonized over the series of actions that brought us to that fatal instant! Questions crop up that have no answers. What if dinner had lasted one minute longer? What if the red traffic lights had been green, or the greens one red? What if Hermi had been driven home by the Fersts? What if I had driven a few miles faster or slower? What if the boy driving that oncoming car had been sober? On and on, I think of these long-lost possibilities that would have brought us to that deadly place a minute earlier or later. But it's a futile exercise. My wife and I were trapped in a crushed automobile.

I never lost consciousness, but the next hour was filled with confusion, desperation, and terrible helplessness. The front of the car had been twisted around to the left so that the steering wheel was forced against my chest and the seatback was hard against my chest, trapping me in a vise. My left arm dangled from my shoulder and was useless. There was no pain, so I couldn't understand why I couldn't raise it.

I reached over, took Hermi's hand with my right hand, and looked at her. "We're going to get out of this," I said. "I know," she whispered.

Outside the car was a chaos of sounds, lights, and rushing figures. Cars were stopping. People were milling around. A police car came. Two ambulances arrived with sirens screaming. My mind twisted back and forth. I wanted to be released from the lock the car had on me, but I also desperately wanted Hermi to be rescued. Whenever my mind swerved to my own escape, a wave of guilt engulfed me.

The door next to me was pried open and my badly injured hip started to slide off the seat. A young police officer knelt beside me and held my hip up with his hands, staying in this strained position for the whole time it would take to pull me out.

A face appeared at the window, and I heard a voice. "We have to get you out before we can reach your wife. The car is jammed against the bank on the passenger side." I've since wondered why the ten men milling about couldn't have slid the car away from the bank, entered the door on Hermi's side, and removed her.

Again came whispers from Hermi: "Oxygen … oxygen … oxygen … oxygen." They were the last words I heard from her.

I yelled out my window, "Get my wife oxygen! Get my wife oxygen! Get oxygen – now!" Whether they were able to give her oxygen, I don't know.

Someone asked me who our doctors were. I couldn't think. If I'd been able to organize my thoughts I would have said, "Get Dr. Wilbur. He lives next door." After Hermi came home a few years before to recover from quintuple bypass surgery (which she did in spades), Dr. Wilbur came over every day to check on her. It was an act of friendship, and he never sent a bill. Would he have saved Hermi that night if I had said his name?

Again an officer peered in at me. "We're going to put a blanket over you to protect you from glass, then break out the windshield. We'll then pull you out over the steering wheel, onto the hood." I have two useless questions that still resonate: Why couldn't they get me through the open door at my side, and how much additional damage was done to my body by pulling me through the front window?

After the blanket was draped over me I heard the blows shattering the windshield. Two men mounted the hood and reached in and grabbed me (I can't remember where) and pulled me out. They put me on a stretcher and immediately took me to a waiting ambulance; the door slammed shut and the siren started. The paramedic bent over me to take my vital signs, and the short ride to West Paces Ferry Hospital began.

The way was then clear to get Hermi out. I was told she talked animatedly to the paramedics as they sped to the hospital. On the way she suffered cardiac arrest, but the paramedic revived her heartbeat with CPR.

A Haze of Disbelief

I have no memory of entering the hospital, and became aware I was there only the next morning. Half away all through the night, I asked, "How is my wife doing?" I was given that frustrating, all-purpose non-answer: "She's doing as well as can be expected."

I lay on my back staring at the unforgiving fluorescent light over my head. There was a window, but a venetian blind closed off any view. Claustrophobia and helplessness engulfed me, and I called over and over for someone to open the blinds. Once it was done I was able to see a sparkling green tree through the slats, and the claustrophobia subsided.

I became aware that my oldest daughter, Terri, was standing by my bed. She took my hand, and with great effort said, "Dad, Mother died last night."

At one level, I accepted Hermi's death; the "doing as well as can be expected" lie had prepared me. At a deeper level, I couldn't grasp the finality of Terri's statement. My duaghter pressed my hand, kissed my forehead, and left the room.

Later I sent a message to the doctor who had attended Hermi and asked him to please come talk to me. I had been told that he'd taken a long time getting to the hospital that night, and it was weeks before he came to see me; I think he dreaded seeing me. When we finally talked, I listened and didn't criticize him. What would have been gained? He seemed greatly relieved when he left, yet another unanswerable question remained: if he had gotten to the hospital immediately, would Hermi have survived?

Lying in that hospital bed, I felt more and more helpless. By great good luck, however, I was attended by Dr. David F. Apple and Dr. Edward C. Loughlin, two of the country's best orthopedic surgeons. They had been called on to treat of the boy who hit us, so after they attended to his relatively minor injury I became their patient. Two years later, when I sought a second opinion on a hip replacement, I consulted a renowned New York surgeon. When I told him that Dr. Apple and Dr. Laughlin would perform the operation, he responded, "So why did you come to me? Apple and Loughlin are the best there are!" I thanked him for his second opinion of my surgeons but said I still wanted his concurrence on whether I needed a hip replacement. He gave it.

A few days after the wreck, I was placed in the confines of an MRI tube in preparation for the operation to repair my shattered pelvis. Over my head was a little decal of Donald Duck, apparently stuck there to comfort the patient. It did nothing for me as I lay in pain on the hard table. Thanks to this experience, when my firm later designed the Scottish Rite Children's Hospital I saw to it that the decor would help children feel they were in caring hands, not under the care of a cartoon character.

While I was surgery, Hermi's funeral was being held at The Temple. The day before, an architect from my office asked if I would like him to take a video. At first I was turned off by the idea, but I decided seeing the funeral might be healing for me in the future. I asked him to go ahead. He filmed the service, along with the beautiful eulogies by two rabbis – but his camera missed the real story: The Temple overflowed with people who were rich and poor, powerful and weak, old and young, white and black – all of whom had known Hermi and been touched by her. She would have been overwhelmed by this show of love and respect. It was the largest crowd since the funeral of the revered Rabbi David Marx in 1962.

When my Yale roommate Edgar Cullman heard of the wreck, he immediately flew to Atlanta in his company plane. At our home he found great confusion. I'm told that he said, "This is chaos. I'm taking charge." Edgar then announced he would stay at the hospital during my operation so that the family could attend the funeral.

Finally back in my room after the operation, I realized my left leg was in traction. When I asked Dr. Apple how long this would last he replied, "Six to eight weeks." A devastating black mood filled my brain. A feeling of dependency and helplessness engulfed me. As I recovered over many weeks, that feeling never left.

Dr. William H. Whaley, a member of the hospital board, were friends – we had served together on the Metropolitan Atlanta Crime Commission and he had given me the medical exam required for my commercial pilot's license. When he heard that I was in the hospital, he arranged for me to be moved to a VIP room at a regular-room rate. The home-like decor in the VIP room was a mixed blessing. Because it had no hospital atmosphere, I had to mentally adjust to the parade of caretakers – a nurse to take blood, a doctor to check me, a housekeeper to change my sweat-soaked sheets.

I had an unsettling experience about a month after I entered the hospital. To vary my outlook, I wanted to see the traffic below on I-75, which ran close by the hospital. So I asked the nurse if my bed could be rolled over to the window. The change made me very insecure, however. Almost immediately I asked to be returned to the regular location, where I felt once more in a familiar environment.

Several experiences at that hospital remain very strong in my memory. One was my request for my bed to be rolled to the window so I could see the traffic on I-75, which I found made me feel insecure. A very positive memory is the hospital staff who were exceptionally attentive for the length of my stay. Every morning the middle-aged black housekeeper would lean over my bed and kiss me on the forehead. "I gotta have my morning sugar," she would say.

I had two fine nurses (my son-in-law fired a third one, who had a grating attitude.) Beaupré Stephens, one of the best, was a kind, intelligent nurse who was with me throughout my stay. Beaupré had one unusual trait – she was a mystic. One day she started interpreting the handwriting of the many people who wrote to me so she could determine their character. When her analysis conflicted with my feelings about a person, I found it very upsetting – and when I asked her to stop, she did. Beaupré, a baseball fanatic, actually was married at home plate in Atlanta-Fulton County Stadium. My firm had designed her wedding site! To come home with me, she suspended a self-imposed resolution. "I don't do home nursing," she said, "but I'll break my rule for you."

The only really bad apple was the male night nurse, who came in for the last few weeks with a soggy, dead cigar clutched in his teeth. He was a "good ol' boy" type in his late twenties. He was always in need of a shave, and his "costume" was a doctor's soiled white coat with a stethoscope hung around his neck. Suddenly I'd be aware that he'd entered the room and was standing silently next to my bed, peering down at me, which left me feeling helpless and threatened.

He was also a poor nurse. One night I had a severe stomachache and he failed to heed my plea to get a doctor. I finally rang the nurse's desk and an MD came immediately. To relieve the gas in my stomach, he inserted a tube through my nose and into my stomach. This disagreeable procedure could have been avoided if my "devil of mercy" (he certainly wasn't an angel) had called a doctor sooner.

As the weeks passed my mental attitude became a matter of deep concern to my general practitioner, Dr. Bernie Lipman. I was having horrific dreams, some of which I still remember. In one, some dark presence or creature was invading my house. As it roamed around the dark interior, the roof started to collapse around me. In another dream I was sliding off the roof of a small shack on the edge of a cliff. In still another I sat on the curb of a street in a European city with Hermi. It was night, but the sky was dark red, stained by the glow from a fire behind a row of buildings. Certainly, enough had happened to me to cause these nightmares, but I was also taking a powerful new sleeping medication – Halcyon, which later was shown to induce severe nightmares.

In the several weeks since the wreck, I had been unable to weep or vent my deep anger. Dr. Lipman called in a psychiatrist, Dr. Michael Haberman, with whom I talked about my dreams and the inability to release my emotions. With one statement, he released me. "With all the medical efforts in your behalf, your constant flow of visitors, and your painful injuries, you have not had a chance to tell your wife goodbye," he said. Finally I wept, and the tension drained from me. Later that night the nightmares stopped – a magic moment. Over the years I've gone back to Dr. Haberman to deal with anxieties I still have as a result of that experience.

Seeds of Recovery

A new and beautiful presence came into my life as I convalesced: Helen Eisemann Mantler. Helen and Hermi were close friends, our children knew one another, and we lived close together. More than once Hermi said to me, "if anything ever happens to me, Helen's your woman." Although Helen is an extraordinarily beautiful woman, their friendship was strong and Hermi never felt threatened by her, nor jealous.

To supplement the meat and potatoes fare of the hospital, Helen rallied our friends to bring a home-cooked gourmet meal every night. This "food chain" was made up of couples, single women, and even bachelors. The last category included Helen's former husband, Bud Mantler; he was an excellent chef, and I looked forward to his soups and milkshakes.

My first provider was Elaine Montag. I had dated her long ago, when we were in college – I at Yale, she at Cornell, the scene of a memorable house party. She had married and divorced twice, and her first husband – Bud Weiss, then president of the Montag Paper Company – asked me to design their house. That first night she came into my hospital room with a platter piled high with Lobster Newburgh, but I could barely force down clear soup. I thanked her and looked away from food that would have sickened me. After Elaine left I offered her gift to the nurses.

Helen produced the first meal I enjoyed. It was a salad with hearts of palm and lump crabmeat. I may have decided immediately that if Helen would have me, she would one day be my bride.

One of the later visitors was an architect I had brought into the firm with the idea that he would take over as CEO once the founding partners retired. In the meantime, his job was to get work. Periodically he would travel to Washington to seek out government commissions for us — yet a year passed and there were no jobs from Washington in sight. We then learned his marriage hadn't interfered with his liaison with a Washington lady. He was spending our money on his extra-marital affair, not on pursuing work for FABRAP. We fired him forthwith. Despite this, the cheater (on his wife as well as our firm) came to comfort me at that time I was just able to briefly sit up in a chair. He broke into tears and told me how rotten he felt over what he had done. "I let you down. I let you down. I let you down," he wailed over and over. So the tables turned. I comforted him tell him that the past was past. By that reversal of roles he left me in a better mood.

Immediately after this guilty visitor left, the wife of a contractor with whom we had worked came in. Drawing on her Catholic upbringing she said, "They're lined up down that hall waiting to see you. It's as crowded as the waiting line at the confessional after New Year's Eve."

I told her how right she was and then about the confession of my just-departed visitor. "I am a lay Jew, not a Catholic priest," I said, "so I doubt my absolution holds any sway with God."

The flood of visitors was very wearing. My nurse set up rules — no more than two persons at a time for no longer than five minutes. I never wanted to turn my friends away, but staying alert for a steady stream of people took a serious toll on my energy.

One memorable visitor was the doctor who was the head cardiologist at a local institution. Since he knew well his superior medical talents and status, he expected to be received as royalty wherever he went. He had been Hermi's cardiologist during her bypass surgery, so we had met several times. One afternoon he participated in a seminar at my hospital, and afterwards came to my room. Controlling visitor access was my baseball-loving nurse, who was told by the distinguished doctor, "I'm in a hurry. I want to see Mr. Alexander immediately." My nurse knew who he was, but she also knew who *she* was.

"Doctor," she said, "Mr. Alexander can see only two people at a time for five minutes. Right now there are two people in the room. You can't go in until they leave."

"Well tell them to leave now."

"I can't do that, Doctor. They are Mr. Alexander's relatives from the West Coast, and they flew in just to see him."

"Well, all right," he said. "I guess I'll wait."

When he finally came in he was most gracious and betrayed no hint of annoyance. In my estimation, my nurse earned the "Gutsy Medal" for 1984.

Another awkward visit came from my daughter Terri, her husband, and their two very young children (the "two persons only" rule was set-aside for family.) In the middle of their stay the phone rang – it was cousin Henry, calling from Eugene, Oregon. Because the youngsters were shouting and running around, I couldn't hear a word my cousin said. My stomach then said to my brain, "If you won't use Alexander's tongue to tell his family to leave, I'm taking over." Seconds later I threw up, and the room cleared. It was a drastic way to empty the room, but it worked.

After a long six weeks, Dr. Apple told me I could be released from traction. This involved removing the steel rod that penetrated my calf and pierced the bone. He laughed when I asked whether I would be anesthetized. "No, you won't feel it," he said. Still, I dreaded the procedure. The doctor was right; there was no pain. After a series of complicated movements he pulled the rod from my leg. Free at last! However, it was weeks before my leg was comfortable. To stabilize my leg at night, I put it back in the cast I'd worn while in traction. I also no longer had to cover my leg with a sheet to shield visitors' eyes from a suspended leg with a rod through it.

"All right, Mr. Alexander," said my physical therapist, "you're going to walk today with the walker. I want you to take ten steps, then turn around and come back to the bed." With great effort, I sat on the edge of the bed and grasped the handle of the walker. I took a deep breath and, with all my will, heaved myself to a standing position. After four steps, I was exhausted, and just made it back to the bed before collapsing. Those weeks in bed had devastated my strength, but it was a beginning.

Some time later I was told I must learn to use crutches. A pair that fit in the armpit was soon delivered, but my badly damaged left arm couldn't handle it. The therapist told he had first considered giving me the new Australian-designed crutches, with hand-holds protruding from the vertical rod and cuffs encircling the forearm. "But if you can't handle the traditional design," I'm sure you can't use the Australian crutch either,"

"Let me try," I said.

To my both my surprise and the therapist's, the newer design worked much better; It allowed me to rotate the left crutch toward my body and take the strain off my left arm. After days of concentrated practice at the hospital, then later at home, I became very adept at using the crutches. I was also introduced to handling a wheelchair. One basic command was "Never, ever sit down or get up without locking the wheels. Otherwise, the chair will roll out from under you and dump you on the floor."

Wheeling Back to Life

My year in a wheelchair was a learning experience, and for months after I came home I had the overpowering sensation that I was about to be catapulted out of the chair. I believe I was reliving the wreck. In one close call, I was almost pitched out of the chair the first time I went from the living room to the courtyard; the stone surface of the court had settled had settled a half-inch below the adjacent wood floor.

A wheelchair isolates you. People avoid you. They're afraid they'll get stuck with you. They don't want to get too close to a sick or disabled person. The first time I went to a meeting in my chair, I experienced all such avoidance first-hand. The meeting was at the Waverly Hotel, which my firm had designed, and had been called to discuss the possibility of mounting an annual show for corporate business planes at nearby Dobbins Air Force Base. When I was wheeled into the room, only two people greeted me in a normal fashion. One was my co-sponsor of the corporate air show. The other was former Georgia governor George Busbee, a pilot and a politician who was at home with the handicapped.

The rest ignored me or glanced at me warily. When we were seated around the lunch table, with all present at the same level, I was accepted. When the meeting broke up, and everyone stood up except me, only Gov. Busbee sought me out to say goodbye.

My experience was universal, and the alienation of wheelchair users was an issue that needed to be addressed. Max Cleland, Georgia's former senator, is confined to a chair, the result of the loss of both legs and part of one arm in Vietnam. In a crowd he reaches out with his good arm, pulls the nearest person to him, and starts an animated conversation. But Max is unique. Thankfully, in recent years wheelchairs that allow users to stand for a good while have been developed – and all I can say is, "It's about time!"

Recovery wasn't just lying around waiting for nature to take its course. Every day I was put through rehabilitation exercises that were demanding and often painful. Rehab covers two areas, the purely physical, and sometimes the occupational. In the first instance, the goal was to increase my range of motion and build up strength. My left arm was still useless – couldn't raise my forearm above my waist, and my shoulder was immobile. A year of painful exercises, which I continued at home with Jim Church, an excellent private therapist, finally enabled me to lift my left arm over my head.

Occupational therapy involved learning how to wash, shave, put on clothes, pull on socks, and tie shoes with my right hand. I also had to learn how to take all my weight on my right leg, and some of this had me sweating.

I also had to learn to use crutches to go up and down the stairs – a dangerous exercise, considering my weak left hip and leg. A long flight of stairs to descend was a terrifying sight.

While in the hospital I became obsessed with the dim memory of a poem: "Say Not the Struggle Naught Availeth," I thought that if I could find it I'd be able to make it through my own struggles. My good friend Don Comstock finally located a copy and brought me the poem, written by Arthur Clough and published posthumously in 1862. During World War II, Winston Churchill had used it to inspire his people and urge the United States to join Great Britain against the Nazis. The first stanza spoke directly to me:

> *Say not the struggle naught availeth,*
> *The labour and the wounds are vain.*
> *The enemy faints not, nor faileth,*
> *And as things have been they remain.*

My own enemies were my injuries and my mental anguish over the loss of my wife, and the poem comforted me. Later, when I was at home but still usiing a hospital bed, I was inspired by Winston Churchill's motto, quoted in the biography *The Last Lion:* "Never give in … never, never, never, never give in."

So, Dr. Haberman, Clough, Churchill, Helen, my family, and my friends helped me survive. Several years later I was surprised to hear from one of my doctor friends who visited but wasn't attending me. When he saw me a week after the wreck, he said that he didn't think I would survive – a shock. I had never thought that my life was in the balance.

My Fight Against Impaired Drivers

While I was still in the hospital I organized the Committee to Combat Drunk and Drugged Driving. Using the Metropolitan Atlanta Community Foundation under the able direction of Alicia Phillip as a resource, I was able to immediately set up my committee as a nonprofit enterprise. A lawyer friend helped write the bylaws, which set a limit of three years on the existence of the committee; I thought the influence born of the 1983 wreck wouldn't last beyond that time, and the last thing I wanted was a committee that was no longer useful and existed only to pay rent and salaries. A budget of $40,000 a year was set up, and it proved to be adequate. Funding was generously supported by a long list of friends and concerned Atlantans.

For my executive assistant I found a gem named Gina Cogswell. She had recently retired as an officer in the Atlanta Junior League, having reached the age limit of 40. Gina immediately wiped out any negative perceptions of the League. She was (and still is) a very smart, energetic, self-starting, superb diplomat. Long-time Speaker of the Georgia House of Representatives Tom Murphy destroyed most people who sought his support, but not Ms. Cogswell. She charmed this bona fide curmudgeon and turned him into a pussycat purring at her feet. In addition, many volunteers worked hard to carry out the efforts of the committee. None worked harder or more effectively than Evelyn Ullman, an old friend of Hermi's.

Denmark Groover, the outstanding leader of the Georgia House for many years, practiced law in Macon, Georgia. Gina was born in Macon, and her family knew Groover well. (Groover was also the politician one who later urged the legislature to adopt my design for a new state flag, the subject of Chapter 14.) A bill calling for stringent penalties for juveniles arrested for drinking while driving was pending in the legislature, and the committee supported it all-out. Gina set up a meeting for the two of us in Groover's Macon office. But when we said we wanted his support for stronger DUI laws governing juveniles, we hit a brick wall.

I'd heard that Groover was a fighter pilot in Pappy Boyington's famous Marine Black Sheep squadron, and to establish some rapport I told him I'd been a Marine dive bomber pilot in the Pacific. Our common Marine combat experience cracked his resolute brick wall. At the same time, he argued that teenagers' reflexes were much better than ours. He also maintained that they were better drivers.

"Mr. Groover," I said, "you're right about reflexes. But teenagers don't have experience or judgment, and they think they're immortal. Who would you rather have on your wing in combat – a 16-year- old, or a more mature pilot in his 20's?"

He didn't answer the question. Instead, he said, "I can't support that bill or vote for it, but I'll tell you how to get it passed." He then named the key legislators and told us how to approach them. We followed his directions, and the bill passed.

At the time of the wreck, Atlanta's Channel 11 TV station dispatched a news crew to record the collision. The cameraman arrived before Hermi was taken from our car and caught on film her removal and her transport to a waiting ambulance. Later, the station's owner, Gannett, produced a documentary showing the effect of alcohol-related deaths and injuries on the victims, their families, and the perpetrators. Our experience was included in the film.

When I had recovered sufficiently, Gina Cogswell and I showed the film to students at all the Atlanta private schools. As I made my introductory remarks the students were restless, inattentive, and whispering. When the film started, however, there was a dramatic change. The message became real, and the students were totally absorbed. After every showing, many would shake my hand and thank me. We were always invited back to address parents and faculty. The adults also became involved and expressed their gratitude.

When I asked the superintendent of Atlanta's public schools if I could bring the message to his students, he refused. He said, "Our schedules are already too crowded, and there's no time for that Gannet video. Academic studies come first."

I later remembered that at some time in the past the superintendent himself had been arrested for driving under the influence. I'm certain he turned me down because he thought my presentation would remind students, parents, and faculty of his own unlawful behavior. It was tragic decision on his part, since some young lives might have been saved.

The film has been shown high school students countrywide and also to persons arrested for driving under the influence. A service group in Atlanta, Families First, used the film to instruct interns from Smith and Spelman colleges. Funding came from the Hermione Weil Alexander Foundation, which was established at Smith College's School of Social Work. After the Committee to Combat Drunk and Drugged Driving was disbanded, I endowed the foundation with the committee's remaining funds with the unanimous approval of the donors.

One of my strongest advocates was State Senator Paul Coverdell, later a United States senator. As a Republican in the Democrat-dominated senate, his support sometimes backfired. In spite of his party, he was a great help. At my request he arranged a meeting for me with Gov. Joe Frank Harris. The governor and his wife were strong opponents of excessive drinking, particularly drinking and driving. When I walked into his outer office, sitting on a bench were Coverdell and Dante Stephenson, owner of Dante's Down the Hatch restaurant and bar, where, I was told, the boys had been served drinks.

Here was Dante, whom I thought had gotten the boys drunk, standing with me in urging the governor to support raising the drinking age, support I thought ironic at best. Recently Dante told my son Doug he was very disturbed that I thought the boy who hit us had gotten drunk at his restaurant, saying both he and his bartender checked the boys' IDs; when he saw they were underage, he refused to serve them. According to Dante, it was a now defunct bar that served the boys a potent drink called Long Island Iced Tea. I later wrote to Dante, welcoming his explanation.

The National Minimum Drinking Age Act of 1984 passed in July of that year, and my committee had been one of many organizations that helped to push it through Congress. A date was set for President Reagan to sign it into law. Coverdell, who was now based in Washington as the Peace Corps, asked if I would like to attend the signing in the White House Rose Garden. Although I was still on crutches, I went. I sat directly in front of the president's lectern in the front row. It seemed to me that the bill the president signed, which required the states to adopt the raised drinking age or lose federal highway funds, was strongly opposed to his philosophy regarding states' rights. I was convinced that Nancy Reagan used her influence on her husband to gain his support.

When I returned to Atlanta I wrote to the first lady and thanked her for the role I was sure she had played. In my letter I told her she and Hermi had been classmates at Smith College, and she handwrote me a warm and thoughtful reply. It ended with, "I'm sure the Lord has a plan for all our lives, but when a tragic, meaningless death occurs as it did to Hermi, it's hard to understand." This was no boilerplate statement. From then on, I changed my feelings toward Nancy Reagan. In the last days of her husband's terminal illness, I wrote to her and praised her devotion to him. It must have been one message among thousands, and this time I didn't receive a reply.

Paul Coverdell and the senior George Bush were hunting and fishing buddies. At the end of the Rose Garden ceremony, Paul said to me, "Come on. Let's go see the vice president." A young woman escorted us to Bush's office in the White House. "The last time I was here," I said, "that carpet was covered with peanut shells." She laughed and said, "Now it's jelly beans."

Politics aside, I found common ground with Vice President Bush. We are both Yale graduates. We were naval aviators in World War II. We both love baseball. And politics never came up. As for Paul Coverdell, his death when he was still a young senator was a loss to the country, to our state, and to me.

The Fate of the Perpetrators

The boy who killed Hermi and injured me pleaded guilty on all counts. Because he was a juvenile, the disposition of his case was never made public. I heard he was sentenced to incarceration in a juvenile institution for alcoholics. He soon went to Dallas to live with his mother, who had divorced his father.

Some time later, on an early Sunday morning, he was stopped on Atlanta's West Pace's Ferry Road in front of the Governor's Mansion. He was charged with eleven traffic violations, including driving with a fraudulent Texas license, and, once again, his blood alcohol was recorded at 0.27 percent, just as when he hit Hermi and me.

I went with my family to his trial. Before the hearing I introduced myself to the judge and told him my history with the boy, now 18. The judge sentenced him to a year in prison. On the way out of the courtroom I passed his family, who were seated in the rear row. They stared at me with virulent malice, as if I had been the killer, as if I were responsible for his sentence.

The boy's father had been charged with a series of violations in connection with the wreck. He plea-bargained, and the charges were reduced to one: allowing his son to operate his car while knowing his license was invalid. I was asked to attend his sentencing by Judge Johnson of the Fulton County Superior Court. Before entering the court, I asked my attorney and the prosecutor about my response if the judge asked me what the sentence should be. "Oh, he won't do that, that's his prerogative," he said. "But If he does," I asked, "what should I say?" He answered, "Ask him to throw the book at the father."

We went into the courtroom. The judge knew Hermi from her service on the Fulton County Jury Commission, and he opened the proceeding with what was, in effect, a eulogy. He said, "Hermi Alexander will never again have the joy of being with her family, of hugging her grandchildren, or sailing with her husband and two daughters. Her death is a great loss to her family, her friends, and her community."

I was upset, thinking the judge's evident feelings could lead the father's attorney to demand a re-sentencing. I whispered this concern to my lawyer, and he assured me that since the defendant had acknowledged guilt the judge could say anything he wanted during the sentencing.

Soon after the court convened the judge called for the defendant, his lawyer, my lawyer, and me to come forward and stand in front of the bench. He then asked me to relate in detail the events on the night Hermi was killed. With difficulty, I gained control of my emotions and reviewed the violent and tragic night, which ended with my daughter telling me the next morning, "Dad, Mom died last night."

The crowded courtroom was deadly quiet as I spoke. The judge thanked me. Then, to the surprise of my attorney and the prosecutor, he asked me, "What do you think should be this man's sentence?" I was standing next to the defendant, a short middle-aged man who looked somewhat disheveled and at a complete loss.

I began, "I have compassion for the boy who hit us. He was obviously raised in a dysfunctional alcoholic environment. He never learned the requirements of leading a responsible life. I have compassion for parents who do all they can to raise their children as responsible citizens but fail. In our society today, raising responsible children can be extremely difficult."

I then turned and looked directly at the father. "I have no compassion for this man. None! He aided and reinforced his son's lawless conduct. He might as well have stood in the middle of Mt. Paran Road and fired a machine gun at us. Judge, I beg you to punish him to the full extent of the law."

The judge then asked my attorney if he had anything to add. "No," he said. "Mr. Alexander said it all.

While waiting for the sentence, I returned to my seat on the front bench. A tall man in his fifties approached me and introduced himself as a physician. "Mr. Alexander," he said, "I want to urge you to forgive the father. It will release you as well as make his life bearable. I was once a skillful surgeon. One fall I was out bird hunting with a friend. He shot wildly at a dove and the pellets hit my right hand, permanently injuring it. I could no longer practice my profession. For months I was bitter and full of anger toward my friend. But finally I realized that I was achieving nothing by my anger. So I went to him and told him that I forgave him. It released both of us, and we remain close friends. Please do as I did."

"Doctor," I said, "the man who shot you was your friend. You knew it was a terrible accident. He was a responsible person and had a fatal lapse in coordination. This father and his son are not my friends. Neither of them expressed the least remorse. It was a wreck brought about by lawless behavior. I cannot forgive the father."

I never have forgiven the father, though my feelings toward the boy softened. One day some seventeen years after the wreck, a friend called me and said, "Did you see in the paper where the DUI who hit you died? He was 28." I do not know the cause of his death.

The judge sentenced the father to one year in the Fulton County Jail. He called me into his chambers and explained that he wished he could have given him a tougher sentence, but the law limited him. I thanked him. To relieve the crowding in the jail, the father was released after only two months. I'm sure that even a night in jail was traumatic to this respected (at least formerly) upper middle class stockbroker.

It has been almost 30 years since that terrible October night on Mt. Paran Road. Time has dulled the anguish, but few days go by that I don't relive that wreck in total recall. I take some satisfaction from seeing how attitudes toward drunks and drunken driving have changed. No longer is there any humor associated with drunkenness and driving drunk; it is now seen as the crime it is. And if it results in fatalities, the driver draws a long sentence.

I hope and believe the Committee to Combat Drunken and Drugged Driving was useful in initiating these changes in Georgia. The Atlanta chapter of Mothers Against Drunk Driving has now become active. It took the place of my committee and continues the fight for tougher laws and public awareness.

The violent death of my wife of 40 years remains a terrible memory. Our marriage had its rough times, as do most successful unions, but our love always prevailed. She was more than a partner; she was a living part of me. Now I am married to another fine woman, Helen Eisemann. I am a most fortunate man, having shared 70 years of my life with two loving partners.

Chapter 13

Helen and Our Blended Family

Helen, thy beauty is to me
As those Nicean Barques of Yore

Edgar Allen Poe, To Helen

Helen Eisemann Harris Mantler took several routes to my heart. As I wrote in the previous chapter, one of the smoothest was through my stomach. When I lay in a Piedmont Hospital room after the October 1983 auto wreck and the loss of Hermi, Helen brought in a delectable salad composed of heart of palm and lump crabmeat, the first meal I enjoyed while convalescing.

After returning home from my two-month recovery at Piedmont, I was invited to a lavish dinner. Although confined to a wheelchair, I went in a tux and wore my tennis shoes (dyed black) over my still-hurting feet. Women, perhaps motivated by their mothering instincts, seemed attracted to my disability and gathered around me. Men seemed threatened by the wheelchair, looked at me with hurried glances, arid kept their distance. One exception was Joe Hutchison, who ran the Atlanta office of Dallas-based general contractors Henry C. Beck and had built two major office buildings I had designed.

We had developed a love/hate relationship as I fought to have our plans' carried out as drawn, but that night at the party, the "hate" part was forgotten. Joe pushed his way to me through the crowd of martini drinkers, smiled and bent down to kiss me on the forehead, and said, "Lookin' good!"

After 40-plus years of marriage, I would find dating uncomfortable. Several divorced or widowed ladies surely saw me as the means of recapturing their happy wedded lives, so I struggled with a dilemma. I wanted their company, but I also didn't want to mislead them; my intentions toward all except Helen were platonic. When I told one of ladies that I planned to marry Helen, she screamed as I left her home, "I hate Helen Mantler!"

My two years as a single man searching for a new life were unsettling and bewildering. But all the while, Helen was my constant "significant other." She had a difficulty accepting my multiple dating, even with my assurance the friendships with other women were platonic. At the time I thought she was being unreasonable, but I came to understand.

I Propose, She Accepts

In 1985 I was 67 and Helen was 63. When we visited my cousin Henry on his ranch outside Eugene, Oregon, he put it to me. "Helen is precious," said this University of Oregon professor of philosophy. "What are you waiting for?" Well, I asked myself, why *was* I waiting?

Back in Atlanta I cast the die, though not in an appropriate setting for a proposal. We were on our way out of the house through Helen's kitchen, hard by the cat's litter box, when I stepped in front of her and asked, "Helen, will you marry me?" She threw her arms around me and softly murmured yes.

The timing of my proposal wasn't accidental. We were on the way to the Round House for lunch, and waiting for us were my three children, Terri, Judy, and Doug, along with Terri's husband Herb and my sister-in-law (Hermi's sister) Terry Lansburgh. Helen and I joined them at the table. Without any prelude I said, "Helen and I are engaged." My children and Herb smiled in delight and rushed to hug and kiss both of us. Terry sat quietly with tears in her eyes, still grieving for her sister Hermi and reluctant to welcome Helen.

Both Helen and I were very aware that marrying in our sixties presented a time limit on living happily ever after; "ever after" wasn't forever. Accepting this reality, we set the date for our wedding just a few months away.

Since our experiences in our previous marriages were very different, we decided to see how that might affect our lives together. So we sought help from a married couple with a joint psychiatric practice, thinking the wife would relate to Helen and the husband to me. But we couldn't have been more mistaken: We left our sessions angry and upset with each other. When I told the psychiatrist who had served me so well in the hospital about our problems with the couple, he said. "If your engagement has withstood those two egocentric analyzers, you and Helen have a very strong attachment."

I had hoped to see beyond our "significant other" relationship to learn how we would relate as a married couple, but Freud himself couldn't have revealed the future to me. The words "I now pronounce you man and wife" would change our relationship. My love and admiration for Helen never wavered, but the stresses of everyday life would have to be absorbed. "Please take out the garbage" is short on romantic overtones.

Failed counseling aside, Helen and I were consumed with planning for the wedding. The choice of a memorable place for this event became a major project I imagined a large room covered with a high, vaulted ceiling with a floor-to-ceiling window at one end. Through the large panes a placid lake stretched below tree-covered hills. We found a location that fulfilled this fantasy: the Greystone Inn, on the shore of Lake Toxaway near Cashiers, North Carolina. The lake had been built by wealthy sojourners from New York, including the Vanderbilts, as a site for the homes of their armies of servants. The lake had been drained for years, but developers saw the potential for large lakeside houses and refilled it.

The history of the inn began when the Greystones, a wealthy, well-traveled couple, visited the area. They had been searching the world over the ideal site for their mansion. When Mrs. Greystone saw Lake Toxaway, her eyes blazed bright and she shouted, "This is it! This is it, by this beautiful lake!" Echoing Mrs. Greystone, when Helen and I saw this scenic, rustic setting we looked at each other, smiled, and in unison said, "This is it!"

The date for the wedding was set, invitations were mailed, and bus transportation from Atlanta was arranged. We asked an old friend, Luther Alverson, a long-time member of the Georgia General Assembly and now a county judge, if he would marry us. He was delighted, but there was a problem; He wasn't licensed to perform the ceremony in North Carolina. The obvious solution, marrying in Atlanta, meant that later in the day we'd we have to repeat the ceremony in North Carolina. It also required absolute secrecy.

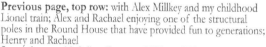

Previous page, top row: with Alex Millkey and my childhood Lionel train; Alex and Rachael enjoying one of the structural poles in the Round House that have provided fun to generations; Henry and Rachael

Second row: with Julian, Doug and Wilson; Wilson, Jed and Julian; a visit with RomanWeil Jr. and his grandson Conrad Laesch of Seattle, Washington

Third row: Rachael, looking so much like Hermi; Doug and me at the dedication of Hermi's Bridge; Wilson and Julian, football players at Pace Academy; Terri with her first grandchild -- and my first great-grandchild -- Hannah Rose Millkey

Fourth row: with baby Jed in 1987; Wilson, Doug, Anne and Julian

This page, top row: Terri and Phil; Alex, Sara, Hannah and Asher Quinn Millkey; with Judy, Katherine Voegeli and Ed

Second row and beyond: Helen and Jed; Judy, Jed and Ed; Four Generations - me, Terri, Alex and Hannah; with Helen, Alex and Sara at their wedding in Hood River, Oregon in 2001; with Rachael, discussing design; with Helen and Rachael at the re-dedication of Hermi's Bridge, 2010; with my nephews, Charlotte's sons, Roman and Ken, and Roman's son Sandy Weil

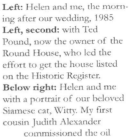

Left: Helen and me, the morning after our wedding, 1985
Left, second: with Ted Pound, now the owner of the Round House, who led the effort to get the house listed on the Historic Register.
Below right: Helen and me with a portrait of our beloved Siamese cat, Witty. My first cousin Judith Alexander commissioned the oil painting for us.
Left, third: With my beloved Helen
Middle: Helen rehearsing a Broadway show
Below Right: Helen and me at my 90th birthday party, 2005
Bottom right: At the re-dedication of Hermi's Bridge, 2010

Left: Helen as "Sparkles", the bank teller in a Georgia Lottery TV ad that made her rather famous about town.

242

Helen's and my blended families at my 90th birthday party, 2008: Bottom - Julian and Wilson Alexander Middle - Carol Martin, Jill Brown, Helen, Me, Judy, Ed Augustine, Ruth Alexander, Anne O'Shields Alexander, Richard Lansburgh, Deborah Adler Top - Alan Joel, Sophie Joel, Art Harris, Josh Harris, George Brown, Terri, Rachael Millkey, Phil Alexander-Cox, Barbara and Rick Adler, Doug

Photo by Stephen H. Moore

Below, left column: Alex Harris with son Will, daughter Eliza and wife Margaret Sartor; Jill Harris Brown with daughter Allie and husband George Brown; Sophie Mantler Joel with husband Alan Joel and daughters Holly and Helen

Below, right column: Cathy Southwick and David Brown on their wedding day; Art Harris with sons Adam Harris and Josh Harris and wife Carol Martin; Jill and George Brown (front seat) with family (from back) - Charlotte, Mary Jane and Mason Walker with Rob and Amy Brown Walker, David Brown and Cathy Southwick Brown, Elizabeth Brown, Allie Brown

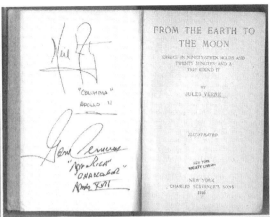

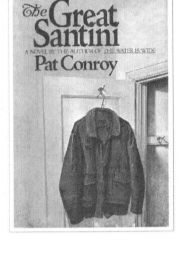

Top Left: With astronaut and first man on the moon, Neil Armstrong, aboard the SS Canberra, 1973, to observe a total solar eclipse off the coast of Africa. I brought along a very old copy of Jules Vernes' *Journey to the Moon*, which he graciously signed while telling my daughter that this was his first solar eclipse ... from Earth. Fellow astronaut Eugene Cernan, the last man on the moon, signed below Armstrong.

Middle Row: Two autographs from Pat Conroy. In the *Great Santini* one he writes that I was his inspiration for the character Col. Virgil Hedgepeth.

Left: Margaret Mitchell inscribed a first edition copy of Gone With the Wind to my Grandmother, who was a neighbor and a friend.

We chose a small, dark-paneled library in the Waverly Hotel for the wedding. Helen and I, along with the wedding photographer Jay Leviton and his wife, gathered in the room at ten o'clock on the morning on December 1, 1985. We were in our places, ready to go – but no Judge Alverson. Thirty minutes late he staggered into the room, red-faced, short of breath, dripping sweat, and highly agitated. Although I'd shown him the room the night before, he was unable to find it. As the architect for the Waverly, I took the blame for his tardiness and calmed him down. "Luther," I said, "I'm the one who's supposed to be nervous. Come on, man, relax." He took a deep breath, wiped his wet forehead, and recited a short ritual. Helen and I were married.

Two buses filled with our families and friends were waiting at the hotel entrance for what was supposed to be a 3-hour trip to the Greystone Inn. We boarded the lead bus, our secret ceremony known only to the judge, the two witnesses, and Helen and me.

Toward the end of the trip, the road to the Greystone spiraled out of a long valley up a steep mountainside as a heavy rain began to fall. The bus drivers wisely chose a longer but safer road but got lost, as were our carefully laid plans to arrive well before twilight. By the time the drivers found their way to the Inn it was almost dark. Then, after several failed attempts to roar up the steep hill to the entrance, they gave up. All the passengers stepped out onto the wet road and slogged up the hill to the Inn. All, that is, except Helen and me. My best man and his wife, Edgar and Louise Cullman, had flown from New York in their private plane. As Helen and I stepped off the bus the two of them drove up in a rental car. "Get in here," he called. Helen's son Alex and his wife Margaret escorted us under an umbrella from the car to the warm, dry and welcoming Greystone Inn.

It was getting dark, and the prized view from the room where the wedding was to be held would be lost if we didn't act fast. I wanted to have the ceremony immediately instead of waiting for Helen to change into her wedding attire.

"No! Absolutely not!" said her daughter Sophie. "Mother, you cannot be married in that rumpled street dress, you have to change." Sophie had spoken. So, as darkness descended and the view of the lake and hills disappeared, we waited. Long after nightfall I stood with Edgar, Judge Alverson, and Bill Rothschild waiting for Helen, clinging to her brother Alex Eisemann's arm, to descend the steep stairs from the balcony. (Rabbi Bill Rothschild is the son of the late Rabbi Jacob Rothschild, revered leader of Atlanta's Temple congregation. Bill is also a lawyer – a graduate of Harvard Law School.)

Finally a radiant Helen appeared on the balcony in a bright turquoise silk, with a camelhair stole wrapped around her shoulders, And her carefully coiffed hair had survived the bus ride. The instrumental quartet I'd retained filled the room with the wedding march as Helen, her brother, and her large family approached us. Preceding them was my 8-year-old granddaughter Rachael Millkey, daintily flinging one rose petal at a time onto their path. The ceremony remarrying us went smoothly. Rothschild and Alverson merged the religious and secular in a soulful and inspiring ceremony. Only many years later did we confess our trickery to our friends.

Helen and I had taken "September Song", from the musical *Knickerbocker Holiday* as our own. Frances, the wife of my Yale friend Dan Hodgson, had a concert-quality voice, and I urged her to sing "our song" accompanied by the quartet. She said, "I'm sorry, I can't do it. We haven't rehearsed," The quartet did play the music, but I missed the haunting line "and these few precious days I'll spend with you."

'The wedding dinner was held in two adjacent rooms. Some of our friends standing in the opening between the rooms, offering toasts, spoke in the warmest, lyrical terms of how wonderful it was that Helen and I had joined our lives together. At the end, the many-tiered wedding cake was rolled in. Wielding my Marine ceremonial sword our hands interlocked, Helen and I cut the first slice.

It had been an enchanting evening even without the view and the poignant lyrics of our favorite song. My own feelings were an ever changing, mix of joy, sorrow and disbelief. It seemed impossible that I, now 67-years-old, was starting a new phase of my life with Helen at my side. How could I be so blessed as to have two such beautiful, talented, extraordinary women accept me as their husband? I felt detached, as though I was an observer watching from the distance. Over the 27 years since, I've never ceased to be gratified and honored that our love has flourished.

My daughter Terri offered Helen and me her second home – a cottage perched on a hill near Cashiers – for our wedding night. Terri's husband Herb had left crumpled newspaper and kindling in the fireplace so we could take the chill off the December night. Helen, not realizing the damper was shut, struck a match and lit the newspaper, which ignited the kindling and filled the room with acrid smoke. It took a long time after the damper and windows were opened for the smoke to clear not the most auspicious start to a marriage that would turn out be wonderful.

I have searched for a way to describe Helen's myriad assets. Now I believe I've found it. In every issue of the classified personal section of the Harvard alumni magazine are glowing self-composed descriptions of women seeking attractive, financially well-established men with or without a Harvard degree. Here's an example from a recent issue:

"Brains plus compelling good looks and a cute dimpled smile ... Finds balance between career and personal life æ radiates warmth and poise.

It occurred to me that an ad similar to these is an apt way of describing Helen. She has one drawback – she is entirely modest. Never would she write such an account of herself. So I'll take on the task of writing the sentences they could include:

"I have many interests: skiing, golfing, swimming, canoeing, sailing, and traveling to faraway places, community service volunteering, and politics."

"Beautiful, radiant, charming, fun-loving. I have also kept my figure. At 105 pounds I can still wear the dresses from my first trousseau."

"I have had a life-long career in acting, appearing on Broadway and in films. I am an artist, working in watercolors, oil, and sculpture and am a museum-quality photographer. I knit and I make pottery."

"I love all animals, and they love me – particularly my Siamese cat Witty, who sleeps on my chest with his paws around my neck."

"Entertaining is my joy. I'm never happier than when there are a dozen people sitting at my dining table with energetic, free-flowing discourse."

"My four adult children are all successful, happily married, and have blessed me with eight remarkable grandchildren.

"There is one obstacle to my search for a handsome, charming, interesting man – I am already married to one." (My own modesty is overwhelming.)

These pretend ads don't do Helen justice, but they're a start.

Helen had been single for sixteen years when we married. Her daughters Jill and Sophie had some adjusting to do as this interloper wedged his way into the family. A long discussion with Jill convinced her I would in no way interfere with her relationship with her mother. Soon we became close. I call her my daughter, never "step-." I admire and love her. She is a shining example of all a daughter, a wife and a mother and a conscientious citizen should be.

Sophie had more to handle. She and her mother lived together for years almost as sisters. She was adjusting to her own recent marriage and leaving her mother's home. I guess I looked like a 600-pound gorilla that had sat himself down between her and her mother. Whatever Sophie did feel 27 years ago (we never discussed her feelings), we now have a close and easy relationship. I enjoy her company and look forward to our times together.

Helen's brother, Alex Eisemann and I quickly abandoned the off-putting concept of "in-law." He was like a brother. His early death was almost as devastating a blow to me as it was to Helen. I miss him.

Our Trip to Europe

When I was free of the wheelchair and used only a cane for support, we traveled to Scandinavia and Italy. The University of Minnesota was sponsoring a group visit to Norway, Sweden, and Finland to research those progressive countries' strict enforcement of their drunk driving laws, Afterwards, Helen and I went on to Venice by ourselves as wide-eyed tourists. As luck would have it, my newly married daughter Judy and her husband Ed were honeymooning in Venice at the time and we spent some fun and memorable days and evenings together.

When the great comic writer James Thurber saw the canals of Venice, he cabled his friends gathered at the Algonquin Hotel in New York "Streets full of water. Advise." My reaction, though profound, was far less witty. I haven't visited all the greatest cities on the planet, but of those I have seen – among them San Francisco, New York, Montreal, Florence, Rome, Paris, London, Copenhagen, Barcelona, and Kyoto – none can match Venice for sheer allure. Helen and I were as awash in it romance as its streets were in the waters of the Adriatic.

By chance, a conference of international city planners was in progress when we arrived. Atlanta was well represented – on paper, at least. One of the Atlanta delegates never attended a meeting; the others seldom came, and when they did they often walked out in the middle of the proceedings. They reasoned they could attend meetings in Atlanta any time at all, but they had to make the most of their stay in Venice.

The unexpected star of the conference was James Rouse, who had revitalized the core of Boston with the redevelopment of the Faneuil Hall Marketplace area. He developed the new town of Columbia, Maryland, on the open fields halfway between Washington and Baltimore. No developer was as highly esteemed as Rouse – a practical dreamer whose motivation went beyond profit to concern for the community. When the organizers of the meeting saw him, they pounced and drafted him as a major participant. All present agreed he made the most valuable, insightful contributions.

On the last day, the absent Atlanta delegate showed up to seize a photo op – a picture of his arms around Rouse and me, proof to his boss back in Atlanta that he went to the meetings. Helen and I, however, were under no obligation to attend. After a few sessions we slipped away to really experience Venice. We spent our days and evenings gliding in the sleek black gondolas through the narrow canals, shopping in the many small shops along the narrow walks, nosing into museums, and strolling around magnificent St. Marks Square, dominated by the tall bell tower. One day we had a memorable lunch with the Rouses, sitting at a restaurant on the perimeter of St. Marks – and happily, Judy and Ed were able to join us.

Every sunset found us on the second floor balcony of the hotel overlooking the Grand Canal. Our gazes alternated between the enchanting scene before us and the enchanting presence of each other. Some writer said, 'See Venice and die." I say, "See Venice and live."

The Alexander Side of the Family

When Helen and I married, my contribution to our new blended family was three adult children and two grandchildren. Now, three more grandchildren and two great-grandchildren from my side of the family have joined the fold.

My eldest child Terri has a master's in special education and teaches preschoolers at St. Anne's Day School in Buckhead. Her happy marriage to Herb Millkey ended with his untimely death in 1988, leaving Terri with two children – Alexander (Alex) and Rachael, then ages 14 and 9. (Tragically, Terri and Herb's second child, Lauren, was born with a lung condition and died after two days.) Terri's inspiring resiliency in the face of adversity carried her through, and she is rightly proud of her children – as am I. Alex earned a PsyD in Clinical Psychology at Pacific University in Oregon and now maintains a private practice in Portland. He also works with the Oregon State Hospital, the state's primary psychiatric facility, and is often called as an expert witness in court cases. He and his wife Sara Morton, a science teacher at the Portland Jewish Academy, presented me with those aforementioned (and adorable) great-grandchildren – Hannah (born 2007) and Asher (born 2011).

Terri's daughter Rachael graduated with a degree in sculpture from the University of Oregon in Eugene. She spent a lot of time there with my cousin Henry, a philosophy professor at the university, and his wife Pat, and grew very close to both, lovingly helping to care for each of them in their final days. In the spring of 2012 Rachael earned a master's degree in interior design from the Pratt Institute in New York, still her place of residence. In a happy coincidence, her stepsister (and fellow artist) is also named Rachel. A ceramist in San Francisco, "Rachel II" is the daughter of Phillip Alexander-Cox, whom Terri married in 1997. Phil teaches art at the E. Rivers Elementary School in Buckhead. As a part-time artist since childhood, I feel lucky to have so many family members connected to the arts, including my daughter Judy.

Judy received her BA in Journalism (with an emphasis on photojournalism) at Boston University and works as a graphic designer, writer, editor, and photographer. In addition, she has succeeded Helen as the president of The Judith Alexander Foundation, the arts nonprofit I discuss in Chapter 15. After the wreck in 1983, Judy moved back to Atlanta, having lived in the San Francisco Bay Area for 11 years, to "circle the wagons", as she puts it, and help me get back on my feet. In 1985 she married Ed Augustine, an attorney and a former assistant to Mayor Andrew Young. Their son Jed was born in 1987 and set out on an adventurous path. After graduating from the Paideia School in Atlanta, he studied at the University of Chicago and earned a degree in Comparative Human Development in 2010. He currently serves as a Peace Corps volunteer in Rwanda, teaching English to villagers in his town of Kinazi and to members of the Rwandan judiciary. Judy and Ed recently visited Jed, and the photos they took made me wish I could make the long trip to see my grandson in such a distant (and beautiful) part of the world and watch him interact with his friends and neighbors in the local language of Kinyarwanda.

My son Douglas, known as Doug and blessed with the middle name of Cecil, was born ten years after Judy, in 1959. He too graduated from Boston University, but with a BA in political science. As I proudly noted in Chapter 19, Doug served two terms on the Atlanta City Council. A long-time transportation policy specialist, he is currently a manager at the Georgia Department of Transportation. His wife, Anne O'Shields Alexander, was born in Japan where her father, a Navy dentist, was stationed. Anne grew up in Atlanta and is a talented writer and editor and teaches English. Doug and Anne have two fine sons: Wilson, who at age 16 is a sports lover and a budding sports journalist as well as a fine athlete, and 14-year-old Julian – a budding actor (and singer), most recently appearing as Prince Eric in *The Little Mermaid* at his school, a soccer player, and just as big a fan of trains as his father was (and is.) Both boys attend Pace Academy and seem to be thriving in every way.

The Alexander side of the family also has no shortage of nieces and nephews, many of them "grand," of course. Those from the family of my sister Charlotte and her husband Roman Weil are briefly profiled in Chapter 6, "Two Careers – Politics and Community."

Hermi's sister Therese (Terry) had two children, Randolph (Randy) Wolff, a talented photographer, and a daughter, the lovely and lively Deborah Wolff. In 1970, Deborah married Arthur A. "Buddy" Adler, a Washington, D.C. investment adviser and founder of Asset Management Inc. Although they divorced, Deborah and Buddy remained good friends until his untimely death in an auto accident in 2004. Deborah's two sons live in Washington: Arthur Alan Adler III, a financial advisor and keen polo player; and Andrew Richard (Andy) Adler, who moved from investment advising to real estate and travels the world in pursuit of deep sea fishing. Both are the fathers of toddlers – Alan of Drew, Andy of Ray. Andy and his wife Nancy Margaret recently welcomed baby Mary Arthur Adler to the fold.

The Eisemann-Harris-Mantler Side

The Southern Crescent, the passenger train from New York, sped and rocked toward Georgia. On board was Josephine Lowenstein Eisemann, her face pressed to the cool window. It was homecoming for her; she was born in Atlanta on then-upscale Washington Avenue, south of downtown.

Josephine's ties to the city had been stretched, then snapped, when she visited New York City as a winsome young Southern Belle. At a Park Avenue party she met a handsome New Yorker, Alexander Eisemann. Eisemann took one look at this lovely Georgia Peach and was forever smitten. A day or so later, Josephine stood at the rail of an ocean-going leviathan bound for Europe when her attention was suddenly caught by a beaming Alex Eisemann, leaping up the gangplank waving his ticket. He was joining his newfound dream girl on her Grand Tour, under the eye of her all-too-dedicated chaperone.

As strict as the chaperone was, she apparently was unable to divert the course of true love. The storybook meeting of Josephine and Alex culminated in a long marriage that lasted until death did them part. As in all long unions, it was not always "happily ever after" but it came close.

Many years later, Josephine's grown daughter Helen, an actress, was with her mother on her first trip South. Helen had taken leave from her Broadway career and was under contract to co-star in a Hollywood film with Victor Mature. Her destiny rode with her and would become evident when she reached Atlanta.

Josephine looked out at the hills flashing by and saw they were tinted with a red glow. As the train entered Georgia she recovered her long-diluted accent and her love of the South. "Come here quick darlin'," she drawled to Helen. "Look out there. Am I really seein' those gorgeous ole red clay Georgia Hills?" Josephine Lowenstein Eisemann was home.

Marcelle Lowenstein, Helen's aunt, was their Atlanta hostess. An accomplished businesswoman, she served as president of the Norris Candy Company, a successful Atlanta enterprise of long standing. Years before the barrier blocking women from climbing the corporate ladder became known as the glass ceiling she smashed through it. As her 25- year-old niece's hostess, Marcelle assumed the role of introducing Helen to eligible gentleman callers, hoping she'd find a suitable mate before the 25-year-old faded into spinsterhood (such a life for Helen was hardly likely, considering her parade of suitors in New York and beyond.)

Arthur Harris, Jr. was the dynamic president of the Atlanta Paper Company, a flourishing family enterprise. He had a huge collection of Napoleon memorabilia and thought he was the Little Corporal reincarnated. He also topped matchmaker Marcelle Lowenstein's list of desirable suitors. His first sight of the beautiful, poised Helen sent him spinning. After a brief exchange of greetings Harris said to her, "I'm going to marry you. Now. Right now!" Helen had met aggressive men before, but they were house cats next to the saber tooth tiger that was Harris. When her breath came back she gasped, "Just a minute! Marriage is a serious decision."

But the irresistibility of Arthur Harris won out. He and Helen wed just two weeks later at the Breakers in Palm Beach; he in tails, she in white. Both approving families, the Eisemann's and the Harris's were present.

Their union was a classic example of the time-honored maxim "marry in haste, repent at leisure" – Helen and Arthur were together only ten rocky years. Yet their problems didn't prevent the arrivals of three gifted children. The first was Arthur Harris III. Like his father, Art would attend Phillips Academy Andover, a top New England prep school. And though he could have followed in his father's footsteps and matriculated at Yale, he chose Duke University. After graduating, Art built a multifaceted career in journalism, television, and writing. After working as an investigative reporter for the *Washington Post* he became a national investigative correspondent with the Atlanta-based Cable News Network (CNN.)

When President George W. Bush, in Kipling's words "tried to hustle the East" by invading Iraq, Art was embedded in my tough old Marine Corps. After leaving CNN, he embarked on a successful career as a freelance writer.

With his first wife, Mynel Yates, Art had two sons – Josh and Adam. Mynel served for years as a physician's assistant in the Atlanta Veterans Hospital with the aging veterans of World War II. Her experience with the ills, aches, and pains of these old men has made her a great source of information to me as I've aged. And she continues to watch tenderly over Helen, who considers her a daughter.

Art's second wife, Carol Martin, is an expert consultant in plastic surgery, a published author and a fierce animal lover. A former model, she is also strikingly beautiful, has a figure to match, and looks far younger than her years. In the spring of 2003, her husband Art was reporting in Iraq and Helen took a trip with daughter Jill and granddaughter Holly to New York. Finding ourselves spouseless, Carol and I decided to have a "date." At our dinner at Chops, an upscale Buckhead restaurant, the staff assumed the gorgeous Carol could only be my young trophy wife. She and I agreed it would be fun to let them "think what they choose to think." and we quietly but gleefully did. Since then we've had no more "dates." Art and Helen returned unscathed from their journeys and reclaimed their rightful places as spouses in residence.

Alex Harris followed his big brother Art to Andover and then enrolled at Yale. Years later it would be Duke that fulfilled his quest for an academic position. He heads the university's Department of Documentary Studies. He is also an outstanding photographer, and not only teaches courses in photography but also founded the photography/literary magazine *Double Take*. His book *The Idea of Cuba* is an insightful look at today's Cuba and its restless people. He has published many other books, some with anthropologist Robert Coles and, most recently, with Edward O. Wilson. Alex's wife, Margaret Sartor, also teaches photography at Duke and is a published author as well. Her book *Miss American Pie* is based on the diary she kept as a teenager in Montgomery, Alabama. With their own teenagers, Will and Eliza, Margaret and Alex spend their summers in an adobe house north of Santa Fe.

Helen's daughter Jill arrived next. For seven years she lived in Amsterdam, where she had a career as a graphic designer. When Jill returned home, the Netherlands national airline KLM hired her for their Atlanta office. She now teaches art at the Fernbank Elementary School. Her husband George Brown was born in China, the son of Methodist missionaries. As a director of the Friendship Force, George travels the world. Their son David recently graduated from Johns Hopkins School of Advanced International Studies (SAIS) and is now with a think tank in Washington, D.C., where he lives with his wife Cathy Southwick, an art historian. Jill and George's second child, Alexandra (Allie) is a scholar in her own right, currently studying Anthropology and Ecology at The University of Georgia, and a fine athlete to boot.

Helen's second marriage was to Marshall "Bud" Mantler, who had been a member of Gen. George S. Patton's staff as Patton's Third Army swept across Europe to victory in World War II. Bud went into the garment business and became executive director of the National Association of Women's and Children's Apparel Salesmen; he also had a gift for growing orchids. In a delightful coincidence, Helen and Bud lived in a spacious house designed by Herb Millkey, whose son Herb Jr., would one day marry my daughter Terri whose bridesmaids carried bouquets of Bud's orchids.

The Mantlers were blessed with a daughter – Sophie, who grew into an adult so like Helen she could be her clone. As an entrepreneur, Sophie opened her own landscaping business; as a designer, she won prizes for two flower-bedecked floats in the 2005 Rose Bowl Parade. Sophie and her husband, realtor Alan Joel, have two daughters: Helen, who graduated from the University of Alabama in 2011 and lives in San Diego, and Holly, now following in her parents' footsteps as a student at the University of Georgia.

Helen and Bud's marriage lasted for ten years before they parted, and once again Helen took on the difficult role of a single mother. For 16 years she went her own way as a successful realtor, all the while following her many interests as she gave love and guidance to her children.

Her grandchildren were just beginning to arrive when Helen and I married. Now there are eight, all living up to the standards of their grandparents' traditional bragging. (They say it isn't bragging if it's true – and in this case, it is..) My children had known me only as part of a couple, and for that reason I think my marriage to Helen was easier for them to accept. In fact, they called her their "bonus mom."

Our Move to Druid Hills

Helen and I quickly decided we needed a new nest to begin our lives together. The Round House had too many memories of my life with Hermi, and every time I drove in or out I would relive the auto wreck by the driveway. We discussed remodeling Helen's house. I drew a scheme for opening up the floor plan and providing better views of the lake in back. Helen never said no, but I sensed that changing so much as a closet would upset her.

We needed to create our own memories – so the search began. Day after day after I returned home from the office, we drove through nice neighborhoods. On one search we drove down Oakdale Road in Druid Hills, one of the city's oldest and finest neighborhoods. The neighborhood had the same designer as New York's Central Park – Frederick Law Olmsted, who laid out a string of linear parks along Ponce de Leon Avenue, the central artery. On Oakdale, a white, two-story timber house set far back from the sidewalk caught our attention. Planted on the lawn was a "For Sale" sign.

Early the next day, a Sunday, we went back to the house. The owner answered our ring and welcomed us in. He told us Neal Reid was the architect. During the 1920s Reid set the standard for gracious houses on beautifully landscaped lots, and 888 Oakdale Road lived up to Reid's best work. After a very short negotiation we agreed on the sale.

Once the house was ours we made a few changes. An upstairs porch became an ample bathroom for Helen after it was enclosed and its floor beams had been augmented with steel. We totally renovated the kitchen and later added a pool to the back yard. Helen went to work on the lot and turned it into a flourishing English garden.

Because security was a neighborhood concern, the privately funded Druid Hills Patrol was organized. It wasn't long before Helen became its president. Two DeKalb County policemen in full uniform checked on houses when the owners were away, answered calls from homeowners who heard suspicious noises, and returned stray children to their parents. They were the "mother protectors" of Druid Hills.

Pinchy, our dog, apparently wasn't all that impressed by the patrolmen. One day they were discussing safety issues with Helen when Pinchy joined them. Then, as canines do, he lifted his hind leg and relieved himself on one of the officer's uniformed legs. Pinchy was not arrested.

The house came with a one-bedroom garage apartment, which we rented to a series of Emory University students; the campus was only is a short walk away. One in particular I remember was an outgoing sophomore from Berlin. We occasionally asked him join us for dinner, and one evening a baseball game lit up our TV. I asked him if he'd ever been to a game, and he said no. A few nights later we were at the stadium watching the Atlanta Braves play the New York Mets. He caught on quickly to the nuances of the game, and the high moment for him was the seventh inning stretch, when the crowd joined in singing "Take Me Out to the Ball Game." Our young German tenant was delighted by the spectacle of 40,000 people singing a joyful ode to a game.

Our time in Druid Hills also had its share of sadness. Just before our first Thanksgiving in the new house, a dark cloud descended when we learned that Terri's husband Herb Millkey was terminally ill with liver cancer and had only months to live. Members of both families (including Herb and Terri) and Helen's family were there for dinner, and we tried our best to celebrate not only the holiday but also Herb's life. I couldn't; a second tragedy so soon after Hermi's death was too much for me. Herb made two poignant observations to me that evening – he said, "Dying is for the birds" and "I'm not afraid of death, but I'm very sad to leave my family." Helen didn't realize the cause of my gloom, but I found little to be thankful for that night.

Months later, a moving van pulled into the drive next door. By good fortune, Bruce Beresford, the director of *Driving Miss Daisy,* had rented the house for his family of three – the film would be made in our neighborhood. Our house had been checked out as a possible home for Miss Daisy, but the remodeled kitchen ruled it out. A period house on Lullwater Road was chosen instead. Helen left a note on the Beresfords' back door inviting them to use our pool and saying she was an available actress. The young Beresford daughter and her mother spent many hours in the pool.

Helen and I were given parts in *Driving Miss Daisy.* I'm sure the pool was a factor. Helen is in the opening scene, sipping tea with director Beresford's wife, and the two watch as Miss Daisy backs her car over a wall in the adjacent yard. Helen also had a speaking part with another woman, but a violent thunderstorm struck, washing out the scene. It was never shot, a real disappointment for Helen.

My role involved nothing but hand clapping. It was filmed in an old mansion that substituted for an elite business club. Dan Aykroyd, as Boolie Werthen, stood at the head of the long table. Jessica Tandy, as Miss Daisy, and Patti Lupone, as Daisy's snooty daughter-in-law Florine, sat across from each other near Boolie.

Dressed in 1930s suits, fifteen or so extras marched in to fill the table with Boolie's friends and admirers, and I headed the line. I'm sure I was expected to go to the far end of the table, but I sat down next to Patti Lupone to make sure I wouldn't be cut from the scene. After we were all seated, Beresford came in.

"I need two younger men at the table," he said,

I was certain I was about to be ejected, but to my surprise George Heery, an architect ten years young than I, was one of the two replaced. George and I had an ongoing joint venture to design athletic facilities, starting with the Atlanta-Fulton County Stadium. When we were together, he always managed to step in front of me if a photographer or a reporter approached. So I took great satisfaction in the only time I was out front. George later told me he felt certain I would be sent out – certainly not he. This added to my pleasure.

In the scene, Boolie was to be presented with a large silver bowl designating him as Businessman of the Year. He would smile and then make a short acceptance speech, after which those of us sitting around the table would applaud. Sound simple? It took over five hours and god knows how many takes before Beresford was satisfied. Aykroyd, who was wringing wet with sweat, blew his lines several times. Thunder rumbled through the windows during one take. While another take was in progress, a phone rang in an adjacent room. At other times, some of the action just didn't suit Beresford. During those long hours, Ms. Lupone never acknowledged my existence; after all, I was just a lowly extra. Ms. Tandy, sitting across from me, was gracious to those around her and spoke with us.

For this ordeal I received $42.38, so I suppose I became a professional actor. But I was never sought after by Hollywood. Side benefits of my one-day career were the calls I received from old friends who recognized me in the film and told me I clapped my hands with the skill of a Marlon Brando. Helen and I have a photograph of us holding a borrowed Oscar as we stood in front a fireplace in Miss Daisy's house. I've had many fantasies in my long life, but appearing in an Oscar-winning motion picture wasn't among them.

Human and Animal Companions

Druid Hills was many miles from the homes of our old friends, but we made many new ones there. Helen, as President of the Druid Hills Patrol, met dozens of neighbors who immediately became her friends. Her daughter Jill Brown and her family lived nearby, and my daughter Judy, with her husband Ed and son Jed, soon moved in behind us on Springdale Road so we certainly weren't isolated.

One new friend was Philip Moise, a prominent lawyer who lived nearby on Oakdale Road. One day we ran into each other on the sidewalk. "Cecil," he said," I'm a Protestant but I know my ancestry is Jewish. I wonder if you can help me locate my ancestors. The only one of distinction was a portrait painter, Theodore Moise." Surprised, I told Phil he had to come with me to my house right away. On the wall of the front hall hung a life-size portrait of my ancestor Isaiah Moses, and the artist was Theodore Moise. Phil was astonished, I gave him the little information I had on the Moise family and suggested he call the Charleston Historical Society for more details.

Every Fourth of July there was a ragtag neighborhood parade led by an out-of-tune, out-of-step pickup band blowing away on a variety of brass horns, a piccolo, two clanging cymbals, and a throbbing bass drum – a reflection of the creative bent of Druid Hills. Just behind, I drove my light blue 1964 Lincoln Continental convertible with the top down. One year a very pregnant Judy sat on the back like a beauty queen, waving royally to no one. A motley group of paraders followed my car singing, shouting, and waving American flags. Families, some with babies in carriages, trotted along in red white and blue outfits. There were no cheering spectators lining the street – everyone was in the parade, including many dogs and one overweight cat.

Speaking of dogs and cats, among the many interests that attracted me to Helen was our love of animals. Helen's constant companions during the years she was single were her two dogs, Clarence and Pinchy. It all started back when Helen's 4-year-old daughter Sophie mounted a vigorous campaign to add a puppy to the household. It worked, and mother and daughter went to the pound and were told there was only one puppy left. "She's sweet," said Sophie. "We'll take her.'

Bea Dunn, a friend and housekeeper who lived with her husband Sam at Helen's home, watched the puppy skidding around the backyard. "I've never seen a female puppy lift its hind leg like that," she said with a grin. "That dog is not a female!" And so he wasn't. He became Clarence, the all-male dog – and he and Helen bonded for life.

In time Clarence needed a canine companion. Helen was playing tennis on a neighbor's court when saw a muzzled puppy running along the fence around the court. "That dog is lost," she told her friend. "I'm going to take him home, then check the neighborhood and see if anyone claims him." No one did, and no one knew anything about him.

She took him (there was no doubt about his gender) home to Clarence, and his pointed, narrow muzzle inspired Helen to name him Pinchy – full name Christopher Pinchy to give him some sense of dignity. Pinchy lacked the soul that made Clarence such a close member of the family, but he had his moments. "Streetsmart" defined him. When the Animal Control van stopped in front of Helen's house one day, Clarence wagged his tail in delight, jumped into the back of the truck to make friends with the captive dogs. Pinchy took one look and ran off into the woods. He knew from experience that he wanted no part of that van.

In his later years, Clarence was plagued with cancer of the jaw. One night he was missing. Much to our relief, a call came from a store in a shopping center several miles away. "Your dog is lying on the walk outside my store. I got your name and phone number off of his collar." When we arrived, Clarence wagged his tail feebly, struggled to stand up, and with my help climbed slowly into the car. Helen and I surmised he knew he was dying and tried to walk back to Helen's home – his home too for most of his life. We knew it was time to say goodbye.

When, the moment came on the cold metal table at the veterinarian's office, Helen and I held Clarence, who didn't struggle but simply looked at Helen with sorrowful eyes. The vet inserted the needle, emptied the syringe, and Clarence's eyes closed in peaceful death. Helen and I patted him one more time and held each other. Clarence is buried behind the gardens of the home on Oakdale Road. Our beloved Pinchy soon joined him there.

At the corner of Oakdale Road and Ponce de Leon in a large, old house lived a dynamic lady in her forties, a woman Helen believed had more-than-friendly eyes for me. And President Jimmy Carter happened to enlist this woman for his Washington staff.

Near the end of his term Carter invited a large group of supporters to a meeting at the White House, and I was among them. Two weeks before the meeting the "dynamic lady" called me. "Cecil," she said, "the President wants the developer Jim Rouse at the meeting. I thought it might help your relationship with Rouse if *you* invite him."

Rouse was the selfsame developer who had joined us in Venice. Years before, during the early days of Carter's first campaign, I had run into him by chance at, of all places, the counter of a New York greasy spoon across from Macy's. A newspaper obscured the face of the man next to me, but I caught a brief glimpse. A worn briefcase resting on the counter, imprinted with the initials "J. R. gave me reason enough to believe it was Jim. " I peered around the newspaper and ventured, "Jim, is that you?"

It was. "Why hello Cecil, good to see you," said Rouse. "I've just been reading about Jimmy Carter. Do you know him? Do you think he would make a good president?" I answered yes to both questions. We then discussed Carter for about ten minutes. As we left the restaurant, Rouse said, "He seems OK to me. I'll get in touch with his campaign."

Over time Jim Rouse became one of Carter's major contributors and a very effective supporter – so, some five years later, he certainly belonged at the meeting being set up at the White House. I sent him a message relaying Carter's wish. To my chagrin, Rouse was deeply offended – the president himself, he thought, should have invited him. I understood his objection but couldn't help feeling I was being put down. It was embarrassing, though there was no long-term effect on our friendship.

I don't remember if Rouse came to the meeting. But I do know that the dynamic lady's offer to help me backfired, and that Helen was pleased.

A Trip to France

By the early 1990s it had been several years since we had donned our "ugly American" outfits and traveled to Europe. Helen wanted to see the hotels in France she had read about in a travel book – reason enough to follow in the flight path of Charles Lindbergh and take off for Paris. I don't know whether we were motivated by wanting to better our relations with my sister-in-law Terry and her husband Richard Lansburgh, or for no particular reason, but we asked if they would join us. They accepted.

Several episodes in what turned out to be a great trip remain in my memory. One was entering the Louvre through one of the two recently opened glass pyramids designed by the star architect I.M. Pei. It was visually exciting, but the sun streaming through the soaring glass walls made it uncomfortably hot. Inside the cooler museum it was reassuring to see both the Winged Victory of Samothrace statue, still breathtaking, and the Mona Lisa, with her mysterious smile undisturbed.

The car we rented had a manual gearshift. Richard drove, and he kept the clutch halfway in all afternoon, effectively burning out the plates. That evening we were on our way to a restaurant when the car suddenly stopped with the engine running full tilt – the clutch was burned out. Luckily there was an auto repair shop nearby. A mechanic, working late, came out, and he and Richard and I pushed the car into his shop.

Terry's uncle, Maurice Hirsch, was a retired desk general and world traveler, and his generous tipping made him welcome in fine hotels and five-star restaurants in major cities. She was sure he would be remembered at LaTour d'Argent, the legendary restaurant across the Seine from Notre Dame Cathedral. Full of confidence, Terry informed the maitre d' that she was the general's niece, only to see him shrug his shoulders, lift his palms, and shake his head. Still, he graciously showed us to our table, and we enjoyed one of the best meals of our lives.

Our most emotionally gripping trip was to Normandy's Omaha Beach, where the Allies drove through fire to land on D-Day in World War II. Richard had been there, just offshore as a Naval officer on board a small ship. And now he was there again, with us physically, while in his memory he was transported back to those fearsome moments, reliving that day of horror more than four decades before. The sight of the acres of white crosses and a scattering of Stars of David across the grassy rolling hills was the somber finale for our day.

As the days passed and we enjoyed many exciting and interesting experiences, Terry began to accept Helen. This had been evident when they held hands as we stood before the Mona Lisa and were moved by her beauty. Terry wasn't Hermi, but I cared for her. When Hermi and I had a crisis in our marriage, Terry urged her not to be so unforgiving – to move on with our lives together. After our trip to France, Terry and Richard and Helen and I were often together until Terry's death, a passing that left me feeling empty.

Reclaiming My Wings

The old flying obsession was still with me. My cousin Ted Levy, a naval aviator and retired admiral, seemed a likely candidate to buy an airplane with. It took some persuading, but he finally came through. Our aircraft of choice was a restored World War II primary trainer, the Stearman. Both of us had flown this two-seat open cockpit biplane in our training days.

Ted and I traveled to the small airfield in Pittsburgh where the plane was kept. The owner took us up to see if we liked this big bird, with its shiny new coat of yellow and blue paint. We did, and put a cashier's check for $15,000 in the owner's hand.

The next morning we decided to fly home – and our first takeoff was almost our last. The small grassy field had no control tower and the runway sloped up in the middle, meaning from either end we couldn't see over the hump. A tattered windsock indicated the direction of the wind. Ted, at the controls in the cockpit behind me, taxied to the downwind end of the runway, swung the plane into the wind, jammed the throttle forward, and raced down the runway. My seat in the front cockpit gave me the first look over the hump, and coming at us was a just-airborne red plane. Not waiting to yell at Ted, I jerked our plane into a sharp turn and we missed the plane by a few feet. An agitated Ted came on the intercom. "That dumb bastard took off downwind! Where did he learn to fly – at Woolworth's? Whew!"

When we reached the mountains we looked for an opening in the clouds. There was none. An alternative was to fly down a river flowing in a valley between two mountains. Flying low over the over the water for an hour and twisting and turning all the while, we at last came free of the mountains and flew out over a rolling landscape.

Turning south toward Atlanta, we had another near miss. A storm over Memphis made us change our route, and we flew at 700 feet under a cloud layer. But wisps of the clouds floated in front and obscured our view. Our charts showed a 1,000-foot TV tower in the area, so we were looking hard to avoid it. Through the mist I suddenly saw the tower, and again didn't wait to tell Ted. I rolled the plane violently on its side and missed the tower, almost hitting the guy wire that anchored it.

Finally, we saw DeKalb Peachtree Airport ahead. As we descended we were so buffeted by a strong headwind that cars on the highway parallel to our flight path passed us. (Humiliating!) The plane bounced twice on the tarmac before settling down. Our worried, exasperated wives were waiting for us at the hangar, and relief mixed with annoyance as they greeted us.

Ted and I found two other pilots, both experienced flyers, who bought into the ownership. The four of us rotated our hours in the Stearman, which was hangared with Epps Aviation at DeKalb-Peachtree. One morning, as Ted was getting into his car, he collapsed and fell to the driveway. He had been hit with a massive stroke. His wife Renata sold his share of the plane.

A few months later I became aware that my hearing was fading, so I quit. Every time I took off I wondered where I would land if the engine quit, so I hung up my helmet and goggles without regret. Fifty-five years of flying was satisfying enough.

On my last flight I circled our house, gunning the engine to entice Helen to run out and wave. She didn't hear it. I flew back to the field, landed, and would have walked into the sunset except it was eleven o'clock in the morning.

Time to House-Hunt

Helen and enjoyed the Oakdale house and its lush gardens. But there was a major problem: Almost every week something quit, broke, or barely functioned. The final insult was the flooding of the basement with a 2-foot-deep pond after refuse clogged a street sewer line. Many of our papers and books were ruined. It was time to move on, I believed, and Helen reluctantly agreed.

We put the house up for sale, but after a year only one offer had been made. It was two-thirds of our asking price, so we took the house off the market. We tried again the following week, and suddenly had a buyer who would pay full price but wanted to move in immediately. It was a classic example of "Be careful what you wish for — you may get it."

Thinking it would be many months before we sold the house, we hadn't made a move to pack up and had no idea where we could find a place to live. At a reasonable pace it would have taken us at least a month to pack, yet we managed to do it (and exhaust ourselves) in seven 16-hour days.

Sophie and Alan returned our hospitality by inviting us to stay in the house they had recently bought. But a hurdle popped up on moving day —convincing the moving company to provide enough van space for our mountain of stuff. In a showdown with the mover, a foot-stomping, exasperated Helen demanded that he send a second van. In the face of this petite tornado, he agreed straightaway. The additional van soon showed up, and off to temporary storage went the material of our lifestyle. It would remain there until we were ready to move into the house we still call home.

Top left: "The Barnes Flag" I designed, adopted by the State of Georgia in 2001. It replaced the controversial "rebel" flag that had flown since 1956, and remained atop the flag poles of Georgia until 2003. It still flies at various places such as The Temple in Atlanta and the main entrance to Lake Lanier Islands.

Top Right: The day the flag was raised over the Capital for the first time. Photo by David Tullis

Below left: The Buckhead Flag that I designed at Sam Massell's behest. I provided several designs that were voted on by a panel of six judges. This was the favorite.

Below Middle: Raising the flag at the Woodruff Arts Center. Photo by Mark Steinmetz

Below Right: Another design for a flag for Georgia. This one was never produced.

Below left: With my daughter Terri on the day of the first flag raising at the state capital

Below middle: Flag raising day with three of my four grandsons, Julian, Jed and Wilson

Below right: Celebrating the flag with Secretary of State Cathy Cox, Bob Rosenthal of Atlas Flag Company (producers of the flag) me and Helen

Chapter 14

A Flag for All Georgians?

Furl that Banner, for 'tis weary ...

—*Fr. Abram Joseph Ryan, The Conquered Banner*

I'm five years old and sitting on my father's shoulders, my short legs wrapped around his neck. It is July 4, 1923 – blindingly bright and burning hot, as only a Georgia summer day can be. Down Peachtree Street comes the parade. Leading the marchers is a Marine color guard holding aloft the Stars and Stripes and the Marine flag bearing the world-and-anchor insignia. Just behind is the band, led by John Philip Sousa himself, trumpeting the stirring notes of "The Stars and Stripes Forever," Sousa's masterpiece.

Peachtree Street is lined five-deep with veterans of World War I (just five years past) and their families and friends, along with regular folks and their kids. As the color guard approaches we wave small flags, clap, and shout. Hats come off, right hands cover hearts, and tears well up in eye after eye. Now Old Glory is in front of me. At my father's command, I yank off my cap and salute. I'm too young to take it all in and to know the full meaning of the flag, but almost nine decades later I remember the thrill of that moment.

Twenty-one years after that memorable July 4th, World War II drenches the world in blood and terror. On a November day in 1944, the Fletcher class destroyer USS *Albert W. Grant* leaves Pearl Harbor. From her mast atop the bridge, the traditional homeward bound pennant flies, trailing from the stern into the ship's foaming white wake. The elongated pennant also reflects the many months the *Grant* has fought in the Pacific, where it survived a near-fatal encounter in the Battle of Surigao Strait. On that fateful day she and her companion destroyers forged into the strait and launched torpedoes at the oncoming Japanese armada at close range. In a sharp 180-degree reversal of her course, she made for the open sea. The U.S. cruiser *Quincy* picked up the *Grant* on radar, mistook her for an enemy ship, and showered her with 6-inch shells. The *Grant* sustained hits from both the Japanese ships and the American cruiser.

The attacks were devastating. Forty-three *Grant* crew were killed and ninty-five wounded. Water rushed through holes ripped in her steel sides and sank her down to her gunnels, her decks awash with saltwater, blood, and oil. Undaunted, the captain ignored orders to take the radio gear from his sinking ship and prepare to abandon ship. Instead, he urged his crew manning the pumps to redouble their efforts. At last the flooding was contained, and miraculously the *Grant* survived.

It is this storied ship that is now homeward bound, and I am standing on its bridge after nine months in the Marshall Islands. As the vessel leaves the Pearl Harbor Navy Yard, the rails of three nearby ships are lined with sailors, their white uniforms bright in the sun. As we pass they raise a chorus of cheers and wave their white caps, urging the *Grant*, with its homeward bound pennant streaming proudly, on into the Pacific on its journey to the United States.

Days later the *Grant* heads into San Francisco Bay. I stand shivering in the cold damp wind with the ship's skipper, Capt. Andy Nisewaner. As we approach the magnificent Golden Gate Bridge, we see a huge American flag rippling on the high cliffs. As one, we turn and salute this bright symbol of home.

This momentary union of the homeward bound pennant and Old Glory still fills me with emotion. These flags were only symbols – but what symbols!

Georgia's Divisive Banner

It was with an understanding of how emotions could be inflamed or inspired by a piece of cloth that I became involved in the malignant controversy surrounding the Georgia state flag. Spurring me all the more was the joyous moment in September 1990 when Atlanta was named host city for the 1996 Olympics, the hundredth anniversary of the modern games. I was afraid the flag, whose dominant feature was the Rebel battle flag's Cross of St. Andrew (a.k.a. the Confederate cross), would destroy Atlanta's hard-won reputation as "the city too busy to hate" once it was seen by television audiences around the world.

What would it say about us that we flew a flag that symbolized racism in the eyes of Georgia's blacks and had been adopted by the Ku Klux Klan as their royal standard in the fight against integration? Thankfully, my fears would not be realized during the Olympics. But that wouldn't stop me from designing a flag that would bridge the chasm between those who believed the Confederate emblem to be sacred and those who saw it as a symbol of racial hatred, violence, and murder.

Many Georgians were aware that the Georgia flag, the third in the state's history, had been adopted in 1956 in the wake of the *Brown v. Board of Education*, which made keeping public schools segregated unconstitutional. Across the South, states choosing to keep the Confederate cross on their flags faced boycotts and economic loss. Most of Georgia's business community wanted the emblem banished, but many were reluctant to say so openly. As he ran for a second term in 1994, then-governor Zell Miller, a tough ex-Marine, had staked his political career on bringing back the less controversial pre-1956 flag. He failed, and the effort almost cost him his re-election.

It was near the end of his governorship that I encountered Miller in the elevator up to the Commerce Club, the hangout for the city's powerful. I told him about the flag I had designed and, sensing an opportunity, offered to show him the cloth flag I had in my briefcase.

He waved a wiry hand at nothing in particular. "I don't want to see any more flags," he spat.

As the elevator stopped and he walked out, he said, "Cecil, you're OK. But as for that flag, Semper Fi." An abbreviated version of the Latin *semper fidelis* ("always faithful"), Semper Fi is the Marine motto. In the corpsmen's rough and tumble vernacular it can also be used in place of an expletive based on a certain reproductive act.

One day in 1995 I was walking out of a meeting of Resurgens, a civic organization named for the anglicized motto of our risen-from-the-ashes city, formed in the 1960s by me and other like-minded citizens as a meeting ground for white and black professionals and businesspeople. At my side was Joseph M. Beck, a prominent intellectual property attorney. We carried out onto the street a conversation about the then-simmering controversy over the state flag. Beck, a Southerner who grew up in Montgomery, Alabama, shares my passion for racial equity. His father is said to have been one of the models for Atticus Finch, the brave white attorney in Harper Lee's novel *To Kill A Mockingbird*.

"If the flag is going to be changed, it should be done by Southerners themselves," Joe said. I agreed, and promised to show him the design for a new flag that could replace the current one. It needed to be free of overtones of racism but also pay homage to our culture and past.

No one inside or outside the government asked me to design the flag, and no one paid me. Also, I eventually transferred the copyright to the state. My original design assembled various icons of our history. In the center was the State Seal adopted in 1799 (which appeared on both the pre- and post-1956 versions), surrounded by thirteen stars representing Georgia's inclusion in the founding states. A ribbon beneath the seal pictured the flags that have flown over Georgia since pre-Colonial days – French, Spanish, English, Revolutionary, Confederate, and the United States. The blue field represents the Blue Ridge Mountains; the red, the state's distinctive clay; and the gold, the precious metal that covers the capitol dome and was panned from the streams around the North Georgia town of Dahlonega.

Joe Beck and I formed a nonprofit to promote the flag and talked it up to organizations and politicians. While many Georgians expressed support, almost no one was willing to do so publicly; such was the fear surrounding the flag debate. The Atlanta Chamber of Commerce, for example, had lost nearly a quarter of its members when its executive board came out in favor of former Gov. Miller's campaign to remove the Confederate cross. Still, Beck and I soldiered on in what seemed to many of our associates a decidedly quixotic effort. Then, in late 1999, things began to change.

Joe and I had been seeking a General Assembly legislator willing to sponsor an amendment to change the flag. Our preference was someone from the conservative and largely rural southern section of the state, the area where support of the existing flag was strongest. When no rural candidate materialized, Beck approached two Atlanta area representatives, and both agreed to take on the job. Soon after we quietly received word that they wouldn't submit the bill in the upcoming session, but that Roy Barnes, the state's new governor, was interested in talking to us.

A meeting was scheduled for April 12, 2000, after the General Assembly had left town at the close of its 40-day session. I arrived at the capitol and met Beck in the stately antechamber outside the governor's office. For what we were told would be a ten-minute meeting, I carried a cloth reproduction of the flag and tucked several paper copies under my arm. After we were ushered into his large office, Barnes entered (alone, to our surprise) and looked on as we spread out the flag on the floor.

It was a strange but oddly appropriate moment for me. I'm a native Southerner whose ancestors arrived in Charleston, South Carolina in 1760. Abraham Alexander served as a lieutenant in the Continental Army that freed the colonies from the oppression of King George III. Almost a century later my grandfather and many other relatives wore Confederate gray and fought against Sherman to defend their homeland as the Civil War convulsed the nation. I had grown up in Atlanta, which we natives proudly called the capital of the New South. I had spent the post-World War II years endeavoring to shape the city's physical appearance as an architect and to influence its political, economic, and racial structure during the civil rights movement. As a Southern Jew in Atlanta, I had seen the polite but often-paternalistic way whites of good will treated blacks, and I was well aware of a system that kept too many blacks in a permanent cycle of poverty. To me, the flag was a means of saying that all of our citizens – black as well as white – were worthy of representation by the state's official banner.

Beck, perhaps sensing that this might be our only chance to influence the governor's decision, spoke eloquently of the flag as a way out of a festering problem and then added, "If we don't do something about the Confederate emblem on the flag, then we're going to have it done to us by others."

Barnes listened intently to every word, but with little or no comment. Nearly an hour later he still hadn't hinted whether he thought this latest idea might fly in the legislature or even if he would support it. Then, as he stood to show us out at the meeting's end, he spoke: "This might just be the alternative I've been looking for."

As Joe and I walked out of the capitol building we talked about where to go from here. I ventured that a next step might be to print up and distribute copies of the flag to every lawmaker. Joe quickly put a stop to that notion in his usual thoughtful way. "No, I wouldn't do that," he said. "We're starting with the governor, and we should leave it with him for now."

Unable to rest in the weeks that followed, I continued to show my flag to the various groups working to change the Georgia banner. The Atlanta chapter of the American Jewish Committee (AJC) had organized a group to study the flag, and even though they didn't support my design I thought I might be able to change their minds. I arrived at their next meeting with a stack of color photocopies of the flag. As I briefly spoke in support of the design and the copies were passed around, I could see that most present gave the design only a casual glance. I also heard one member snort, "This will never fly."

After a reception (polite for the most part but discouraging) I made my way out of the meeting and chatted briefly with the guest speaker, State Rep. Calvin Smyre, an African-American and outspoken opponent of the post-1956 flag. I handed him a copy of my design and recounted my meeting with Gov. Barnes and his positive parting comment. Smyre's only response was a grin.

I wasn't the only Alexander on a mission. My son Doug, then a member of the Atlanta City Council, had organized a citizens' group to push for the adoption of a new flag, and they rolled out bumper stickers and buttons promote it. Support for the idea of returning to a pre-1956 design of the flag was slow in coming, but the need was greater than ever.

Design by Committee

One chilly morning in January 2001, my office phone rang. The voice on the other end of the line belonged to Jerry Grey, Gov. Barnes's deputy chief of staff. "Mr. Alexander, I need to talk to you about your flag," he said. I knew just how serious his call was going to be.

"Certainly. I can come to the capitol," I said.

"No," he replied. "I'll come to see you."

He wasn't just being polite. Grey arrived at my office less than an hour later, and we sat down to discuss the design that I had conceived for a new Georgia flag back in 1993.

Grey, a young, businesslike African-American, quickly came to the point: My flag design was going to be presented to the General Assembly as part of a bill that would remove the Confederate cross-bearing flag adopted in 1956.

As we talked about my design, Grey's main focus was its ribbon of small flags stretched across the bottom containing the various banners that had flown over Georgia since pre-colonial days. We also talked about the wording in my flag. When he left I had the feeling that changes were in the offing, changes that would garner the support of the state legislators currently in session.

My design would ultimately undergo alterations that resulted in more than half a dozen new versions. With every change something would be added to the flag that its proponents knew would ease the concerns of one or many of their fellow legislators. As these men and women worked at introducing and passing bills and budgets for a wide range of issues, the flag question quietly made its way around the capitol.

An important former state legislator, Denmark Groover, had fought passionately for the 1956 flag glorifying the Confederacy. Now, half a century later, he became a decisive proponent of change. Addressing the House Rules Committee, he said, "As former governor Marvin Griffin's one-time floor leader, I humbly say to you that had I not been in favor of the 1956 flag, it wouldn't have passed. It is for that reason I presume to speak to you. Now it matters little what the motivation was. Our state flag has come to be the most divisive issue on the political spectrum, and it needs to be put to rest. Only you and your courage can do so."

As a World War II Marine fighter pilot from Macon, Groover had strong credentials as both a Southerner and a patriot. A majority of the General Assembly followed his lead and stepped forward into the future, not backwards into our contentious history.

Still, much had to be done to make the flag acceptable to Georgia lawmakers. The lineup of past Georgia flags adorning the new design was changed to include the 1956 banner with its Confederate cross. A bad idea, I thought, but I assumed that the flag bill's handlers knew best, so I consented.

As each revision was ordered I made the alteration with the aid of a local graphics firm's computers and a Georgia Tech imaging lab. As work continued, I became increasingly concerned about the cluttered look of the flag. Along with everything else, an amendment in the House added the words "In God we trust." Afterwards I said to the legislator who had introduced the amendment that I thought the additions were creating a hodgepodge out of an already busy design. He responded, "It got us five votes." No matter what the architect in me might think, my practical side had to admit that these changes were necessary and therefore tolerable.

I also knew that my original design had started out in 1993 as anything but a pure work of art. I had conceived it as a compromise from the very beginning — not by any means the best and cleanest example of flag design, but a banner that could represent Georgia without embarrassment or controversy.

The Rest of the Story

The call from Deputy Chief of Staff Jerry Grey had been my first indication that a movement was afoot. In the days to follow there would be many emotional ups and downs as the legislature took up the bill for consideration.

The flag bill passed the Georgia House, but ahead was a tense week-long wait for action by the Senate — a week filled with rumors, arguments, and threats. So divisive was the issue that real violence wasn't out of the question. On the day of the vote, guards ringed the capitol to fend off any "flaggers" (die-hard Confederacy sympathizers) who might try to storm the building.

Helen and I left early for capitol the morning of the vote, anticipating a large crowd. We were right. Stone-faced guards lined the broad granite stairs on the west side of the capitol where we entered. In front of those stairs stands a statue of Tom Watson, whom Georgians sent to the both the U.S. House of Representatives and the Senate. Watson started his political career as a populist, but after losing elections as a pro-black candidate he became an avowed racist and anti-Semite. In fact, his newspapers fed the poisonous anti-Semitic atmosphere during the 1913 Leo Frank trial, as noted in Chapter 1. Were he alive, I thought, Watson would be fueling the rage of the flaggers.

Helen and I went through a thorough search that made today's airport screenings seem lax. We then proceeded to the second-floor governor's office and once more had to be all but frisked. The reception area in the governor's ornate office is designed to impress with its high ceilings, paneled walls, rich carpets, and oil portraits glaring down at visitors. Loud noises from the street below drew us to the high windows at one end of the suite. Looking out, we saw the broad, tree-lined avenue beyond the capitol lawn filled with swarms of backfiring motorcycles. The unidentified riders all wore black leather clothing and German-style steel helmets. My thought was, "What the hell does that bunch of reactionaries think they're doing?" A member of the governor's staff set me straight: The motorcyclists were campaigning for rescinding a law requiring them to wear helmets. All right, I thought: if they want to bust their heads, I'm all for it — except we may have to pay their hospital bills later.

Word went out that the Senate was about to vote on the flag. We rushed to the Senate chambers and found a place to stand at the edge of the room. It was difficult to follow the voting, but at the end there was no question: Georgia would have a new flag — a flag I had basically designed — as soon as Gov. Barnes signed the bill.

Helen and I went back to the governor's office to join in the self-congratulations. If it had been a locker room we would have poured champagne all over one another. It was great day! No violence had occurred and the image of a more progressive Georgia seemed assured. Raising the flag over the capital was a proud moment for me and for those who had offered encouragement and support. Many of us thought it was the end of the matter, and that Georgia now could turn toward more important issues, such as building better schools and attracting more jobs.

At the celebration, a smiling Calvin Smyre approached me and recalled our meeting at the American Jewish Committee. After embracing me, the black state representative admitted that that at the time of the AJC meeting he knew my design had been chosen but the governor had sworn him to secrecy. "He told me the week before that your flag was it. But he said, 'If you tell anyone, you're toast,'" he recalled with a laugh. Rep. Smyre also said he'd heard all the AJC's members' adverse comments about the flag and had a hard time suppressing his amusement. If only they had known!

The flaggers at large, however, were angry – and they mobilized. The flag became an even more divisive issue in the upcoming governor's race, which was a face-off between Democrat Barnes and one of the strongest Republicans ever to mount a challenge in Georgia: Sonny Perdue. Across the state, particularly amid the red clay and pine trees of Middle and South Georgia, a seemingly endless number of yard signs popped up challenging the incumbent. It seemed that more than just members of the Sons of the Confederacy were opposed to Barnes's replacement of the old flag. More worrisome to the Barnes camp was the increasing number of Perdue signs appearing in traditionally Democratic yards.

The state's power establishment was firmly behind Gov. Barnes, and donations from the business community were filling his campaign coffers – so how could he lose to the under funded and little-known Perdue, himself a former Democrat? Georgia hadn't had a Republican governor for 130 years, and many thought there wouldn't be one now. Everyone, it seems, was wrong. Perdue swept to victory and Barnes returned to his law practice in Marietta.

In hindsight, it's difficult to say just how much the flag issue hurt Barnes in his reelection bid. Other issues, including educational reform that had stirred up the state's powerful teacher's lobby, no doubt played a role. Then there's the fact that Georgia, after years of attracting hundreds of thousands of new arrivals from outside the state, just wasn't as solidly Democratic. In suburban counties like Cobb and Gwinnett was a whole new class of SUV-driving Republicans ready to vote for the moderately conservative Perdue. And the flaggers believed he was a kindred spirit. Once in office, however, Perdue sidestepped the issue by proposing an entirely new flag. That wasn't enough for the flaggers, who demanded a return to the 1956 battle-flag design or a public referendum.

In 2003 Gov. Perdue authorized House legislators to come up with yet another new flag, which would be pitted against the Barnes flag in a public referendum. The new one was modeled on the Stars and Bars – the first Confederate flag, in use from March 1861 until May 1863, when commanders realized that from afar it could be mistaken for the Stars and Stripes. A circle of stars representing the eleven Confederate states was set in a blue field in the upper left corner, and three broad stripes – two red ones at the top and bottom and a white one in the center – filled out the rest.

The new design was a stealthy choice: The Confederate legacy was apparent to some black Georgians and Civil War buffs, but most were willing to allow it because it wasn't widely recognized as such and wasn't linked with the Ku Klux Klan or other racist groups. In addition, the State Seal of Georgia was centered in the circle of stars. Even many Georgians who had supported Gov. Barnes's flag openly supported this neo-Confederate version.

I was, however, appalled that Georgia would even consider flying a flag recalling the worst period in the state's history. What a travesty to commemorate slavery, Sherman's burning of Atlanta and his "War is Hell" march to the sea, and years of oppression of Georgia's black citizens!

One day a few weeks before the referendum I received a slick, expensive mailing urging support for the new flag. To my dismay, former mayor of Atlanta, U.S. congressman, and UN ambassador Andrew Young, a stalwart fighter for civil rights, was one of the most prominent supporters. Backed by a sizeable war chest gathered from the business community, the flag had no shortage of endorsements, including a strong one from former president Jimmy Carter. Except for a limited mailing I sent out, proponents of the Barnes flag had little to say.

The referendum came in March 2004 as part of the presidential primary, As vote counts trickled in, the new Perdue flag was ahead more than four to one, and it became the decisive winner. The banner I had originally designed was abruptly hauled down at the capitol, and the thousands of copies that had been manufactured were locked away, consigned to the dustbin of history.

Not surprisingly, the vote didn't settle the issue for the flaggers. They claimed Gov. Perdue had promised to include on the ballot the pre-1956 flag with its large display of the Confederate cross. They nailed up anti-Perdue posters for the next election, posters emblazoned with "Sonny lied."

Although my design is no longer is Georgia's official flag, I take solace from three sources. First, my flag did replace the divisive 1956 flag, with its ties to the Klan and other racial extremists. Second, the Kennedy Profiles in Courage Award was presented to Gov. Barnes in recognition of his flag, and Helen and I attended at the ceremony at the Kennedy Library. Third, Gov. Barnes's official portrait hangs on the wall outside of the Georgia governor's office, and his flag is clearly visible in the painting – so Perdue had to pass by it every time he entered or exited his office. Ha!

When I first sketched out the design for that flag I was motivated in part by the famous quote uttered by Sir Winston Churchill: "If we open a quarrel between the past and the present, we shall find we have lost the future." I place my faith in the hope that we will put our quarrels aside and move forward confidently. The demise of the Barnes flag wasn't an ending; its creation was the beginning of a more enlightened era.

Some day in the future Georgia will have a flag heralding the future; the Civil War and its terrible aftermath may finally, and thankfully, be forgotten. In fact, I've designed such a flag. It displays a stylized version of the red clay hills of Georgia and the date 1776, the year the state joined the Union. The flaggers will probably say the use of red is Communist. I don't know what I can do with this design, and I have a feeling no politician will touch it, not in the foreseeable future, at least.

Chapter 15

We Move to Rivers Road

And these few precious days I'll spend with you ...

— Kurt Weill, September Song

The year was 2000, and our search for a new house succeeded sooner than we expected as the new century dawned. I was driving down Rivers Road, a short but beautifully wooded street just a block off busy Peachtree, when I saw a For Sale sign in front of a large New England house painted in a pleasing shade of yellow and topped with a mansard roof.

The owner answered my knock at the door, and she took me through the house – four bedrooms with the master suite downstairs, a large living room, a dining room, a well-appointed kitchen, a family room, and four and a half baths. The front yard was lined with a forest of trees, and a creek ran though the property. The small backyard wasn't a problem, since Helen and I were empty nesters.

I thought I'd found our new home. Responding to my call, Helen drove over from her daughter Sophie's house, which was just around the corner. She put aside some misgivings after a tour. "What's the price?" she asked.

It was $400,000 — half what we were paid for the Oakdale Road house In Druid Hills. After exchanging nods, Helen and I told the owner we wanted to buy the house and asked when we could move in. "Next week." she said. We followed with, "It's a deal."

After we completed the home-buying transaction, a major problem came to light. The neighborhood sewer line ran under the house from one end to the other, and the sellers had failed to disclose this disturbing fact. Helen was so outraged she was ready to void the purchase.

Finding themselves subjected to some legal persuasion, the sellers consulted an engineer and agreed to reroute the sewer line. It could've been run underground at some extra cost, but to save a few bucks they snaked a large cast-iron pipe supported by concrete-block columns through the beautiful side yard.

To block the view of that aboveground abomination, we erected a tall wooden fence. This meant obtaining a permit from the city, which came with an order that made me grind my teeth: We had to stain (not paint) the fence. Not a word from the city about that big open-air sewer pipe, but our fence had to be stained! We planted fast-growing trees along the fence, but still had traded a hidden sewer pipe for a now not-so-pretty side yard.

For the six months it took to renovate the house, Helen and I had to camp out. After several weeks with her daughter Sophie and her family, we thanked them for taking care of us and moved to the Bennington, a mid-rise apartment on Peachtree Street and Lindbergh Drive. The rental unit had two bedrooms, a living/dining space, and an ample kitchen. Our view from the fourteenth floor was an ever-changing mural of downtown Atlanta as the sun moved across the arc of the sky and darkness brought out a kaleidoscope of twinkling lights.

Our stay at the Bennington was very pleasant. The rooms were comfortable, the staff attentive and friendly. It was also just a few blocks our new home, making it an ideal place to wait out the construction work. Except for minor changes and a coat of paint, I thought the house was ready. Wrong!

Helen envisioned some major changes, additions, and renovations, and I became her draftsman. Her first priority was expanding the dining room so our children, their spouses, and our grandchildren could all dine together. The wing on the right side of the house was extended to give Helen a dressing room, a large closet, and a bathroom off the master bedroom. The two small windows in the front of the living room were replaced with a bay window that would provide light, a view of our front-yard forest, and space for our piano. The kitchen was remodeled with new equipment, and a wet-bar linked the living room with the master bedroom. On the second floor, I added a drafting room as a workspace.

Our contractor was nicknamed Sawhorse. That horse didn't gallop – it didn't even trot. Many months went by before the remodeling was done. We gladly put Sawhorse out to pasture, moved into our yellow New England house, and began a new phase of our lives together.

Friends and "Friends"

Our next-door neighbor, Marshall "Skip" Beebe, had just come back to Atlanta from Hartford, Connecticut. Coincidentally, my Yale roommate, Edgar Cullman, had once retained him to manage his office park, part of the Cullman family's 6,000-acre tobacco farm in the Connecticut River Valley. Skip took over at a bad time. A recession was settling over Hartford with dire consequences for the city's major businesses and insurance companies, a prime source of office park tenants. His efforts to rent offices failed, so he and Edgar parted. Skip and I spoke briefly about the Cullman's tobacco farm in Connecticut but soon moved on to less painful subjects. I enjoyed his company and was saddened by his sudden death in 2011 at age 67.

Our whole neighborhood was full of "good people" who were polite when we passed them, kept beautiful yards, drove a BMW or Mercedes Benz and sent their children to elite private schools. Yale, Harvard, or Princeton stickers adorned many bumpers. The neighborhood was also a Christian enclave, with three large churches only a block away.

Soon after Helen and I moved in, we invited all the neighbors for a buffet under a tent. Some hundred of our new neighbors joined in. We soon came to the disappointing realization that our being in the neighborhood didn't assure a busy social life with the neighbors, like we had in Druid Hills. Many a night our street would be filled with shiny automobiles for a party somewhere nearby, but our invitations must have been lost in the mail.

Still, we developed ongoing friendships with some of the neighbors and stayed busy inviting our intelligent, fascinating, racially diverse, and some-times controversial friends over for lively dinner parties, whether new friends or old.

Helen had entertained on the stage, and she was no less an entertainer in our home; hardly was the classic tableware whisked away when more was set on white linen lit with candlelight. And on such a night in the mid-1990s, a once-in-a-dinnertime "event" was nigh. At one point the conversation turned to what is called Freaknik, a spring break festival frequented by students from historically black colleges. Some of the participants antagonized the community with behavior that's probably not so unusual in spring break havens such as Panama City Beach but were out of place and sometimes unsettling to city people. One of our guests, a lovely young black woman, was offended by the conversation and let it be known in no uncertain terms. Her scowling assertion "You are all racists!" put a damper on the rest of the evening and largely limited the conversation to "Please pass the beans." Our protestations that the race of the youngsters had nothing to do with the disgruntlement fell on deaf ears. Helen and I felt her comment was ironic, considering our life-long dedication to civil rights issues.

Perhaps on nights like this, it occurs to me, some of our neighbors may have wondered where *their* invitations were.

Family Near and Far

One advantage of the Rivers Road house was a real joy – the proximity of two of our daughters. Terri's house overlooked the neighborhood duck pond just across Peachtree; Sophie's house was a short walk away from ours. We had left Judy and Jill in Druid Hills, so it was especially nice to have Terri and Sophie to fill their places. We were also happy we could see Sophie's daughters Helen and Holly more often. Helen's only Atlanta cousin, Bill Lowenstein, lived with his wife Suzy in the nearby Park Place condominium, and once a month he came by and took Helen to lunch.

Alex Eisemann, Helen's brother, was a most welcome visitor when he traveled down from Westport, Connecticut. His optimism, smile, and energy took over our house and made it sparkle. When we visited Alex in Westport, we contended with two loud-barking dogs and an overweight cat – a cat that was allowed (even encouraged) to prowl on the kitchen counters where food was spread out, much to our disgust. Disgust would turn to acceptance when our Siamese cat Witty, the family member I describe below, took over our kitchen counters.

Another Alex in our lives is Helen's son. When a student at Duke University, Alex found a scrapbook filled with watercolor sketches done by Helen when she studied typing and shorthand. Her father had told her, "You want to be an actress, but actresses starve; you'd better have some back-up skills." So she enrolled in secretarial school. Studying shorthand put her to sleep, and to stay awake Helen drew about 80 fanciful critters inspired by the shorthand symbols. For some 50 years they lay dormant in her scrapbook, and at Helen's request, Alex sent the scrapbook to Atlanta.

When I saw the watercolors I was fascinated. "Helen," I said, "these are great; there's nothing like them. Let's have them made into stuffed toys. Every kid in the world will want a bunch." In due time, 6,000 made-in-China replicas of twelve of the plushies, which Helen had named Squinkles, arrived and were stored in our garage.

A little later we met a poet and author at a Yale event in New Haven, and Helen showed him pictures of the different characters we'd had manufactured. Amused and intrigued, he volunteered to write couplets for each individual character that would be printed on tags and attached to each toy.

Our marketing efforts didn't generate the torrent of orders I expected — it's been more of a trickle. Helen's daughter Jill sold several hundred to the children in her public school art program, and a local drugstore sold many of them at Christmas. The biggest disposal was the gift of 600 Squinkles to the Marines' Christmastime Toys for Tots drive. Two illustrated articles about Helen and the Squinkles were published, and I haven't given up. I still think Mr. Hi Hooter, with his orange hat pulled over his green face, can become the next Paddington Bear.

In the 1980s I became friends with a relative I never even knew I had. I received a note from Henry Clay (Hank) Moses, the freshman dean at Harvard. Hank's great-grandfather, also named Henry Clay Moses, was the brother of my maternal grandfather Judah Touro Moses. I don't know how he found me.

Moses was a practicing Protestant who was raised in Saudi Arabia. His father was employed with Aramco in that country and had deemed it wise to sever any connection with Judaism while living and working there. Hank matured with no knowledge of his Jewish roots, but once he learned of them he wanted to know more.

Before long Helen and I were invited to a meeting in Cambridge at the Harvard School of Design, and we called Moses to say we'd like to meet him. Hank and his wife invited us for dinner at their historic brick row house just off Harvard Square. As we discussed our ancestry that evening, Helen was pleasantly surprised to see how strong a resemblance Hank bore my first cousin Ed Wolff, another grandson of Judah Touro Moses.

A few years later Hank and his family moved to New York, where, from 1991 to 2009, he was headmaster of the prestigious Trinity School on Manhattan's Upper West Side. While looking through old family papers one day I came across a calling card addressed to my parents from Mrs. Henry Clay Moses I, and it included her New York address. Her house was in the same block as Trinity School! I sent the card to Hank, who told me he looked at the house where his great-grandmother lived every day on his way to Trinity. Hank died in 2008, a loss I feel deeply. Our unexpected friendship had become a valued part of my life.

A former family member I must include is Witty the cat. Helen missed her pets, so when a stray Siamese cat sat in our driveway one day, she fed it. My love of pets was limited to dogs. Cats bit, scratched and did their own thing – not my kind of "best friend." I said to Helen, "Feed this little beast if you must, but that is an outdoor cat. Don't bring him inside." A month later Witty (as in Kitty Witty, as Helen called him) was in the house, sleeping curled up on our bed and a fully licensed member of the family.

Siamese cats are known vocalists, filling their space with penetrating "yeows." Witty took cat talk to a new level. He had a three-word vocabulary: "owwttt" (out), uttered when he wanted to go outside; "ellloo" (hello), when he greeted us on his return; and "eeete" (eat), his demand to be fed. Helen's brother Alex was a non-believer when we told him about our loquacious cat. In a phone conversation he said, "Oh sure, and I suppose he's fluent in Siamese." After a week of staying with Witty and us, Alex changed his mind. "That damn cat does talk," he said as he bid us goodbye. "He's amazing!"

Rest, Recreation, Responsibility

The time had come, I knew, for me to give up my toys. The first to go was my Stearman biplane. As I wrote in the previous chapter, I hung it up when I could no longer clearly hear the instructions from the tower. Next to go was my 27-foot Erikson sloop, which I gave to charity. The last was the 1964 Lincoln Continental convertible, sold to raise money for the Atlanta Committee for International Visitors (AVIC.) No more toys – not even in the attic.

Helen, an avid reader, enjoyed the lively meetings of her book club and often went to lunch with friends – among them Evie Wolff, Barbara Kaye, Virginia Hein, Martha Heyman, and Roz Sandler. Eleanor Massell, perhaps Helen's closest friend, died several years ago, a death that left both Helen and me deeply saddened.

Helen continued acting in films and TV commercials. After her cameo in *Driving Miss Daisy,* as recounted in Chapter 20, she had a more substantial part in *The Price of Heaven* (1997), featuring Cecily Tyson. Two of her commercials are particularly unforgettable. One, for Georgia Railroad Bank & Trust, was a period piece shot in a train station in North Georgia with an old locomotive hissing steam across the platform. In one scene Helen hands a bright red bicycle down from the train as a Christmas present for her delighted grandson; in another she gives a check to her husband and admonishes him, "Now Henry, do be prudent."

More recently she starred in a commercial for the Georgia Lottery. The scene opens with Helen as a bank teller wearing a plain high-neck dress and her hair in a bun as she welcomes a handsome young man to her window. He hands her a huge check, having just won the lottery. Helen blinks at the check, says "Just a minute please," disappears behind a wall, and returns, now with flowing hair, a low-cut dress, heavy makeup, and a come-hither smile. "My name is Edna, but my friends call me Sparkles," she whispers. "And I have a hot tub." Many people who remember the commercial call Helen "Sparkles" when greeting her.

Helen is also a horticulturist with a mystical relationship to flora. Working with her for many years was Robert Barrow, who left the tree business to become a gardener. Twice a week he plants, waters, fertilizes, and performs all the other services required to keep Helen's garden beautiful. Helen regards Robert as much more than her gardener – he's her loyal friend.

Robert was with us on the sad day we put an end to our dear Witty's suffering. Our little companion's cult of admirers wanted to tell him goodbye, so we invited a dozen friends to our house for a wake. Robert said to Helen, "I've never been to anything like this before; how should I dress?" Helen said, "Neither have I. Wear what you like." Robert came in a dark blue three-piece suit. All the guests had some endearing story to tell about Witty. With laughter and tears, it was a happy-sad event.

Witty's ashes are buried in our backyard, under a sleeping ceramic cat. Nailed to a tree beside him is a plaque we brought from France – *Chat Gentil,* it reads. My late cousin Judith Alexander was one of Witty's great admirers. She commissioned a New York portraitist to paint Witty, and the painting of the intelligent, alert cat hangs in our study. Our second Witty, although greatly beloved, has never entirely taken Witty the First's place.

The dozen-plus years of the twenty-first century have gone well for us, in spite of a 2011 bout with pneumonia that laid Helen low for few months and the hit my finances took in the Great Recession. Thankfully, both Helen and my accounts recovered.

In 2006 Helen took the reins of a newly minted nonprofit, the Judith Alexander Foundation. Cousin Judith was a unique innovator in Atlanta's diverse art world. A gifted artist herself, she chose to direct her talents to furthering the careers of other artists, starting in the 1950s when she opened a gallery in the smaller of the two houses her father built on Peachtree Road, the one Hermi, Terri, Judy, and I had lived in for six years. Here she introduced to art lovers from across the Southeast the works of such artists as Franz Klein, Robert Motherwell, and Jackson Pollock.

In the late 1970s Judith opened the Alexander Gallery on East Paces Ferry Road in Buckhead, a showcase for self-taught, or naïve, artists from Georgia and the Southeast. Her prime discovery was the elderly black artist Nellie Mae Rowe, who lived in a small wooden house in the suburb of Vinings. When Judith first met her, Rowe crafted three-dimensional yard art and painted distinctive pictures of people, animals, birds, flowers, and trees in what she called her "playhouse." Judith supplied her with high-quality paper and implements, and Rowe's work blossomed. Her first exhibition, at the Alexander Gallery in 1978, was followed a year later by a one-woman show at the Parsons/Dreyfus Gallery in Manhattan.

Rowe died in 1982, but her art lives on. In 1998 she was given a one-woman show at the Museum of American Folk Art in New York City, and Atlanta's High Museum of Art maintains the Nellie Mae Rowe Room to exhibit her individualistic artworks.

In 1987 Judith took an apartment in the Flatiron District of Manhattan to be near her sister Rebecca (long afflicted by multiple sclerosis) and divided her time between New York and Atlanta. Not long after Becky's death in 2004, Judith died in her sleep. Her brother Henry went on to establish the Judith Alexander Foundation (JAF) and asked Helen to be its president – a job at which she excelled. Board meetings are held in our house on Rivers Road. Recipients of the foundation's donations include Artadia, a New York-based nonprofit that annually awards grants to seven artists in selected U. S. cities and connects the awardees to a national network of galleries, museums, and collectors. In 2009 the JAF helped make it possible for Atlanta to join Boston, Chicago, San Francisco, and Houston as the fifth Artadia city.

So, just as Nellie Mae Rowe's art was discovered and lives on thanks to my late cousin Judith, Judith's contribution to the arts lives on through the foundation that bears her name. I am also pleased that when Helen chose to pass the torch of the presidency of the Judith Alexander Foundation, it went to my daughter Judy.

Chapter 16

Some Final Thoughts

The shadows are lengthening for me. The twilight is here. My days of old have vanished ... Their memory is one of wondrous beauty ...

— Gen. Douglas McArthur

In spite of Tom Brokaw's assessment, my generation is not the "greatest" (Washington's was by far), but we certainly experienced the greatest changes since man invented the wheel. When I was born in 1918 much of what is now around us and taken for granted wasn't even imagined.

A great deal of scientific discovery was still lying fallow in unborn brains; inventors were improving on earlier inventions, World War II and many lesser engagements hadn't been fought or the future's terrible weapons conceived. The social revolutions — women's rights and the civil rights movement — were incubating. The world beneath the seas, space near and far, and other dimly seen realms of earth were unexplored by man or his robotic devices. Communications were confined to the telegraph and the radio. The money made by star athletes and entertainers and bankers was within reason. Obviously, the list could go on and on.

Today the innovations that ensued are as integral to our lives as the pot-bellied stove was to our ancestors. And all have had an impact on my life — some of them profoundly. Those I will cite here are not in order of importance; I don't know how to rank them because they dominated my thinking and my actions at different times.

Life Then and Now

Communication is a good place to begin. Sitting here on the desk is my cell phone. I hate the damn thing. After years of ownership I'm still an ignorant user. The phone's noisy ring demands immediate attention no matter what I'm doing – eating, talking, reading, attending a play or lecture (and being lectured if I forgot to turn off the sound.) I don't text with the phone, I don't listen to music on it, and I don't use it as a camera. I don't dare tax it and my intelligence with more demands.

Following close behind but bigger (so far) is the laptop computer, with its stupid illogical language. I've just given my *Encyclopedia Britannica* to a library. Who needs it, I'm told, when all you want to know is on the Web? Maybe so, but out of the thousand references there, the information I want eludes me. Computers demand obsession – we can't go out, we can't come in, we can't go to bed until we check our e-mails. When we want to send an e-mail, we have to lift the cat off the warm comfortable (for her) keyboard. To know someone's address, you need a lot more than a street number and a zip code –you need an e-mail address, a fax number, a home phone, a business phone number, a cell phone number, and a hash tag (not me!)

Around the time I was born, radio began to invade American homes. It didn't enter mine until my senior year in high school; Dad had thought it would interfere with my homework. I'm sure it would have, but I found many other distractions.

Television showed up at my father's house just after the end of World War II with a postcard-size screen, no color, and lots of "snow." Football games and the fascinating test pattern were the primary offerings in those early days. But what do we see today? News is telecast 24 hours daily – a stupefying repetition of murders, rapes, wrecks, child molestation, celebrations, suicide bombings, frauds, scams, financial disasters, malfeasance by executives, strikes, torture, diseases, obesity, and endless unintelligible commercials.

Yet TV does have something for me. I watch Atlanta Braves baseball when I ought to be working – and when I channel surf and intercept an interesting History Channel documentary, an Animal Planet show that intrigues me, or a well-remembered classic film, I'm hooked. I also delight in booing and hissing the political screamers such as Bill O'Reilly or Sean Hannity, and I occasionally take in a significant political speech or event. I rely on the *New York Times* to keep me informed.

I have become "hearing impaired," which is to me a useless euphemism for "deaf." In my ears are two hearing aids that cost $6,000 but garble sounds and make much of what I hear unintelligible. Only background noises come through loud and clear. I've yet to hear anything but "Here's your bill" at a restaurant, never the recitation of the night's specials.

Transportation has improved in some respects. In 1918 dirty non-air conditioned trains, pulled in jerky starts and stops by a loud coal-burning locomotive, hauled exhausted passenger between cities. Now electric or diesel-powered locomotives carry comfortable passenger cars and freight over the same steel rails, but it's still exhausting. My last trip was a disaster. The train swept around a curve as I was returning to my seat and hurled me to the floor. The result was a dislocated hip replacement and another operation.

As mentioned before in this book, Mark Twain (he's that good) said, "Everybody talks about the weather, but nobody does anything about it." Well, we can't yet control hurricanes, tornadoes, or blizzards (to hear the meteorologists talk on TV, they're working on it), but we can control the heat to an extent – we call it air-conditioning. The house I grew up in was built years before it came along. A small electric fan stirred the humid air around my bed as I sweated away the night. Work in a hot office was constantly interrupted by brow mopping. Although it's rarely recognized, the advent of air conditioning for our homes, businesses, and automobiles was the invention that made Atlanta (and the rest of the South) habitable year around and set the city on the path to becoming a powerful financial center. It enabled us to compete with northern cities.

At the beginning of the 1920s choices of automobiles were very limited. The Model T Ford (any color, just so it was black) was the most widely seen car making its noisy way through low-trafficked streets. Now, as we all know, unmanageable many-colored fleets powered by mighty engines creep along our highways and roads at the pace of an elderly walker. A rare open highway invites the restless driver, probably coerced by television commercials, to jam the pedal to the floor and hurl his four-wheeled weapon at terrifying speeds, weaving around frightened drivers and often ending in a heap of crumpled metal, smoke, and death.

Only fifteen years before my birth year the Wright Brothers struggled into the strong storm-generated wind at Kitty Hawk, North Carolina, with their wood-and-fabric plane pulled by a sputtering engine, and changed our world forever. World War I, with its fighters and bombers, accelerated the advance of the flying machine, but it was many years before "pilots of the purple twilight [dropped] down with costly bales," as prophesied in 1840 by Tennyson, and passengers in supersonic projectiles crossed the Atlantic in just three hours.

We are living longer (I am an example) but in spite of science, medicine, and skilled doctors and robotic surgeons, living forever escapes us. Some believe that with the exploitation of stem cells and a little luck (would it be good luck or bad?) we might do just that.

Taking Measure

Living longer can be a mixed blessing. We're around to enjoy our children, our grandchildren, and the pleasures of life. But the loss of mobility, the many diseases of aging, mounting drug costs, and the hours spent in doctor's offices and days whiled away in hospitals aren't so enjoyable.

The fascism, bigotry, anti-Semitism, and injustices rampant after World War I have survived my 94 years and show few signs of abating. It is remarkable that this nation has evolved from acceptance of lynching as "justice" for blacks to the election of an African-American as president, but racism still lives on.

As I look back, I'm less than satisfied with my accomplishments. I was a competent creative architect, but the goal to be a "form giver" who set a strong direction in design escaped me. I stuck a tentative toe in the waters of politics but was never a fighter in the dirty pit of elective office; still, a term or two as mayor of Atlanta would have been a real trophy. I did, however, advise mayors and legislators and help set Atlanta on a progressive road, and this I find gratifying.

Flying obsessed me, and I became a skilled pilot. I look back on my many hours in the air in both war and peace as a high point in my life. I have no regrets that I didn't have a career as an airline pilot, which I thought would bore me or scare me to death. Sometimes I do regret I wasn't an astronaut; I would like to be able to look up at the moon and say, "I've been there."

My most gratifying efforts were putting aside prejudice and hatred. I sought justice for blacks and spoke out against our terrible treatment of American Indians. I also came to terms with my feelings against the Japanese, who in my youth were our vicious enemy. Most profoundly, I worked hard to overcome my Deep South racial attitudes based on white superiority and the view of blacks as less than fully human.

Germans have turned away from their Nazi past and expressed deep remorse for the horrors of Nazism, and I'm able to forgive today's young Germans. But I cannot forgive the dwindling survivors of those terrible days. How could a highly civilized, educated, cultured people accept Adolf Hitler as their "god-like" leader? Perhaps given similar circumstances, any people could dip into the gloomy pit of man's inhumanity and become Nazi-like. It could happen here, I'm afraid, unless good men and women are forever watchful.

Several significant changes in my outlook have come to me as I accept the fact of my own mortality.

Man is, I am certain, an animal; no more, no less. We are at the top of the chain – more intelligent, more self-aware, more inquisitive – but still an animal. Compare our bodies with the mammals around us, our pets. With cats and dogs we share a similar skeletal frame, the same internal body organs, two ears, two eyes, and a mouth with a tongue and lined with teeth. What about tails? We have them, if only vestigially. Recently, I read that a cat's brains are very similar to those of humans. When as I watched our Siamese cat Witty live through his days, I knew this must be true.

As my relationship with animals evolved, eating them became difficult. I never hunted with a firearm or a bow and arrow; killing a defenseless creature for sport had no appeal to me. I hunted only for food, with my wallet as my weapon, buying slices of beef or lamb at the butcher's so I could disassociate them from the living beast. Hypocrisy was part of my diet. Today I can no longer pretend the meat in the glass counter wasn't once part of a cow or a lamb. I'm not yet a total vegetarian, but I'm well on my way to joining the herbivores.

Two drives we share with all living things is the desire (obsession) to survive and reproduce. Even the tiny flying insect avoids my slap. And there is inconvertible evidence all around us that they reproduce.

Man's curiosity is cited as evidence of our superiority. I believe our curiosity is a way of seeking survival. We look over the hill to see what danger is there, we go into space seeking a refuge if some day the earth is about to be destroyed. Dogs walk in circles around their nest in the wild to rid it of snakes, and they'll be on board if mankind takes off in a space ark as a massive meteor hurdles towards earth.

My most disturbing reassessment is my denial of the dogma of Judaism or any other man-conceived religion. I believe deeply that there is a powerful intelligent force (call it God, if you will) that created this mysterious universe governed by the laws revealed in all their intricacy by scientists dating back to Newton, Darwin, and Einstein. Surely that force isn't mindless, but I haven't accepted that it is a loving presence within all of us. I wish I had the faith the ball player has when he crosses himself and prays to his Lord to let him hit a homerun. Doesn't God, no matter which god, have more serious problems than the success of a home run hitter?

In spite of all my doubts, there is one steel cable that binds me to life — the love I share deeply with Helen and with my children and their children, their mother Hermi, Helen's children and grandchildren, our friends, and the memory of our departed families and friends. If love is a mystery, it's a mystery that makes me a believer that I'm here for a purpose.

At one time I saw glory in fighting. I'm still proud to be a Marine, but now I see war as the pit of human endeavor. While I still believe World War II had to be fought to save humanity, I think if wiser men had shaped the peace after the First World War there would have been no rise of Hitler or Mussolini. Tennyson (him again) predicted that at last peace would prevail. In *Locksley Hall* he wrote, "Till the war-drum throbb'd no longer, and the battle-flags were furl'd / In the Parliament of man, the Federation of the world."

The United Nations is the so-called Parliament of Man, but the war drums still throb and battle flags still fly over attacking armies. Albert Einstein, a strong advocate for world peace, was a pessimist about man. He said, "As long as there is man, there will be war." And as long as there will be wars, we had better have a strong and ready Semper Fidelis Marine Corps. At the same time, the drive toward violence must be contained or we will destroy all life and the earth itself.

Thank-Yous Past and Present

As I end this part of my memoir I want once more to recall the positive and joyous role Edgar Cullman, his mother, his father, his brothers Joe, Arthur, Louis, and his sister Nan had in my life since Yale (so fortunately for me) made us roommates some 75 years ago. His parents opened their home to me as if I were one of their own.

In every crisis in my life Edgar was there, and never more than in 1983, when he immediately flew to Atlanta after our car wreck. He brought order out of chaos and stayed with me during my operation so my children would feel comfortable going to Hermi's funeral. And there were many, many happy times when Hermi – and later, Helen and I – were their guests at the Connecticut farm. Never will I forget Edgar, after flying with Louise through violent weather, standing with me as best man when Helen and I joined our lives. The lines in Yale's song "Bright College Years" – "But time and change cannot avail to break the friendships formed at Yale" – have a living reality as they apply to Edgar and to me. Thank you "Dear Old Yale"! Edgar died in mid-2012, and words cannot express how much I miss him.

As a final note, I am filled with satisfaction that Hermi's Bridge, which spans the Chattahoochee River near Vinings, was restored after a ten-year campaign for its repair. I am deeply grateful to the Path Foundation and to Cobb County Commission Chairman Sam Olens, the force behind this project – a most fitting memorial to my late wife's efforts to bridge the troubled waters of racial intolerance.

I am also gratified that Helen Eisemann Alexander's many accomplishments and joie-de-vivre are celebrated by the display of beautiful Moulthrop bowl I donated to the Woodruff Arts Center in her honor.

I couldn't conclude this book without expressing my great debt to those who helped put it together. Randy Southerland has for six years been my advisor, critic, and editor. His support kept me struggling to keep on when, without it, I would have quit long ago. Thanks Randy! I'm also grateful to Fred DuBose, a board member of the Judith Alexander Foundation and formerly the Editorial Director of Reader's Digest Illustrated Reference Books. Fred cast his seasoned eye over the manuscript, organized it, put an index together (no small task!) and added finishing touches and details. I thank my daughter Judith Alexander Augustine, who worked closely with Fred, oversaw and coordinated the publishing of the book and designed the covers. My granddaughter Rachael Millkey and her dear friend Michael Vadino contributed a cover design idea that I thought very handsome which is represented on the title page of *Part 2, The War Years*.

Finally, I offer a warm thank-you to those folks who helped refresh my memory of various details: Rebecca Hatcher, Barbara Kaye, Tiffany Merchant, and Harry West.

I may be advanced in age, but the beautiful words of Robert Frost's *Stopping by the Woods on a Snowy Evening* still capture the emotion I feel profoundly as I come to the end of this memoir:

The woods are lovely dark and deep.
But I have promises to keep,
And miles to go before I sleep,
And miles to go before I sleep.

Cecil Alexander
with Randy Southerland

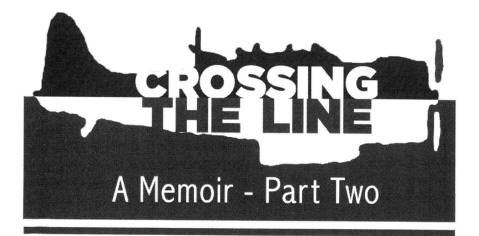

CROSSING
THE LINE

A Memoir - Part Two

The War Years
1941- 1945

Dedication

To my squadron mates, the members of the Ace of Spades Marine Scout Bomber Squadron 231 (VMSB-231) who shared in the adventure, especially Skipper Elmer Glidden and Executive Officer Homer Cook.

Acknowledgements

I am forever grateful to my wonderful wife of 27 years, Helen, who has encouraged me every step of the way in the writing of this memoir. When things were darkest for me, she brought me back to life.

I am indeed a very lucky man to have spent so many happy years with two outstandingly beautiful, bright, loving and supportive women – two women, Helen and Hermi, who were the best of friends – by my side, in my life.

My children and their spouses, my grandchildren and even my great-grandchildren (although they couldn't know it) have provided valuable perspective and inspiration throughout my adult life. My "bonus kids" – Helen's children, their spouses, and grandchildren – have been very supportive as well.

I am very appreciative of Randy Southerland, Fred DuBose and my daughter Judith Augustine for the roles they played in the creation of this book.

More thorough acknowledgements are in *Crossing the Line, The Awakening of a Good Ol' Boy*, Part One.

Table of Contents

Foreword

Days of Risk and Reward

In the opening pages of this second part of *Crossing the Line,* I recall that as a boy I was obsessed with model airplanes and becoming an ace pilot some day. I never could have dreamed that fresh out of college I would be stationed in the Pacific as third in command of the famous Ace of Spades Marine Air Corps squadron.

In the chapters that follow I recount how I learned to fly lumbering seaplanes, the sleek SBD (Scout Bomber Douglas), F4U Corsair fighters, and other craft. From the Civilian Pilot Training Program (CPTP) in New York State and Pennsylvania to instruction for flying DC-3s in Texas to carrier-landing training in Hawaii, I most definitely earned my wings. And those wings would be put to use first in California, then at Ewa Marine Air Corps Station near Pearl Harbor, and finally in the Marshall Islands, where I flew 62 dive-bombing missions and more than a hundred search missions over Japanese-occupied islands.

I also trace my personal life during the war years, from California to the Marshall Islands to North Carolina and Memphis, with the rare bad egg and "a few good men," and one wonderful woman: my sweetheart, then wife, Hermi Weil.

Chapter 6 is devoted to our post-war landing in New York and then in my home town of Atlanta, while the final chapter recounts a trip with Hermi to the Marshall Islands some four decades after I served there – a chance for Hermi and me to contemplate my Pacific War days and their place in my roller coaster of a life.

Chapter 17

Soaring with Eagles, Preparing for War

For I dipp'd into the future
Far as human eye could see
Saw a Vision of the world
All the wonder that would be.
Saw the heavens filled with commerce
Argosies of magic sails
Pilots of the purple twilight
Dropping down with costly bales.

—Alfred Lord Tennyson, Locksley Hall

It is early fall of 1942. I am in the right-hand copilot's seat of a Douglas DC-3, the aircraft that made air travel available to the nation and to the world. We are flying over Atlanta, directly on course to intersect Atkins Park, the small neighborhood where I spent my early years.

I remember it well. I looked over at the captain, Jimmy Gott. He was commanding this Penn Central Airlines DC-3, which had been converted from passenger to cargo configuration for the duration of World War II.

"Captain Gott," I asked, "can I fly this thing? We're on course to fly over my old Atlanta house where my father lives. I'd like to see if I could find it and signal my dad."

"You've got this bucket of bolts," Gott said as he lifted his hands off the yoke and gestured for me to take over. Looking down through a light haze, I located our position and we were directly on course to St. Charles Place. I pushed the yoke forward and eased the plane down to a thousand feet as we approached my house, clearly visible in the amber glow from the streetlights. I sawed the throttles back and forth and the engines alternately purred and roared. The front porch light of my house flicked on just before we passed over.

The next day I called my father from Miami, where Gott and I had spent the night. "Hi Dad," I said. "We flew directly over 1111 St. Charles Place last night about 9:30. I gunned the engines to signal you as we approached. The front light came on. Did you hear us? Did you see us?"

"Well what do you know," he answered. "I heard a plane approaching, flipped on the front light, and rushed out on the front lawn. I knew it had to be you! Sure enough, this large plane came very low over our house with the engines. I waved with both arms, watched it fly away, and then went back inside to be greeted by Snuff's loud barks. He convinced me that must be you up there, and it was!"

So what alerted my father? Do I have to revise my nonbelief in ESP? Or was it just coincidence and an alert, proud father standing there on the lawn? How about my Scottie's barks?

Our flight down to Miami from Atlanta with an empty plane was routine except for unexpected, one self-induced event. The plane was purring along. Its muted roar was very conducive to sleep. I thought Captain Gott had taken over the controls and he thought I was still flying. We both went to sleep. With a start, we woke up simultaneously. Penn Central Airlines had no autopilots in its planes (too expensive). Without guidance, our DC-3 went into a sharp, twisting climb. It was almost on its back when we became alert. Recovery was easy, and fortunately there were no passengers demanding an explanation for our unorthodox maneuver. I think it was at that point that I decided flying for one of the commercial airlines wasn't a promising career. Being either scared to death or bored to death didn't appeal to me as a lifetime occupation.

Our adrenaline dropped to normal after a few minutes and Gott said, "OK, I've got it. You can go back to sleep."

Some time later, we approached the Miami airfield. Gott called the tower operator to announce our arrival and ask for permission to land. The operator was a woman. This annoyed my captain, who was used to man-to-man communication. He thought a female couldn't possibly be capable of directing air traffic at a major airport. To suggest his annoyance, he followed all his communications with, "Ma'am." "Yes Ma'am. You say we're clear to land? Is that right, Ma'am?" This patronizing approach didn't please our lady operator. Under her breath, thinking no one could hear, she hissed in a whisper, her lips away from the microphone, "Bastard!" The expletive came to our earphones loud and clear. Jimmy burst out laughing and said in his microphone, "Thanks, Ma'am. You have my number." The operator laughed too, cleared us to land, and directed us to a parking area. Thoroughly worn out, we took a taxi to a downtown hotel and were soon asleep, this time flat on our backs in bed, not climbing into thin air.

Why I Learned to Fly

How did I come to be sitting at the controls of a DC-3 in that night sky over Atlanta? It was the realization of a boy's dreams; of a kid who didn't just admire, but who wanted to BE Charles Lindbergh; a boy who built balsa wood and Japanese tissue paper models of the warplanes of the Great War; a boy for whom flying became a life long obsession; who made the soaring stick-built, rubber band-powered models of Lindbergh's *Spirit of St. Louis*.

Learning to fly was also an order from Bob Jacobs. For the summer of 1940 he was my boss at his firm of Kahn & Jacobs Architects in New York City. "Cecil, there's a war coming," he said, "and I want you to have the skills to save this country and particularly to save my ass, which I hold most dear."

"Yes?" I asked.

"President Roosevelt has set up what he calls the Civilian Pilot Training Program and he wants a large backlog of pilots for the war he knows is coming. There's a CPTP program out at Roosevelt Field on Long Island. I'll give you all the time off you need to take the course."

"Oh, I've always wanted to fly," I said, so I'll look into it for both of us, not just to save your rear end."

That afternoon I drove my 1940 Buick Special convertible (which cost $1,100 new) with the top down, of course, out to Long Island for an interview with the Dervend Flying School at Roosevelt Field. I found the owner, Zeke Dervend, at a broken desk in a dilapidated wooden hangar on the edge of the dusty field.

"Sure," Dervend said in his heavily Austrian accent, "Just sign here. You're in." Dervend had flown against the allies in World War I but wanted to be with a winner this time.

For the rest of the long, hot summer, I struggled out of bed at the Yale Club in Manhattan at 5:30 am, sometimes after a very late date had left me with only a couple of hours of sleep, and drove out to Roosevelt Field to learn to fly. After an hour or so in the air, I drove back to Kahn & Jacobs and worked until 5:00. I then drove back to the field for more flying and finally back to the Club.

Shortly after my course began, the Civilian Pilot Training Program was thrown off Roosevelt Field for being a hazard for the regular air traffic. After a string of Austrian expletives, Zeke Dervend went searching for an alternative field. Not far from Roosevelt he found a vacant cow pasture where he relocated his operations. Dangerous high-tension lines bordered one end of the pasture.

I was sorry to leave historic Roosevelt Field. It was from there, on a murky morning in 1927, that Lindbergh had taken off for Paris. The first night I slept at Roosevelt Field, I was in the room where Charles Lindbergh had tried desperately (but unsuccessfully) to catch a nap before his flight. He was without sleep for 24 hours before he took off, and he battled desperately to stay awake for another 33 hours in his long flight across the Atlantic.

To express our annoyance with our removal from Roosevelt Field, we named the new field "Wendell Willkie International." Willkie was the charismatic Republican running against Franklin D. Roosevelt, who was seeking his much-disputed third term as president.

Clearing the hay from a pasture that was soon to be an airfield, was both a story and a photo opportunity for a local Long Island newspaper. I still have the three-column article with a shot of me pitching hay into a truck under instructions from the photographer, who disapproved of the measly portion of hay I put on the fork. Never have I pitched hay since that day 70 years ago; nor have I wanted or needed to.

Throughout that hot summer I went aloft in a yellow Piper Cub with my Lithuanian instructor, Paul Saltanis. (To add a tragic footnote, Saltanis, later a pilot for Eastern Airlines, was killed when his plane crashed into the Potomac River after take-off from Washington National Airport.) He was a good instructor, although at times I had trouble understanding Saltanis's version of English. Some of this cleared up when I realized that his "f" sounds became "p" sounds. For example, "focus" became "pocus," as in "Pocus your nose on the horizon."

The Piper was a very light, fragile-looking, underpowered trainer. It was little more than a kite with a sewing machine-powered engine and was easily thrown around by wayward air currents. Still, despite its unimpressive looks, it did the job not only for me but also for the thousands of pilots trained in it, many of whom became military pilots later.

My solo was a tense and exciting circuit of the field. The vacant front seat was very, very empty. Stretched out in a lounge chair, Saltanis was at ease on the ground. Like every pilot on his solo, I heard my instructor's disembodied voice speaking to my inner ear.

From the moment I taxied out to take off, I heard, "OK, throttle all the way forward. Lift off. Ease back on the throttle. Level off. Look out for the plane at one o'clock. OK, downwind at 500. Slow, slow, pull the nose up – up, level your wings! OK, you're down. Whew! Now do it again."

This came from Saltanis, who had walked to the plane after I landed. He reached in, shook my hand, and sent me up again. One more time his voice took me around in a successful circuit. Now I thought myself a seasoned aviator with ten hours aloft; all of 15 minutes or so alone – solo. I could not have guessed how much more I would have to learn.

I remember a couple of things from that summer. After I soloed, I wrote to my Dad and told him I was learning to fly. I hoped that if he knew I was competent to solo, he wouldn't worry.

He reacted with two displays of support. First, he flew to Montgomery to visit my sister. It was his first flight. (We later compared our tense feelings before our "firsts." Both of us wondered, "Why am I doing this?") He then took a train to New York, out to Willkie Field, to watch me fly for the rest of the summer. I found a room for him at a local hotel.

At first he told me he thought the little Piper Cubs looked like fragile toys. After many times watching these unlikely flying machines carry students aloft and land them safely, he came to completely respect the Cubs.

At the end of August I passed my final check ride and was awarded my private pilot's license. I recently showed my 1940 license to a Delta pilot.

Several times, he looked curiously back and forth from my worn face to the worn license. "Hey," he said with a grin, "which one of the Wright Brothers checked you out?"

In a rush of pride for my accomplishment, my father gave me a Lindbergh Longine Hour Angle wristwatch. Two years later, during World War II, I took it overseas, along with four other wristwatches. The watch and the compass in the Lindbergh Longine would be vital instruments for over-water navigation.

In the fall of 1941 I entered the graduate architectural program at MIT, and the school-related CPTP was operating out of Logan Airport, still the major airport for Boston. The plane used for earning a commercial license had an open cockpit. Duncan McDougal, my instructor, was a taciturn, humorless, demanding bastard of Scottish extraction. I was flying every morning, usually after working into the morning hours at my MIT drafting board. After four or five hours of restless sleep, I would get up at 5:30 am. All my reflexes had evaporated, and what I had done easily at Roosevelt Field was now nearly impossible.

Boston's Logan Field juts out into the bay, and at the edge of the field was a sharp 15-foot drop to the water. A strong downdraft struck intermittently just before the plane approached the vertical bank at the runway's end. In my nearly comatose state, I often failed to anticipate this downdraft and come in high.

I failed once too often, and it took a burst of the engine to get the plane up to field level.

"Alexander, before you leave, come and see me at my office," said McDougal. I knew it would be bad news. "Alexander," he said, "you're not going to make it. I'm washing you out of the program. Good luck with your architecture. You'll never make an air pilot."

There was no use pleading exhaustion or offering any other valid excuse. "OK," I said, "so long and thanks," then walked out. If he'd worn a kilt, as should a proper Scot named Duncan McDougal, I would have pulled it over his head and kicked him front and center.

Several weeks later I heard that Harvard also had a CPTP course and it was open to MIT students. I drove down to Squantum, Massachusetts, where Harvard was operating its training program. I approached the senior instructor. When he heard I'd been washed out at MIT, he said, "Forget it. I'll take you up and see whether you can fly." So, on a typical cold, gray, overcast winter day in Boston, we took off.

The dirt field was adjacent to the Navy's field in an area close to the present-day location of President John F. Kennedy's library. The Navy tried to stop Harvard from using the bordering field, which they thought interfered with their flying. To make the point, they drove vertical steel rods across the field. The next day, all the rods were flush with the ground. The Harvard trainees had been busy driving the stakes into the ground during the night. The Navy surrendered. Navy could beat Harvard in football, but not in stake-driving.

From the hours spent in a similar plane at Logan, I felt more or less at home in the Waco UPF-7, a biplane often used as a training plane in the 1940s. I had the controls at takeoff and climbed into the freezing air to 5,000 feet. "OK," the instructor said, "let's see what you can do with this old crate." At that point, I had no training in aerobatics, except for entering and recovering from a tailspin. However, while sitting at the controls of a plane in the hangar I had gone through the motions (and memorized) a flight manual's instructions for maneuvering a loop and a slow roll.

"So," I thought, "what's to lose?" I put the nose down to pick up speed. With the throttle wide open, I pulled the stick back, putting the plane in a vertical climb and then farther back until the plane was on its back at the top of the loop. The biplane went over the top and down. The engine, now idling as I pulled back the throttle, came out of the dive and closed the loop. It was a perfect maneuver.

The instructor in the front cockpit turned his head around. Grinning, he yelled, "Hey! Nothing wrong with that. Who taught you?"

"Nobody," I said. "That was my first loop. I read how to do it in a flight manual."

"All right," he said as he laughed above the engine noise, "show me something else you read about in the manual."

So I tried a slow roll, a much more difficult maneuver than a loop. It was very sloppy, but I made it around 360 degrees without falling out of it. From the instructor, I got a thumbs-up and a grin. "Let's go down!" he shouted. I put that Waco in a tight spiral, lost 4,000 feet in a hurry, circled the field, cut the engine, and glided into a passable landing.

"You're in the program," my new friend said. "Whoever it was that washed you out is a piss-poor instructor."

A Setback Set Right

My triumph was short-lived. The Civil Aeronautics Administration (CAA, now the FAA) found out I was starting over after having been washed out.

311

That bureaucracy searched its manual and decreed that I couldn't continue. I was through forever with Civilian Pilot Training Program.

My father was outraged. He wrote to our congressman, Bob Ramspeck, and asked him to intervene. Ramspeck tried, but to no avail.

Two years later Dad sent the congressman a copy of my commission, which designated me a Marine second lieutenant and a qualified naval aviator. He pointed out what fools the CAA were to have kicked me out. But he didn't stop there. Over the years my father continued to send the congressman clippings about my combat in the Pacific, my medals, promotions, and my promotions from operations officer to executive officer to squadron commander. I felt sorry for Ramspeck because he did try to help and should have been spared the flood of mail.

Dad often said, "If those ignorant bureaucrats had had their way, think what a great pilot our Marines would have lost." He stopped short of saying that we might well have lost the war without me, but I'm sure he thought it.

A year or so later, after I had won my Navy wings, I checked into American Airline's training program at Fort Worth, Texas. Its purpose was to instruct Navy and Marine pilots to fly DC-3s. There, in the line with me, was my Harvard CPTP instructor. We were delighted to see each other. My Navy wings vindicated his evaluation of my flying ability.

We were assigned rooms in the long wooden Bachelor Officer's Quarters (BOQ). Every night, my Harvard friend would stop by my room to urge me to join him in his quest for willing and able "babes." Since I was unofficially engaged to my future wife, I turned him down. I relented one evening, however, when he really urged me to come. "OK," I said. "What the hell. Let's go."

We found our "babes" in a bar. In our cars, we went our separate ways. My date and I were busily engaged in testing each other's libidos when we arrived at a point of "go or no go."

"Clara," I said, "I don't want to get you pregnant and I don't have a rubber, so we'd better stop now." She glared at me with fire in her eyes. In one swift move she swung the car door open and leaped out. With her spiked heels clacking down the concrete sidewalk, she stalked away. I couldn't blame her. Being brushed off by a sorry second lieutenant was more than she could take.

When I was at MIT, a couple invited me to come to New York for dinner one Saturday. At the table with us was a Jewish couple, just escaped from Nazi Germany; they somehow had been granted admission to the United States. The husband was fluent in English. He told, in all its horror, the story of what was really happening to the Jews in Germany, Poland, and Austria. It was a life-changing experience for me. I lost all interest in architecture. I wanted to fight the Nazis *now*, not wait for the U.S. to enter the war.

That late spring, on my way home from MIT, I went back to the Dervend Flying School. I told Zeke about what had happened to me at MIT and at Harvard. He growled at me and said, "If you were having trouble at MIT, why didn't you come here so we could have straightened you out?"

"Well," I said, "I was in school; I couldn't take the time, but how about seeing if I can qualify for a commercial license now?"

He took me up and checked me out. "You are ready to go," he said, and sent me up with a CAA check pilot. I flew through all the maneuvers without a hitch. Now I was a qualified commercial pilot.

The next day I went to the Marine Air Terminal at New York's LaGuardia Field. There, where the Pan Am Clippers docked, was the recruiting office of the Royal Canadian Air Force. Four RCAF flying officers greeted me. When I told them that I had an A.B. from Yale, one year at MIT, and held a commercial pilot's license, they jumped out of their seats. One of them shoved an enlistment paper and a pen at me. "Here," he said. "Sign here!" I drew back and said I needed to think it over. Then one of the pilots stood in front of the door with his arms spread wide. "You're not leaving until you sign up," he said.

"Oh yes," I said. "I'm going to check out the U.S. Navy first. I'm not signing now, but I may be back. Come on. Let me out of here."

The door blocker slowly stepped aside, shook my hand, and said, "We hope you'll come back. We need you."

I've often wondered what my fate would have been if I had joined the RCAF. The legendary Battle of Britain, where outnumbered RAF pilots flying Spitfires and Hurricanes turned back the German bombers, had saved England. Their great historical contribution was immortalized by the words of Winston Churchill who said, "Never in the history of human combat was so much owed by so many to so few." Still, there would be many more years of aerial fighting, but my guess is that I wouldn't have made it into combat. Rather, I probably would have spent the war ferrying planes from Canada to the British Isles.

As soon as I reached Atlanta I went to the Navy and the Air Corps recruiting offices. I'm not sure why I decided on the Navy. Maybe their "Wings of Gold" had more glamour than the "Silver Wings of the Air Corps." More likely it was my distant cousin Stanford's influence.

Captain Stanford Moses, USN, was one of the first Navy pilots. In the early 1920s, the terms of the Naval forces' agreement among the United States, Great Britain, and Japan actually required that the U.S. scrap some of our major ships. This wanton scrapping included the cruiser that Capt. Moses commanded. When his big ship was sunk, he decided that aviation was his future. At the advanced age of 50 he took flight training at the Navy's Pensacola Air Station and never looked back.

Moses commanded the Navy's first flight to Hawaii from California. He also served aboard the Navy's dirigible, the *Shenandoah*. Fortunately, when this mammoth airship broke up in a line squall and crashed, he wasn't on board.

The few Jewish officers in the Navy were subject to discrimination. As a young ensign, Moses had run a launch aground in a fog. When he came up for promotion to admiral, this trivial incident was used to deny him the rank, while Protestant officers with similar lapses were promoted.

Captain Moses was a hero to me. Telling him what censorship would allow of my experiences, I periodically wrote to him during the war. I'm sure he played a major role in my decision to become a naval aviator.

Cmdr. Nordhouse, who was in charge of recruiting for naval aviation in Atlanta, gave me an enthusiastic welcome. It almost matched the welcome I had from the RCAF back in New York, but without any threats. This time I said yes.

A physical examination was required. When the flight surgeon looked at my feet, he drew back in mock horror. "My God," he said, "they're as flat as a carrier deck. You'd never make it in the infantry, but I don't suppose you need arches to push rudder pedals."

The second near miss was my left arm, which I had crushed at the age of five; two operations left me with a crooked arm with a restricted range. The flight surgeon once again bent the rules, this time accepting a deformity. The Navy was desperate for pilots, particularly those rare birds who had both a commercial license and a college degree.

Ready for Takeoff

The three dimensions that encompass flight are from an alien world. Human beings are flatlanders. Even scaling Mount Everest doesn't separate mankind from the earth, which we're held fast to by gravity. We're amazed at the distance Michael Jordan can jump, but he quickly returns to earth (he couldn't hit a curve ball, either, by the way).

Learning to fly and be comfortable in an airplane starts with learning to be at ease with moving in the air's three dimensions. It requires overcoming all of our natural instincts. It is an artificial adjustment to a dangerous environment. Only many long hours of flying can overcome the rational fear of being in the air. When I reported for Navy service at Atlanta's Naval Air Station with CPTP flight time under my belt, I was already on my way to being at ease in the air. I also knew the fundamentals of flight – taking off, climbing, turning, letting down, landing, and being constantly prepared for an emergency. What I didn't know was the "Navy Way," which required absolute precision. If the instructor said, "Climb to 3,000 feet," he meant exactly 3,000, not 3,005. If he said, "Fly a course of 15 degrees," he meant 15, not 14 or 16.

Landing procedure was different from my past training as well. The Navy wanted all of its pilots to know the requirements for carrier landing. The approved procedure was to fly downwind, parallel to the runway, at 500 feet or more. When the plane was exactly opposite to the end of the runway, the pilot cut the engine and entered a 180-degree descending half-circle to the end of the runway. The plane had to be absolutely through flying when it touched down, and this required gradually pulling the stick back while the plane was a few feet over the runway until the plane stalled, lost its lift, quit flying, and the tail wheel hit the runway. The grounding of the two front wheels followed seconds later.

The front wheels on our trainer were very close together, making the plane unstable on the ground. The long lower wing could easily scrape the runway and force the plane into a ground loop, swinging the plane around in a tight, fast circle. A long row of those yellow biplane trainers was lined up on the ramp. For my first flight on that bright, early fall day in 1941, a chart indicated my plane assignment. The heavy parachute, hanging from my shoulders, banged against the backs of my knees, turning my walk into a clumsy waddle as I went toward my plane. My instructor, Lt. William Wolcott, a Marine and a graduate of the University of Virginia, was waiting for me. I saluted him, shook his hand, and climbed into the rear cockpit. Standing on the wing beside me, he asked, "Have you ever flown a plane before?"

I said, "Yes. I have my commercial pilot's license."

"Good," he said with a grin, "we can have some fun."

With Wolcott at the controls, we took off and headed west. Dropping down to about 10 feet, we were over the muddy water of the Chattahoochee

River. Wolcott opened the throttle wide, and the plane banked and turned on the river's twisting, three-lined path. Above a road was an old steel bridge supported by 15-foot-high trusses – and we headed directly toward it. Suddenly, the engine cut out and we were on a collision course.

My legs were pummeled as Wolcott yanked his stick back, which was synchronized with mine. This sent the plane soaring just over the bridge. We headed for a landing in a plowed field but didn't land. My instructor pushed the throttle forward and we climbed back to a reasonable altitude.

A small mirror giving Wolcott a view of my face was mounted on a wing strut. Its purpose was to show the instructor the student's reactions. Yes, the near-collision with the bridge turned out to be a trick (one I thought was great). If a student's face was twisted in terror, the instructor made a mental note that the candidate probably wouldn't make it through the flight course.

A similar test involved Stone Mountain, just east of Atlanta – an ancient outcropping of granite some 600 feet high. But before I describe the aerial training test, I'll expound briefly on Stone Mountain's history.

On one face of the mountain, a memorial to the Confederacy had been carved. The original sculptor was Gutzon Borglum, the very talented artist who later carved the four presidents at Mt. Rushmore. After a fight with the Daughters of the Confederacy, who proposed the idea for the carving in 1909, Borglum was fired. He broke up his plaster models and left, and the faces of Lee and Jackson remained his only legacy.

Subsequent sculptors weren't nearly as talented as Borglum. These sculptors destroyed his work, and heads of the South's two great generals lie in broken shards at the base of the mountain. My lasting regret is that the mountain was broken into at all. It is a beautiful work of nature, and the memorial should have been put at its base. One unfortunate legacy of Stone Mountain is that it lured hooded Ku Klux Klansmen, who burned huge fiery crosses on its summit.

Thankfully, the history of the mountain wasn't in an instructor's mind as he flew the biplane directly at the carved heads of Generals Lee and Jackson. At the last second, he would turn the plane on its side, jerk back the control stick, and quickly turn the plane parallel to the mountain. This maneuver almost rolled the plane's wheels on General Lee's granite face. If the student hadn't ducked down in the cockpit by then, the assumption was that he wasn't frightened and would probably be good Navy material.

Another aptitude test was the student's reaction to a sharp-banked turn. If he leaned into the turn the way he would on a bicycle, he was OK. If he leaned away, he would have trouble flying

Occupying my days were flying, ground school, and close order drill, where I lugged a heavy old 1903 Springfield rifle. A major effort in the training was preparing a student to land a plane if the engine quit. Over and over, Wolcott would yank back the throttle without warning. This would shut the engine down and make me responsible for finding a field where I could land.

We never actually landed, but I was expected to approach the field I had chosen. I then had to glide down to it a few feet above the ground. When he was certain I could land, Wolcott would open the throttle and we would climb away from the field.

One day, after I had one cut run after another, I decided to turn the tables. We were flying at about a thousand feet, and I was at the controls. Without warning, I cut the engine. Wolcott looked back at me. Grinning broadly, I held my hands high over my head. Then I tapped my helmet and pointed to him as I mouthed, "It's all yours!" He grinned and took over the idling plane. He picked a field surrounded by tall pine trees.

With only a few feet of clearance, we approached the field and headed straight at two pines. He then opened the throttle wide. At the last minute he pulled back sharply on the control column and we climbed up through the limbs of the pines. The noise of the limbs hitting the wings' taut skin was very unsettling. In fact, it was almost a disaster. We leveled off at about 2,000 feet. The instructor could talk one-way to the student through a tube – the Gosport tube, attached to the earphones worn by students.

"Hey," Wolcott yelled into the Gosport tube. "Look at our left wing! There's a limb caught in the wires! I gotta get that out of there before we go home. You fly it, and I'll get out on the wing and get it loose."

I was flattered that he trusted me to fly while he wing-walked, but I was also apprehensive. Suppose he fell off? What would I say when I landed, even if his chute functioned and he managed to land safely?

All went well. He pulled the limb loose and let it slip off the wing. After he settled back in the cockpit, he called me again.

"Hell, we can't go home yet. There's a hunk of pine trees tangled in the landing gear. Do you know any out-of-the-way small field that doesn't have tower control where we could land and remove that tree?"

I nodded yes, patted my helmet, and took over. There was a small field I had passed many times on my way to the Atlanta airport, and I circled it once. Then Wolcott took over to land. As we approached he said, "I hope the landing gear doesn't collapse." We made a short, safe landing on the dusty field. Wolcott taxied off to one side of the landing area and cut the engine. We both got out. From out of nowhere, five or six young women suddenly appeared and ran in our direction. Several of them had cameras. So, while I worked to free the landing gear, Wolcott posed for the photographers. With his chin held high and his eyes on the far horizon, he had the look of an eagle. Wolcott was every inch the heroic aviator, while I, assigned to the hot, dirty work of getting the pine limbs out of the wheels and landing gear struts, was every inch the lowly Seaman Second Class.

When I finished, Wolcott graciously saluted his new admirers. We climbed back into the cockpits and took off for the base. As soon as we taxied to the line and stopped the engine, Wolcott quickly filled out the flight report with no mention of pine trees. He then walked swiftly away.

I was left to tidy things up. Inspecting it carefully, the mechanic in charge of the plane walked slowly around it. Stopping abruptly in front of the left wing, he said, "What the hell is all that green stuff smeared on the left wing's leading edge? Where have you guys been? What the hell did you do?"

I lied. "That was on there when we took off, wasn't it? We just had a normal flight."

"Yeah," he said. "I don't think so. I think you flew through a tree. Help me wash it off and I'll forget it."

December 7, 1941

As the weeks passed, we all became convinced we were going to war with Japan. Each of us chose a date for the start and put money in a pool to be paid to the winner. I don't remember which date I picked. I do know I didn't win.

I was invited for lunch with a date to the Neely Farm, and it was a Sunday like all the rest. The farm was the home of Frank Neely, who had married Rae Schlessinger, my cousin. Frank was CEO of Rich's, Atlanta's leading department store, and later served on the Atomic Energy Commission. He was a part of every positive development in Atlanta. His farm was spread along the Chattahoochee River, and dairy cattle peacefully chewed their cud while waiting to be milked and artificially inseminated. Rich's Tearoom was a ready purchaser of Neely Farms milk, and Neely was also trying to convince Georgia's farmers that artificial insemination was a quick way to develop outstanding herds.

Lunch was over. The Neelys excused themselves for a nap. My date (nicknamed Nertz) and I were lounging on a sofa in the middle of the very spacious living room. She was widely known for doing headstands, with her skirt dropping to the floor. She was demonstrating this to my admiring eyes when Frank Neely raced into the living room. "Cecil," he said, "you'd better listen to a report on the radio."

I followed him into the bedroom where the radio was playing. It was Sunday, December 7th, 1941, and the excited announcer was reporting the Japanese attack on Pearl Harbor. President Roosevelt later proclaimed it was "a day that would live in infamy." My reaction was one of deep relief. There would be no more uncertainty, and the die was cast.

"Cousin Frank," I said, "I don't want to hear any more. I'm sure they'll soon order all military personnel to report to their bases. Nertz and I are going to take a walk."

At about five o'clock, I drove up to the base after taking my date home. Several rows of guards flanked the road, and they stopped every seaman and asked him to show his weekend pass. Those who had gone AWOL were restricted to the base until they went to an advanced base or were washed out. Luckily, I had a pass.

That night, long lines formed at the only two pay telephones in the barracks – every man was eager to talk to his family and his girl. Finally, at around one in the morning, I reached a phone. First I called my father. I told him I was glad the uncertainty was over. He told me he was proud of me and wished me well. Then I called my special girl, Hermi Weil, in New Orleans. It was an emotional exchange of deep feelings and a long discussion of what the future might hold. From the guy next in line, repeated pleas of "Come on, come on" finally ended our conversation.

At exactly zero seven hundred hours on Monday morning, the entire corps was assembled in the hangar. Cmdr. J.J. Schieffelin, who was in charge of training, strode in. Someone yelled, "Attention!" We all sprang to our feet.

This World War I veteran was a member of the special Yale University Naval Aviation Unit. Tall and erect, with a commanding voice, he inspired awe as he said, "At ease, gentlemen." We relaxed somewhat. "Gentlemen," he continued,

"I am about to read you a list of the capital ships in the Japanese Navy." He then read a long list of the enemy's carriers, battle ships, plus heavy and light cruisers. He stopped short of naming their destroyers and submarines. When he finally finished announcing the strangely named ships, he called us to attention. "Gentlemen," he said, "I name these enemy war ships not to cause you concern, but wish you good-hunting! At ease." Then, disappearing under the huge American flag that hung at the entrance, he turned and strode from the hangar. Later that morning we were reassembled to hear President Roosevelt pledging to the nation that we would recover from the attack on Pearl Harbor and carry on to victory.

An order was issued. It stated that the student pilots would patrol the bases every night. We were issued 1903 Springfield rifles that kicked like giraffes when fired. The first night I was assigned to patrol the inside of a chain-link fence bordering Clairmont Road, a well-traveled artery. My orders were to yell "Halt" at any car coming down the road after eleven o'clock. If the driver didn't stop, I was to fire in the air. If there was still no reaction, I was to fire at a tire.

Shortly after 11:00 a speeding car came down the road. At the top of my lungs I yelled, "Halt!" But on this cold night in early December, the driver had all his windows rolled up and didn't hear my command. So, obeying orders, I fired into the air. That sharp sound penetrated the closed windows. The car came to an abrupt stop, leaving black rubber skid marks on the pavement.

The driver's door banged open, and out came the executive officer of the base in a fury. He bounded toward me, the image of indignation. Halfway to where I stood with my rifle at port arms, he slowed down. It must have hit him that I was carrying out his orders. With the chain-link fence between us, he stopped in front of me. Then, in pure "militaryese," said, "Seaman, report to the Officer of the Day. Say that you discharged your weapon in accordance with orders!"

"Yes, Sir!" I said.

By the following night our orders had been changed. There would be no more firing of rifles. Within a week the commander acknowledged that the Japanese were not an immediate threat, and the guards ringing the base were disbanded. We not only considered this a victory but welcomed the return of a full night's sleep.

Early one morning the corps was ordered to assemble on the ramp outside the main hangar. Cmdr. Schieffelin appeared with an elderly, carelessly dressed man in civilian clothes. In his clipped tones, Schieffelin said, "Gentlemen, I have the honor to present to you Sgt. Alvin York, American hero of World War I and holder of the prestigious Medal of Honor! He will address you." We shrugged to attention at his command.

York won us over immediately. "Hey – relax, you guys. At ease. You'll all outrank me in a couple of months anyways." I've forgotten much of his rambling discourse, but his major point has stayed with me. "Look," he said, "don't you go out there thinking you can win this war with one bomb. You know, we'd have won World War I even if I hadn't captured those Germans; even, for that matter, if I hadn't been in the Army at all. Being a hero is just dumb luck. It's being in the right place at the right time. Just look out for your own ass and don't stick your neck out, except for your buddies." Though Cmdr. Schieffelin was visibly unhappy with York's choice of words, we were delighted and applauded for at least five minutes. We were ready to award the sergeant a second Medal of Honor.

Another morning, after we'd finished the usual vigorous calisthenics, Schieffelin told us, "Men, pair off. We're going to have an Indian wrestling elimination match. You know what Indian wrestling is? You face each other about 5 feet apart. Each extends his right foot until they touch. Then grasp each other's right hand. At the go command, you try to force your opponent to move his extended foot by manipulating his arm with yours, throwing him off balance. The winners of each bout will wrestle each other until only one of you is left."

I'd been Indian wrestling since age 10 and knew all the right moves: Relax completely while the other guy tries to throw you; when he stops, give a sudden sharp pull to the side, and your opponent will lose his balance, his extended foot will move, and you'll win.

Using this technique, I was the last one standing that morning. I was the winner. "Alexander," Schieffelin said, "I'd like to take you on." "Yes sir!" I replied. We went at it. In about a minute, I had not only dislodged his foot – I had thrown him down on the hard asphalt paving.

As I pulled him back on his feet, a somewhat muffled cheer went up from my fellow seamen. "Well done, Alexander," Schieffelin growled as he marched off. Very briefly, not even for 15 minutes, I was a hero. To his credit and my relief, the commander didn't hold my humiliation of him against me. Perhaps it was because we were both Yalies.

The days passed with monotonous sameness except for the flying. We had a crash course in Navy and Marine lore: John Paul Jones; Admiral Farragut;

"Don't give up the ship!"; "You may fire when ready, Gridley!"; "Damn the torpedoes, full speed ahead!"; "The Marines have landed and the situation is well in hand." We learned when to salute and whom to salute. We did close order drills with the heavy Springfield rifles. We learned something about aerodynamics and internal combustion engines. We learned to recognize Japanese ships and airplanes, more or less.

All of this would be re-taught and amplified when those of us who didn't wash out went to the Jacksonville, Pensacola, or Corpus Christi Naval Air Stations. Once I learned the Navy way, flight instruction was easy for me. I loved to fly. That I was being paid for flying was hard for me to believe, even if my pay was a pittance.

Because of our plane's narrow landing gear and the placement of the lower wing close to the ground, there was a constant danger of the wing tip dragging as we landed. Any damage wasn't to the plane; instead, it was to the pilot's ego and wallet. If you dragged a wing you put $10 in a kitty. If you completed the course without dragging, you collected $50. Landing in a heavy crosswind one day, I came within inches of dragging. But I gave it full throttle, picked up some speed, and was able to recover. The students watching from the line thought they had a dragger, and were very upset when I recovered. They jeered me as I walked away from my plane. I gave them a broad grin and the finger. I held up my other hand with the fingers spread indicating I was going to win fifty dollars.

Cadet Days in Jacksonville

Finally, some time in January, the survivors in my class were deemed ready to move up for more advanced training. My name was on the list to go to the Jacksonville, Florida, Naval Air Station. This suited me fine. I was glad I wasn't going to Corpus Christi, Texas, which was far from home and hot.

Jacksonville wasn't ready for us. No airplanes. Our impatience was readily assuaged by the activities available to us. These included horseback riding, tennis, golf, and swimming. Dating Jacksonville's loveliest was at the top of the list. We now were officially aviation cadets, wearing uniforms similar to the Navy officers'. The glamour of our crisp blues with gold trim was a very good opening to make dates. War was raging in Europe and the Pacific, but we were enjoying a relaxed vacation with the fighting far away.

Housing for cadets was excellent. In a long, low building, two men were assigned to a room with two beds, two desks, a sink, and an ample closet. I don't remember if it was air-conditioned; most likely, it wasn't. In the winter and early spring months, our concern was with the cold, not the heat. Much to my surprise, Jacksonville was no tropical paradise in the winter.

We had a Cadet Club, and its bar was open to everyone. While I was there, the president of the club was Joe Kennedy, Jr. He was later killed at Peenemünde while on a dangerous mission to destroy the German installation for building V-1 and V-2 rockets. His plane was loaded with explosives. As I remember, he and his crew were to bail out after they crossed the Channel. Their plane would be guided to the target by radio, beamed from a plane. The plane exploded in flight while Kennedy and his crew were still aboard. All were killed.

Of course, in 1942 Kennedy's name carried no special weight. Few of us knew that his father was the pro-German ambassador to Great Britain. I certainly didn't. He did all he could do to keep us from aiding the British.

My contribution to the Cadet Club was a large oil painting of a PBY Catalina. The cadets, most of whom wanted to be hotshot fighter pilots, derided this lumbering flying boat. Even so, I thought the plane had a certain beauty, and I was happy it was on display at the club. I recovered it years later, long after the war.

Planes finally arrived in Jacksonville (to us, "Jax"), and the idyll came to an end. It was back to the stick and rudder, instructors, yells through the Gosport Tube, calisthenics, marching, and ground school. The planes we flew were rugged biplanes – Stearmans painted bright yellow, with a forgiving wide landing gear unlike the unstable narrow gear on the N2S planes in Atlanta. Dragging wing tips was a remote concern.

Before I could fly I had to take another physical. The flight surgeon saw my crooked left arm with its limited range. In disbelief, he said, "How the hell did you get in this program with that arm?"

"Sir," I said, "I already had my commercial pilot's license. The first physical examiner knew my crooked arm didn't keep me from flying, so he passed me."

He looked hard at me. "Mr. Alexander, if this station was under attack by Japanese planes, would you take off and engage them?"

"Sir," I responded. "It is my understanding that none of the planes on the station have guns, so it would be a suicide mission. Even so, I'd rather be in the air than on the ground. Yes, if I could get a plane I would go up."

The surgeon looked at me, fingered his stethoscope, and said; "I see you're a Yale graduate with one year at MIT. Hmmm ... hmm ... All right, I'll give you a pass."

So my physical exam – including a courage test, my education, and my body parts – made the grade. I fervently hoped that if I were ever in real need of a doctor it would not be my convoluted examiner. While I was in the service, every time I had a physical, my crooked arm caused concern. As my service flight time built up, however, it became a non-issue.

Auxiliary fields surrounded the main field at Jax, where more basic training with the Stearman was conducted. I was assigned to Cecil Field, which was not named in my honor. My efforts to find this other Cecil, with whom I shared this unfortunate name, were fruitless. Every morning we would pile into a huge barn-like truck for the trip to Cecil Field. Then we'd return to the main station the same way each evening.

One of the most exacting maneuvers at the auxiliary field was landing with an idling engine in a 25-foot-diameter circle. It was drawn in white lime on the ground. You were allowed to slow the plane down by "fishtailing" – moving the rudder from side to side; you couldn't side-slip to lose altitude. A dozen or more planes would all try to land in the circle simultaneously, since no priority was assigned. Truly a game of "chicken," it was as potentially deadly as avian flu.

When the instructor was sure a student could do the maneuver solo, he landed the plane, got out, and stood with other instructors to assess his student's efforts. One time when I was waiting my turn to land, two students who were flying solo approached the 25-foot circle ahead of me; neither would give way. They locked wings, and one of the planes was thrown out of the circle. The other was a wreck with a broken wing, but lying within the circle's circumference. Neither pilot was hurt. Cursing, with fists ready to break each other's jaws, they leaped out of their planes and went after each other. A wild fight ensued and lasted until a couple of instructors pulled the students apart. Bloody noses and black eyes were the student's souvenirs of battle.

The instructors of the two were in a state of shock; at least one was. The other one was jumping around yelling, "That's my boy! That's my boy with his plane in the circle!" That the Stearman was a total wreck didn't bother him.

I never learned what became of the two cadets. Since the maneuvering of all those planes landing at once was a situation ready-made for crashes, they probably continued in the program. If their fight became known, they most likely would be severely disciplined for that rather than for their tangling of wings.

Ground school was a necessary evil. From quickly flashing slides, we were supposed to recognize Japanese planes and ships – but the fleeting images left us baffled. To show us we could interpret the slides if we worked at it, the instructor would insert a quick flash of Betty Grable in a swimsuit. With her magnificent curves and "come-on, buddy" looks, she was a favorite World War II pin-up wherever American servicemen were stationed. Proving the instructors point, we all recognized her (and how!). After many sessions, we could even recognize the enemy's ships and planes, though they totally lacked sex appeal.

A sleep-inducing drill was learning both audio and visual Morse code. The audio was projected through earphones, with the dots and dashes sent by wire from a record. The speed could be varied. A blinking light that was exposed for long and short intervals sent the visual communications. Drowsiness overpowered us when we came in from the cold air surrounding our airborne planes to the hot, stuffy classroom heated by a potbelly stove. To make matters worse, the droning of the code, which we tried our bet to understand and write down, put us very close to sleep.

We had a compelling reason to stay awake, though. To get off the station on weekends, we had to increase our speed week by week. The thought of free weekends served as a real incentive to fight sleep. At the end of the course, the audio Morse code became a language, and we interpreted the sounds as easily as we did English. I never was as fluent with the blinker.

Teachers Across the Board

Another class dealt with internal combustion engines and aerodynamics. I was shocked the first day when I saw our instructor. He had been my cadet commander in ROTC when I attended Boys High School. Back then I had been drawing posters for school events, and he had seen some of them. One day the Boys High big-shot said, "Cecil, I want you to make some drawings of various situations involving combat. You do that, and I'll see that you are promoted to a cadet lieutenant." I made the drawings and he used them, but I was never promoted.

When he saw me all those years later, his face broke into a nasty broad grin: He had a patsy in his class. I became the target of all his jokes and I was always called on to answer the toughest questions. At the time, only a few engineers knew anything about jet engines. I had read an article predicting that jets would eventually replace the propeller-driven engine, and during a class discussion I mentioned this article. The instructor laughed derisively. "Come on, you're dreaming. No way will a jet engine work. Forget it. An airplane needs a propeller, now and forever." I was very interested in the subject matter, but I could have managed very well without him.

I often wondered if he recalled his poor prognostication in later years as he sat back in one of the many jet planes he must have flown in. Yet my negative attitude toward the instructor had a positive effect: Knowing that he was certain to call on me to embarrass me, I diligently prepared for his class and, in turn, made top grades. More important, I acquired a solid grasp of the aerodynamics of flight and how the engines delivered their power. The last day I said to him, "Ensign, I'm still waiting for the promotion you promised me at Boy's High, but it's a little late." I don't think he remembered. He looked blank. I saluted and walked out.

Our Physical Fitness instructor was a true celebrity: heavyweight boxing champion Gene Tunney. In the Twenties he won the title from Jack Dempsey in the much-disputed "long count." Dempsey had floored Tunney, who lay crumpled on the mat. The referee started his knockout count but realized Dempsey was still standing over Tunney; he then waved him to a neutral corner and started the count over, giving Tunney a few more seconds to recover. At the count of ten, Tunney was back on his feet and went on to win the fight.

In an entirely unexpected attribute for a heavyweight boxer, Tunney was an avid student of Shakespeare. So learned was he that the legendary Professor William Lyons Phelps at Yale brought him in to lecture his class on Shakespeare every year. But this history meant nothing to us. The former boxer's condescending manner toward the cadets and the rigors of the tortuous exercises he invented turned us all into Tunney-haters. Where was Jack Dempsey when we needed him?

Flight training gradually progressed from the Stearmans to more powerful and less forgiving aircraft. We flew the Vought OS2U Kingfisher, which was originally designed as a seaplane with two long pontoons. After wheels were substituted for the pontoons, the OS2U became a rugged, stable land plane.

In our first experience with formation flying, we flew the Ryan FR Fireball. It was a low-wing, aluminum monoplane. The Ryan Company had manufactured Lindbergh's Atlantic-crossing *Spirit of St. Louis,* so our version had a very romantic appeal to me.

Formation flying is a difficult skill to learn. It was mandatory to approach the plane you joined up with at exactly the right speed – too slow, and you'd never catch up; too fast, and suddenly the lead plane would loom huge and you had to duck under it to avoid a collision. With much practice, I learned how to join up and it was never a problem.

One day I was in a formation flight when, as we approached the field, a low cloud layer began to cover the ground. The instructor spotted a hole in the overcast and dove down through it, leaving the students on their own above the clouds. Somehow we all came down safely, either through breaks in the clouds or just diving through them.

When the brass found out the instructor had deserted his students, they gave him immediate orders to the Pacific. At the Cadet Club, we drank to our Judas-like instructor's departure with satisfaction. When he was in the air, we wished the Japanese, "good hunting."

I had a near crash in the Ryan of my own doing. The day was very hot, and air rose from the steaming asphalt of the landing mat. As I came in to land I eased the stick back, pulled the nose up, and slowed the plane for landing. I was looking straight ahead. Suddenly I realized the hot air had lifted the light plane 30 feet or so in the air; if it stalled, the nose would drop and the plane would crash into the ground, undoubtedly killing the pilot – me.

I caught on fast enough to save myself. I pushed the nose down and opened the throttle, just missing the dreaded stall. But I almost hit the nose of the plane on the mat. At that last instant I pulled back on the stick, the plane leveled out, rolled its wheels over the asphalt, and gradually came to a stop. There was a phrase for this mistake: "He had his head up his ass and locked." That day my head fit snuggly.

For those of us who won "up checks" on our formation flying, flight instruction progressed to SNJs. The SNJ was a sleek metal low- wing monoplane that looked like the Navy's combat fighters and had many of the same flight characteristics as well. Some pilots flew a similar plane, designed by Curtiss, which was regarded as a death trap. Those who were assigned to SNJs, as I was, considered themselves fortunate. Those who were assigned to the Curtiss felt they were doomed.

The syllabus for the SNJ was similar to our previous instruction. In spite of its evil tendency to ground loop (an embarrassing, unintended maneuver I had escaped), the plane, with its powerful engine and fine flight characteristics, was a joy to fly. Those of us who flew the SNJs thought that we were real hot shots, ready for anything.

The survivors of the SNJ and Curtiss programs were ready to move on. We filled out a form requesting assignment to a particular operating squadron, including fighters. Those who were assigned to fighters left Jax for a Navy base farther south, where they would be subjected to a hard, rigorous course in battle tactics. This was the World War II version of *Top Gun*.

Because I didn't have the blood lust, the kill-or-be-killed love of war, or the thrill of the hunt I believed were necessary traits of a successful fighter pilot, I applied for instruction flying PBY Catalina seaplanes at Jacksonville. A big, lumbering whale with wings, the PBY had been designed in peacetime to fly from Los Angeles to Catalina Island. The Navy used it mainly for patrolling and rescue missions.

Its fuselage was shaped like a boat's hull. The huge wings spread out from a short streamlined tower mounted on the fuselage above and behind the pilot's cabin. This tower accommodated a crewman who could give the pilot directions when he was taxiing on the water. On either side of the tower, on the wings were two engine nacelles with propellers well clear of the water. At the tips of the wings were small floats that were deployed down from the wing for landings, takeoffs, and taxiing and kept the plane from tipping over.

The pilot and copilot sat in the extreme front of the plane and had an excellent view both ahead and to either side. In the fuselage were the navigator's table, a galley, the head, several bunks, and two large plastic bubbles for machine guns. The PBY cruised at a slow 105 knots. Its controls were very heavy, and the pilot used both hands on the control column to pull the beast up during takeoff. In the Pacific it proved its value many times over. It picked up a multitude of downed pilots, flew reconnaissance patrols, and even launched torpedo attacks in the Solomon Islands.

I once again came close to a fatal wreck. I was on what I thought was my last PBY check flight, seated on the left side of the cabin. To my right was the instructor, seated with his legs crossed as he scanned a girlie magazine. As I came in for the landing, the surface of the water appeared as a windless, unruffled sheet. In such conditions it was very difficult to judge altitude, and bouncing the plane off the water wasn't unusual. I had done it before; after a bounce, the correct procedure was to wait until the plane slowed down and then slowly pull the nose up, which would stall the PBY into a satisfying, deep splash as it landed.

In my enthusiasm to land the plane correctly, I didn't wait for it to slow down. I quickly hauled the yoke back, which brought the nose straight up into the air. At some 75 feet up we were very close to stalling and diving into the unforgiving water.

Out of the corner of my eye I saw the instructor explode out of his calm demeanor. He threw his feet on the rudder pedals, grabbed the yoke with his right hand, and pushed the nose down. With his left hand he shoved the throttle hard forward, accelerating the idling engines to full power. We recovered, and the instructor landed safely. He leaned over to me with fire in his eyes. "What the shit were you doing? You were doing OK until you nearly killed us. That bit of stupid flying earns you a resounding down check. You need more instruction."

Thankfully, I was successful the next time I was checked. On a hot July day in 1942, I became a second lieutenant in the Marine Corps, with a naval aviator's "Wings of Gold." I left Jacksonville for two weeks leave, which I split between Atlanta with my father, and New Orleans, where I courted Hermi.

My Month in Texas

The phone rang in the hall of the Bachelor Officer Quarters at Meacham Field in Fort Worth, Texas. I picked it up and voiced the usual greeting, "Hello." A female voice answered, "Hi." We were off to a great start. Here I became more involved. "To whom do you want to speak?" (I probably said, "who", but in print that looks very ungrammatical.) Back came a soft purr, "You, honey." I dropped the receiver. When another fellow came down the hall I told him, "Someone wants to speak to you" and handed him the phone. I hope it was the beginning of a meaningful relationship.

Yes, Fort Worth was a very hospitable city, but that wasn't why I was there. I was there to learn to fly DC-3 transports. After my promotion to second lieutenant I was ordered to the month-long training program, which American Airlines had set up for Navy and Marine pilots. The instructors were well-seasoned commercial pilots with thousands of hours in the air.

My last check flight in Jacksonville was in a PBY with Navy Lt. Perry as the check pilot. In contrast to my near disaster with the preceding check pilot, I performed perfectly for him. "Hey," he said. "You can really handle this bird." As a result of my performance, he wrote a letter to his friend, a senior American Airlines pilot named Sam Ross, and urged him to instruct me.

His letter, which I've kept all these years to feed my ego, stated in part: "Lieutenant Alexander, who had some work with me here in Jacksonville, is one of the most promising young air pilots I have ever seen. I would like to see him entrusted to your capable hands."

Ross was one tough, demanding SOB, but I learned a great deal from him. On our first flight, he nursed the slow-climbing DC-3 up to 3,000 feet. To familiarize me with the plane's flight characteristics, he put it through a series of stalls, with different configurations of the plane's appendages: wheels and flaps down, wheels down, flaps down. Then, with the wheels and flaps up and both engines idling, he had me repeat the maneuvers. He then took over and pulled back the yoke at the top of the control column. This raised the nose until we slowed to stalling speed. Stalling comes on when the airflow over the wing is so slow there is no lift. The nose drops suddenly. The pilot must push the yoke forward, diving the plane until it restores the lift and the plane can resume level flight.

But Ross had a surprise for me. As the plane stalled with the engines idling, he kicked the hard right rudder and pulled the yoke back in his lap. The DC-3 fell off in a tailspin. After a couple of turns, he took his hands off the yoke and his feet off the rudder pedals. He turned to me and said, "You got it." I knew how to recover from a spin in a small plane, but this was a large twin-engine transport. There was nothing for me to do but apply the same technique I had used in the small Stearman biplanes. I kicked the rudder hard in the opposite direction of the spin and shoved the yoke all the way forward. To my vast relief, the airplane stopped spinning and entered a dive, from which I quickly recovered. This brought the DC-3 to level flight. Ross looked at me with a tight smile on his lips. "I just wanted you to see this here aircraft ain't no old lady." I was convinced. My pulse rate gradually returned to normal.

A little later, my pulse went up again. Preparing to land, Ross had taken over the controls of the DC-3. Meacham Field had high-tension wires at the end of the most-used runway, which we were approaching. About a mile out, Ross pulled back the throttles and we glided down toward the field. Lower and lower we dropped.

To make the engines carry the plane up over the wires I expected Ross to shove the throttles forward. But he didn't move, and instead just looked at me with that same tight smile. I'm not sure what my expression conveyed to him, but if he could have felt my accelerating pulse he would have been pleased. Suddenly he reached for the handle that controlled the landing flaps and forced it down; with the flaps extended, the wings had much greater lift. The plane rose swiftly and easily cleared the wires.

After we landed Ross said, "I showed you that maneuver so if you're ever caught with no power behind wires or any other barrier, you'll know how to get over it." The lesson stayed with me, but fortunately I never had make use of it.

In addition to flying, we had long hours of ground school and a hot, frustrating time in the Link trainer. If the devil wanted to severely punish wayward pilots who've been sent to his everlasting care, he would put them in a Link trainer for eternity. The Link was an early crude design of a simulator. Its appearance was comical. The fuselage was about 5 feet long, with stubby wings, a ridiculously small rudder, and elevators. When an opaque enclosure was placed over the pilot's head, the tight cockpit became claustrophobic. The Link trainer had the look of a boy's toy, but it wasn't that much fun.

The cockpit had a full instrument panel, rudder pedals, and a control stick. This unlikely simulation of an airplane was perched close to the floor on a single column filled with wires. The Link had absolutely none of the feel of an airplane in flight. It moved with lurching jolts, and a sound I still remember was the high-pitched sighing of the pressurized air that moved the Link in response to the changes I made with the controls.

The point of this ordeal was to teach instrument flying the use of instruments only when there was no visibility. An instructor sat at a table that bore a large chart. In response to the pilot's control changes, a stylus attached to a mechanism moved a pen drew a pattern on the chart, showing the instructor whether the student was accurately following the maneuvers required for an instrument landing. Although it taught the mechanics of instrument flying sufficiently enough, the Link process was totally devoid of any enjoyment – so much so that instrument flying in a real plane, with its natural feel, was a great relief.

The most valuable lesson the Link taught was to never to rely on your senses when flying on instruments, since your body could falsely interpret pressures generated by a plane in flight. For instance, if your plane suddenly heads straight for the earth, your body can tell you aren't pulling out of the dive – so you overcompensate and pull back too hard on the stick. This misguided action actually makes things worse. Unless you completely ignore your feelings, believe only your instruments, and react immediately, you and your plane will end up in what's justifiably called the "graveyard spiral." If a pilot can use the Link, which relies solely on instruments, to master this lesson, it's more than worth the miserable experience.

A few days before I'd left Atlanta for Fort Worth, I was a guest at a War Bond fundraising breakfast. Sitting next to me was the CEO of Robert & Company Architects and Engineers. He was Chip Robert, who was not only CEO but also owner of the company, the leading Atlanta engineering firm at that time. I was wearing my very new Marine uniform with my second lieutenant gold bars and Navy wings. In response to his questions, I told him I had orders to the American Airlines School in Fort Worth.

"Fort Worth," he said. "I have a close friend there, Amon Carter. I'll write him and tell him to call you." I later discovered it was like having an introduction to the King of England, John D. Rockefeller, President Roosevelt, Winston Churchill, and Babe Ruth all in one. Carter was Mr. Fort Worth, with an abiding hatred for Dallas. Dallas referred to Fort Worth as Cowtown, not a neighborly thing to do to a city whose borders almost touched your own.

After I arrived in the city I received a hand-delivered letter from Mr. Carter, inviting me to dinner with his daughter. His home was an impressive, well-designed mansion. His daughter, Ruth, was also impressive and well-designed. ("Beautiful" would be the better adjective.) During dinner Mr. Carter let me know that his hospitality extended to his generous offer that I date Ruth. This I did on several well-remembered evenings. I was restrained in my approach, however, because I was unofficially engaged to Hermi.

Amon Carter's son, whom I believe was with the Eighth Air Force, was shot down while piloting a bomber over Germany and was listed as missing in action. Carter Sr. hadn't received any information about what happened to his son after his plane was hit. Did he parachute safely? Did the Germans capture him? Did French resistance fighters rescue him? Only questions – no answers. Over the fireplace in their palatial home was an oil painting of the lost son in his uniform, displaying his Army Air Corps Wings on his chest. An overhead light illuminated the painting was never extinguished while there was no word of his whereabouts. Several months after VE-Day, I read in the Atlanta paper that Amon Carter, Jr. had been found in a German prison camp in reasonably good health. He was headed home. I wrote to his father, offering my deep and sincere congratulations for this joyous end to his three-year vigil.

It was early one morning, about 5:30. After a long date, a 3:00 a.m. session in the Link trainer, and a night of little or no sleep, I was in the command pilot's left-hand seat of a DC-3. I was practicing night landings. Watching my less than alert effort, the ever-present Sam Ross sat by me, hints of annoyed concern in his eyes. After each practice landing, I swung the plane around and taxied back to the end of the runway for another takeoff.

To reduce the number of takeoffs and landings my fatigued body and brain would have to endure, I was taxiing very slowly. The second time I was dragging back, Ross shouted, "I got it!" He pulled the plane off the runway, idled the engines and set the brakes. Then he leaned over toward me and put his arm on the seat back behind me. In a low growl he said, "Do you want to fly this thing or don't you? If not, we'll go to the hangar right now!" His angry question woke me up with a swift rush of adrenaline.

"Sure I want to fly," I said.

"Then fly this damn thing and don't drag ass taxiing back after you land." Now wide-awake, I nodded yes, and taxied rapidly back to takeoff. Somehow I made it through the session, which lasted until daylight, without crashing. I did "crash" soon after on my cot back at the BOQ, finally waking up at noon.

The previous night's date was my last until Hermi came to visit her cousin in Oklahoma City. Somehow I thought I could get a ride there in a DC-3. I must have been hallucinating. My means of getting there was in my sleek little Buick convertible. It was a long drive from Fort Worth, but the power of love seemed to shorten it.

When I arrived at the cousin's home and Hermi saw me, she was visibly upset. I was wearing my Marine khaki uniform, and she had wanted to present me in my dazzling Marine whites. I'm still not sure whether it was me or my whites that she fell for.

Winding Down with Sam Ross

After the weekend in Oklahoma, I had little time left in Texas. But that didn't mean less hard work with Ross. One of his oft-repeated drills was practicing instrument approaches, using the signals sent out from a radio tower. This required a keen ear and absolute concentration to detect the "cone of silence" as the plane passed over the tower where its signal faded out. The pilot then knew exactly where his plane was. He could then begin the involved procedures of flying prescribed headings; making 180 degree turns while losing altitude at exactly 300 feet a minute. There was no time for daydreaming. Adding to the problem, Ross invariably cut the power to one engine in the middle of this demanding procedure, complicating it.

Only once did I lose it. One night I was flying a turn with the plane banked over some 45 degrees. A grasshopper had bummed a ride and was perched on the pedestal between the seats. At a glance, I saw this insect jump straight up—not from the angle we were flying, but 90 degrees above the earth below. Totally disoriented, I had a serious attack of vertigo. To restore my equilibrium I stopped the turn and leveled the plane. Ross looked at me with incredulity. "What the fuck are you doing?" My grasshopper excuse only added to his anger. Somehow I survived, and so did that aeronautical insect.

At the end of the month-long session in Fort Worth I was taking a check ride. This time, thank god, it wasn't with Ross. As I approached my final landing, a fellow student named Dick Dominick, whom I recognized, suddenly ran out on the middle of the runway's end. He did this to take a picture of the plane landing. He faced me with a decision – not about his safety, but about what would be the check pilot's reaction to my decision. Should I advance the throttle and go around for another landing, or should I go ahead and land? There was no comment from the check pilot, then or later. I went for the landing, clearing the photographer by a few feet, and brought the plane down for a rough landing. My decision must have suited the check pilot, since gave me an "up." I still have the photo Dominick took.

I never measured up to the glowing introduction that Lt. Perry gave Ross about me. Part of the reason may have been the pressure his letter put on me to be perfect. Years later I was reading an excellent book by Ernie Gann about his airline experiences. Writing about his early flying as an apprentice co-pilot, he mentions that the captain he flew with was named Ross. At one point, he was landing the plane through some foul weather with low clouds hanging over the runway, and just as Gann lined up the runway Ross leaned over and started striking matches an inch in front of his eyes. Gann jerked his head away, could finally see the runway, and made a decent landing. He demanded of Ross, "Why in the hell did you light those matches?"

"Someday your plane may be on fire," Ross answered. "You'll remember the matches and know you can handle the situation." I think that later Gann actually did land a plane on fire, for which Ross's flaming matches had, I'm sure, well prepared him.

I wrote Gann, telling him of my experiences with Sam Ross and asked if his Ross was the same man. His response was, "You know there cannot be but one Ross in the air, or for that matter, in the world. Yes, I'm sure it was Sam."

As I left Meacham Field, I took a last look at a badly wrecked DC-3 lying in front of one of the hangars. It was there when I arrived, and here's what had happened. The plane, carrying two students and an instructor, was barely airborne when the instructor cut one engine and the flat propeller blades created considerable drag on the plane. Over the front windows were two red buttons; when one was pressed it would "feather" the indicated propeller – that is, rotate the blades in line with the plane's direction, greatly reducing the drag. The student in the front seat reached up and punched the wrong button – the one for the good engine, which disrupted the propeller and made the engine lose all thrust. Abruptly, neither engine was functioning. The plane stalled, fell off on a wing and crashed, killing the instructor and the student beside him. The student in the jump seat survived to tell what had happened.

After that fatal wreck, things changed. If the instructor stopped an engine, the student touched the correct button but would not push it in. The plane could fly with an unfeathered idling propeller, a much safer solution.

The DC-3 was known as a "forgiving airplane," but that wrecked plane lying by the hangar indicated there were deadly limits to its forgiveness. The image of that wreck stayed with me throughout my flying days.

The final week of training, we each received orders for our next, very unusual duty. It was to report to one of the operating airlines for experience flying as co-pilot on their regular schedules. My assignment was to the (now defunct) Penn Central Airlines, operating out of Washington, D.C. Our schedule of two days on and four off, which conformed to that of an airline pilot, would give me ample time to hop a train to Northampton, Massachusetts to visit with my number one girl, Hermi, at Smith College. It was a long, hot, enervating ride, but it was worth every discomfort.

The only unsettling memory I have was my neglect of my father's birthday on September 10th that year. He let me know in a vivid way how hurt he was. "I was home, completely alone on my birthday, and not a word from you," he said. I swore then that if I ever had children, I would never say something like that to them. So far I haven't. The reason I forgot his birthday was my ardent pursuit of Hermi, a fact I didn't pass on to my father. Somehow I didn't think it would assuage him.

At the beginning of this chapter I recalled flying a DC-3 over my father's house in Atlanta on the way to Miami. I said that I would explain how I happened to be sitting in the right-hand co-pilot's seat of a DC-3 that night. Starting with my civilian pilot training in New York and Massachusetts, Navy-Marine training in Florida, American Airlines schooling in Texas, and finally flying with Penn Central Airlines out of the nation's capital, I think I have told the story.

On to Southern California

After two months at Penn Central, I had new orders. It had been a time I thoroughly enjoyed – both the flying and my trips to Smith College. Now Southern California beckoned.

My new orders were explicit: Report to the San Diego North Island Naval Air Station. I had left my car in Fort Worth when I went back to Atlanta on leave, and there wasn't enough time to pick it up and drive across the desert and the mountains to San Diego. So one of the Marines who'd been with me in Fort Worth agreed to make the drive.

When I saw my cherished car in San Diego I went into shock – the driver had been hit by a desert sandstorm. All of the paint was stripped off the front of the Buick, and the windshield was so pitted that, once the storm passed, my friend had to crane his neck out of the window to see the road. To have it fixed cost me what was then a fortune for a second lieutenant; somehow my insurance didn't cover sandstorms.

I had arrived in San Diego after a miserable trip by train – much more than miserable, in fact. Because there was no air conditioning, all of the windows were open, allowing grit, dust, and miscellaneous garbage to fly into the car. The insipid, greasy, cold food made you wonder if it was really worth waiting in the long line to the dining car. Since I was unable to reserve a berth (they were in short supply), I spent the four- or five-day trip, sitting upright in the rigid seats in the day coach.

At one point a large rat appeared and perched on the seatback in front of me. A small middle-aged woman occupied the seat, and the passenger next to her saw the rat and advised her of imminent danger. In a matter of seconds he lady sprang up and went down the aisle screaming for the conductor. In a while he showed up and tried to calm his frantic passenger as she was finally able to let loose: "A rat, a huge rat, was on the back of my seat!"

His reply left her less than mollified. "Thank you for locating him, Madam," he said. "He has been dodging me, and I need to collect his fare." The victim didn't join in the laughter that erupted. The rat, perhaps dodging the conductor who wanted to collect his fare, disappeared for the remainder of the trip.

At long last it was the end of the line – San Diego. As the tired train jolted to a last stop, the brakes screamed and squealed. Another Marine pilot and I left the train together. We had similar orders: to report before midnight to the Marine Officer of the Day at North Island. My companion said, "I'm tired as hell. I'm going on and report in, so I can sack out for 12 hours."

"Well," I said, "I'm bushed too, but I'm going to hang around San Diego until later. I'll see you out there. Sleep can wait." I checked my baggage, and after waiting at the end of a long line for the cab I shared with three other Marines, I headed for downtown.

After leaving the cab I walked around downtown San Diego "wearing my architectural hat" and criticizing all that I saw. Around 7:00 the light faded and I found a good restaurant, where I tried to apologize to my stomach for the sickly train meals I'd dumped into it. I still remember the steak, baked potatoes, spinach, ice cream, and coffee I consumed. As another reward for those tiresome days spent crossing the country, I took in a bad movie. Around 10:00, I headed out to check in with the Officer of the Day. He took my orders, assigned me a room in Bachelor Officer Quarters, and told me to report back at 0800 the next morning. When I hit the sack, sleep came instantly.

The next morning, as I walked along the dock on my way to check in at the OD's office, I heard someone calling my name. It was my buddy who checked in early. He was standing above me on the stern of a transport tied up at the dock. The ship was headed for Guadalcanal. My delay signing in gave me another six months in California. His early arrival sent him to the hellhole of Guadalcanal. He did not come back. As tragic as this twist of fate was, it made me think nobody should ever dismiss the advantage of sightseeing, a good dinner, and even a lousy movie.

Soon after I arrived, Capt. Bell, my roommate at Fort Worth (he had been promoted to major), showed up. He greeted me warmly.

"Alex," he said, "I'm taking a transport squadron of DC-3s out to the Solomon Islands. Nothing would suit me better than to have you come with me. But you told me you want to fly B-25s, and a B-25 group is being formed at Santa Barbara. I can get you in if you want to go."

I said, "Nothing would suit me better than to be in your outfit if you were flying bombers. I hate to turn down going out with you, but I joined the Marines instead of the Navy so I could fly B-25s. So I'll accept your offer to get me in the B-25 group."

There is one very negative aspect of flying a DC-3 in combat – no machine guns. The pilots and crew carried 45 automatics in shoulder holsters and a hunting knife strapped to the calf, hardly effective weapons to hold off a fighter. That was it. The logo for the transports well reflected this vulnerability. The round shield displayed two crossed 45 automatic pistols, and around the perimeter was a Latin phase that translated "In clouds we trust."

If Japanese Zeroes attacked an unescorted DC-3, clouds were the pilot's only refuge. Often the skies were clear, and down went a transport in flames. But it was the chance to fly B-25s, not the DC-3's vulnerability, which influenced my decision. Bell and I shook hands and wished each other happy landings. He was a real friend, as good as his word. Soon my orders to Santa Barbara arrived.

I drove my repaired convertible with its brand new windshield to Santa Barbara and checked in. My orders made a profound change in my plans: There was no time for marriage, a turn of events I'll elaborate upon in the next chapter.

After several weeks spent waiting, with nothing to do, the word came down – our planes were being assigned to a group on the East Coast and my group was to be disbanded.

Chapter 18

The War Can Wait

That old black magic has me in its spell.

— *Harold Arlen, "That Old Black Magic"*

Immediately after my orders to join the B-25 group in Santa Barbara came through, I called Hermi in New Orleans. In those days telephones came in two pieces – the receiver, which was put to your ear, and the speaker, which was at the top of a short column attached to a circular base resting on a table or desk. The receiver was hung on a U-shaped hook extending from the column when the phone wasn't in use. Black was the universal color. Long distance calls were rare events. Usually these calls told of deaths, disease, accidents, or other major catastrophes. On rare occasions the wires hummed with glad tidings: graduations, promotions, new jobs, births, and weddings. The wires sang in the last category when I called Hermi.

"Hermi! Hermi," I said. "I have new orders that will keep me stateside another six months."

"Oh, Alex, what are we going to do?"

"Get married!" I announced.

She whispered breathlessly, "Ohhh, Alex! Ohhh, Alex! Ohhh, Alex! Ohhh, Alex! When? Where? Ohhh, Alex!"

"Right now," I said. "As soon as we can. I'll see if I can get to New Orleans."

Hermi's folks were not enthusiastic. I heard they had said my life expectancy as a Marine pilot was minuscule and that Hermi would be left a 20-year-old widow. I've always suspected that the real reason was that no mortal man was good enough for their daughters. They had already helped terminate their older daughter Therese's wedding plans at least twice. Nevertheless, Hermi was in love, there was a war on, and she was then (and would forever remain) a lady not easily swayed from her chosen path. This time was no exception.

I cleared the guard at the Santa Barbara Marine Corps Air Station after the long drive from San Diego, then checked in with the Officer of the Day (OD). He assigned me a single room in BOQ, where I met a few of the pilots who were also joining the B-25 group.

The next morning I went at eight o' clock to group headquarters, where I met the commanding officer. He was a tall, affable Marine major who gave me a strong handshake and a warm "Welcome aboard, Lieutenant glad to have you here with me."

He then went on to explain the present situation. "We haven't received any B-25s yet. They should arrive in three weeks. All we have now are five SNJs (a trainer). You and the other guys can fly for a few hours each month to qualify for flight pay and get familiar with the area. Other than that, just report in every morning, and the rest of the time is yours. Just be back on board by eleven o'clock each night."

"Major," I said, "since we don't have any planes yet I have a request. I'm getting married to a New Orleans girl. Her mother badly wants to have the wedding there. I would like to go to please her. Can it be done?"

"I don't have a problem as long as the B-25s don't come in. You can have one week basket leave when you set the date."

"Basket leave" was unrecorded time off. Papers were drawn up authorizing the leave in case something unforeseen happened, but the documents remained in a basket on the CO's desk. If all went well, the papers were destroyed when the officer returned. The leave was entered on his record only if something caused him to overstay it. It was an under-the-table way of doing someone a favor who might not be eligible for an authorized leave — my situation exactly.

I called Hermi with the good news: I could go to New Orleans for our wedding! The planning for Queen Elizabeth's coronation barely exceeded the detailed and elaborate course of events then planned by Rosetta, my future mother-in-law. Several hundred expensive engraved invitations to the wedding were sent out almost overnight.

Waylaid Plans

Then it happened, as with so many well-laid plans of mice, men, and Marines.

"By the way, Lt. Alexander, you have to clear your leave with the general."

This upsetting directive came from the CO several days after I had been given the all-clear to New Orleans. "But sir, I've already told my wife-to-be I'm going to New Orleans."

"Sorry. The general has to OK it."

In clean crisp khakis and brilliantly shined shoes, I went to the general's office and stated my case. The general heard me out and then said, "I can't let you go. You just had two weeks leave when you were commissioned. That's all you're due for another year."

"But General," I said, "I didn't know you would have to clear my leave. I told my fiancée I could go. Her mother has already sent out invitations and made big plans. She will be one unhappy mother of the bride."

"Lieutenant, it will be good for her and even better for you. It'll show her she's not the boss. I did the same thing to my mother-in-law, and we've had an excellent relationship ever since."

A third long distance call – a very tense one – relayed the general's refusal. Not only was the New Orleans ceremony aborted but also the revised plans called for Hermi, her mother, father, and sister, and my father and sister to make the long, hot trip from the South to California.

Now *I* became the planner. I arranged for a private room for the ceremony at the Ambassador Hotel in Los Angeles. Since its opening on New Year's Eve in 1921, this grand hotel had been a Mecca for the rich and famous of Hollywood, including such stars as Clark Gable, Joan Crawford, and Claudette Colbert.

The most prominent reform rabbi on the West Coast was Edgar F. Magnin, the long-time leader of Wilshire Boulevard Temple, whose family owned I. Magnin & Co., a chain of elite retail establishments. He rather reluctantly agreed to officiate.

My first try at choosing a best man was a humiliating experience. One of the pilots at Santa Barbara went out of his way to be friendly and thoughtful. A few days after his initial gestures, he asked if he could borrow my car to drive to San Francisco for a date.

"Sure pal," I said. "Just be careful."

How could I turn down my new friend? So, when I was considering a candidate for my best man I thought first of him. "Would you," I asked, "be best man at my wedding?"

"No way," he said, "why would I want to stand up with you?"

"Well you've been very friendly ever since we met, so I thought you might like to do that favor for me."

A flash of revelation hit me.

"Hey, you just buddied up to me so you could borrow my Buick; you're some friend."

"Yep, that's it; I wanted your car," he smirked.

"Asshole!" I muttered. "See you around."

At least the jerk was honest, and he had the prudence to never asked to borrow my convertible again.

My next choice was Phil Field, a fellow I had met in training. He was an accomplished artist and a fellow Ivy Leaguer. Phil came from one of the First Families of Virginia (FFVs) and lived in His Lordship's Kindness, an estate owned in colonial times by the third Lord Baltimore. Phil immediately agreed to my request. Two years later he was shot down at Guadalcanal, screaming into his open microphone as his flaming torpedo bomber spiraled down at high speed to dive into the dark waters. Hermi and I remembered him whenever there was a beautiful sunset, saying Phil must have painted it.

Tying the Knot in L.A.

The afternoon of the wedding, Harold Weil, my future father-in-law, asked me to have a drink with him before dinner. We went into a bar in the hotel, picked two stools, and faced each other with drinks in hand.

"Alex," he said, "I want you to know we like and admire you. Our only hesitation about the marriage was the idea that because of your dangerous flying you might not survive the war and could leave Hermi a widow, " a restatement of what I had heard indirectly. After looking away for a moment, Harold said "We welcome you into our family."

I guess he and Rosetta had decided that while I might not be good enough, good manners demanded they be gracious. I thanked him as we touched glasses to confirm his welcome.

In time, I became very close to both of Hermi's parents. Hermi complained later that if she and I were having an argument, her mother always took my side (which shows how reasonable a person Rosetta was).

On January 20, 1943, late in the afternoon, the wedding party gathered in the appointed room at the Ambassador Hotel. Hermi was dressed in a form-fitting satin wedding gown, a veil atop her well-set hair. I wore my Marine dress blues set off by the USMC's shiny brown leather Sam Browne belt (that's the diagonal over-the-shoulder belt named for a 19th-century British officer), Phil, my best man, was similarly dressed. My soon-to-be sister-in-law and mother-in-law looked beautiful in their magnificent gowns.

The only outsider at the ceremony was Julius Dreyfous. Julius, an architect, lived across the street from the Weils in New Orleans. He was now stationed near L.A. in the Army. so was invited to the wedding. He had lost two wives in accidents. Of course, in 1943 it wasn't even a remote idea, but after Harold's death, Julius and Rosetta would marry. So, in a strange twist, he was unwittingly a witness at the wedding of his future stepdaughter. What's more, Dreyfous and I would one day collaborate as architects on a movie theater in New Orleans.

Rabbi Magnin took himself very seriously. He made no effort to be gracious and convivial, and there was no mistaking his attitude that performing this wedding was a great favor on his part. He conveyed this in spite of Rosetta's effort to inform him that the Weils of New Orleans were top-drawer and entirely worthy of his rabbinical favors.

After Hermi and I kissed at the end of the short ceremony, I turned to look at our families. Hermi's relatives were all in tears. My father and sister were dry-eyed and smiling. We cut the wedding cake with my Marine sword.

The next morning, after breakfast, Hermi and I drove to our cottage in Santa Barbara. To my mother-in-law's vast disapproval, my father came up to see us for several days, staying at a local hotel. Rosetta thought the newlyweds should be left alone, but I understood my father's motives. His only son would soon be in deadly combat, and this could be our last time together. He made himself welcome by taking us to a fine restaurant for dinner the two nights he was in Santa Barbara. Since Hermi knew nothing about cooking, these two meals were most welcome. In time she became an excellent cook, specializing in New Orleans cuisine.

High on my list had been finding a place for us to live. An agent referred me to a cottage on the crown of Eucalyptus Hill overlooking Santa Barbara. When I saw it I knew we had to have it. The tiny house was located on a cul-de-sac above a broad green valley sweeping down to the blue sea in long billows of high grass. It was built of white wood and was protected from the road by a low white picket fence. Large windows opened to stunning natural views. The owner was a tidy and very friendly woman in her middle years. She was pleasant, but reluctant to let me rent the cottage.

"I know what will happen," she said. "You're a Marine. You'll be here a couple of weeks and then you'll be sent somewhere else. And I'll have to start all over again."

"On no, Mrs. Manning," I said, believing every word. "I'll be training in Santa Barbara to fly B-25s. It won't take less than six months."

A lovely photograph of Hermi, a large bunch of roses, and my Southern sweet talk finally won Mrs. Manning over. I agreed to pay two months rent in advance. At $80.00 a month, the rate was steep for a second lieutenant, even with the addition of flight pay. But price wasn't a consideration – romance had taken the wheel.

An added attraction was our neighbor, a concert violinist named Spalding. Mrs. Manning introduced us. I told him my bride was an accomplished violinist, and asked if he could give her advanced instruction. "Certainly," he said.

In selling our marriage to my future mother-in-law Rosetta, she herself a symphony-quality violinist, I mentioned Spalding. She was pleased, but Hermi was not. Practicing the violin on her honeymoon wasn't her concept of a romantic pursuit. Mr. Spalding became, therefore, just a friendly neighbor whose beautiful music we heard from time to time.

As I said before, Hermi had never learned to cook, despite having been brought up in a household where good food was a must. My own culinary skills were limited to scrambling eggs, frying greasy bacon, burning toast, and squeezing orange juice.

I quickly taught her these far-from-Cordon-Bleu skills. We were set for breakfast, but lunch and dinner remained problematic. Between the bedroom and the kitchen was a small open pass-through. One morning I was struggling into my uniform while Hermi was making our usual eggs and bacon breakfast. Suddenly from the kitchen came a loud report and the smell of smoke and flames. I rushed into the kitchen to find Hermi standing there frozen in shock, an empty frying pan dangling from her hand.

"Are you OK? Are you OK?" I shouted over my pounding heart.

"Yes," came the feeble reply.

"What happened? What the hell happened?"

"I wasn't thinking," she said. "I turned on the gas and went around getting the eggs and bacon ready. Then I lit a match and the gas exploded."

"My God," I said. "I don't know why you aren't burned. Badly burned!"

I hugged her and kissed her tear-streaked face. I turned off the gas and opened all the windows. That day we ate cold cereal for breakfast.

Dinner usually consisted of food I sneaked away from the noon chow at officer's mess hall. Once or twice a week we drove down to Santa Barbara for a decent meal.

At least Hermi could answer one of the other Marine wives' cooking questions. This naïve young lady from Little Rock was trying to follow a recipe in a bride's bible, *The Joy of Cooking*. "Hermi," she said over the phone, "I jes can't remember, which is the yolk of the aig?" As I remember, she fed her husband nightly on parsley sandwiches when he came home from the base.

Our Move to a New Base

Our landlord Mrs. Manning was all too right. The B-25s our group was supposed to obtain never arrived and went to a group on the East Coast instead. Our dejected skipper called all the pilots together to tell us the group was disbanded. We would all be transferred to El Toro, the Marine Air Station south of Los Angeles near Laguna Beach, and then be assigned to either dive-bombers or torpedo planes.

So Hermi and I packed up our limited belongings and piled them in the trunk of my Buick. We took a last look at our fairytale cottage, wound slowly down Eucalyptus Hill to the coastal road, and headed south to El Toro. The beauty of that drive along the coast was no compensation for being jerked away from our lovely house. On one section of the coast, heavy storm waves had eaten away the shore, leaving a dozen houses tilted down into the ocean. It was a sobering sight, but it didn't stop us from wanting to rent a beachfront house.

Our search for house in South Laguna Beach came to a swift and happy end. It was a two-story, square stucco box cut into the top of a vertical cliff directly over the white waves crashing into the large rocks 80 feet below. Across the sparkling waters we could see Catalina Island, shrouded in a light mist.

The rent was 50 dollars a month — much more easily handled by my Marine pay than the Santa Barbara cottage. Entry to the house was down a rocky path at the end of a paved road terminating in a long flight of weathered wooden steps. At the bottom of the stairs, a short bridge led to the small entry to the upper floor. Inside on the right was a dark closet with narrow stairs beyond, leading to the lower floor. The kitchen was on the left and a spacious combined living-dining room spread across the front. This room was surrounded on three sides by large glass windows with views out to Catalina and up and down the coast. Downstairs were a bath and two musty bedrooms — not too appealing, but the first floor overcame any less desirable features below.

A decade after the end of the war, Hermi and I went back to see the house. The owner, a writer named Wells from Charleston, South Carolina, and the owner of a Ford dealership, welcomed us. He had completely remodeled the house and had built a guesthouse where a dilapidated garage once stood. He made us at home in the guesthouse where we spent the night. Hermi and I were charmed with the changes and said, "Let's retire here." I asked Mr. Wells to let us know if he ever put the house on the market.

Two weeks after we returned to Atlanta we received a letter from Wells saying he had sold his Ford dealership, was leaving South Laguna, and the house was for sale for $125,000 (a heavy price in 1956). We had already told him we were building a house in Atlanta, so he knew we probably weren't ready to buy; in his letter he said he was merely letting us know, as he had promised. I wrote back, thanked him, and confirmed his supposition that one house at a time was all we could handle.

The remodeled house was later featured in *Hillside Homes,* a West Coast publication. In addition to the plans and photographs of the remodeled house and guesthouse was the plan of the house when we lived there. I've heard the site itself is now valued at several million dollars, with the house thrown in.

Our stay in the little stucco house was enchanted, and nothing in our later life together ever matched the romantic experience of those short months perched over the blue Pacific. At night we delighted in watching the dappling patterns of light on the ceiling caused by the reflection from the fluorescent waves breaking below. Monet would have been inspired.

Still, we lived on the knife's edge of danger. Every morning when I left to fly we knew I might not return. Dive-bomber training was perilous, and many fatal crashes marred the Marine airmen's efforts. Our squadron lost more airmen in training than died in combat.

One day around noon, two Marine pilots rang our doorbell. Hermi, who was alone, saw them through the kitchen window; her knees went limp. What other mission could they have but to tell her I had crashed? Their smiles reassured her that they weren't bearing bad news. I don't recall why they came by, but I do know my demise wasn't the reason. Maybe these two hungry bachelors just wanted to have lunch with my very attractive wife. And feed them she did.

Food rationing placed a severe limitation on entertaining. Some weeks after our arrival at South Laguna I invited my commanding officer, Elmer Glidden, and the executive officer, Homer Cook, for dinner. Hermi stood in line for hours at the butcher to buy a minuscule remnant of beef. When I came home she showed me the "steak" that was to be the main course.

"Oh no, Hermi," I said, "even if you and I don't touch it that's only enough for two bites for each of them." She was indignant. "I waited in line for hours for that meat. It took all our ration points for the month. It just has to be enough!" After she calmed down, I persuaded her to supplement the tiny steak with macaroni and cheese.

Our guests enjoyed her company – a welcome change from the all-male dining at the base. Hermi told them that the names of the three senior officers in the squadron Elmer, Homer, and Cecil must strike paralyzing terror in the hearts of the enemy.

Homer laughed. "Maybe the Japanese translation sounds more fearsome," he said.

Our guests left, if not full at least happy.

Ghouls in the Closet?

Some time later I found out that the large dark closet at the entry to the house terrified my 20-year-old bride. She was sure all manner of weird creatures worthy of "Dreams of the Rarebit Fiend" (a popular comic strip of the time) dwelled in that dark forbidding space.

Every two weeks I was assigned military police duty in the nearby town of Santa Ana. It was a dangerous assignment. Each night the numerous bars were crowded with throngs of drunken – and usually rowdy – sailors, Marines, and airmen. Anyone wearing a different uniform from yours was, per se, a "lousy mother fuckin' bastard" or worse. Drunken brawls were almost inevitable.

My job was to plunge into these bars, with a large and deadly looking .45 automatic riding low on my hip, to break up fights, handcuff the struggling ringleaders, and conduct them to a waiting paddy wagon. Fortunately, I had help in the person of a 6-foot, 5-inch tall, 250-pound, strong-as-a-gorilla master sergeant. While I watched, he did all the manhandling. Without him, short of cocking my pistol, I could never have done my duty.

It was early morning when I came home after one of these Santa Ana sorties that I learned about Hermi's fear. She wouldn't go near the front door closet, and even a glance at it terrified her. What she feared was in it I don't know; it was certainly more than the coats hanging quietly. I discovered just how young and childlike my wife was.

After that experience I put a substantial lock on the closet. Before I would leave, we'd inspect the closet, shining a flashlight into all the dark corners looking for ghoullies. Convinced it was empty, Hermi allowed me to lock the door and give her the key before I walked out. Hermi was never convinced that those dreadful critters wouldn't materialize, locked door or not, once I left the house.

Hermi's days were much more pleasant than those fearsome nights. They were filled with shopping, visits with other Marine wives, and stretching out on the beach to enhance her suntan. She was convinced that only bronzed skin could mean the benefactor enjoyed good health. On one of Hermi's visits to New Orelans, the Weil's black cook, shielding herself from the blazing sun with an umbrella, saw Hermi in her bathing suit lying in the backyard. In her musical accent she said, "Ain't it funny. Miz Hermi, that you're white and wanna be black. I'm black and wanna be white."

To get to the sandy beach in South Laguna, Hermi had to scramble down a steep, rocky path from our house. For hours, until the sun began setting, she read books and wrote letters, the cold quiet waves lapping near her feet. I think she particularly enjoyed writing her friends back east at snowbound Smith College, in far-off Massachusetts, about the countless joys of sunning on the beach in southern California.

On to Hawaii

After too short a time, our squadron was ordered to pack up to ship out to Hawaii. The night before I left for the ship at San Diego, Hermi helped me fill a duffel bag with enough stuff to overburden all the shelves in one of today's big-box stores. If I had gone to the Pacific a second time, a toothbrush, a bar of soap, a razor, extra socks, undershorts, and a couple of shirts and pants would have been all I would have taken.

There was one rare lighthearted moment in the grim job of shipping out. As I packed my footlocker the night before, Hermi saw I was taking five watches, among the most valued navigation tools for pilots. With a twinkle in her eye, Hermi asked brightly, "OK, I know where you can wear four wristwatches, but where will you wear the fifth?" This came from a young, just-married woman of twenty, who later revealed a strong streak of naiveté.

Hermi and I found saying goodbye was unreal. We couldn't – or wouldn't – realize that I was headed for combat; that I might be badly wounded or killed; and that it was possible we might never see each other again.

One last time she drove me out to El Toro from our fairytale home hanging from the cliff over the sea. My last glimpse of her that dark night was of her hand caught in a shaft of light, waving goodbye from our Buick as she drove off. Later in the morning she headed down the coast to San Diego, where her father waited at the Hotel del Coronado to join her in driving across the desert to New Orleans. A new era had begun for both of us.

Then came the new orders: Report for assignment to either a dive-bomber or torpedo squadron. Some 30 to 40 other pilots joined me, all of us tense as we awaited our assignments. Nobody wanted torpedo bombers, which had a deadly reputation. In the Battle of Midway, an entire Navy squadron was shot down in an attack on the Japanese carriers. Only one man survived – Ensign George H. Gay, Jr., who had dropped out of Texas A&M University to fight for his country.

To my great relief, I was assigned to the Vought Marine Scout-Bombing Squadron 231 (VMSB-231), just back from some hard fighting, flying dive-bombers from Henderson Field on Guadalcanal. Now I would begin my training to use an airplane as a weapon. I would become a hunter, and I would be hunted.

Chapter 19

Getting Ready

Heard the heavens filled with shouting
While there rained a ghastly dew—
From that nation's airy navies
Grappling in the central blue.

— *Alfred Lord Tennyson, Locksley Hall*

In early 1942 I joined the Marine Scout Bomber Squadron 231 (VMSB-231), the famous Ace of Spades unit stationed at El Toro Marine Air Station, south of Los Angeles near Laguna Beach. It was the oldest flying squad in the Marines and had already participated in two decisive World War II battles. During the Battle of Midway, fought June 4-7, 1942, six months after the Japanese attack on Pearl Harbor, the 231 attacked the Japanese carriers bearing down on Midway. (In the interest of accuracy – and for the benefit of WWII buffs – the 231 was temporarily designated as VMSB-241).

The squadron had just received Scout Bomber Douglas aircraft (SBDs) and had no time to train for dive-bombing. The skipper, well aware his pilots weren't prepared for diving attacks, led his squadron in a shallow gliding approach to the ships. As a result, the vulnerable airmen made no hits, and half their the planes were shot down. Navy SBDs from our carriers came to the rescue. In the end, four Japanese first line carriers were destroyed and U.S. forces won the Battle of Midway – a turning point in the war at sea.

Soon after, VMSB-231 was ordered to Guadalcanal. Here conditions were terrible. There was nightly shelling by 16-inch shells and bombing attacks. Malaria, limited medical supplies, bad food (some of it moldy Japanese rice), rain, and mud-filled foxholes made life tenuous and miserable. Despite this horrendous environment, the 231 and other squadrons did their part to keep the Japanese at bay.

Compadres at El Toro

Some of the veterans of Guadalcanal were still with VMSB-231 when it was sent to regroup at El Toro, then still under construction. The unit's skipper, Elmer Glidden, had won two Navy Crosses, a medal not lightly awarded. When the commanding officer was lost at the beginning of the Battle of Midway, it was Glidden who led the 213 back safely, after dark, to the tiny, blacked-out atoll. As commanding officer at Guadalcanal, he led the 231 on attack after attack against Japanese shipping and ground forces.

Glidden graduated with a degree in engineering from Rensselaer Polytechnic Institute in the early 1930s, and the only job he could find in those Great Depression days was selling curtains. With no regrets, he left that uninspiring job to join the Marines and would win his wings several years before World War II began.

The executive officer, Homer Cook (whom I write more about later), strafed the Japanese ships coming down the passageway between the islands of the Solomons chain, including Guadalcanal, and drove them back. At the end of many months, Guadalcanal was secure and planes flew from its Henderson Field to patrol sea-lanes used by vital cargo ships headed for New Zealand and Australia.

The third veteran, Dale Leslie, was an excellent pilot who became my trusted and most likable friend. He was shot down at Guadalcanal. Crashing at sea and his gunner dead, Leslie bailed out of his riddled plane at 500 feet. He stripped to his shorts and held his shoes in his teeth by the shoelaces as he swam more than a mile to Guadalcanal's western shore. Exhausted, he crawled into a small cave hollowed into a bank and fell asleep. Voices awakened him. After venturing into the brushes in front of the cave he spotted three Japanese soldiers sitting on the cave's roof. He quickly ducked back in. Soon the roof of the cave began to collapse under the weight of the soldiers. Leslie struggled to his hands and knees and braced the roof. For several hours he held up the three soldiers until, at last, they left.

Leslie would remain trapped behind enemy lines for much of his weeks-long trek to Henderson Field, across mountainous terrain on the other side of the 2,050-square-mile island, He stole food from a native fire when no one was around. In a kind gesture that could have come straight from the pages of James Michener's *Tales from the South Pacific,* a white planter fed and clothed him and directed him toward Henderson.

After five weeks, Leslie stumbled into his tent and fell on his sleeping bag. His mates, believing him dead, had divided up his belongings – a knife, a canteen, a pistol, and other gear. When Dale demanded they return his stuff, they refused. "You're dead," they said. "You don't need these." After a while, they admitted he was alive and gave him back the loot.

Another friend, First Lieutenant Bud Blass, was a "mustang," the name given to Marines who had been promoted from enlisted status to officer. Bud was the smoothest flyer in the squadron. He never took foolish risks, but he always pressed his attacks to dangerously low levels, which he considered his job. When we college guys sat around drinking beer and discussing why we were fighting, Bud would remain silent. At the conclusion of our sophomoric theories, he would put an end to our surmising by saying "We're fighting because there's a war on." Although Bud never went to college, he was the best-read man in the squadron, not to mention a man well-versed in logic.

To grade the officers in their outfits, commanding officers periodically sent fitness reports to headquarters. The last question (and the most telling) was "Would you want to serve with this man in combat?" It should have been modified for aviation units to read "Would you want to fly on this man's wing?" Although I would have easily answered, "Yes," for all four of these veteran pilots – Glidden and Cook and Leslie and Blass – the man I was most comfortable following was Bud Blass.

Also at El Toro were a few veteran non-commissioned officers. One, Sergeant Strange, a gunner, often lived up to his name. I was very gratified when, after flying with me, he asked if he could be my permanent gunner. This was a strong vote of confidence, since the gunner's survival depended entirely on the skills and judgment of the pilot. Strange was my gunner for a year and a half, but we exchanged hardly a word beyond the discourse required while flying.

A distinguishing mark of all these men was the green pallor of their skin, a side effect of the drug Atabrine, a manmade malaria-fighting substitute for quinine. All the new pilots who, like me, were about to undergo multi-engine training were green from inexperience, not from Atabrine. There was much to learn, and we had to overcome a deep anxiety (come on, Cecil, it was *fear*).

After months of training as a twin-engine transport pilot, I would now learn to pilot an airplane as a weapon. No longer would my aircraft be a large DC-3 transport plane, flying straight and level, with no guns, bombs, or torpedoes. No longer would the comforting presence of a senior veteran pilot be next to me in the orderly cabin of a plane built originally for flights of peace.

Dive-Bombing Drills

My new plane would be the SBD (Scout Bomber Douglas), built by the Douglas Aircraft Company to conform to the Navy's specifications. Those specifications described a plane capable of entering a vertical dive at 12,000 feet, more or less, releasing bombs at low altitude while still in the dive, and recovering from the dive in a sharp pullout close to the ground. Straight and level speed wasn't required, so the SBD cruised at 150 knots. In a vertical dive with flaps deployed, the plane zoomed at a constant 250.

To protect the crew and strafe the enemy, the SBD had two 50-caliber machine guns, both forward-timed to miss the blades of the slowly revolving propeller when firing. The gunner, whose weapons were two 30-caliber machine guns, manned the rear cockpit. The guns were mounted on a circular "scarf ring," which allowed the gunner to swing them around to fire through an arc of 180 degrees. This arc took in the tail of the plane, which was at risk of being shot up by friendly fire from the gunner's weapon. It happened.

The SBD, officially called the Dauntless, was more accurately named "Slow But Deadly" by the pilots who flew her. And deadly she was. In the critical Battle of Midway, through a combination of luck, daring, and skill, carrier-based SBDs led by the aviator (and future rear admiral) Wade McClusky sank four of Japan's massive carriers, but not without a terrible loss of their first-line pilots. Still, Midway broke the back of the Japanese aggression at sea, and the Dauntless/Slow but Deadly, manned by gutsy, skilled men, was the weapon that brought off the victory.

The plane may have been as dauntless as its name, but in the cockpit was a daunting array of dials and misplaced levers. One surprising perk for the pilot was an automatic pilot, which was used in scouting missions. It was "caged" — that is, made inoperative in dives. But it wasn't always reliable. My automatic pilot engaged once without warning out over the Pacific, sending the plane straight down from a thousand feet. I recovered almost at the top of the waves, my heart beating at top speed.

The most inopportunely placed levers were next to each other on the right side of the cockpit. One lever activated the landing flaps, the other the dive flaps. The knobs were slightly different shapes and in different colors: black and orange. But with leather gloves on to protect our hands from fire, we couldn't feel the difference. Nor could we spare more than the quickest glace to check for the correct color. We lost two pilots and their gunners in training when, while slowly approaching for a landing, the pilots deployed the dive flaps instead of the landing flaps; this slowed their planes precipitously, causing a stall and sending their SBDs spinning into the ground. The accident reports assigned the crashes to "pilot error." It was not. It was "cockpit design error."

The original bombsight was a short, black tube about an inch in diameter and with crosshairs on a glass lens at the end of the tube. In the last stages of the dive the pilot put the tube at one eye and tried to center the target in the crosshairs, adjusting slightly for wind forces. He then released the bomb at a low altitude. Later, a safer and more accurate gun sight similar to those in fighters replaced the tube. The pilot could now look around and keep track of his altitude, glancing only periodically at the sight.

For protection, a heavy steel sheet was placed behind the pilot seat. There was also an inch-thick, foot-square sheet of bulletproof glass backing the windshield, protecting the pilot from shrapnel or anything else coming head on.

The SBD was equipped with both a tail hook used in carrier landings and very primitive radar, which was operated by the gunner. In a failed attempt at camouflage, the top of the plane was panted dark blue to blend with the ocean when seen from above, and light gray on the bottom to blend with the sky when seen from below. If this fooled the Japanese, their eyesight must have been tremendously deficient. I never had any difficulty seeing our planes, whether I was above or below them. The camouflage made for an interesting color scheme, but nothing else.

Clockwise from top left:
Hermi in her wedding gown. Both our
daughters wore the same gown on their
wedding days;
Married ! And a certificate to prove it;
Newlyweds;
Mr. and Mrs. Cecil Alexander, January 20,
1943, The Ambassador Hotel, Los Angeles,
California.

Walking with my father on Peachtree Street in Atlanta,
before shipping out to the war.

Ace of Spades Squadron, 1943. Top row from left: Cecil Alexander, Tom Hennesy, Unidentified, Commanding Officer Elmer Glidden, Dale Leslie, Judd Bell, Henry Graydon. Bottom row:Unidentified

Captain Alexander in SBD dive bomber, Marshall Islands, WWII

Shorty McSnorter with Cecil in the cockpit of the SBD

Life on Majuro Atoll during WWII

After a few familiarization flights around the field to become more or less at ease in the SBD, along with an intense study of the Pilot's Handbook, we were officially deemed ready to become dive-bomber pilots.

To start our training, we first "tail chased " – an exacting maneuver intended to condition the novice to handle the SBD in all altitudes and positions. The leader of the chase, always one of the veterans, led five fledglings on a wild ride. Loops, Immelmanns, slow rolls, snap rolls, vertical reverses, and Chandelles were all on the agenda and were executed in rapid succession. I won't describe these aerobatics. Non-pilots need only know that they were the disorienting, nauseating antithesis of straight and level flying. The pilots, closely following the plane in front, struggled to stay in position while trying desperately to emulate the leader's wild maneuvers.

We beginners chased tail for days until the control movements became instinctive, without requiring conscious thought. Now we were ready, in theory, at least, to point our planes straight down in a vertical dive, the Pacific's hard, unyielding water coming up at us at an alarming rate.

Glidden led my first dive-bombing run. We flew out over the ocean for several miles, and the gunner threw out a yellow dye marker. The stain from the marker spread an iridescent yellow patch against the dark blue ocean and would serve as our target. We climbed slowly into the thinning air at 13,000 feet. Whitecaps came and went on the sea below.

Each plane carried a mailbox-sized container under its right wing. In it were several small practice bombs, used to simulate the real thing. When one of them hit the ocean, a plume of smoke was released, marking the drop's accuracy.

Since takeoff at El Toro, we had been flying in the usual V formation, a plane on either side of the lead plane. The tips of the wings of the two planes deployed on the leader were held 4 to 5 feet out from the elevator at the tail of the leader's plane. At a hand signal from Glidden, the plane on his left slid to the right under the lead plane, then under mine to fall into position on my right elevator. We were now in a column, ready to dive.

Glidden and his gunner yanked open their Plexiglas-covered cockpits. I followed suit and opened my cover, and my gunner and the crew flying on my right opened theirs. The cold air streamed around my windshield and into the cockpit. I saw the yellow stain below. Glidden was almost right above it. He rocked his plane from side to side, signaling he was about to dive. His plane suddenly rolled over to the left until it was upside down. In a shallow arc the nose fell toward the ocean and the plane entered its dive.

Startled by his abrupt departure, I hesitated momentarily before I realized it was time for me to follow. I moved the control stick rapidly from side to side, rocking the plane, as had Glidden before me, to signal to the pilot on my wing that I was on my way down. Then I rolled the plane over, pulled back the control stick, and dropped the nose toward the ocean. My adrenaline was pumping. There was only intense concentration, not fear, as I reached for the lever to deploy the dive flaps, then pulled back the throttle to idle the engine to ensure the speed in the dive would stabilize at about 250 knots. The controls would become progressively heavier, and pullout from the dive would have to start 3,000 to 4,000 feet up. Accurate bombing required releasing the missile at no more than 2,000 feet.

I saw Glidden's plane boring down in front of me, looking as though it would never pull out. Then, when it seemed he was about to hit the water, he recovered from the dive. A bomb hit instead, and a plume of white smoke rose from the center of the stain.

Now I raised my goggles and put my right eye snug against the cold rubber guard at the end of the telescopic sight. Stories of pilots who became fixated as they gazed through that tube flashed through my mind; oblivious to danger and their altitude, they flew on down and crashed. I looked away from the tube to glance quickly at my altitude – 3,000 feet and unwinding fast. Back on the tube, I saw the target sliding under the crosshairs – Now! I jerked the lever to release the bomb, pulled back on the stick, closed the flaps, and pushed the throttle wide open. I was in an almost vertical climb, following Glidden's plane. I looked out. The wings were still attached. Whew! It would take many dives before I was confident that the wings wouldn't fly off on their own as I recovered from a dive.

"OK," I thought, "that's over. Now we can go home." To my dismay, when I asked my experienced gunner why we were climbing back up instead of heading for the coast, he replaced over the Intercom, "Sir, there are six bombs in that container. I think we'll have to dive five more times."

"Oh my God," I thought. "How can I get out of this and back to those straight and level DC-3s?" Of course, I couldn't.

Somehow I survived five more dives. I don't know if any of my bombs hit the bull's-eye, and I didn't care. If I sound unenthusiastic, I was. At the end of those six dives, it would have been a hard sell to convince me that I would ever enjoy dive bombing. The day came when I did, and I was one of the best at dropping a finned projectile on targets less than 25 feet in diameter. I'm also eternally grateful that none of my targets were civilians. It is disturbing enough that the enemy military installations we targeted were manned by men who may have had wives and children back in Japan.

A practice dive is exhilarating and dangerous. It is not the same, however, as the death-dealing experience of diving in combat. In the next chapter, "Off to Majuro," I attempt to reveal my attitude, my feelings, and the sensations of the act of destruction that is a dive-bombing attack.

Extra Exercises

In addition to dive-bombing, we were trained in ground support and simulated carrier landings. "Hairy" was a term we used to describe something so dangerous it caused your hair to stand up, and ground support that involved smoke screens to shield the infantry qualified as hairy.

I flew on Bud Blass's wing to an area near San Diego, where the ground Marines were on maneuvers. Our assignment was to lay a smoke screen in front of the "friendlies" to obscure them from the "enemy." This required flying almost at ground level while twisting and turning to miss hills, trees, and buildings. It made dive bombing seem tame. After about an hour, we had exhausted the smoke we carried in canisters and left for El Toro. I was more than ready.

Another ground support session, devoted to the simulation of bombing and strafing enemy forces advancing across a field, was much less exacting. Our gunners had a bucket of small cloth bags filled with flour. As our planes flew low over the field, the gunners threw the bags at the running Marines playing the enemy. I saw one of our bags hit a man between the shoulders. It sent him crashing flat on the ground, his rifle spinning away in the air – one very "dead" Marine. He looked up and shook his fist at us.

Wild flying, known as flat-hatting, and decidedly off-color language had become commonplace as Navy and Marine pilots trained along the coast from San Diego to San Francisco. To handle this outbreak, fighters with "Police" stenciled on the fuselage were sent to patrol along the coast. If he detected a miscreant, the "cop" pulled alongside the plane and signaled "thumbs down" while shaking his head; the violator was then supposed to land at San Diego and turn himself in.

One day, as I pulled out of a flour-bagging dive, a patrol cop joined up with me and flashed thumbs down. I vigorously shook my head "no" and peeled away from him. I was carrying out orders, and my dives were entirely appropriate to my mission. I'm sure the cop had noted my plane's number, so I fully expected a summons from San Diego. None came. Perhaps the pilot realized I wasn't flat-hatting after all.

A few days before we shipped out to the Marshall Islands by way of the Ewa Marine base in Hawaii, I was sent on a mission to stock up on whiskey for the officers. (Enlisted personnel were limited to beer.) My destination was the Naval Air Station at Alameda, California. On the way, I stopped at El Segundo for fuel. My takeoff was delayed when the airfield was closed for the initial flight of the Lockheed Constellation, a twin-ruddered transport. I minded not at all, sitting by the runway with my engine idling, as I watched that beautiful bird lift off on its first flight. Green and brown netting was spread out around the field and completely covered Lockheed's building. Placed on the netting were lightly built replicas of houses and other buildings along a pattern of fake streets. It was a very convincing *trompe l'oeil* designed to foil Japanese bombers.

At Alameda I left my plane on the flight line and walked to a large warehouse. I was shown a row of large wooden crates marked "Aviation Spares," with our squadron designated to receive them. The office manager assured me the crates were full of bottles of bourbon, not airplane parts, and that they would be on board the ship we were scheduled to sail on.

The Alameda field is located adjacent to Oakland, close to the east end of the long Oakland Bay Bridge. After being assured our whiskey was on its way, I taxied out, was cleared for take off down the runway, and headed for the bridge. Just as I lifted off, the engine lost power, backfired violently, and barely kept the plane airborne. I was out of runway. There was nothing to do but fly straight ahead and make a water landing. Just when it seemed I was going down, thankfully the engine cleared up and full power came back– but I was too close to the bridge to turn. My only course was under that low bridge just skimming the water. I made it, cursing heavy "aviation spares" as I did.

From then on, the return flight to El Toro was uneventful. I thought my daredevil flight should have earned an Air Medal or at least a Good Conduct Medal. None was forthcoming. Could it be because flying a seaplane under the Bay Bridge wasn't all that unusual? The first time it happened is still remembered. In November 1935, Pan Am's Martin M-130 clipper, dubbed the China Clipper, took off from the waters of San Francisco Bay on what would be the first scheduled air mail flight across the Pacific. Weighed down with close to a ton of mailbags, it wasn't able to clear the Bay Bridge, then under construction. So the pilot flew it beneath it through a harrowingly narrow space, drawing a gasp from the huge crowd that had gathered to watch the takeoff. "China clipper" would become the generic name for all Pan Am's clippers, which were pressed into military service in World War II.

The last phase of our training was in field carrier landing. This land-based maneuver simulated landing on a carrier deck. Missing was the pitching and rolling of the carrier, but adding to the danger on land was flying just over the trees and dodging a windmill in our flight path. Another factor that couldn't be duplicated was the speed of the approach. In both landings, real and simulated, the pilot flew just above stalling speed.

At sea, the carrier makes 20 to 30 knots into the wind that usually blew 15 to 20 knots directly down the deck. This meant that the plane, slowed down by the wind and slowly catching up to the carrier, is approaching the deck at only some 20 to 30 knots relative to the carrier. On land, however, the wind could be coming from any direction, and the runway certainly wasn't moving. So bringing a plane down on a field involved handling much greater speed – not necessarily a hazard, but far different from an actual carrier landing.

In both instances, a landing signal officer (LSO) with two circular paddles directed the plane on its final approach. The pilot watching the moving paddles saw whether he was flying too fast, too slow, above or below the correct glide path, whether to cut the engine and stall in for a landing, or whether to wave off and go around again. The LSO also checked to see if the pilot had let his tail hook down, since without it there could be no landing. When the tail hook caught the cable stretched across the short deck, it slowed the plane as the cable unwound and finally brought the plane to an abrupt stop.

At first it took a great act of faith and confidence for a pilot to put his life literally in the hands of the LSO, who was totally in control of the final approach. The only exception was when is the pilot was uncomfortable with the approach, broke away, and went around again.

As an approaching plane crossed the stern, two signals were essential: First, the LSO's "cut", which the pilot had to obey unless he had to go around for another try. Second, the LSO's "wave off," which signaled that either the plane is so far out of position that a safe landing was impossible or the deck hasn't been cleared of the plane just ahead. After a few landings, we pilots had no concerns. I never saw the landing signal officer make a mistake.

Time went quickly. We were well trained. We were also a team, and our training had become almost routine. As a break in the monotony we were occasionally challenged by a flight of Air Corps P-38s – the large, beautiful forked-tail fighter. A group of three to six from a nearby base would fly over El Toro. The Marine fighter pilots rushed to intercept them, going up to see if we could survive a real fight encounter with our slow- flying SBDs. Our tactic was to get behind the P-38s, whose machine guns fired forward and left the tail unprotected and vulnerable to attack. Because the SBD could fly more slowly than the P-38 and pull a much tighter turn, we were often able to get on the tail of the "enemy" and theoretically shoot it down.

This was a great confidence builder. We were ready, we thought, to dog-fight those Japanese Zeroes. We never encountered P-38 fighters during our time in the Pacific, but who can say we wouldn't have sent them spinning into the ocean had we been challenged? It's probably a good thing we never had to find out.

One bright morning, a sprawling gaggle of 24 SBDs roared over the field and circled for a series of ragged landings. They were our new planes flown in from the Douglas factory, piloted, we learned later, by inexperienced civilian pilots. When the last plane landed our sighs of relief could be heard for miles. We were in business!

As the navigation officer, I was responsible for aligning the compasses correctly. This was done by a procedure called "swinging the compass." A large compass rose was painted on the concrete tarmac with the compass points correctly aligned. One at a time, I taxied a plane over the rose and lined it up with the compass points painted on the concrete. Then, pushing hard on the brakes to keep the plane from rolling, I advanced the throttle until the engine was running at cruising speed, which generated magnetic impulses affecting the compass. Using a small screwdriver, I adjusted some small magnets on the compass to correct the deviation caused by the engine.

As I recall, the procedure of covering the 360 degrees of the compass had to be followed 24 times at 15-degree intervals. And this was required on all 24 planes! It took a week of 8-hour days to do this exhausting, boring job. When

I finally finished, I thought I owned those planes, that a part of me was a vital element of them. Later I found out I had no ownership whatsoever.

At last, after many weeks of training, our orders for overseas duty arrived. We packed our squadron's gear and gassed up the planes to fly to San Diego. There the *Kitty Hawk,* a converted railcar transport, was ready to take us to Hawaii. The last night, as I mentioned before, was time for personal packing and saying goodbye to wives or sweethearts.

We flew our SBDs down to North Island, the Navy's field at San Diego. There the planes were loaded on the *Kitty Hawk,* tied down in the hold to the rails recently used to carry freight cars across the Great Lakes.

Finally loaded, our ship slipped her moorings and headed out to sea, followed by a cloud of squawking seagulls. A small but fat Navy blimp circled overhead, on the lookout for Japanese submarines. On our way to the Pacific, I took a long last look at the Hotel Del Coronado, where Hermi waited. The finality of our goodbye now became real. I went into my cabin, locked the door, and wept.

Oahu as a Way Station

The long trip to Hawaii was boring for the officers. We read tattered, dull books, old torn magazines, or played Acey Ducey (the Marines' name for backgammon) for low stakes in the hot tiny wardroom. Whenever someone entered or left the room after dark, the single unshaded light bulb went out to preserve the ship's mandatory blackout. This on-again, off-again bulb reminded me of a bit from one of Charlie Chaplin's silent skits. Charlie had failed to pay his electric bill, so his power was cut off. Outside his apartment window was a flickering Broadway sign. Chaplin plugged his lamp into the sign, and as it went on and off so did his lamp, making his effort to read his newspaper a hilarious stop-and-go affair.

The enlisted men were not bored. They were desperate. A non-stop poker game dominated by a talented card shark was raging below decks. The shark, in real life a sergeant, had cleaned up, winning every hand. When our CO Elmer Glidden heard about it, he ordered the sergeant, under threat of demotion, to give back three-quarters of his loot. I think if Glidden hadn't acted, the sergeant, stripped of his ill-gotten gains, would have been thrown overboard one dark night and found himself swimming with real sharks holding a full house – not of cards but of saber-sharp, flashing teeth.

A lot of talk from the old hands assured us a Navy band would be at the dock in Honolulu to serenade us ashore. We thought they were making it up for our gullible benefit. To their surprise and our delight, as we approached the pier we saw a large Navy band in crisp white uniforms, their brass instruments sparkling in the sun.

As we walked down the gangway they blasted out the Marine Hymn, "From the Halls of Montezuma, to the shores of Tripoli. . . ." At the end, they shouted, "Semper fidelis, welcome Marines!" in full-throated unison.

Our stay in Hawaii, at the Marine Air Station at Ewa on the island of Oahu, was short and rather uneventful. Much to our dismay, the new SBDs that had come with us in the *Kitty Hawk* were snatched away by the Navy for carrier duty.

On a more personal level, I found it unsettling to walk Ewa's streets, which were crowded with people who appeared to be Japanese. Some probably were Chinese or Polynesian, but a third of the population was Japanese. They were completely loyal Americans, but how could you know? Reminders of December 7th were all too evident at Pearl Harbor, where hulls of ships lay in the water and the shoreline was covered by thick black congealed oil. Major Glidden told me that on that infamous December day in 1941, he was at Pearl Harbor and was shaving in front of a small mirror when Japanese Zeroes attacked the base and fired at the barracks. One bullet went through the roof of Glidden's barracks, zinged close by his ear, and smacked through the mirror that had just held his reflection. I don't know when or where he finished shaving.

The most traumatic event during my stay on Hawaii didn't directly involve me. Barracked next to me was Jim, a Marine pilot, waiting for his B-25 medium bomber to arrive from the mainland. It was coming as deck cargo on a tramp steamer. My neighbor had been waiting for days, and finally the phone rang with great news. The ship with the plane had docked at Pearl Harbor.

"Let's go see it; come on with me," urged Jim. We borrowed a Jeep and drove the 17 miles to for Pearl Harbor, the accelerator all the way down. As we stopped alongside the ship, Jim's plane was being swung on a crane cable before being lowered to the dock. Jim clapped his hands, did a little dance, and yelled, "Here it is! Here's my plane at last!"

Just as the bomber cleared the deck the cable snapped, and Jim's beautiful new airplane dropped some 60 feet to the concrete dock. When the plane hit on three wheels the wings broke away and the two engines fell off. Then the B-25 with drooping wings just sat there, a forlorn, quivering wreck.

Jim couldn't believe it. He looked at the remains in shocked horror. Then he slumped down on a crate, buried his face in his hands, and sobbed. He was beyond comfort. A drink at the Officers' Club later that day set him off again. I slipped quietly away. Even Hallmark couldn't have created a sympathy card to help Jim handle his loss. I don't know the end of the story.

Still another unfortunate event was my first encounter with a tense racial situation. In short, white Marines and black soldiers tangled on a bus in Honolulu and I, a second lieutenant, was the very junior but most senior officer present. Some indoctrination!

Of course, there were plenty of bright sides to our stay too. Used to food and gas rationing on the mainland, I was pleasantly surprised to see there seemed to be no controls in Hawaii. I ate my fill of thick steaks. Later I found out the steaks were buffalo, not cow, but no matter. Since fuel was also in abundance, Bud Blass and I took a Jeep drive around Oahu, much of it through acres of tall sugarcane fields and pineapple farms. We stopped at the large Dole Pineapple plant, which boasted fountains of pineapple juice, rather than water, to quench one's thirst.

The high point – literally and actually – was the Pali, the pass over the mountain ridge bisecting Oahu. The view is awe-inspiring. To the north, the blue Pacific stretches to the horizon; to the south, the ocean stretches beyond the white city of Honolulu and the landmark of Diamond Head. Wind constantly blows there, so strongly some men throw their hats off the cliff thinking the wind will blow them back into their hands, I didn't try it: if I lost my cap, my head would be left bare and would put me "out of uniform," an unpardonable condition for a Marine officer.

Also in full supply in Hawaii was film for our home movie cameras, another item unavailable in the States. I bought six reels and mailed them home to Hermi. She put them to good use, creating a documentary of her life on the home front in New Orleans.

On to Midway

I don't recall whoch mode of transportation took the whole squadron to Midway. My mode was a Caribbean United Fruit banana boat converted to a troop transport. Midway lies some thousand miles northwest of Honolulu. It is the next to last island in the Hawaiian chain, which, as it spreads northwest, is made up of many small reefs, atolls, and islands.

Our trip was uneventful. The interior of the ship was poorly ventilated and stiflingly hot, so I slept on deck in my sleeping bag, drifting off to the gentle rocking of the ship and the low growl of her engines.

Midway showed up on schedule. We entered the narrow channel between the only two inhabited islands in the circular reef – Eastern on the right, Sand on the left. There was no tugboat, and the captain turned his ship toward the dock at considerable speed. He reversed the engines too late, and the ship the dock with force. The wood pilings were knocked at an angle, leaving a gap between the dock and the ship. Still, the gap was easily bridged by the gangplank, which we walked down to go ashore.

One of the dockhands laughingly told me how they adjusted to compensate for the captain's poor ship handling. "His one route is between here and Hawaii, so he comes in often. We bring him in on alternate sides of the dock. Next time when he hits the pier on the other side, it will straighten it up."

A couple of months later, I heard that the newly attached ship's doctor, whom I knew and liked, was on the same transport docked at Sand Island. I went on board to see him at noon – chow time. The ship's captain sat at the head of the table and wasted no effort on pleasantries.

"Lieutenant," he asked me. "Are you a pilot flying those SBDs?"

"Yes Sir."

"Well, goddamn it, your squadron gives us lousy submarine cover, and some of you enjoy making low dangerous passes at my bridge. You've got to tell your skipper I want that stopped. Now! Do you understand me?"

"Yes Sir, I will."

Like the captain's demeanor, the lunch was lousy. I did have a good visit with the doctor after we left the table; we sat out on deck in the warm air and began shooting the breeze.

Since I'm not a geologist, I probably shouldn't attempt to explain the origin of the Hawaiian islands, and if you are a geologist please skip my amateur efforts. Actually, what follows is my understanding as the result of extensive reading of theories by qualified scientists.

In the 19th Century, Charles Darwin planted the seeds of a theory that is still accepted. It makes sense to me, and following is what we know now and how Midway fits in.

The long chain of islands stretches from Hawaii, the Big Island, for over a thousand miles northwest to Kure, a small atoll that is the oldest of the islands still above the sea. Sixty miles southeast of Kure is Midway, a name that now echoes down our history like Concord, Bunker Hill, Gettysburg, Appomattox, Pearl Harbor, and Guadalcanal. Midway's age is estimated at 25 million years, give or take a millennium or two.

An example of the chain's creation is even now in progress deep in the ocean southeast of the Big Island. Loihi, a seamount (submerged volcano) that was thought to be old and inactive was found in the early 1970s to be a young and active, It ejects a massive flow of hot lava that is building a conical island now some 10,000 feet tall, and whose top is less than a mile beneath the surface. Many thousands of years will pass before Loihi breaks through the ocean's surface.

All of Hawaii's islands rest on the Pacific Plate, the subsurface land mass moving northwest at about 3 inches a year and carrying the islands, but not the vent, with it. The Pacific plate is the source of the so-called ring of fire surrounding the Pacific basin; its eastern rim forms the San Andreas Fault. As the plate carries an island northwest, the connection to the vent is broken, causing the volcanoes to become extinct. For example, five volcanoes rise on the Big Island, three of them active and two dormant. But northwest of the Big Island, the worn-down volcano Diamond Head, on Oahu, broke away from the vent and is extinct.

Eventually the volcanic mountains subside, leaving a ring formed by its walls below the ocean's surface. Over thousands of years live coral attaches to the rim and eventually emerge a few feet out of the water, with Midway as an example: It is a circular atoll composed of a ring of narrow, low lying islets and measures some miles in diameter all told. Fortunately, nature left a channel into the lagoon between the two largest islands, Eastern and Sand. The channel was dredged to accommodate large ships and submarines.

The Navy fortified these two islands during World War II. In the past, Sand Island served as a coaling station for ships on the voyage across the Pacific. It was also a way station for the communication cables spanning the ocean and a refueling depot for the large Pan American China Clippers that landed in the lagoon. During the war, Sand became a submarine base with advanced repair facilities to service submarines returning from attacks off the coast of Japan. Under a large coral bunker, the Navy installed a command and communication center, which continued to make use of the trans-Pacific cables. The cable messages, which the Japanese were unable to intercept, played a vital role in the Battle of Midway.

Eastern Island was developed as an airfield with three coral runways. Hangars, a power station, barracks, mess halls, and repair shops were built around the runways. There was also a primitive Officers Club, where many drunken pilots tried to escape reality. Some humanitarian planner included a motion picture theater in the cluster of buildings. Films were shown 24 hours a day, and most of them were old and cracked. They regularly broke during a showing but gave a moment of relief from the enervating life on Midway.

Midway's Feathered Aviators

The Navy wasn't the best form of entertainment on the island. The star performers were the birds of Midway — thousands of birds soaring in the wind, nesting, mating, dancing, raising their chicks, clouding the air above, and covering all available land. They made Midway unique, and fascinated all of the higher-order residents stationed there.

With its 7-foot wingspan, the soaring Laysan albatross is the royalty of the many species of birds on the island. "Gooney bird," the demeaning nickname for these magnificent fliers, certainly wasn't an assessment of their airborne abilities. It came from their ungainly waddle on the ground, their hilarious mating dances, and their failure to extend their webbed feet for the first landing on the atoll after months at sea, which caused them to tumble, disoriented, head over feet for many yards.

Gooneys spend much of their lives at sea, flying hundreds of miles in search of squid, their favorite food. They bring back the squid and regurgitate this dainty dish into the open beaks of their chicks. (Helen, who became my wife after Hermi's death, had a look of disgust when I described the process. I pointed out that no grocery carts or plastic bags were available.) Goonies take up residence at Midway, Laysan, and other islands to nest, mate, incubate, and hatch their one big egg. The newborn chick is taught to fly by example, a long and difficult process.

Norman Harrower, one of our pilots, was a Harvard graduate. It pained him to see the slow progress the chicks made toward becoming airborne. Why not, he thought, give them the advantage of a Harvard education?

A sign soon appeared along one runway. "The Harvard Gooney Bird School of Flight," it read. Underneath was inscribed "Professor Norman Harrower."

Norman's training method was strictly practical — no theory, no intellectual investigations. He banded six of the chicks to identify them and enrolled them in his school. For hours at a time he would lift each of the fledglings by their wingtips, run into the wind and launch them from above his head. In a short time his students were flying. It was several weeks before the baby gooneys that hadn't been schooled were airborne. Harrower proudly proclaimed that his training showed the superiority of a Harvard education.

Many more species of seabirds nest on Midway, all of them magnificent flyers. As we watched, we envied their ease and grace. The beauty of the lot is the bosun bird, with its pure white wings and body and a single long tail feather tipped in red. The tail feather turned out to be the birds' curse. Before World War II, Japanese poachers killed thousands of bosuns for their tail feathers, which were in great demand for ladies' hats and garments.

The bosun flying technique is unique. For long periods the birds face into the wind, their wings spread wide and moved just enough allow the birds to allow hovering over the same spot. We would have been a bunch of happy pilots if our SBDs could have hovered like those bosuns.

Shearwaters were also at Midway in great numbers, and were called "moaning doves" for a good reason: they moaned. The sound was like a thousand babies wailing or, as many believed, a more unsettling source. A widely accepted myth was that the moans were the pleas of the souls of dead seamen who had drowned when their ships wrecked on Midway's reef.

On a windy, stormy night I walked out on the deserted reef. I wanted to be alone with my thoughts of Hermi. The piteous cries of the shearwaters surrounded me. A disturbing thought came to me: Maybe it wasn't a myth. Maybe those eerie cries were from the souls of those lost mariners. The howl of the wind and the thunder of the breakers joined the moans. Under the low black clouds I became a believer. Then came something that hadn't happened since I was a kid listening to a camp counselor reading Edgar Allen Poe's *Fall of the House of Usher* as we young campers huddled around a fading fire: The hair on the back of my neck stood on end.

It was time to leave that desolate, eerie place. In the distance I saw the glow of yellow lights from our quarters spilling out on the coral. I didn't run exactly, but I certainly didn't amble toward the light. Sure, I knew it was only those damn birds crying, but why was I so relieved to be back at our barracks, back among the living?

One sailor became so agitated by the moans he went berserk one dark night. He ran wildly about where the birds were nesting, swinging a baseball bat and screaming, "Die, you fuckin' birds! Die!" He clubbed hundreds of them into small bloody masses of feathers. Exhausted, he fell to the ground sobbing.

The next day he was shipped back to the States, where a panel of psychiatrists would examine him to determine if he was insane. In Europe, General George S. Patton slapped a soldier who was in a hospital after a nervous breakdown, and only Eisenhower's leniency saved him from being relieved of command. The bat-wielding soldier on Midway was lucky not to be in Patton's army, or the general would have smacked him to a pulp.

The frigate birds circling high over the reef were scavengers; they let the other birds do the hard work of fishing. When these large black fowls see a bosun, shearwater, or any other bird returning from the ocean with a fish clutched in its talons, it folds its wings and dives toward the homeward-bound carrier. When the carrier becomes aware of the plummeting marauder, he springs open his talons, releasing the fish. The frigate bird snatches the falling meal out of the air and swiftly flies with it back to the nest.

All those soaring birds had been on Midway long before man came ashore. They will, if we don't ruin the planet or kill all wildlife, be there long after man has run his course, his mechanical flying machines reduced to scrap. In 2009 President George W. Bush designated the western Hawaiian Islands as the Pacific Remote Islands Marine National Monument, an act that ought to preserve these treasure and the birds for years to come.

During the war, the birds and the Marines shared Midway on both the ground and in the air. But unlike the birds we were there to finish our training in any badly distressed SBDs left after the battle; to search for enemy submarines and ships; to escort our own subs to protect them from friendly fire; and to attack and destroy any Japanese fleet trying once again to capture the Midway islands.

Tsunamis and Submarines

We had been stationed on Eastern Island about a month. I was Officer of the Day, which involved, among other duties, receiving encoded messages from Honolulu, messages that had to be immediately decoded. One day the phone rang and a voice said, "Stand by for an encoded message on your telegraph." The key started clacking away and the operator translated the dots and dashes to coded words on his pad. The message was repeated. I pulled out our codebook and frantically interpreted it. The translation made me gasp:

"Large Japanese task force headed Midway from north. Take all necessary steps to drive back the attackers."

Leaving the clerk to call the other units, including the submarines base, I raced in a Jeep to rouse Major Glidden, our commanding officer. It was about two o'clock in the morning, but the sleeping major was immediately alert when I read him the message. He had been there before. In an SBD on June 4, 1942, he attacked the Japanese carriers during the Battle of Midway.

It took Glidden only a few minutes to throw on his clothes, and we ran down the hall to the Bachelor Officer Quarters entry lobby. The island commander, a Navy lieutenant, was staggering around naked, enveloped in a haze of alcohol. When he saw Glidden he said, "What the hell are you doing? I give the orders, I'm in command here!"

Glidden stared at him, strode over, put his hand over the lieutenant's face, and gave a hard shove. The drunken officer staggered backward, hit the wall, slid to the floor in a sitting position, and passed out. Someone later threw a towel across his lap to preserve what was left of his modesty. He sat there for the duration of the crisis, totally oblivious. He was soon transferred.

Glidden immediately called the pilots and gunners together for a conclave. The squadron was divided into two sections – one led by Glidden himself, the other by Homer Cook, the executive officer. At that time I was the navigation officer for the squadron.

It had occurred to me earlier that flying for hours over water to intercept a ship – and returning perhaps with no radio direction and probably after dark to a blacked-out tiny atoll or a carrier – required the highest degree of navigation skills. I made it my business to learn all I could about the mathematics required to plot a course and ways to judge the wind. Every day I brought Midway's pilots and gunner into a makeshift classroom and drilled them on navigation. I was so obsessed with accuracy that just finding a small island didn't satisfy me. I aimed for a particular bay or promontory on that island. And if I missed by more than a mile, I felt I had failed.

Homer Cook was aware of my hard earned skills. "Alex," he said, "I want you on my wing so we'll be sure to find this damn island after the strike." I was gratified by his expression of confidence, but I wasn't happy with the responsibility.

Glidden ordered all of us to check out our planes, run up the engines, check the fuel using a dipstick rather than the unreliable gauges, see that our cockpit and navigation lights functioned, and, most important, to be certain we carried a 500- pound bomb under the plane. He then told us to bunk down on canvas cots next to our planes. There was no further information about the enemy, and PBYs, the big flying boats, made searches out to the north with no sightings. We settled in for an uneasy sleep.

At 5:00 in the morning, just before daylight, I was jolted awake by the roar of our SBD engines being run up and checked out. Getting dressed wasn't a problem; I slept in my flight suit without even taking off my heavy shoes. A Jeep brought coffee and rolls to us from our mess hall – hardly a great last meal, which it would certainly be for some of us if we dive-bombed a heavily armed Japanese task force.

Later in the morning we heard planes approaching. They were, to our relief, Navy fighters sent from Oahu to bolster our air power. Were we glad to see those shiny new Grummans come down on Eastern Island!

More waiting. Tempers flared. Nerves tightened. Stomachs growled. No news – just "standby," "be alert", and "keep the guns and planes at the ready."

Then came the crushing climax (anti- isn't a strong enough prefix). Yes, a Japanese convoy of ships had been seen north of Midway, but it wasn't headed our way. It had been sent by the Japanese to evacuate the Aleutian Islands and was on its way back to Japan.

My emotions were as mixed as if they had been poured into a Waring blender. Great relief that I wouldn't be diving in a battered SBD at a mighty battleship or carrier (while under aerial attack from enemy fighters) mixed with deep disappointment that I wouldn't have a chance to bomb a ship – my mission in full measure after months of training. Someone defined "mixed emotions" as "watching your mother-in-law drive off a cliff in your new Cadillac." Since I truly loved and admired my mother-in-law, the Waring blender analogy I've chosen is more appropriate. It is also not likely to offend the blender.

The Navy fighters flew back to Oahu and we went back to the same dull, monotonous, energy-draining routine.

Music to Our Ears

Soon after the faux alarm, there arrived a wonderful alleviation for the dreariness of our existence. The father of one of our pilots, Lt. Arthur was, I believe, one of the producers of the great musical *Oklahoma!* He sent out to us a 78 rpm record of the entire play. We had an electric turntable in the Ready Room, but how we came by it I've forgotten.

All day and far into the night we played the great songs: "Oh What a Beautiful Mornin'," "The Surrey with the Fringe on Top," "I Caint' Say No" and the joyous title song "Oklahoma!" We wore the grooves in those platters down to deep canyons.

Another favorite was "Skylark", a plaintive ballad in a minor key. I think the vocalist was Hoagy Carmichael. If the lyrics "Have you seen the valley green?" didn't make you incurably homesick, you were an emotional rock.

There was a battered, out-of-tune, upright piano in the wardroom. Lt. Cal English, an excellent pianist, either played his own compositions or knocked out our favorite tunes by Berlin, Kern, Rodgers, Gershwin, and Porter whenever he could. He also sometimes adapted the original lyrics of these great composers to our situation. One of his adaptations used me as the butt, much to my discomfort. The source of that well forgotten satire was entitled "Throw That Pistol Down," and how the joke came about follows.

The second island southeast of Midway was the uninhabited atoll of Lysianski. Periodically we searched that barren strip to make sure the Japanese weren't occupying it. I had just skimmed over the island, saw nothing alive but birds, and was leading my wingman back to Midway. The SBD was being flown by autopilot, the engine purring away. I was relaxed, almost asleep, when the sudden sound of the propeller running wild got my attention. The propeller was controlled by a governor that maintained the pitch of the blades set by the pilot at different angles for takeoff, landing, or cruising. The governor had broken and the propeller went almost flat, its rpm below safe limits.

Several days before, our exec Homer Cook told me he had a similar occurrence. Fortunately, he said, he was lined up to land and was able to make a safe landing. If he had been away from the runway he added, he would have had to ditch (make a water landing). Memory of that conversation concerned me as I headed in my SBD for the blue Pacific 500 feet below.

The pilot's manual gave detailed instructions on preparing for a water landing. To prevent the gunner from being trapped in his cockpit by the two machine guns mounted just aft of the cockpit, he should detach them and drop them overboard. We were down to about 200 feet when I said to my gunner over the intercom, "We're ditching, Sergeant. Throw out your guns." "Yes sir," he said, and reported shortly that that the guns were gone.

It occurred to me that, flat as it was, the propeller was pulling the plane ahead. I leveled out, and much to my relief the SBD stopped its descent and maintained our altitude about a hundred feet above the surface. So at that low altitude and dangerously slow speed, we made it back to Midway.

I called the control tower, reported an emergency, and was granted a straight-in approach. The landing was normal, but the reception by the CO was anything but.

"Why in hell did you throw those guns out? They cost 15 thousand dollars, and they may take that out of your salary. You should have waited until just before you hit the water."

Homer Cook was with us. I looked at him and told Major Glidden what he had told me about his experience. "Homer," I said, "You told me you couldn't stay airborne when your prop governor broke, right?"

"No," he said, "I never said that."

But he had said it. I admired Cook and thought he was a fine Marine, but I still haven't forgiven him for changing his story. He could have spared me a large amount of grief.

So that's how my experience became fodder for the musical Lt. English's satirical lyrics. He re-titled "Throw That Pistol Down" as "Throw Those Thirties Down," a reference to the discarded 30-caliber guns. I've blanked out the lyrics, but the gist of them still burns. The several verses painted in detail that I had lost my cool and panicked, when actually I was methodically following the correct procedure. Every time I went into the Ready Room and English was there, he sat down at the piano and played that damn tune.

Threats, Lessons, and Subs

Only twice during my four years of active duty in the Marines did I come close to a fistfight. In fact, I was eager to have at it. This was based on two opinions of the power in my right hand. I was training for a boxing tournament at Yale, boxing with my Atlanta friend Bob Ferst. (Gerald Ford – yes, the future president – and a student then at the Yale Law School, was my coach.) We had been at it a few minutes when I saw an opening and landed a hard right to Bob's face that rocked him. It seemed strange then, and still does, that he said, "I'm hurt. Come on at me, take advantage of that right." In preparation for the tournament he was, I assume, urging me to be aggressive even at his own expense.

After my sophomore year at Yale, my cousin Henry and I spent a week at Osceola Camp in North Carolina, where we had gone as young campers. A counselor at the camp, Joe Murnick, was the captain of the UNC Chapel Hill boxing team. Some overeager (from my viewpoint) would-be promoter arranged an exhibition bout between Joe and me. We had been trading light punches with our gloved fists. It was truly an exhibition until some time in the third and last round, I fell back against some women seated in chairs around the ring. My chin went up, and Murnick landed a hard left to my Adam's apple – very painful. It stopped my breathing for a long minute and became infuriated. From that point on I was in a real fight, throwing every punch I could at him.

Joe and I were showering after the match. He said, "Hey man where did you get that right? It hurts like the devil." So I had two endorsements of the power in my right hand.

I would have welcomed the chance to use my right in both of the following encounters. The first incident was at the base in Atlanta while I was in training. One of the other would-be pilots was giving me a verbal going over. I went back at him. Anger escalated, and I cocked my fist. A friend pulled us apart and said, "Knock it off. If you two guys get in a fight, they'll wash you both out." We were being trained to fight and kill with airplanes, but fistfights were off limits. The irony was inescapable.

The second occurrence was at Midway, over a much more serious matter. As part of our training we made firing passes at a canvas sleeve pulled on a long rope well behind a tow plane. Six planes would line up above and behind the tow plane. One after the other, we would dive down in an arc firing at the sleeve with our two machine guns. It seemed entirely reasonable that you waited until the plane in front of you was well out of the way before you made your own firing run – reasonable, yes, but at least in this one incident, ignored.

I had just finished my run and was pulling away from the sleeve when I saw a stream of tracer bullets racing past my cockpit. Tracers leave a trail of fire to show the gunner where his shots are landing. There was no doubt that the pilot behind me was firing his machine guns while I was still exposed.

When I landed, I taxied my plane next to the plane that fired at me. Not even waiting for the ground crew to put chocks in front of my wheels, I struggled out of my parachute, jumped out of the cockpit, and raced to the offending plane. The pilot was just climbing off the wing. I grabbed him by his collar with my left hand and cocked my right fist. I was in a rage. "You son of a bitch, you fired before I cleared the target, and your tracers went right by my cockpit!" I yelled. "You could've shot me down or killed my gunner or me! I'm going to beat the hell out of you!"

A mechanic grabbed me and pulled me away. "Calm down sir, you'll be in trouble if you hit him." He was right; I turned and stalked away. I never spoke to that trigger-happy bastard again. The Japanese were our official enemy, but I had one of my very own – one I loathed much more than I did the Japanese.

One of our youngest pilots taught the squadron two vital lessons – but unfortunately, in death. On a moonless night with overcast skies, a takeoff from Midway was a chancy procedure. There were no lights beyond the runway, and the horizon couldn't be seen. The solution was to rely entirely on the instruments until you had climbed to a safe altitude. Also, our planes had recently been equipped with shoulder harnesses; this was in addition to the broad seatbelt, which had been standard for years. The harness protected the pilot from butting his head on the instrument panel or the bombsight if the plane came to a sudden stop. The younger pilots thought using the harness wasn't macho. John Wayne certainly would never wear one.

It was one of those very dark, cloudy nights when the pilot in question turned onto the runway and accelerated down its length for takeoff. Just after he left the runway, he called his gunner on the intercom: "Hey man, its black out here. I've got vertigo. My instruments are all haywire. We're going down. Hold on!" The plane plunged into the black water.

The gunner survived the crash. The pilot did not. The gunner later told our skipper that as soon as he freed himself from his cockpit he swam around to the front cockpit to check on his pilot. He was dead, his head impaled on the bombsight's tube. The plane rapidly sank, leaving the gunner afloat in his life jacket. A launch spotted his flashlight and picked him up. A shoulder harness would have protected the pilot's head and an instrument takeoff would have kept him airborne – and alive.

Two lessons even the most immature "nothing-can-happen-to me" pilots learned: Use your instrument for night takeoffs and buckle your shoulder harness – macho be damned. After all, John Wayne fought his many battles of the war on film from the comfort and safety of a studio. Vertigo wasn't his problem, and shoulder harnesses weren't needed in an actor's canvas chair.

The anticipated Japanese attack had yet tot come, but now we had another deadly warning. A violent underwater seismic disturbance had occurred in the ocean floor near the Aleutian Islands, setting off a tsunami racing toward Midway at 600 miles an hour. (We called it, in error, a "tidal wave,") The roof of the power station on Eastern Island and a manmade low hill on Sand Island were the only areas well above sea level, so all of the patients in sickbay were hoisted on stretchers to the top of the power station. In addition, rubber rafts were taken out of the planes, inflated, and placed close to the barracks; this didn't qualify as a precaution, but pilots and gunners were asked to volunteer to man two SBDs to search for the tsunami north of Midway. Being airborne seemed much more desirable than waiting on the ground for a 30-foot wave to sweep me away. I shot my hand up ahead of all but one other pilot, and he and I were chosen. I was to fly on the wing of the worst pilot in the squadron. He was senior to me. He couldn't be bothered with navigation, a rather useful skill for flying miles out over the ocean and finding your way back to low-lying Midway. No matter, I would navigate for both of us without telling him.

In our separate planes we headed north from Midway in the direction of the distant Aleutians, armed with excellent charts for determining wind strength and direction from the appearance of the ocean. The large waves below us sent foam cascading down their backs into the wind. The wind force and direction at the surface usually were the same for a thousand feet or more in the air. We were at that altitude. I entered on my chart, "wind 35 knots from 90° (east), the plane's compass heading of 0° (north)," and I calculated our true direction as affected by the wind.

From time to time I looked down to check the wind and search for the tsunami. After about an hour I looked below and couldn't believe what I was seeing. The wind had swung 180° and was now blowing from west to east. The waves were exactly the same height, but the foam was sliding west into the wind. To make sure I was right, I had my gunner throw out a smoke bomb. When it landed it floated and a trail of smoke streamed out. And yes, the smoke's direction showed the wind had swung completely around. I entered the change on my chart and recalculated our new heading.

There was no sign of a huge breaking wave. After we reached the point where calculations placed the tsunami and saw nothing, we reversed course to return to Midway. When we arrived at the spot where Midway was supposed to be according to the other pilot's navigation, there was just ocean. He hadn't realized that the wind had changed. He was lost. My own navigation indicated we were about 20 miles east of Midway – and there it was, a dark line on the horizon. I called the navigator and pointed toward Midway. We were soon there with nothing to report.

While we were gone, the tsunami had hit Midway exactly on time based on its progress of 600 miles per hour. But its energy was spent. The much-feared massive wave was only 3 feet high. Unlike the failure of the Japanese to attack, I had no mixed emotions about the failure of the big wave to material-ize, only great relief.

A meteorologist laughed when I told him about our unsuccessful search for the tsunami. He said "When a tsunami is over deep water there is no wave crest; it is only a long swell. The huge vertical wave forms when it reaches shallow water. From the air it could never be identified. Yours was a fool's mission." I answered, "All right, from your viewpoint it was a fool's mission, but that search got me off the ground, safe from the tsunami. I think it was a brilliant mission."

Now I return briefly to Midway's feathered aviators. After all the amuse-ment the gooney birds had given me, I was saddened by a fatal (to the bird) encounter I had with one of those beautiful albatrosses. The wind was blow-ing down the shortest of the runways. To get off the ground in time I was applying the brakes hard while I brought the engine to full power before takeoff. Just as I released the brakes and the plane started to roll forward, the gooney glided across the runway into the fast spinning blades of the SBD's propeller. Nothing survived but a few feathers. I shut down the engine to inspect the propeller, and there was no damage. Charles Lindbergh, who in his latter years had become a conservationist, said, "Given a choice between airplanes and birds, I would take the birds." I agreed then, and I do now, only more so.

Before my story moves on I will try to capture the magic of one early morning flight. The dawn was just beginning to bring its light to ground level when I took off. Overhead, a blanket of gray clouds stretched to the horizon in all directions. I climbed up through the clouds and, after a few minutes, burst into the clear air. The cloud layer below, a turbulent mass of deep valleys and high peaks, was lit by the rising sun in colors ranging from white to pink to dark purple. I dropped down into a beckoning purple valley and guided my nimble plane through a canyon of clouds. Then, at the end of the canyon, I again climbed above the clouds, which now looked like long rolls of solid, multi-colored mist. In all too short a time the sun rose and turned the pastel colors into blinding white. The magic was gone, but the vision of that flight has never left me.

At ground level, one of our assignments was to rendezvous with our submarines returning from patrols off the coast of Japan. It always amazed me that the subs surfaced exactly on time at the exact coordinates they had radioed ahead would be the rendezvous point. Most of the returning submarines had a broom attached to the periscope, indicating a clean sweep. Every ship they encountered was sunk.

The submariners loved to fly, and we loved to eat their choice chow. A deal was struck: fly with us and we will eat with you. Stan Kaplan, our intelligence officer, liked the food but wanted to know more about the submarines. When the boats came into Midway, an exacting test was run on them. Stan went out on one of these dives and found that the captain took the sub down below its designed depth to see if it leaked! Pails were put under any leaks and the location was noted. When I heard about these test dives, I decided I would confine my submarine experiences to eating their fine food while the boat was safely tied up at the dock.

There was another encounter between SBDs and submarines. One of our pilots was searching for Japanese subs when he saw the dark form of a submarine on the surface in an area where our subs weren't allowed. The pilot thought if it wasn't ours, it must be theirs and decided, "I better drop my surface fused depth charges on it before it dives." He made a low pass, but both his charges missed and landed well away from the sub. A sailor, obviously an American, came out of the conning tower to frantically wave off the attacking SBD. There was a complication: Our skipper was on board the submarine.

When he came ashore, he sent word to the pilot who had dropped the charges to report to him immediately.

"How the hell could you miss?" he demanded. "That sub was on the surface and dead in the water. How could you miss?"

I was embarrassed to have to admit it was one my planes. Forget that the skipper could have been killed if the drop had been accurate. His only concern was embarrassment over his pilot's poor marksmanship. The squadron crew's remarks on his statement varied from "Stupid!" to "Courageous!" – none made to the skipper's face, of course.

Our Return to Oahu

After five months on the tiny historic atoll, the squadron was ordered back to Oahu. Our relief was flying out in the whale-shaped Curtiss C-46 transports. My brother-in-law Roman Weil was with the relieving squadron. I asked the skipper, Elmer Glidden, if I could fly out on the last plane so I could see my brother-in-law when he landed. It was beyond his understanding (being a bachelor I suppose) that anyone would want to see his brother-in-law, but he said "OK."

Roman's plane lost an engine several hundred miles out from Midway. The heavily loaded C-46 couldn't maintain its altitude and steadily lost altitude as it headed for Midway. To lighten the plane, the passengers formed a chain and threw everything that wasn't a vital part of the plane out the wide cargo door.

The last cargo to go was some heavy crates of bourbon. Throwing those precious bottles out was a deeply traumatic experience for those on board, particularly my brother-in-law, who regarded bourbon as elixir of the gods. But with the weight gone, the plane avoided a water landing, leveled out at 300 feet, and wobbled its way to Midway.

Roman and I met briefly, exchanged our latest word from home, shook hands, wished each other luck, and said so long. We didn't guess we would soon be together in the Marshall Islands.

Storing our squadron and personal gear on the C-46s for our return to Oahu required controlling the weight and the distribution of the load (lost engine or not). In control of weighing was the same tsunami-seeking pilot who couldn't find Midway. I'm not sure what motivated him, but he cheated on the weight, reducing the pounds for each item well below the amount shown on the scale. Maybe he was afraid his footlocker would be left behind, but this list had to be given to the pilot, and for good reason.

Knowing the plane I was in was heavily overloaded, I had a bad case of white knuckles as we went down the runway for takeoff. The plane lifted off with just a few feet of runway left. By the time we reached the Ewa Marine Air Station, most of the fuel had been consumed, reducing the plane's load to a safe figure. We landed without incident.

Midway had been exciting and boring at the same time. We perfected our dive-bombing there and improved our gunnery, sufficient training for our next move to the Marshall Islands, where enemy anti-aircraft fire would become a serious factor and would bring our long months of preparation for combat to an end.

Chapter 20

Off to Majuro

And if I take the wings of the morning
and dwell in the uttermost parts of the sea
Even there shall thy hand lead me ...

— Psalm 139

On an ordinary day in early 1944, it was just one more uneventful afternoon at the Officers' Club in Honolulu. Or so we thought. "Captain Alexander, a phone call for you," came booming over the PA system. I ambled over and picked up the receiver. "Alexander here."

"This is Major Glidden. Alex, we're shipping out. Round up the most sober pilots; a bus is on its way to take you back to Ewa. We have to fly our planes to Ford Island immediately to be put on board the *Gambier Bay*. That's the carrier that will take us to Majuro in the Marshalls."

"Yes sir," came my answer.

I was immediately cold sober. I went around picking the pilots who seemed to be the least under the influence and told them what was up. We all flowed into the bus waiting outside and raced out to the Marine Air Station at

Ewa. Our planes were waiting, their engines idling. The pilots grabbed their parachutes and life vests and were taken by Jeeps to the SBD dive-bombers.

I led an erratic, under-the-influence flight of a few minutes to Ford Island. We landed, miraculously without incident, and taxied to the dock where the *Gambier Bay* was waiting. One after another, our new aircraft were hoisted aboard by a crane and latched down on the short deck of the carrier. A number of Corsair fighters were already aboard. We left Pearl Harbor the next morning at sunup. Behind us were the remains of the U.S. fleet destroyed on December 7th.

Major Glidden had made a tough decision. I'm not sure what his criteria for dividing the squadron were, since about half of the pilots and enlisted men were already on their way to Majuro; they had been assigned to direct the loading of the squadron's gear, except for the planes, on a rusty old cargo ship. That was bad enough, but they themselves boarded the old crate for the slow, hot, boring trip to the Marshalls. Along with the gear and personnel, the cargo ship carried a heavy load of anger and bitterness.

In contrast, the three senior officers – Elmer Glidden and Homer Cook and I – were all going on the *Gambier Bay*, truly a glamorous passage compared to the tramp steamers. It was a long time before the pilots on that cargo ship got over their hard feelings toward those of us who sailed on the carrier, especially me, whom they considered their equal.

A destroyer accompanied us to protect the ship from submarines. This was the first, or "shakedown," voyage for the crew of the *Gambier Bay*. They had never launched a plane; we had never flown off a carrier – a bad combination, I thought. The shortness of the deck meant that planes about to take off required a catapult, a cable stretched across the deck and hooked to the plane. One at a time, the planes were hurled forward as the cable was sharply pulled in by hydraulic power with a loud booming sound. It was very unsettling waiting to be catapulted by that green crew as I prepared to take off for Majuro.

My time came. I sat in the cockpit, a bundle of tension, my head pressed back against the rest to absorb the shock of takeoff, my left hand hard against the throttle. The SBD was shaking with the engine at full power, the throttle opened wide. The SBD was about to be catapulted, but I was a creature of habit and forgot. I pressed my feet with all my strength on the brakes, holding the plane against the force of its full throttle and creating a potentially disastrous situation. As I gave a salute to the launch crew, the signal that I was ready to go, I suddenly realized what I was doing and quickly let go of the brakes, my muscles still recall the feeling. What would have happened if the brakes had been set? I'm not sure, but I think the tires would've burned off the wheels as the plane skidded across the deck and plunged into the water.

As my plane left the deck, a flight of four Marine Corsair fighters flew close across the bow in front of me. I had barely attained flying speed and had to throttle back to avoid a collision. After they passed I was tumbled about by their slipstreams. Later, on Majuro, I heard the fighter pilots laughing about their exploits and the hapless SBD pilot's predicament. It was four to one, but I let them have it, telling them what I thought of their reckless flying. I'm sure it had no effect, except to heighten their enjoyment.

The runway on Majuro, built of live coral scooped out of the lagoon, was still under construction. I landed short on the surface, which was rough but fine. When I left the plane on the line and walked to the operator's tent, a bunch of angry, glaring pilots confronted me. At first I was surprised by their reception. Then I knew why. These were the guys who had come out on the cargo ship, and they wanted me to know how they felt about their mistreatment.

The object of their envy, the *Gambier Bay*, would turn out to be ill-fated. In late October 1944, during the Battle of Samar (part of the second Battle of the Philippines), it was sunk. Admiral William F. Halsey, in command of an American task force, was lured away from protecting the fleet of destroyers and small carriers (including the *Gambier Bay*) by a ploy of the Japanese. They sent a small force of ships north of the Philippines and Halsey, in an erroneous tactical decision, went after it. His abandonment resulted in the destruction of the unprotected carriers and other ships.

In the short time I was on the *Gambier Bay* I met a few of her officers. The sinking of that ship carried a personal sense of loss for me because of the deaths of those men I had only briefly known but came to respect and admire.

Majuro was now home not only to my VMSB-231 squadron but also a second dive-bombing unit, two fighter squadrons, and the crews of patrol and rescue flying boats (PBYs). When the key atolls of the Marshall Islands had been invaded by the Marines, there were only a dozen Japanese soldiers on Majuro, who quickly surrendered – no dying for the emperor. But it was flanked with fortified Japanese-held atolls: Mili to the south; Jaluit to the southwest; Maloelap, Wotje, and Bikini to the north; and Kwajalein and Enewetak to the northwest.

Until our bulldozers cut their ugly swaths, Majuro was a dream of an island paradise. Coconut palms, twisted pandanus, and breadfruit trees covered the islets forming the narrow circling reef. It and its neighboring atolls have a violent geological history similar to that of the Hawaiian Islands. The dazzling white of the coral surrounds the blue-green water of the lagoon and holds back the ocean. An atoll born in violence is truly one of nature's masterpieces.

There is only one passage into Majuro's lagoon, 20 miles long and some 10 miles wide. This large, deep body of water easily provided anchorage for a huge U.S. task force during World War II, complete with carriers, battle ships, cruisers, and destroyers. Our encampment was a small islet adjacent to the runway. Housing was wooden-floored screened rooms elevated off the ground by sections of palm tree trunks. A head, the mess hall, a first-aid station, the squadron office, and a volleyball court completed the village. Sounds of the surf and the rustling of palm fronds were a constant backdrop.

We caught rainwater off the roofs in barrels for washing, shaving, and laundry. Serving as washbasins were steel helmets, inverted in holes cut in several long wooden planks; small green lizards liked the cool shelter of the helmets and usually had to be run out before we could wash. Showers were made possible by a stream of water from an elevated barrel we filled periodically while standing on a rickety ladder. Some of us used natural cloud-generated rainfall for showers. All too often, just as we had covered our bodies with soap, the rain would stop. A dive into the saltwater of the nearby lagoon washed off the soap but left the skin a sticky, salty mess.

Prep for an Attack

The islets were connected by coral causeways, and a one-lane road ran from one end of the occupied islands to the other. A parallel taxiway was built on Majuro when the sole runway was bulldozed. This passage was lined with revetments (embankments) formed of coral, and it was here the planes were parked.

Headquarters for the various squadrons and the aircrews' Ready Rooms were also here. Nearby was a cluster of large round fuel tanks, painted a mottled green and black to blend in with the palm trees when seen from the air. To prevent burning fuel from running across the area if a tank was bombed, each tank was surrounded by a circular mound of coral. So much for camouflage. From the air, the dark tanks surrounded by the white coral stood out like bulls-eyes. No Japanese plane ever flew over Majuro while I was there, so the fuel tanks survived their inviting markings.

One interesting feature of Majuro was a cluster of beautifully built Japanese wooden buildings. We used them in various ways. One served as the Officers' Club, where the whiskey I had arranged for at Alameda was consumed. Canned beer, in a large mound surrounded by barbed wire and secured by armed guards, was the enlisted men's recreational drink; it was distributed at measured intervals to the thirsty enlistees. Compared to the hellholes of Europe and the South Pacific, Majuro was a paradise. The only interruptions in this beautiful existence were the required strikes and searches and boredom.

The squadron was gathered after dark in the Ready Room, which occupied the entire area of a square wooden structure with green plastic screens; a canvas tent overhead served as the roof. Along one wall were wooden bins filled with parachutes, one-man life rafts, and the yellow life preservers we called them Mae Wests, so named because the shape they took when inflated resembled the actress's ample bosom.

The pilots and gunners were seated in rows on rough wooden benches. In front of the crews hung a single light bulb illuminating two maps. One was a small chart of the entire Marshall Islands chain, the other an enlarged detail map of Jaluit. This was the location of our target for tomorrow's strike – the squadron's first attack.

Stan Kaplan, the intelligence officer, opened the briefing, pointing out on the map Jaluit's location 120 miles southwest of Majuro. He gave us the compass headings there and back and pointed to the specific target, a cluster of wooden warehouses. He concluded with the weather prediction (clear) and the winds aloft at various altitudes (variable).

Then Kaplan gave us a brief political history of the Marshalls, which we listened to impatiently. The gist of it was that the islands were in German hands until 1914, when the Japanese, many of whom saw the islands of Micronesia as a natural part of the Japanese empire, invaded and took over the Marshalls as part of a larger imperial expansion. The United States and Great Britain launched years-long diplomatic negotiations with Japan and, as a result, in December 1920, the Council of the League of Nations approved a mandate that all former German colonies north of the equator in this part of the world would be administered by Japan. Jaluit, tomorrow's target, was the administrative center of the Marshalls. (What Kaplan couldn't have known was that after the U.S. won the War in the Pacific it took possession of Micronesia – now the Trust Territory of the Pacific Islands.)

Kaplan also told us that the Japanese built a seaplane base on Jaluit, but there were no runways. Its rim of coral islets surrounded a large deep-water lagoon able to accommodate carriers and battleships. Its defenses against air and attacks from the sea were in-depth and powerful, hardly a reassuring prospect for us on our first mission.

We recorded all the data on our navigation chart boards, which we later inserted in slots under our plane's instrument panel. The charts could be pulled out in flight for continuing navigation. Kaplan was followed by our commanding officer, Elmer Glidden; then Homer Cook, the exec; and by me, now the operations officer for the squadron. Glidden and Cook discussed tactics. I displayed a list of plane assignments for the pilots and drew a diagram of the location of each SBD in the flight's formation.

It was a hot night, but that was only part of the reason I was soaked in sweat. I was tense and I was scared – not just of Japanese gunfire but whether I would measure up to the Marines' high standards on this, my first mission. After I finished we walked in silence to our tents, each of us alone with his anxieties and fears but eager to at last strike a blow at the Japanese.

Early the next morning we again assembled in the Ready Room, put on our Mae Wests, slung our heavy parachutes (atthached to equally heavy folded life raft) over our shoulders, and got in our Jeeps. The Jeeps, those magical all-purpose transports of World War II driven by enlisted men, took the pilots and gunners bouncing and skidding over the rough coral to our assigned planes.

The weather prediction was right. There wasn't a cloud in the sky. In the order of our place in the formation, we taxied to the end of the runway. Each plane carried a 500-pound bomb under its fuselage. The tower cleared the flight for takeoff. At short intervals we swung our SBDs from the revetement out on the airstrip and, with the throttle forced wide open, rolled down the runway slowly gathering the speed needed to liftoff into the hot, light air.

The lead plane, flown by Glidden, climbed slowly as he turned back toward the field, allowing the following SBDs to catch up and slide into tight formation. I led a section of three planes trailing Cook's section of three. After the mission he gave me a thumbs up for holding my section in tight formation with his throughout the flight. All these years later I'm still pleased with his compliment.

After about an hour of flying on a southwest heading, I saw the thin dark line of Jaluit resting on the distant horizon. A few miles out, Glidden swung his plane toward the south end of the atoll. The large formation followed as we climbed to 12,000 feet. Within sight of the warehouses, our target (and our planes in sight of the Japanese), Glidden led us down in a shallow glide, then picked up speed as we made our approach. Flying through black puffs of exploding anti-aircraft shells, we accelerated in a wide circle toward the target. Glidden peeled off in his dive, followed by the two planes in his section. Cook was next. The SBD in front of me rolled its wings from side to side to signal its departure, then rolled over on its back and fell into a vertical dive. A column of planes was now diving on the warehouses.

Bombs Away

It was time for me to go. Reacting to my signal, the plane on my left slid under me and joined up with the plane on my right wing. Below me I saw the target sliding under the panel of the left wing. I rocked my plane signaling my dive, opened the hatch, idled the engine and spread the dive flaps, and rolled over and pulled the nose down. At regular intervals I heard sharp explosions as I dove. I thought my engine was backfiring, but I looked around and saw large billowing bowls of black smoke split seconds before I heard the noise. They were, I learned later, 40-millimeter shells, their fuses cut to follow our planes down as we dove. "What in the hell, I thought, what are you bastards trying to do – kill me? Don't you know I'm a nice guy with a wife back home? Sure, I'm dropping a bomb on you, but that's just my job!"

That fanciful phase passed in a hurry. I flicked on my gun sight and picked up the target in its crosshairs. I took a quick look at the altimeter. It read 2,500 feet and was unwinding fast. At 1,500 feet I pressed the red button on top of the control stick to release the bomb. I then pulled violently back on the stick to recover from the dive, jerking and skidding the plane to foil the gunners. I twisted it toward the ocean out of range of the Japanese guns. I don't know where my bomb landed.

I had heard two loud metallic twangs as I pulled out of the dive. A machine gun bullet had hit my right wing and lodged in the self-sealing fuel tank located there. The second shot cut through the cockpit under my seat and, in exiting, tore a hole in the side of the fuselage. The hole in the wing was too large for the tank to seal, and on the flight home a white stream of vaporized fuel flew from the tank. I recovered the bullet when the mechanics changed the wing, and still have it – somewhere. Three days later the plane was again flight-worthy.

Only a poet, a philosopher, or a great writer should attempt to put into words the emotions felt in a dive-bombing attack. Antoine de St. Exupéry, author of *Flight to Arras*, and William Butler Yeats, who wrote *The Irish Airman Contemplates His Death*, would have been well qualified, but neither, as far as I know, ever flew a dive-bombing mission. It is true that St. Exupéry was an experienced pilot who flew dangerous reconnaissance missions into Germany during World War II, but his flying was level and at high altitudes. As a writer I'm certainly not in a class with either St. Exupéry or Yeats. However I did fly 60 missions, so bear with me while I attempt to capture on paper what dive bombing was like.

There is, as far as I know, no other human activity that prepares a pilot for rolling a plane into a nearly vertical dive plunging toward land or sea at high speed, dropping a bomb at very low altitude, and pulling out of the dive while gravity slams him down in the seat. Perhaps some dangerous endeavors come close: the ski jumper racing down a snow covered wooden scaffold, automobile racers, the circus's human cannon balls, the high wire tightrope walker, the deep-sea divers or the parachutists. All are close, yes, but missing from their dangerous pursuits are bomb-dropping and enemy gunfire. Killing or being killed. Acts of total destruction.

As I approach the target, all my thoughts are focused on getting in position for the dive. There is no place for emotions. I am in a fragile dive bomber 2 miles above the earth and am about to drop deadly explosives on living beings or, if I'm hit, fall to the earth in a flaming wreck. Fear is there, but it's locked away in a shadowy area of my brain. I've become a taut container of knots of muscles and nerves. My arms, legs, hands, and feet respond to the demands of flying totally by instinct. I am not conscious of ordering any movements. They are as automatic as breathing.

My eyes are riveted on the target, which I see over the gray cowl of my plane. I am a fierce eye in the sky – a huge mechanical eagle plunging toward its prey, its deadly talons extended. I check and check again: Am I in good position for a precise and accurate drop? Is the plane flying straight? If it is skidding, will the bomb be thrown wide of the target? Have I made allowances for the wind? What is my altitude?

A fast debate rages in my brain as my altimeter slips past 2,000 feet: "Drop the bomb now?" "Go lower? If lower, how much?" The target bursts large in the sight. End of debate: "Now! Now! Now! Drop the fucking bomb and get the hell out of here!" As I push the release button, my priorities abruptly change. The attack was my job, the mission the Marines pay me to do. Escaping is my own job; I am self-employed. Fear comes out of its hiding place, but I hold it in check as the plane abruptly curves out of the dive. The giant hand of gravity forces me hard against my seat and blood leaves my brain. I yell, and yell again. In a movie called *Dive Bomber,* Navy carrier pilots stumbled out of their planes and blacked out on the deck. That was ridiculous, but the image stays with me and I yell even though the risk of blacking out is virtually nil.

I run a gamut of intense machine gunfire as I dodge and weave toward the sea. Then relief floods my brain. We have made it beyond enemy fire. My plane is flying. I am alive. I am not wounded. Everything with my gunner is fine. Gradually my intensity subsides and I relax. I inhale the warm solid air. I join my flight section and we head for home.

My description doesn't apply for all 60 of my bombing dives, but it does to any that taxed my emotions to the limit. And it certainly describes my first dive that day at Jaluit.

Compared with what dive-bombers faced on missions deep into Germany, at Midway, or in the Solomons, my missions in the Central Pacific were a walk in the park, a relaxing stay in the vacation islands. This may have been true for those of us who were neither wounded or killed, but don't say that to the families of the pilots or gunners whose remains are trapped in broken planes at the bottom of the Pacific or scattered across those deadly atolls.

As we demolished more and more of the Japanese gun installations, our missions became milk runs – routine flights. But, as James Michener wrote in the chapter "Milk Run" in his great *Tales of the South Pacific,* it was no milk run for a pilot the day he was shot down.

When actively engaged, however, we were the precursors of today's so-called smart bombs. Our brains were the computers, the planes the guided missiles, the bombs the warheads. Our brains were subject to diverting fear and were often unable to process all the data storming in. Our planes weren't steered in the dive by automatic gyroscopes but by the sometimes uncertain movements of the pilot's hands, his feet, and his blinking eyes. The bomb was, in the end, launched in freefall subject to wind and erratic flying – not a part of the plane (thank god), as it is with a smart bomb.

I wasn't a war lover, but I enjoyed dive bombing and was good at it. If I had to repeat World War II, I would still want to be a dive bomber – but only with SBDs, not the F4U Corsairs our squadron would eventually fly. I loved that plane. I flew a #10 SBD and called it "Hermi the Swoose." A popular song of the time was "Alexander Is a Swoose – Half Swan Half Goose." I combined my wife's name with the Swoose named Alexander and stenciled it on a piece of the cowling of my plane. I recently gave it to the William Breman Jewish Heritage Museum in Atlanta.

Assignments and Procedures

As operations officer for my squadron, my duty was to schedule pilots and gunners for the various missions, both bombing and reconnaissance. The pilots were very critical of my assignments. At first they wanted bombing missions and were very unhappy if they couldn't get them, directing their ire even at the other pilots. Enthusiasm later waned. The missions became boring but still dangerous.

Four pilots who had been shot down and rescued had had it. Every time I assigned them to a flight, they talked our flight surgeon into grounding them for mythical illnesses. This created a problem. The other pilots, by then very ready to stay grounded themselves, raised hell about having to fill in for the four malingerers. I went to Dr. Peradi, the flight surgeon, telling him that grounding those four was tearing the squadron apart and asking if he would please stop. "Alex," he said, "these guys ought to be relieved. They ought to be sent back to the States. Being shot down has shattered their nerves. In fact, you all should be sent home. But I understand your problem. I'll stop grounding them."

The normal procedure for attacking was for a flight of F-4U Corsair fighters to strafe the target and surrounding gun emplacements first, each firing their six 50-caliber machine guns with a hail of steel that drove the Japanese into their slit trenches. But when the last plane had left and the firestorm was over, the Japanese rushed back to their weapons entirely unopposed, ready to shoot down any oncoming dive-bombers. The Corsair fighters were good for our morale, but I don't believe they actually suppressed anti-aircraft fire.

Two of the Corsair fighter pilots who accompanied us are of special interest. John Glenn, the future astronaut and senator and the first American to orbit the earth, flew from Majuro. Years later I met him at a fundraiser in Atlanta when he was a Democratic candidate for president. We were at a gathering held in the garden of one of his wealthy supporters. His host had heard about his obsession with strawberries and chocolate syrup and provided a huge bowl, which Glenn consumed almost by himself (I gave him an assist). I had brought with me some snapshots of wartime Majuro, which I showed to him. "Senator," I said, "we were stationed together on Majuro but never met. If

I had known then you would become an astronaut, a senator, and a presidential candidate, I would certainly have jumped in a Jeep and run down to your squadron to meet you." His famous grin was his response.

Later I tried to interest Glenn in the miserable post-war plight of the Marshall Island natives – health problems brought on by exposure to radioactive fallout from the U.S. testing of nuclear weapons in the Marshalls, including the island of Bikini. But I never saw, to my disappointment, any evidence he investigated this sad situation.

The other pilot was Charles Lindbergh, who made history when he flew solo from New York to Paris in 1927. He had resigned his Army commission when he became heavily involved as a leader in the America First movement, which sought to keep the United States isolated from the war in Europe. President Roosevelt regarded his efforts to halt assistance to the British against Germany as close to traitorous. When the Japanese bombed Pearl Harbor and Germany declared war on the U.S., Lindbergh immediately tried to reclaim his commission. Roosevelt blocked him. As an alternative, Lindbergh worked with Henry Ford in his warplane production and with Pratt & Whitney, a manufacturer of excellent engines.

In this latter capacity, Lindbergh went first to the Solomon Islands and then to the Marshalls to instruct Marine pilots how to achieve maximum fuel economy from Pratt & Whitney engines. As a civilian, he should never have flown in combat, but he did. In the Solomons he shot down one Japanese plane; in the Marshalls island of Kwajalein, where he was stationed, he led fighter planes as escorts for our dive-bombers.

After the war Lindbergh published his flight logs. A comparison with my own missions indicated we had flown together on four strikes. In spite of all my negative feelings about his suspected anti-Semitism, he was still my boyhood hero. I am still proud to say I flew in combat with Charles Lindbergh.

After the fighters and dive-bombers had completed their attacks, an SBD armed with a camera arrived with the purpose of taking photos that would be used by our Intelligence office to assess the effectiveness of the attack. Every gun on the atoll was aimed at the single unprotected dive bomber as it dove down, with the gunner in the rear cockpit aiming his primitive hand-held camera at the target. The Japanese, now totally unopposed, had a fear-free field day. It is obvious why none of our pilots wanted these missions.

It was on one of these photographic missions that Homer Cook, our executive officer, was killed. We were near the end of our tour, and by that time the facilities on the enemy atolls were pulverized and photos were almost useless.

I had assigned one of our less aggressive pilots to photograph our attack on Wotje. Cook was known as a perfectionist, and when he heard who was taking the flight he exploded. "Hell, that guy won't go lower than 5,000 feet. Headquarters will see these dive photos taken out of harm's way and raise hell." Homer ran to his Jeep and dashed to the end of the runway. He swung in front of the lead plane as it taxied out to take off, shook his head, and held up his hands. The column stopped. Racing to the end of the line, he leaped from the Jeep, vaulted on the wing of the photo plane, and ordered the timid pilot out of the cockpit. "I'm taking this flight," he yelled, and slipped into the parachute the now-departed pilot had left, fastened his seat belt, and shouted into his mike to the flight leader, "OK, let 'er roll."

It was this flight, a flight devoid of any meaning in the course of the war, which would be Cook's last. Homer was an extraordinary man — a brilliant leader who radiated energy. Before enlisting he had earned an engineering degree from Georgia Tech, and he was 17 when Tech's president put the diploma in his hand.

Early the next day, without clearing it with the skipper, I flew to Wotje with Ernie Dunn, a very capable pilot, in a second plane to see if we could find any sign of Cook. There was none.

Across the atoll in heavy mist we saw a large flying boat low over the water. It looked to us as if it might be Japanese. We pushed our throttles wide open and, after a long chase, were positioned just behind it at 500 feet above. As we were poised for attack, two things brought me up short. I saw a white star, the U.S. insignia, on one of the wings and recognized the seaplane as a Navy Martin PBM Mariner. I then saw the turret on top of the plane swinging its twin 50-caliber machine guns straight at us. Dunn didn't realize the plane was a PBM and that we were about to be subjected to friendly fire; without waiting for me to lead, he had peeled off in a diving sweep toward the lumbering seaplane, clearing his guns as he readied the attack. I grabbed my mike and started screaming. "Knock it off! Knock it off! Ernie! Ernie! Ernie! It's ours, it's ours!"

Dunn heard me just in time and broke away. Years later, at our first reunion, he recalled the encounter. With a grin he said, "Thanks; you saved my ass. I certainly could have been shot down, but if I had destroyed that PBM and survived I would have been better off dead."

Elmer Glidden gave me a bad time for searching without his permission, in spite of the fact he loved Cook like a brother. Dunn and I never told Elmer about our abortive encounter with the friendly PBM. Why get more pounding?

A fellow squadron member helped uncloud my memories of the loss of Homer Cook. Tom Hartmann had been one of the first Princeton students to volunteer for service in World War II and, after a long teaching career, retired in his native New Jersey. Tom agreed with my account of what happened that day but added some more information. He had taken off in his SBD for Wotje, but engine trouble forced him to return to Majuro before the attack. When he heard Cook hadn't returned, he sought out George Lane, who had been on the flight. They immediately flew back to Wotje to search for Cook. Lane (a Texan, if memory serves), had seen Cook flying at an extremely low level, probably under 500 feet, back and forth over the target taking pictures. His plane was under heavy ground fire.

Lane didn't see him crash, but he thought Cook's plane had to be in that area. With Tom on his wing, they duplicated Cook's flight several times – the same low pass over the target. Heavy fire, probably machine guns, covered their path, but there were no hits. After seeing no signs of a wrecked SBD Lane said, "Let's go home." Sixty-two years later, I could still hear relief in Tom's voice when he told me, "We finally got the hell out of there." My search with Dunn was flown from a much healthier altitude.

A False Alarm and a Wish Fulfilled

North of Majuro, I was test-flying a plane that had just overhauled. The sky was overcast, and a veil of mist hung over the ocean. "Good god," I yelled to my gunner, "look at that!" Coming out of the mist was a huge fleet – carriers, cruisers, battleships – all protected by airplanes and headed directly for Majuro. Were those ours? Or were they Japan's? The clouds and mist made it impossible to tell. I decided I couldn't take a chance, since they were only an hour or less away from Majuro.

In the clear, and not taking the time to encode my message, I radioed, "Many unidentified ships and planes bearing due south 20 miles out headed for Majuro." Then I repeated the message and was ordered to continue tracking the fleet to see if they were friend or foe. The pilots on Majuro were alerted and rushed to their planes.

I took my plane down to 500 feet and flew toward the ships. With a burst of relief as drew closer, I saw they were ours. I radioed in the news and headed for our airstrip. The huge task force entered the Majuro lagoon and dropped anchor, and the planes followed me in on the airstrip.

The task force commander's failure to notify our island commander that his armada was heading for Majuro was a terrible oversight. But it wasn't the only time the Navy failed to communicate, starting with the events leading up to the Pearl Harbor attack. One particularly horrendous failure occurred in the last days of the war. The ship that had brought the atomic bomb to Taiwan, where it was loaded on the *Enola Gay* to be dropped on Hiroshima, was on its way to the Philippines. No one at the Cavite Naval Base knew she was coming. When the ship was halfway there, a Japanese submarine sank it. It went down quickly, leaving hundreds of sailors swimming in the shark-infested waters. Many hours later, after the Navy became concerned about the missing ship, the location was pinpointed and rescues began, although too late to save most of the crew. Of course, nothing tragic happened in my encounter with the fleet approaching Majuro, but friendly fire might well have been exchanged if I hadn't happened to spot it.

The arrival of "my" task force brought several improvements to our monotonous daily existence on Majuro. Among the many warships was one hospital ship. It wasn't the doctors, medicines, or operating rooms that caught our attention. It was the nurses – real, live, female Americans! I don't know if any contacts with our pilots went beyond lively conversations (mine did not), but I wouldn't bet against it.

A Yale buddy, Jimmy Israel, had access to a PT boat used by his PBY squadron to go to and from their seaplanes. It became a water taxi for us in the evening, taking Jim and me to the floating "entertainment district." We would visit the ships, calling up to the sailors to find out what movies were showing onboard that night. When we found one we liked, we would tie up to the ship and climb a ladder to join the crew on deck. Our favorite theaters were on some eight or ten destroyers; their tenders tied closely together, making it easy for us to walk from ship to ship. Sometimes the crew shared ice cream with us – a real treat. War is hell, but not on those evenings.

Leisure-time pursuits were one thing, but our purpose at Majuro was another. At this point I badly – obsessively – wanted to sink a Japanese carrier. That would be the ultimate goal, the justification for all those practice dives and attacks on static land-based installations. Sure, a carrier would be bristling with anti-aircraft guns and guarded by fast moving, deadly fighters – the respected and feared Japanese Zeros. It also would probably be surrounded by a ring of destroyers sending up a blazing curtain of fire. Talk about being in harms way! No matter, I felt invincible: Just let me get one of those Japs in my sights! I'll drop a thousand-pound bomb that will bore through the flight deck and explode in the middle of high-octane fuel and stored bombs, sending the ship plunging to the ocean floor in a matter of minutes.

I never saw a Japanese carrier or, for that matter, a destroyer, cruiser, battleship, or submarine. Only once did I have at a Japanese craft, a poor stand-in for a warship. At rest on one of Jaluit's islets was a long narrow wooden ship, its bow resting on land and stern jutting out into the lagoon. It was probably a cargo ship bringing supplies to the neglected Japanese on Jaluit. I was leading a section of six planes. At 10,000 feet I rolled into a dive, determined not to miss the undefended ship below. At 2,000 feet I could see the pattern of wood planks of the deck so clearly that the black caulking sealing them together was visible. I kept boring down the long axis of the ship, its image fixed in the center of my sight. There was little wind, and I was in perfect position.

At 1,000 feet I released my bomb – it couldn't miss. I closed the dive flaps, pushed the throttle wide open, and climbed vertically away. Looking down, I saw a large explosion tear a gash in the center of the ship and set it on fire. There was no doubt it was *my* bomb exploding, and my gunner confirmed it.

No, it wasn't a carrier, and it wasn't twisting and turning to dodge my bomb, but it was a ship, and I had destroyed it. There was one problem. The photo plane, for some damn reason, missed the burning ship and took pictures of the open sea, so I didn't have pictorial proof. But all the pilots and gunners on the attack witnessed my feat, which earned an Air Medal, the only medal I won that meant anything to me. Years later, when I visited the Marshalls with Hermi, I tried to charter a flight over Jaluit to see if I could see the remains of my trophy. But unfortunately, I could not.

Hermi at Home

Speaking of my wife, while I was in the Pacific, Hermi was in New Orleans working for Higgins Aircraft, a subsidiary of Higgins Industries. With a semester of drafting at Smith College, she had the only training in her department except for the manager. She was also the only female. Her job was to correct the second original prints sent down by Curtiss-Wright Company in Buffalo, with a constant stream of change orders. Her desk was in the rear of the drafting room, and when she went forward to speak to the manager through the center aisle, all work stopped. All eyes were focused on the rear view of her undulating, swinging walk. (Not without reason did I call her "Legs Alexander.") So that the male studs in the room would be less distracted, the manager soon moved Hermi's desk to the front of the room, facing her admirers.

The move also gave Hermi easier access to the manager. One day she asked him about some notations on the blueprints. "Bob," she said, "on the plans from Curtiss-Wright, some of the fittings are labeled 'male' and others 'female.' I don't understand. What does that mean?"

The manager was a true Southern Victorian, a protector of innocent young women. Though embarrassed, he somehow answered the question to Hermi's satisfaction. I doubt he used hand gestures. This enlightenment, as telling as it was, did not save the subsidiary. General Eisenhower said that Higgins Boats, which manufactured the landing craft used in Normandy on D-Day, won the war. Higgins Aircraft, however, never produced a plane.

There was one other naïve question Hermi asked. She mailed this one to me when I was stationed in the Marshall Islands. "What does it mean," she asked, "when the guys say, 'Hermi, you're built like a brick shipyard?'" I explained, "By substituting a 'p' for the 't' in 'ship,' and 'yard' for 'house,'" the guys clean up the colloquial name for a privy." I told her a brick privy would be expensive and very rare, and that relating her figure to one was a supreme compliment and an indication that she was very special.

Hermi was well aware of the effect her figure had on men. She was also aware of her (somewhat) heavy sister's very beautiful face. "Therese," she would say to her, "with your face and my body, it's too bad we aren't one girl." Therese was not pleased.

Hermi was so displeased with Higgins's failure to produce planes she finally quit and began volunteer work with the USO. And, after I got home from the Pacific, it didn't take long for her to be completely at ease with the meaning of male and female fittings.

Chapter 21

Missions to Mili

Those that I fight I do not hate

—W. B Yeats, An Irish Airman Forces His Death

As far as I know, the Marshall Islands atoll known as Mili has been in the head-lines only twice, most recently in 2000 with the publication of the book *The Search for Amelia Earhart,* by Fred Goerner. The author's theory (and I do mean theory) is as follows:

Earhart and her navigator Fred Noonan, who in 1937 attempted flying a twin engine Lockheed Electra around the earth near the equator and disap-peared over the Pacific, were photographing Japanese fortifications on Truk and Jaluit in the Marshall Islands at the request of President Roosevelt. Making a water landing in the Mili atoll lagoon after running out of fuel, the two were captured by the Japanese, taken to their base on Saipan, and either died there of disease while being held as prisoners or were executed as spies.

The other time Mili made headlines preceded Goerner's Earhart theory by six decades. During the War in the Pacific, from late 1943 into 1944, American forces conducted a series of bombing raids on Japanese fortifications on Mili,

Kwajalein, Enewetak, Jaluit, and other islands of the Marshall chain. And I know for a fact there was nothing theoretical about it. I was there.

These islands were referred to as "bypassed," a term I use throughout this chapter. Admiral Chester W. Nimitz, commanding the Pacific Fleet from his headquarters in Hawaii, knew that invading them could amount to a bloody mission on the order of the battles of Midway and Guadalcanal, both fought in 1942, He reasoned, correctly, that if the fortified islands were bombarded daily and left to wither, they were not likely to constitute a threat.

Before attacking Pearl Harbor In December 1941, the Japanese worked hard to fortify Mili – with 92 tiny islands, the second-largest atoll in the Marshalls. On the main island they built three coral runways that crisscrossed in the middle and stretched the length of the island. They also constructed numerous supporting facilities, including hangars, barracks, a radio station, ammunition bunkers, gun emplacements, and trenches. Mili was massively defended by Japanese anti-aircraft guns, machine guns, and shore batteries.

Unique among these weapons were several 8-inch guns captured from the British at Singapore in the early days of the war. The British pointed these guns to the sea to repel invaders; they couldn't be swung around to repel a land-based attack. Whether the guns played a role or not, the surrender of Singapore was a devastating humiliation for the British. Not until British tommy-guns drove back the vaunted Nazi Afrika Corps led by General Rommel at El Alamein did the Brits recover their fighting spirit.

Mili was often designated as my VMSB-231 squadron's target. In view of its powerful concentration of artillery manned by skillful, experienced gunners, it wasn't our favorite destination. In addition to bombing attacks at dawn and near sunset, we flew two-plane reconnaissance missions around the rim of the large atoll. We searched for any sign that personnel reinforcements or supplies were being delivered by submarines, but never found any evidence for it. Eliot Morrison, the venerated historian of the United States Navy, did find evidence. He wrote that in March 1944 a Japanese sub unloaded 60 tons of supplies at Mili. A little later, a submarine 1-184 brought food and ammunition from the port of Yokosuka In Japan. In spite of these two supply efforts, the garrison on Mili came close to starving by the time it surrendered.

On search missions over Mili, our planes were always greeted by heavy anti-aircraft fire. It was rarely effective, but it certainly kept us from regarding those flights as pleasure jaunts. More effective (and more dangerous by far) were the dive-bombing attacks we mounted every few days. Our targets – the runways, hangars, gun emplacements, and other facilities – were gradually pulverized, but the intense anti-aircraft fire continued to the end of our tour.

It was on one of those attacks that my friend Jud Bell had a devastating experience. His plane dove just before mine, so I had a good view of his ordeal as I followed him down. Jud dropped a 500-pound bomb on a large gun revetment. I let mine go seconds later. As Jud pulled out of the dive, what was a deadly 40-millimeter shell hit the plane's nose. Fiery streamers flashed out through the engine's cowl flaps, and the plane was immediately enveloped in black smoke. I had to skid to one side to dodge the smoke so I could fly alongside Jud's burning SBD. As flames surrounded the cockpit, Jud struggled out, weighed down by his parachute and life raft. He then stood on the wing clutching the rim of the cockpit for a few seconds, trying to see if his gunner had jumped. The pall of smoke enveloped the rear cockpit. I couldn't see the gunner, and Jud was surely even more blinded.

There were only seconds to spare before the crashed. Jud jumped off the wing, his chute opened quickly, and his feet hit the water within seconds, Fortunately, a guard rescue destroyer was soon at his side. A sailor threw him a line and quickly hauled him aboard.

The next day the destroyer took Jud back to Majuro. He was wounded and had lost blood, but none of his cuts were deep. It took only a few minutes in sickbay for the squadron doctor to patch up his face and arms, using butterfly bandages rather than stitches.

After his wounds were dressed, Jud came into my tent and sat down next to me on my cot. He was distraught. "Alex", he said, "you were on my wing; you saw the whole thing. I tried to roll that damn plane over so Jack [his gunner] could drop out. You know it's hard as hell to climb out of that back cockpit. That crate wouldn't roll. I yelled at Jack to jump but he didn't answer. When I got out on the wing I tried to see if he was still in the plane, but the smoke blinded me. That fire was really hot, so I bailed out. I jumped. If I could have rolled that plane, Jack would be alive. I'm OK, I guess, but I'll never forget Jack was killed. I left him to die. He depended on me, he trusted me, but I let him down. I'm alive; he's dead. I'll never, never get over it."

For years after the war at our reunions, Jud would always talk about his gunner. "Alex," he would ask, "were you ever unable to roll your plane? If I had been able to roll Jack would be alive." My efforts to help him find peace were futile: "Come on Jud, I'm sure the cables to your ailerons were shot away, and you never could have rolled that plane. You jumped at the last minute. For god's sake, you did all you could. Forgive yourself, Jud." He never did. The Purple Heart that his wounds earned him only added to his guilt.

The senior President Bush had a similar experience. He was the youngest American naval aviator in World War II. He jumped from his burning torpedo bomber not knowing if his two crewmen had escaped. His ordeal is recounted in the book *Flyboys*, by James Bradley, the son of one of the Marine flag raisers in the famous photograph taken on Iwo Jima. Bush and Bradley went back to the island of Chichi Jima, where Bush was shot down. The author interviewed him there for a video documentary. He spoke with deep distress when talking about the loss of his crew. His reaction was the same as Jud's. Forget that one was president of the United States and the other an employee in the State Department; their sorrow and unwarranted guilt never ceased to plague them.

In contrast, I had narrow escapes at the worst. One came on Majuro right after my plane's engine had been completely overhauled and new piston rings were installed. To seat the rings and check out the engine's performance, I took the SBD up to run the engine at modest speeds. It would take several hours of boring circling to do the job. As I took off I saw a towering, dazzling cumulus cloud over the field. To stave of the boredom of flying nowhere in particular, I climbed up above the cloud's base, circling around the billowing, cottony mass. The beauty of the cloud and the sheer joy of flying enraptured me for hours.

Suddenly I was brought back to reality. My plane was violently jolted. An anti-aircraft shell had exploded much too near the SBD. I looked around. I was surrounded by dirty black exploding shells. "What the fuck is going on?" I asked myself. The answer was all too clear – I was directly over Mili Atoll. For a long minute I couldn't figure out how the hell I got there. A couple of hours before, I was circling that same cloud over our friendly base on Majuro. Then it hit me. Out loud I said to myself, "You're an idiot, it was a strong wind that got you here. It blew that cloud you were circling from Majuro to Mili. You never looked down until the explosions woke you up!" I didn't hang around. Forget pampering the overhauled engine. I shoved the throttle all the way forward, rolled the plane into a tight turn, and got out of the Mili gunners' airspace.

Those gunners surely were delighted to have my slow-moving, unescorted SBD floating in their sight. After I escaped unscathed, their joy must have quickly evaporated. They possibly considered committing hara-kiri. From my viewpoint I was ready to award them lifesaving medals cast in gold.

My close friend and aforementioned movie buddy, Jimmy Israel, was stationed with the Navy on Majuro. He was flying PBYs, the large, slow-flying boats that accompanied attack missions to rescue any pilots or crew who went down at sea. The PBY was the same plane I flew in training at Jacksonville, and Jimmy knew I was checked out in it ("checked out" was slang for "familiar with"). "Alex," he asked me, "Would you like to be my co-pilot on a rescue hop to Mili?"

"Great," I said "Let's go!"

After a long, lumbering takeoff from the Majuro lagoon, Israel gave me the controls. I swung the heavy PBY around to a heading for Mili. Overhead the attacking flight of fighters and dive-bombers were on the same course. We circled off the main Mili Island, watching our planes strafe and bomb the Japanese installations. None of our planes were hit, and they joined up after the attack and flew back to Majuro.

Free of our rescue responsibilities, and just for the fun of it, I flew low and close to the shore to see what I could of the island's fortifications. By low I mean 20 feet or less above the water. While I was watching, I saw two plumes of white smoke shoot up out of the palm trees just beyond the beach. Seconds later, two explosions close behind our PBY sent up large geysers of foaming seawater. Suddenly, two more plumes, two more splashes, even closer this time.

"Let's get the hell out of here!" yelled Israel. I swung the plane around, shoved the throttle to the stops, and fled out to the open ocean. "Those bastards are firing fucking coastal guns at us!" I said. "Your big old tub makes a great target. As slow and low as we were, one of those geysers could have sunk us. They wouldn't have wasted those big shells on my little SBD." I forget what I was flying. "You take it, Jimmy – it's all yours!" Israel laughed, took over, and flew us home.

An A-Hole of an Officer

Among the Marine Corps' "few good men" were some bona fide assholes in command roles – officers who somehow avoided detection, but only initially. Invariably, before they had done too much damage, they self-destructed, lost their commands, and the corps moved on. For a time on Majuro, our squadron had an executive officer who more than fit the bill. This incompetent little tin god attempted to establish his authority by issuing ridiculous orders.

One of his misbegotten acts was in response to my report on a routine Mili search mission. Following is what I reported, but I'll save his response for later, after recounting four incidents when the exec, to put it kindly, made a fool of himself.

On that particular mission over Mili, I spotted a native outrigger canoe sailing in the lagoon well away from land. Gliding down low to the wake, I flew close by it. There was no doubt the six men in the canoe were natives. They all stood up and pumped their arms over their heads in the Marshall Islanders' sign for "friend." I dipped my wings and flew away. Back at Majuro, I reported the encounter to Stan Kaplan, our Intelligence officer. As required, he sent it on to group headquarters, where the ever-watchful group executive officer saw it. His reaction and subsequent order was all out of proportion, but first I'll recount four previous incidents signaling the measure of this man.

Incident number one:

Before his elaborate quarters were constructed, the exec stayed in our enclave. The squadron head was a screened-in row of round holes cut in wood planks that served as toilet seats. Under these seats was a trench 4- or 5-feet deep. After nature had been appeased, the user shoveled lime through the hole to cover his deposit. Every morning after breakfast, a gasoline-fueled fire was started in the trench to burn up its contents. As the fire burned, and for some time after, heat and smoke made the head unusable. This did not sit well with the executive, who could not sit well on those hot seats. Steaming with righteous fury, he told Elmer Glidden, our commanding officer, to stop burning out the head right after breakfast. "It's against nature," he said, "to make it unusable just after I've eaten!" Glidden complied. In honor of the executive officer, the order became known by our squadron as "The Royal Shithead Decree." After the exec moved to his own quarters, the post-breakfast hot seats were reinstated.

Incident number two:

Natural functions weren't involved in this order: "Attention! Attention! Attention!" One night the exec, whose rank was lieutenant colonel, was being badly beaten in an impromptu bourbon-soaked wrestling match with a burly second lieutenant. The junior officer had the exec bent over in a one arm vise-like headlock while he painfully ground the knuckles on his other hand into his scalp. It was at this point that our struggling leader, unable to break free, resorted to military protocol with his screams of "Attention!" Instead of standing at attention, the junior officer flagrantly disregarded the order and kept up the knuckle-gouging. The tent full of pilots, all in varying degrees of alcoholic enlightenment, briefly stopped laughing and pulled the victor away from his victim.

The junior officer expected dire repercussions. None came. The exec, probably embarrassed when he sobered up and became aware he shouldn't have been in a drunken brawl with underling, let the humiliating encounter fade into myth.

Incident number three:

Our intrepid exec's next foray took him into "campus planning." Our tents were scattered at random to take advantage of shade under the tall palm trees. This offended the exec's sense of military order, so he had a bulldozer cut a rigidly straight street through the trees. The offending tents on their wooden platforms were set on either side in precise rows under the tropical sun. Within the confines of the squadron we named the street "Shithead Boulevard," but no one had guts enough to put it up on a street sign. There was no shade now, but military rigidity reigned supreme.

Incident number four:

Twice, our brilliant executive officer ordered strikes against non-existent airstrips on Jaluit. The first time, his superior, Elmer Glidden, said nothing, and we directed our bombs at a gun emplacement. The second time the order was issued, Glidden went to the exec and advised him that his orders to bomb runways on Jaluit couldn't be carried out because there *were* no runways.

"Are you certain, Major Glidden?"

"Yes sir," " replied his superior.

"Well then, select a suitable target," said the exec.

Again, "Yes sir." If there is such a thing as a sarcastic salute, I'm sure Glidden snapped one off as he left the exec's office.

Now back to the canoe on the lagoon incident, which I referred to a few paragraphs ago:

This blow up resulted from the report of my failure to attack the native canoe in the Mili lagoon. The executive officer summoned me to group headquarters and grilled me intensely. The only instrument not used in his inquisition was a rubber hose to beat a confession out of me. It wasn't necessary. I told him without coercion exactly what I had or had not done.

"Captain Alexander," my inquisitor said, "you neglected your duty. You could only surmise that the occupants of that canoe were not Japanese. Your duty was to sink that canoe and kill its occupants! Today," he continued, "I'm issuing orders that all canoes and any other small craft must be sunk with all hands, whether you pilots think the occupants are natives or not. Your serious dereliction will be permanently recorded in your records at Marine Corps headquarters in Washington, D.C."

Glidden was supposed to submit a written report of my dereliction. If he did, which I doubt, it never made it into my records.

When the vicious order was issued, the pilots shrugged and ignored it, except for one overeager war lover who had led a two-plane reconnaissance at Mili. His wingman told us that he broke away from formation when this gung-ho warrior of a leader dove down with his machine guns firing at a defenseless outrigger carrying natives. After several passes, all the natives were dead and the canoe a shattered wreck. When the story of this assault spread through the squadron, we were revolted and angry. From then on we froze the guy out. We spoke to him only when necessary.

Our group executive officer had compiled an outstanding record: He stopped the post-breakfast head burning; he was defeated by a junior officer in a drunken wrestling match; he had moved our living quarters from the shade into the tropical sunlight; he had twice ordered attacks on phantom runways; and he ordered the slaughter of friendly natives. Soon his commanding officer caught on that the executive officer was not only incompetent but vicious. The CO immediately cut orders to send this sorry human being back to the States.

But I'm not through with the exec's exploits yet (yes, there were more). Later in this chapter you'll read about how the famous cartoonist Robert Osborn, who created a bungling Navy pilot called Dilbert, came to eat dinner with our squadron one night and saw our exec as the embodiment of Dilbert the moment he laid eyes on him.

Hard Truths, Close Calls

It was on a reconnaissance flight, this one well into my Pacific tour, that I fully realized my ultimate mission was killing. I was leading a two-plane search mission to Jaluit. The Japanese had long since figured out the times when these flyovers took place. Therefore, when we appeared, the atoll looked deserted; there was absolutely no activity. This time, I thought, I'll fool them.

After flying over the lagoon, I led my wingman in a climb headed back toward Majuro until we slipped into a cloud. I looked over at him and pointed back toward the lagoon, after which we made a fast turn amd dove out of the clould at high speed toward the water.

A large launch with a group of men on board was just leaving the dock. As I dove toward the launch, I flicked on my gun sight and charged my 52-caliber machine guns. At a height of 1,000 feet or so I pressed the trigger. But nothing happened. The guns were jammed. On these searches we carried two depth charges, primarily to attack submarines. The charges could also be set to explode on contact with the water or any object. With no guns available, I turned to the depth charges, adjusted the switch for surface explosion and, at some 500 feet above the launch, released them.

We were under heavy fire from shore-based guns, but the launch carried no weapons. As the charges dropped I looked down at the boat, now close below. All the men were frozen rigidly in place, their pale faces turned up toward the deadly depth charges. I jerked my plane into a sharp climb, twisting and turning to confuse the gunners attacking me from the shore. Safely out of range, I turned and looked back. The launch was gone. Only a smear of black oil marked its grave.

The image of those faces peering up at me has never left. Years later, as I walked the streets of Japanese cities, I wondered if any of the people I passed could have been the mother, father, wife, or children of those men. In some of my other missions I probably killed and maimed, but only that day did I see my victims as human beings. So thoroughly had I trained, so many dives had I made at inanimate targets, that when initially confronted with targets manned by living beings, it hadn't been driven home that I was dealing death. The encounter with that launch forever branded this truth deep into my mind.

At the same, the reality of war and what was a stake made me do what I had to do. One day skipper Glidden told me, "Alex, I want you to work up a 'hunter-killer' tactic for sinking submarines at night." The objective was to create more spirit in our squadron and raise morale. Months of bombing the bypassed islands had left the pilots and gunners feeling endangered but somehow bored and listless. Our attitude was well expressed by a pleading song written by pilot Cal English, a clever musician. Here's all I remember: "Oh, the SBDs stink and the pilots all drink and Zed always sends us out wrong. Oh, Major, we've been here too long!" ("Zed" was the code name for the radio dispatcher who ordered the pilots out on missions.)

"Hunter-killer." This military term stirred the blood, and belongs in the hallowed realm of those historic orders that sent men into death's jaws: "Don't fire until you see the whites of their eyes"... "Come on you bastards – do you want to live forever?"... "Don't give up the ship!"... "They shall not pass!" I soon realized, however, that there was nothing blood-stirring about

409

my assignment. Practicing the attack method I masterminded was interesting the first few times, but it soon became stultifyingly routine. We never had a chance to actually attack a submarine, but I'm sure if we had, our interest level would have gone up off the chart.

During practices, one plane dropped a flare to light a smoke bomb already dropped; the smoke represented a sub. Three planes on either side of the "sub" climbed to a thousand feet and made alternate runs over the target, dropping small practice bombs representing depth charges. There was no way of knowing, of course, if this would have destroyed a submarine. As the flare died out, we joined up and flew back to the base. Our morale was still low, and our boredom intensified. I had reconciled myself to these meaningless forays when I was jolted out of my semi-coma by a near collision one night.

Majuro served as a "plane pool" for the Navy's carriers in the Central Pacific. From time to time, Navy pilots were brought in on DC-3s to fly planes back to a carrier, replacing aircraft lost in accidents or combat. One side of the Majuro runway was lined end-to-end with these planes, but the narrowness of the island left little room for them; only a few feet separated their noses from the rush of planes taking off and landing. After sundown, that lineup was a dark and menacing presence, but we accepted it without concern as just one more hazard of our trade.

My lack of concern changed abruptly that night. As the lead for a hunter-killer practice mission, I was racing down the runway toward the black night at the end. About a third of the way down I heard a loud bang that came from beneath the left wing; a tire had blown. The SBD swerved toward those silent Navy planes, and I stamped on the right brake. Luckily, I had just accelerated to flying speed so was able to barely lift off, clearing the parked planes by only a few feet. Gradually, the plane gained altitude and I took over the hunter-killer exercise.

My mind wasn't with the practice. it was full of concern for my landing at the end of our maneuvers. In fact, my concentration was so poor I got lost. I didn't know where our base was. To cover myself, I called my wingman.

"Ernie," I radioed, "take over the lead. I blew out a tire on takeoff. All the planes should land before I come in, just in case I block the runway."

"Roger," he acknowledged.

I followed Ernie back to Majuro. No one, not even my gunner, knew that the peerless squadron navigation officer had let his anxieties take over and made him lose his way.

410

Cecil climbing into the cockpit of the SBD for another mission

Cecil with crew of SBD - Kneeling: mechanic; Standing, gunner, Sgt.
Strange; Ace of Spades logo can be seen to the left; Markings on the
fuselage represent the number of missions this particular plane had flown.

Cecil receiving the Air Medal from General Wood
Majuro Atoll, Marshall Islands, 1943

Left: The Air Medal; Center: US Navy Aviator
Wings; Right: Distinguished Flying Cross

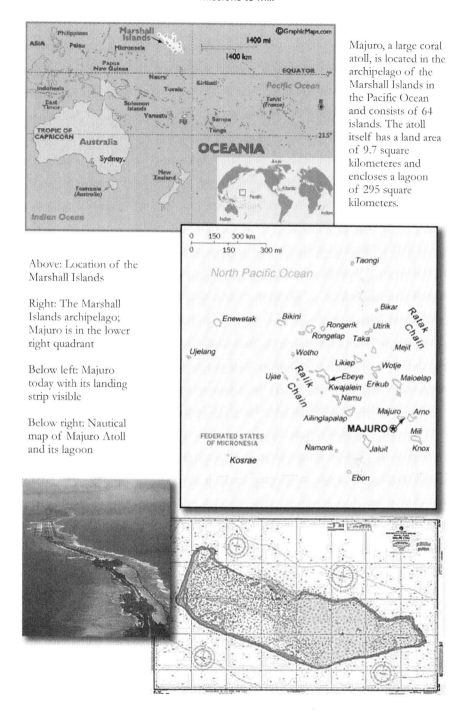

Majuro, a large coral atoll, is located in the archipelago of the Marshall Islands in the Pacific Ocean and consists of 64 islands. The atoll itself has a land area of 9.7 square kilometeres and encloses a lagoon of 295 square kilometers.

Above: Location of the Marshall Islands

Right: The Marshall Islands archipelago; Majuro is in the lower right quadrant

Below left: Majuro today with its landing strip visible

Below right: Nautical map of Majuro Atoll and its lagoon

413

During my 1982 return to Majuro, I met a Japanese veteran who was on a similar journey. Here we look at my wartime photos.

Hermi's and my 40th wedding anniversary,
January 20, 1983, celebrated at Atlanta's 57th Fighter Group
Restaurant. I wore my flight jacket; Hermi wore the fur-collared
coat she had worn the day we were married.

Now I approached the landing, the runway directly in front of me. I brought the plane down slowly, landing lightly on the right wheel while holding the left wheel as far above the runway as I could. The plane slowed, and the deflated left tire came slowly down and made contact with the coral runway. The flat tire locked the wheel and swung the plane to the left, threatening the same line of Navy planes I'd narrowly missed on takeoff. With all my strength, I stamped on the right brake pedal. The plane straightened out and, after a long bumpy ride, came to a halting stop near the end of the runway.

With a deep sigh, the whitest of knuckles, and sweat dripping off my nose, I climbed out of old #10. A ground crew pulled the plane off the runway. The next morning, a spare wheel was substituted for the damaged one, making the plane ready to go. My blown tire and escape from a wreck was a major topic at the mess hall that day – but as were most such events, it was soon forgotten, consigned to the archives of squadron happenings.

From time to time, headquarters kept us occupied by dispatching us on nighttime harassment strikes. Our mission was to disturb the sleep of the Japanese, with small bombs and empty beer bottles as our weapons. We released the bombs at random across the bypassed islands, visible on even the darkest night because they were surrounded by the luminescent ocean. At the same time, our gunners threw out the empty bottles that whistled loudly on the way down. I doubt these missions shortened the war by even a millisecond.

Returning from one of these faux daring missions, I saw what later would be called a UFO – an unidentified flying object. I was leading a flight of six planes back from Jaluit, and there were no islands below us. Off to the right I saw a large ring of orange lights slowly drifting down. Our Majuro radio contact confirmed that there were no planes or ships in the area. So UFO's they were, ahead of their time. All six crews saw the mysterious lights, perhaps dropped by aliens from outer space or, more likely, from a high-flying plane undetected by Majuro's radar. But to me it was a UFO.

R & R On-Site and Away

Between missions there wasn't a lot to do. We played volleyball or poker and swam in the lagoon with the barracuda, huge jellyfish, and killer whales. Washing our filthy shirts, shorts, and pants was another diversion.

I had brought along a box of pastels and a roll of velour paper, so I was able to resume drawing. My first effort, which took several days, was a life-size portrait of Hermi drawn from a photograph. Commanding Officer Glidden, after seeing if, asked me to do a pastel of him from life. He had a fine chiseled face with a strong jaw and fiery blue eyes, a great face to draw. I think I captured him. Many years later I donated the portrait to the National Marine Corps Museum in Quantico, Virginia.

Sleeping and eating were two other not very demanding occupations. We had an excellent, creative cook. Spam, a compressed mixture of ham and we-didn't-want-to-know-what-else packed in tins, was a daily staple. Our chef presented this unappealing food in many different forms, some of them even delicious. My good friend Bud Blass raised rabbits whose ultimate fate was to be the essence of what he called "bunny stew". I wouldn't touch it, since those rabbits were almost pets. It would have been like eating my dog or cat.

I remember one lunch, not because of the menu but because of my guest. He was Robert Osborn, a great cartoonist who had come ashore from a visiting cruiser. Osborn, a few years older than I, had also graduated from Yale. We both drew cartoons for the *Yale Record*. The Navy assigned him the job of illustrating their Patrol Sense pamphlets, accounts of stupid flying accidents taken from the Navy's accident reports and intended to warn their pilots. Osborn created an unforgettable character he called Dilbert, an unwittingly inept pilot caught up in all sorts of moronic misadventures. One I clearly remember depicted a pilot who tried to take off in a TBF (a torpedo bomber) with the plane's wings folded behind it. Osborn's drawings followed the TBF down the runway until it crashed into a steaming pile of debris. Osborn also drew a wizened, ranting old pilot he called Grandpa Pettibone, whose main purpose was to react to all of Dilbert's fuck-ups. Pettbone's response to the folded wing episode was so violent he shot up and out of sight at the top of the page.

Osborn and I were in the middle of our meal when our hapless squadron executive officer, the one known for his stupid orders, walked in. He passed by us without a glance and settled alone at a table in the rear of the room. "My god," Osborne said in a whisper. "I've been looking all over the fleet to find the real life Dilbert, and there he is, right in this room!"

"You are dead right, I said. "He's an accident always happening. He makes your Dilbert look like a Jimmy Doolittle or an Eddie Rickenbacker. But how could you tell? You only saw him walk by."

"Well," Osborn said, "It's like a father knows his long lost son. Dilbert just sticks out all over him. And he's your exec? God save VMSB-231!"

As promised previously in this chapter, here are some more of the real-life Dilbert's exploits: pulling his plane out of dives so violently he bent the fuselage on two of them (they went to the junk pile); breaking the canopies of two parked planes on either side of him and breaking the wings of his own plane in the process; losing control of his plane on takeoff and just missing a collision with several parked planes (he was adjusting his seatbelt). I'm sure there were others, but I've forgotten.

During the years we were on Majuro, each pilot was able to take two trips to Honolulu for rest and recuperation – better known as R & R – lasting an all-too-short week. The long, slow flight to Honolulu was made in an old DC-3. We sat facing each other on metal bucket seats up against the cold aluminum sides of the plane. There was a stop for fuel at Johnson Island. An airstrip, a few random buildings, and a lagoon full of sharks were all that the bare island had to offer, but it was halfway to Hawaii, and that was what mattered.

Near Honolulu's Waikiki Beach was the Chris Holmes Estate, an imposing cream brick mansion surrounded by green lawns and coconut palms. President Franklin D. Roosevelt stayed there when he came out to meet with the senior Pacific area commanders during the war. In preparation for the visit of the commander in chief, agile Hawaiians climbed all the palms to cut loose the coconuts and drop them to the ground. It wouldn't be good PR if a newspaper headline blared, "President Roosevelt Killed by Falling Coconut at Chris Holmes Estate." No such fanfare or precautions preceded our stay at the estate, but we were wined and dined like celebrities.

The staff arranged a dance for the pilots one night, with a high-powered band brought in from the Royal Hawaiian Hotel. Floating about the house and grounds was a bevy of Honolulu's loveliest debutantes, clad in beautiful, lacy gowns. But where were the Marines? All too soon they came piling in from a fleet of taxicabs, each with one of the city's earthiest prostitutes on his arm.

End of the dance. The debs fled into the night, the band packed up its instruments in disgust, and the lady in charge, her voice like an erupting volcano, screamed, "Get those filthy women out of here! NOW! NOW! NOW! OUT! OUT! I say NOW!!!" So much for an elegant ball with fair ladies and handsome knights just descended from clouds of glory. It was the first and last time the Marine pilots resting at the Chris Holmes were treated as gentlemen – officers perhaps, but not gentlemen.

My second R & R trip to Honolulu came near the end of my tour overseas, although I didn't know then that my time in the Pacific was short. On this trip our "home" was the Alexander House (unfortunately not related) located by the ocean near Diamond Head. It was a much less formal setting – a one-story timber house sprawling across the grounds.

I wanted a mascot for 231, and in the Honolulu phone book found a listing for dog kennels. To my delight, one of them sold Scottish terriers. I had had Scotties all my life, starting with Rosay Macaboy, a present on my fifth birthday. In a borrowed car, I drove to the kennel on the city's outskirts. Most appropriately, the owners were from Scotland. They took me to a fenced yard where several wiggly puppies were enjoying life.

After looking them over one at a time, I made my choice and carried him into the office and put him down. There was a long sofa along one wall. The puppy ran to it and peered under the seat. Then, barking loudly, his tail crooked over, he ran back and forth in front of the sofa. I was mystified until one of the owners pointed to a large mirror stored behind the couch. The Scotty saw his reflection and thought it was another dog. Never before or since have I had a pet notice its own reflection. (I have, however, had a Siamese cat who occasionally watched TV, particularly lions or tigers on the Animal Planet channel.)

I put down $80 in cash, tucked the puppy under my arm, and headed for the plane. But what would I name him? Inspiration didn't come until I was out over the Pacific on the way back to Majuro, and here's how. Military pilots in World War II carried a roll of dollar bills, and after landing at airfields they made fast trips to the bar. The airmen signed one another's dollar bills as keepsakes and named them "short snorters" for the short snorts of whiskey they consumed. I realized that our long flight to the Marshalls qualified my Scotty pup for a short snorter dollar bill. And since he had no pockets or an allowance, why not name him Shorty McSnorter? (The "Mc" connected him to his ancestral home in Scotland.) He became known in the squadron as Snorter.   •

It soon became evident he was a one-man dog – mine. He wasn't at all interested in being a mascot. So I was stuck with paying for him, and we were stuck with each other for the rest of his life. I loved that dog, and I think he returned my affection.

•

Back to Reality

How near I came to what we World War II pilots called "buying the farm" as the result of a Japanese bullet, I don't know. But there were two incidents unrelated to gunfire that came close to finishing me off.

Although our cabins on Majuro were surrounded on all sides with plastic screen, very little air could penetrate the heavy mesh. To help ventilate the stuffy room, I propped the jerry-built canvas roof to the 2 x 4s supporting it. But my choice of a means to hold the roof up was – there's no other word for it – stupid. I used a trenching spade with a razor-sharp edge designed to slice through hard ground. I don't recall how many nights I went to sleep with that fine substitute for the Sword of Damocles balanced some 6 feet over my cot.

It all came to a violent end one windy morning around dawn, when a jagged blue flash ripped through my brain as a sharp blow hit my forehead. The wind had dislodged the tool and sent it falling straight at my head. I called to my roommate, "Please come here. I'm hurt pretty bad." He took the few steps across the floor and stared down at my bloody face and the jagged flap of skin on my forehead. "Christ!" he said. It was light enough that I could see the look of horror on his face, which didn't help my state of mind.

"Please go get the doc," I said, "I need him." He ran out the door and was back in a few minutes with our flight surgeon, a Guadalcanal veteran who had just joined our squadron. He had seen much, much worse than my wound down in the Solomons. "OK, hold this towel on your forehead," he said. "We're going to sickbay." He asked my tent mate to round up the medical corpsman and have him meet us at sickbay on the double.

I lay down on the examining table while the doctor poured iodine in the wound. It stung like hell, and I let out a yell. The corpsman had by then come on the scene. The doctor said to him, "I came on board just yesterday. I don't know where anything is. Where are the sutures?"

"Sir, we don't have any. All surgery is done at the group sickbay. All we treat is jock itch, blisters, and stomach upset."

The doctor answered, "To hell with that. He's not going anywhere. I'll close the wound with butterfly bandages. We don't have any of those either? Well, dammit! Give me those scissors and that adhesive tape. I'll make them myself."

An hour later he was finished and the wound was neatly bandaged. Sulfanilamide had just come into use against infection, and he gave me a handful of pills with directions for taking them. They gave me hallucinations, so I didn't finish the course. But the makeshift butterfly bandages did a fine job and there are no lingering signs on my forehead of the 4-inch cut the doc skillfully patched up that morning.

The second time I had too close a call was much more dramatic. It could have killed three innocent people including me (I was innocent). In the final months of my tour at Majuro, our SBDs were recalled and we were issued F4U Corsairs to use as fighter bombers. The single-seater Corsair was a magnificent aircraft, as beautiful as it was deadly. The powerful Pratt & Whitney engine, the R2800, rotated a propeller 14 feet in diameter and pulled the plane through the air at (for those days) an astounding 400 knots. Land-based Corsairs had seen extensive service in the Solomons, and after the problems with their dangerous carrier landing characteristics were worked out, they were used extensively on our carriers.

To accommodate the arc of the huge propeller and eliminate the need for a very long landing gear strut, the Vought designers came up with a unique solution. For about 7 feet on either side of the fuselage, the wings angle down. At this point the direction changes and the wings slope up, forming the shape of a gull's wing. It is at this transition, the point closest to the ground, that the short landing gear is located. Another, unforeseen, characteristic of the Corsair was the howling scream it produced in a dive – a terrifying sound. It so intimidated the Japanese that they called the Corsair "Whistling Death."

Toward the end of the war, some senior Marine ground officers transferred to aviation. Two majors joined VMSB-231, now VMFB-231 (the FB stood for Fighter Bomber). They knew it all, or so they thought. It was my unenviable job to qualify one of them to fly the Corsair. To help him understand the fighting plane's characteristics, I engaged the major assigned to me in mock dogfights. A mandatory rule of these competitions was never to engage a third plane. As we went at it some 10,000 feet up, I easily maneuvered to a position on the tail of the major's plane, thanks to my hours piloting F4Us; in actual combat, my six machine guns could have sent his plane down in flames. Looking back in his rearview mirror, my student saw I was on his tail. To try to escape, he rolled his plane over and pulled it into a "split S," which brought him down in a half loop. I followed close behind, just below the plane's tail. As we came out of the dive, his plane blocked my view forward.

What I saw as he pulled up at the end of the half loop was an SBD only a few feet away and headed straight for me – a huge, deadly apparition. I skidded my plane sharply to the left and, with a jerk of the control stick, knocked my right wing down. An instant later the two planes flashed by each other, our wings so close the compressed air between them shook my plane like a cat with a live mouse. Man, was I scared! I broke off the dogfight and went off in a quiet corner of the sky to get my nerves reassembled.

The major outranked me, but that was a matter of no concern to me. I was furious. "Good god, man, you almost killed me! What in the hell were you doing diving on that SBD? We almost hit head on. I told you, goddamn it; never, never engage a third plane in a dogfight! I'm through. You'll have to find someone else to work with you." He looked at me with no sign of remorse, said nothing, and walked away. Two weeks later I received orders back to the States, and they were almost too late. I had been only a few inches away from being trapped in a wrecked Corsair at the bottom of the Pacific for eternity.

Some of my attacks were very frustrating. Often, neither my gunner nor I was sure whether it was my bomb that hit or one that missed the target, so close together were the drops. One frustration on my list was my dive at the Wotje Atoll radio station. I saw my bomb hit in the middle of the station's flat roof. A large cloud of dust burst up. "Hot damn, I called to my gunner. We hit it right on the button!" In a few seconds the trade winds had cleared the dust from the site. The radio station still stood. My bomb's only effect was to leave a large shallow crater in the 3-foot-thick concrete roof. I could only hope the concussion had broken some vacuum tubes in their radio sets.

The radio station wasn't the only Japanese structure on those islands encased in 3 feet of concrete. On Maloelap was a large concrete ammunition bunker rising some 30 feet above the coral surface. A joint strike of fighters and dive-bombers was launched to destroy it. Our SBDs carried 500-pound all-purpose bombs, and three of the Corsair fighters had armor-piercing bombs hung under their fuselages. A new technique called "skip bombing" had been developed. In these attacks, the plane raced at top speed toward the target almost at ground level. At the last possible instant, the pilot released the bomb, which maintained the plane's high speed as it crashed into the target.

Several of our dive-bombers hit the target, but without doing much damage. We pulled away and circled to watch the F4Us attack. At over 400 knots, not more than 20 feet above the ground, the first plane raced toward the bunker. I saw the armor-piercing bomb released and smash at high speed into the Maloelap bunker's concrete wall, but I couldn't see if the missile had penetrated it.

The pilot of the attack plane sped straight up directly over the target. At about 3,000 feet he rolled the plane over so he could see what his attack had accomplished. At that instant, a huge fireball and a mushroom cloud shot up (a much smaller precursor of the atomic blast at Hiroshima). All of the tons of explosives stored in that bunker had detonated at once.

The shock wave from the blast smashed into the Corsair hovering above, and the fighter was slung straight up a thousand feet or more. Later, the pilot, still a quivering mass of jelly, reported his experience to his intelligence officer. "Hell, when that shock wave hit my plane I didn't know what was happening," he said. "The stick was jerked out of my hand and I was banged around the cockpit. When the plane stopped shooting up I had to settle my nerves and get my breath back before I could see if I still had something to fly. That rugged old 'Hose Nose' was in one piece, so here I am. That's the last time I'll hang around to see what I've done." I had had a dugout-level seat from a safe distance and saw the whole thing. What a show!

Off Limits, Within Limits

It had to happen – sex came to VMSB-231. Our very efficient master sergeant was caught in a compromising embrace with a private who was his clerk in real life. The sergeant was demoted to private at once and sent back to the States to stand trial. His departure left the squadron's paperwork in turmoil. It was never straightened out. There must have been a lot more sodomy on that womanless island, but only our sergeant was caught. I would have been tempted to overlook his dalliance if I had been the CO; he was too efficient to lose.

The Japanese bypassed islands were now a threat only because their soldiers could aim anti-aircraft fire at our planes; otherwise, they were useless. Glidden had been transferred to a desk job back in Honolulu. He was succeeded by Maj. William E. Abblitt, a good man who would later earn a Legion of Merit award for valor in Korea. But he was no Elmer Glidden. In fact, there was only one Elmer Glidden in the entire corps – truly a one-of-a-kind leader.

Long after our arrival at Majuro I was working with our squadron records when we picked up an electrifying message. VMSB-231 was to pack its gear immediately for relocation to Guam. At last we would be able to attack some meaningful targets. With enthusiasm we hadn't had for months, we threw our gear into wooden crates and dragged them to a pier for loading onto a ship. There we waited. No word. And waited. No word. What had happened? In a word, nothing. We were ordered to unpack; we weren't going anywhere. Our morale hit the depths.

That there was fighting going on farther west without us was brought home one day. As I noted before, Majuro was used as a pool for planes that would replace damaged or lost aircraft from the Navy's carriers. Even though there had been a decisive victory – the "Great Mariana Turkey Shoot," the nickname for the U.S. invasion of the Mariana Islands during the June 1944 Battle of the Philippine Sea – the Navy still lost many planes that needed to be replaced with no time to spare.

More than once we asked the Navy to let us fly the idle planes lined up along the runway, but permission was denied; we might scratch them or dirty the windshields, I suppose. But suddenly all that changed. The Navy acquiesced, and my squadron was assigned to the previously untouchable fighters, dive-bombers, and torpedo bombers. Our orders were to fly them to Enewetak, the site of a very busy Navy base, in short order. With pilot handbooks in hand, we sat for hours in the cockpits of the unfamiliar planes trying to locate the vital dials and levers. That was all the preparation we had – no check flights.

The day after the dispatch arrived, we took off for Enewetak. The plane I was assigned was the huge lumbering SB2-C, the dive bomber then replacing the SBDs. Because of an unfortunate characteristic, a tendency for the tail to break off in dives, SB2-C wasn't overly popular with the pilots. Of course, I wouldn't be diving the beast on the way to Enewetak, so I had no fear of losing a tail. A twin-engine Lockheed Electra bomber acted as the navigator for the large, undisciplined clusters of pool planes. These ungainly messes, several of which were headed to Enewetak simultaneously, looked like a queen bee followed by her swarm.

Our fuel limitations required a stop at Kwajalein, about halfway there. Since we weren't flying in formation, there was no priority for landing. We came at the runway and played chicken until the most tenacious pilot prevailed and landed. The remaining pilots, some of whom no doubt chickened out, circled to try again. It took several hours for all the planes to land.

At Enewetak we went through the same ordeal, but even more tangled. In the middle of our landing, a flight of heavy B-24 bombers returning from a distant mission showed up and demanded to land before their gas ran out.

Besides fighting off our own planes, we now had go between the bombers that landed at wide intervals. Somehow, with three exceptions, we landed the Navy's planes without incident.

We stayed one night on Enewetak. I was waiting for a chance to run across the very busy runway when a Jeep driven by a Navy lieutenant commander pulled in front of me, off to one side. He was impatient. The stream of planes seemed endless. With a loud "Shit!" he slammed his Jeep into reverse and cut the wheel hard over, all without looking behind him. The Jeep headed straight for me, but I was able to jump out of its path.

"Hey, Commander," I yelled, "Watch where you're going – you almost hit me." He momentarily braked, turned his head, and yelled back, "You watch where you're going, Marine." His arrogance left me speechless and wanting to punch him. I guess when you mobilize millions of men, even All-American boys, you're going to drag in some real jerks.

Weather was no more than a minor problem in carrying out our flights. While showers were almost a daily occurrence, they were widely spaced. Dodging them on our missions was easy – just circle around. I remember one exception that could have brought me down. Six SBDs were scheduled for a nighttime "keep 'em awake" strike on Wotje. A low layer of dark clouds covered the sky, and I went up to see if the flight should be called because of the weather. We were cruising along at 2,000 feet. I looked down at the placid ocean. Just off to the left I saw on the surface a large circle of turbulent water. I had seen such circles before, ones caused by schools of fishes in a feeding frenzy.

When I looked up I saw I was headed straight into a towering waterspout – a tornado at sea. It was the base of the spout that roiled the sea in that whirlpool, not fish. The top disappeared into the clouds 3,000 feet above the ocean. I rolled my plane into a fast turn, just missing that tower of destructive wind. It was time to go home, it was time to land, and it was time to call off that night strike. The meteorologists say that the wind force in a waterspout is a great deal less than in a tornado. I wasn't at all eager to find out if they were right. I've since seen other waterspouts at sea, but at a great distance, which suits me fine.

Waning Days in the Marshalls

"CB" was short for Construction Battalion – both the unit that constructed the Navy's facilities and the battalion's members. One of the CBs I took with me on a few test flights (he loved to fly) had salvaged a small Higgins landing craft after the Marines took Majuro. "Alex," he said, "I'm going out to Laura Island to see the natives. Want to come?" It sounded fine – a great way to break away from the boring routine.

I met him at the dock. He carried a large box full of Coke bottles, canned turkey, Spam, C-rations, and fruitcake. At the end of a long 20-mile ride, we went ashore on the beach at Laura Island. Near the lagoon was a thatch-roofed hut supported by 8-foot-tall coconut log posts. The CB put some of his food-stuffs in a canvas bag, which he slung over his shoulder, and climbed the well-built ladder to the hut. In the dim indoor light we saw a handsome old brown-skinned man sitting cross-legged on a mat. He greeted us with a smile and a wave. Language was a problem, but not insurmountable. I started in naming the atolls – Mili, Majuro, Allinglapla, and so on – and he repeated them to me with a broad grin and nods of recognition.

When the canned turkey came out of the bag, language was no longer a barrier. My CB handed it to our host, who then reached for a silk scarf hanging from the roof, a scarf adorned with Japanese characters and the red rising sun. It was the kind of scarf the Japanese pilots wore around their heads under their leather helmets, and the pilots regarded as sacred. The old man probably had taken it from the body of a pilot who had crashed on the island some time in the past, and may not have realized its significance.   With gestures, my companion asked if he could take the scarf in exchange for the turkey. The old man nodded and waved his hand to indicate, "Yes, take it."

I had noticed the scarf when we entered the hut. It was a prize that I really wanted, but Marines were forbidden to trade with the natives. Either the CBs had no such restrictions or my companion ignored them. I gnashed my teeth when he tucked that scarf in his jacket. But I didn't leave empty-handed. In my house are three small, round, beautifully woven fans hung in a frame – the souvenirs I was given by that bronzed-skinned, white-haired old man almost 70 years ago.

My CB friend invited me to join him in another adventure – this one underwater, and a lot more dangerous than our trip to Laura. He had scavenged a discarded hot water tank from somewhere, and, using an acetylene torch, had cut one end of it into a passable diver's helmet. It fit across the wearer's shoulders and was cushioned by a strip of hose attached to the bottom rim. A thick glass faceplate was installed so the diver could see. On top of the tank were two fittings for intake and return air hoses.

I must have been really bored when I said yes to his invitation to try out his rig. The two of us, with the helmet and a manual air pump, motored in a small boat out to one of the coral heads that rise in the lagoon. My diving outfit was shorts; tennis shoes; leather gloves; the helmet, and a web belt hung with window sash weights that would allow me to stay submerged. I put the heavy, uncomfortable helmet over my head. The CB tightened the straps under my armpits to hold the cylinder on, checked out my weighted belt, and began pumping air into the helmet. I stepped out on the peak of the coral head and carefully and slowly started inching down, with a signal rope tied around my wrist.

The scene underwater was magical. Schools of brightly colored tropical fish darted by, and fan coral waved in the current. But a jellyfish with its 20-foot poison-tipped tentacles wasn't far enough away to suit me, and a barracuda with rows of sharp teeth flashed by but paid me no attention. On the coral mount I found footholds and handholds as I descended. At about 30 feet down I was feeling for a coral knob to hold with my left hand. I grabbed a convenient object without looking – and through my leather glove it didn't feel like coral. I looked, and it certainly wasn't. It was the head of a huge, deadly moray eel. I jerked hard on the signal rope. With help from the CB and my adrenaline-charged muscles, I climbed fast to the surface. The CB quickly took off the helmet. "What went wrong down there?" he asked. "A moray eel," I said. "I accidentally put my hand on its head."

That was the end of diving for me. I had done it, and it scared the hell out of me. I never tried it again, even when scuba gear became available. I don't even enjoy snorkeling.

Time moved at various tempos overseas. There were the long months away from home, there were the long days just waiting, there were the shorter hours flying to and from our targets, and there was the very short time I was actually under fire. But it seemed much longer. On a bombing strike there was no anti-aircraft fire except directly over the enemy's islands. I never clocked the time, but I would guess it was never more than 15 minutes, more likely 10 minutes, that I was a target. Based on that, during my 60 missions I was under fire only 10 to 15 hours during my year in the Marshalls. Of course, my wife and my father worried about me every waking hour and probably in their dreams. They couldn't know that for most of the time I lived overseas, I was safe.

As the days passed and the excitement of dive-bombing strikes lost their glamour, time slowed to the pace of an inchworm. Every morning I wondered, "Is this the day I'll get orders stateside?" It finally happened.

I was dozing in the Ready Room when a clerk broke in on my nap with, "Captain, it's here – your orders home by the first available transportation."

"You're sure?" I asked.

"Yes sir – here it is. I typed out the radio message"

"What do you know?" I replied. "I thought headquarters had forgotten me."

Now I had to wait for that "first available transportation." It finally came in the form of a Fletcher Class Destroyer, the USS *Albert W. Grant*. It was headed for San Francisco after almost being sunk in the Philippines in the Battle of Surigao Straits. Pilot-musician Cal English and I asked the ship's captain if we could bum a ride with him. "Sure. There's plenty of room," he answered. "We lost 50 of the crew in the Philippines."

It was an emotional trip home on that battered ship, and in Chapter 19 I write about it in detail. One discovery I made on that voyage was that flying was a hell of a lot better duty than being thrown around on a destroyer as it rolled and pitched across the Pacific.

My brother-in-law Roman came to my tent to say goodbye. He was, I knew, happy for me, but the sadness that he wasn't going home too was imprinted deeply on his face, an image I have never forgotten.

So my months in the Pacific came to an end. Those days were highlights of my life. I knew what was expected of me and I thought I lived up to the expectations. There was no doubt in my mind that after a few months stateside I would ship out again to a more critical arena, probably Japan itself. (Without the atomic bomb, I would have.) In the years since I have taken a realistic look at my wartime contribution. The 15 tons of bombs I dropped on those bypassed Japanese islands could have stayed in an arsenal in the United States and we would still have won the war. But I'm glad I was there as a part of the country's vast effort to destroy the evil forces of tyranny.

Still, my contribution to the victory over Japan was microscopic. Today when people find out I was a Marine pilot in World War II, many say, "Thank you for your service." I am embarrassed by their gratitude.

Another post-war observation I've made is very depressing. When I encounter people who appear to have no sense of appropriateness in dress, public conversation, and civil interaction with others (nor, most likely, even a thought of doing anything good for humanity) I think, "My God, did I put my life on the line to make this country safe for these bums?" But when I think of my family and the fine people I know and have known, I am at peace with my role in the war.

Chapter 22

Down to Earth

Soldier rest! thy warfare o'er,
Sleep the sleep that knows not breaking ...

— *Sir Walter Scott*

When the USS *Albert W. Grant,* the battle-scared destroyer that brought me home from Majuro, docked at the naval base on San Francisco Bay's Mare Island Naval Shipyard, I was the first one to elbow my way through the crew to the gangplank. After being surrounded by water for many months, what a great feeling it was to put my feet on land that stretched 3,000 miles before reaching the Atlantic!

In one hand was the "toolbox" secreting my Scottie, Shorty McSnorter, who had lived with me on Majuro. With the other hand I held my duffel bag filled with uniforms, shoes, and other gear. A bus was available to take me off the base and into San Francisco.

I was concerned that if the guards at gatehouse knew I had a dog they would grab him and put him in indefinite quarantine. So, as we drove across the base, I kept McSnorter's box on my lap with the lid closed. Fellow sailors who noticed snorting and whining were very curious about the contents of the toolbox; it certainly wasn't tools they heard. Immediately after the bus cleared the guardhouse and I was free of military control, I opened the lid. The Scottie was overjoyed, his tail wagging furiously and his head held high as he snapped off bark after bark. At this joyous sight the busload of sailors clapped and yelled "Right on!" (short for "right on target").

Although our destination would be New Orleans, Hermi stayed with friends in San Diego as she waited for me. When I called from Honolulu to tell her I was on the way to San Francisco, she took the train to Los Angeles and checked in at the Ambassador Hotel, where we had been married; I left word there to let her know what train I would be on coming in on. As I walked up a broad ramp from the train I saw Hermi standing at the front of a large crowd, waving wildly at me and grinning with joy.

Just before I went overseas I had been in a San Diego bar talking to a weather-beaten Naval aviator just back from carrier service in the Pacific. I said, "I'll bet your folks were overjoyed to hear from you."

He looked down at his drink.

"Well, I haven't called them yet – I haven't even called my wife."

"Why not," I asked.

"Combat changed me; I feel like they are strangers. It'll take time for me to make the adjustment."

As I walked up the ramp in the Los Angeles train station that conversation came back to me, and I understood. The attractive, excited Hermi waiting for me may not have changed while I was away, but I had. I almost felt I was approaching a stranger.

When I reached her we hugged briefly, disappointing the crowd of cheering people who had expected, I'm sure, a tearful, passionate kiss. Only when we settled in a taxi did I reach out, pull her to me, and share a long kiss.

We checked in at the Ambassador Hotel with memories of our wedding all around us. As soon as we settled in our room Hermi called her folks in New Orleans and excitedly said, "Oh mom, oh dad, Alex is here! He looks great! He hasn't changed a bit!"

That last sentence hit me. What did she mean I hadn't changed? For almost a year and a half I had lived in an all-white male world except for glimpses of nurses, Pacific Islander women, and the debs I saw briefly in Honolulu. Sixty times I had rolled my dive bomber into a near vertical dive, not knowing whether I would live or die. Nothing in my former life compared with the fearful exhilaration of that plunging cascade into a hail of fire. And, I had killed and wounded possibly many hundreds of human beings, which still haunts me.

Day after day there was the crushing boredom, the insistent crackle of the palm trees in the never-ending wind and the same barely edible Spam-laden food. I felt years older than I did when I sailed from San Diego. I was sharply aware of the fragility of life – that I was mortal, that death could take me at any moment. I knew that the deaths of my comrades were real. I might look the same, but the naïve, callous Marine who waved good-bye to his beautiful young wife was forever changed. It took time for me to accept Hermi's warmth and love as I had before. She too must have changed while living through the long months alone, listening every night to the same wistful love song played on the wind-up music box I gave her.

After we waited in line for hours at the train station, the exhausted ticket agent sold us a lower berth on the next train to New Orleans. Hermi and I gladly shared the berth on the long, hot trip, eating miserable food. We stopped, stopped, and stopped at every desolate small town across the great southwestern desert. Days later, the train squealed to an ear-splitting stop in the New Orleans terminal. Hermi's folks were there to meet us. As her mother Rosetta took me in her arms, I at last felt accepted as her son.

A Mysterious illness

A few days of attentive in-laws, soft beds, great New Orleans food, and obliging servants to wash my clothes and make our beds came all too quickly to an end. We piled our suitcases into the trunk of our sleek black Buick convertible, said our goodbyes, and took off for Montgomery, Alabama, on the way to Atlanta.

Hermi and I were stopping in Montgomery to spend a couple of days with my sister Charlotte. I brought her loving greetings from her husband Roman, who had bid me a sorrowful farewell when I left him that day on Majuro with his Marine detachment.

The second night we were there, I woke up in the early morning burning with fever. A dose of aspirin exchanged the fever for overpowering chills. After going through this sequence twice and developing a volcanic headache, I decided I'd better be examined at the Army Air Corps Hospital at Maxwell Field (there was no Navy hospital in the area). The doctor let out a low "Christ" when the thermometer he drew from my mouth registered 105°F.

"Captain Alexander," he said, "I know you're a tough Marine, but you are a very sick Marine. I'm putting you to bed. We need to find out what's causing that high fever and the headache." In case I was contagious, I was assigned a private room. I waved an uncertain goodbye to Hermi as I was led down the hall.

Just days before, I was a picture of health in New Orleans. I have a picture to prove it, one showing me beaming and in great spirits as I sat on a wall by Lake Pontchartrain. The sudden onslaught of fever was bewildering.

Every other day a nurse with a large needle came to draw blood for lab tests, and this went on for several days. Nothing showed up. I was given no medication. The doctor would look in, feel my forehead, check my chart, shake his head, and raise helpless hands. I accused him of taking my strong Marine blood to inject into the weakling Air Corps pilots.

A tentative diagnosis was that I might have undulant fever brought on by drinking unpasteurized milk. But I heard no more about it. Only when I was checked out after six weeks did I find out that at one point the doctors didn't think I would survive, the reason they had waived visiting rules and let Hermi spend her days with me.

My room looked out on a parking area. After the doctors and nurses made their mid-morning rounds I would pull the shade half way up as a signal to Hermi, who was parked outside my window, that it was OK for her to come in. I also had another constant visitor. Every night a small mouse would wake me by running across my face and then jumping in the wastebasket and rustling the thrown-away papers. He kept me unwanted company for the duration.

My neighbors in the room next to me were eight B-17 pilots back home after twenty missions bombing Germany. They were a wild bunch, suffering from shell shock (today called post-traumatic stress disorder, PTSD). They had seen too many of their buddies spiral down in flames. Over several weeks they began to quiet down, so much so they were allowed to go to the movie theater on the base. Along with the feature was a newsreel showing American B-17 bombers being shot down by the Germans. It brought the pilots' own missions roaring back. They went screaming into their room, pounding on the walls and throwing furniture at the windows. Doctors came running and quieted them with shots. The next day one of the pilots slashed his wrists, but survived.

I was never aware of such violent behavior by Navy and Marine pilots. The Air Corps pilots stationed in England left more familiar surroundings to plunge into a hail of fire. And when those who made it back left the base, the contrast with their American counterparts in Germany was dramatic: They went into nearby pubs where girls were plentiful and there was music and food. It was almost like being home. In the Pacific, we pilots never escaped the war except for brief times on rest and recuperation trips – so, unlike the pilots in Europe, we never had to adapt to the change from hellfire to civilization. We certainly became war weary, and some pilots pled sickness to escape from combat. But I think living constantly with the war without change kept us sane.

The nurses at the Army Air Corps hospital in Montgomery kept a chart of my temperature at the foot of the bed. After a month, my fever started a slow, steady decline. Then it abruptly went to normal, then back up to the line on the chart. The doctors who had thought I would soon recover were very puzzled.

Hermi had her own thermometer, and her chart didn't record any sudden descent to normal; the daily drop stayed right on the descending line. She told this to the doctor. "Well, I know what happened," he said. "The nurse failed to record your temperature one day, and to save herself any embarrassment she put in 'normal.' Forget it, you're steadily recovering." After a week of normal temperature, no headache, and some recovery of energy, I was to be released.

I went to the office of the Air Corps major who had the title Head of Medicine. He had kept careful watch over me, and I liked him.

"Captain Alexander," he said, "do you know what you had?"

"Some doctor said it could be undulant fever," I replied.

"It wasn't. We don't know what the hell was wrong with you. That's why we never gave you any medication."

"Thank the Lord it wasn't undulant fever," I said. "I was told if it was I could never fly again. Man, that really depressed me. It was like a black cloud hovering in my brain."

"Well, Captain, I wish you well."

Then, with a grin he said, "We couldn't afford to have a Marine die in an Air Corps hospital. I would be terrible for inter-service relations."

He clutched my shoulder and shook my hand with a long-held grip. I smiled, saluted, turned, and left.

Atkins Park and Points North

With the unexpected medical adventure behind us, Hermi and I were back home in Atlanta and turned into my long remembered house on St. Charles Place in Atkins Park. At the front door my beaming, tearing, too-proud father crushed me in his arms.

"Welcome home son! Welcome home! Come in! Oh do come in!"

He then hugged Hermi, his competitor, lightly and brushed her cheek with a fleeting kiss. Standing behind him was his indispensable housekeeper Bernice. She reached for my hands with both of hers.

"Welcome home, Mr. Cecil. I'm so glad you're safe home."

So began a few days of kisses, hugs, and suffocating adulation from relatives and friends. It was with profound relief when, after three days, I said, "Dad, it's been great! What a welcome you gave us! But we'll have to shove off in the morning. I have to check in at Cherry Point day after tomorrow." As I backed the Buick out of the driveway, we waved goodbye to my father, who stood on the sidewalk with tears streaking his face.

Two days later we drove into New Bern, North Carolina, a town time hadn't forgotten; time had never been there. With its tree-bordered streets, blooming gardens, and stately classic houses, with a soft wind curling through it all, it was almost a cliché. But all its doors were shut. There were no For Rent signs, no real estate offices.

I've always believed that when you want something, you start at the top. In New Bern that meant starting with the mayor. I found out where she lived (yes, a female mayor in the 1940s South). We walked the path to the door of her neat, narrow, three-story brick home, set in front of the frisky black Neuse River. A petite, stylish, middle-aged woman answered my knock and then greeted us with a warm hand, a friendly smile, and "I'm the mayor of New Bern. Can I help you?"

"I've been assigned to Cherry Point," I said. "We're looking for a room to rent." I glanced up at her inviting gray-brick home. "Do you have one?"

She seemed startled at my straightforward request.

"Oh no, Captain, I'm sorry we don't. But I think you may find one in that large wooden house over there."

She pointed down the street to a house almost hidden behind a small forest of oak trees. "Thanks," I said. She wished us good house hunting and a pleasant stay in New Bern, and then waited until we walked away before softly closing the door.

"Yes, we have a room. It's in front of the house on the third floor. You share a bathroom and a small kitchen in the hallway with two other Marine couples." This was our greeting at the door of the house the mayor had indicated.

Hermi and I exchanged nods. Without looking at room or asking the price I said, "We'll take it." The landlady then led us to a large, high-ceilinged room with a king-sized bed, a sofa, two chairs, and a desk, all softly lit by three lamps. I've forgotten the rent. Except for the shared bathroom, we were very happy with our new home.

The road to Cherry Point ran through Morehead City and was long, narrow, pothole-filled, and bumpy. The base was large and active. Planes were taking off and landing in swarms – but I wouldn't be piloting one for several months. My duty was to sit all day on a cracked leather sofa in a Ready Room, waiting for assignment. Torn old magazines and comic books afforded a little relief from the stultifying waiting.

"The colonel wants to see you, Captain," said the sergeant who sat at a desk in the room.

Those welcomed words shocked me awake as if I'd dived into a cold lake. I struggled out of the sofa and walked across to the colonel's office. He was like a god with silver leaves on his collar, and in his beefy hands he held my assignment to an active position.

He never looked at me, and instead directed his gaze at papers on his desk. "Captain Alexander," he said, "you will be the commanding officer of the Headquarters Squadron at Bogue Field. You will report to the C.O. there at 800 hours tomorrow. Here are your orders."

He pushed a pile of papers across the table, swiveled his chair around to the cabinet behind him, and said, still never looking at me, "Good luck Captain. Semper Fi."

"Yes Sir!" I snapped off a salute directed at his back, did an about face, and left his office. I was one happy guy to leave that stuffy room with its baggy furniture, but only semi-happy with my assignment. C.O. of a headquarters would make me the fearless leader of a covey of lackadaisical file clerks with their typewriters as weapons and little else. At least I would have a plane to fly the four hours a month required to earn flight pay.

Getting to Bogue Field from New Bern added at least 45 minutes to the trip. Hermi was glad I had a job, but the alarm going off at 5:00 in the morning didn't please her. We would share cups of coffee, she would shuffle back to bed, and I would slip into the Buick and drive the potholed road to Bogue.

A short, thin, smirking lieutenant colonel asked me into his office. He introduced himself as the executive officer of the group. "Sit down, Captain. I want to tell you what I expect from you as C.O. of my headquarters squadron.

First the men, including your officers, will always be in correct uniform; no rolled up sleeves, no soiled trousers, ties two-blocked, and always covered outdoors. Got it?"

"Yes Sir."

"Our grounds will always be policed. A discarded cigarette on the ground is, as far as I'm concerned, a capital offense; if I catch the man who threw it down he'll be court martialed. Weekend passes have to be earned. A single demerit, and that man doesn't leave the base. You will conduct close order drill every day for at least one hour. I will not accept any paperwork with erasures or corrections; it will be typed and retyped until it's flawless.

"Your squadron has these missions: One, assemble all directives, orders, and correspondence in alphabetically designated files. Two, see that all incoming correspondence is answered within 24 hours without fail. Three, you will preside over court martials; there is a backlog to be tackled immediately. We have three amphibious Grumman bi-planes to be used for rescue service. There are six pilots in the squadron, and two are assigned to each plane. They are responsible for its maintenance – fuel tanks topped off and ready to fly. There is a Curtiss dive bomber in the hangar that you may use to get in your four hours a month of flight time to qualify for flight pay. You will require my permission for any additional flying. You will be on board every day but Sunday at 800 hours and remain until 1900. Any questions?"

"Yes Sir. Where can I put my gear, where can I sleep if I need to stay overnight, and when can I meet the squadron?"

"I'll call the squadron to assemble at 1400," he said. "After that you may meet with your officers." He answered my other questions, one with "Your office is directly across the hall. Keep your door open."

"Yes Sir!" I snapped my heels, saluted, did a crisp about-face, and marched out of his office.

Good God, I thought, how did I draw that tub of shit masquerading as a Marine? At least I knew what I was going to have to handle. He lived up to my first impression the entire time I was under his command; so at least I knew that he was consistent.

That afternoon I introduced myself to the platoon of clerks, mechanics, and guards that I would command. To give myself a little glamour, I told them I was just back from combat. I repeated the lieutenant colonel's directives and added a few of my own, one being "On time is five minutes early" and "to err is human, to forgive is divine, and neither of these directives is my policy."

I told them they looked like a good bunch of Marines and I looked forward to working with them. I asked the six pilots to come into my office and be at ease.

"Men," I said, "I'm sure you know our mission is rescuing downed men at sea flying those Grumman Ducks. Are you all checked out in the Ducks?" They all shook their heads no.

"Well," I said, "our first order of business is getting checked out. Lt. Everett you're the first. Tomorrow, after the plane has been run-up, I want you to take it up a couple of thousand feet and practice stalls and a couple of chandelles. Then fly over to Bogue Sound and land it. Don't stall it in; fly it slowly until it meets the water. If it's dead calm tomorrow, you won't go. I flew PBYs at Jax, and I know if there isn't some wave action it's impossible to judge your height above a flat, glassy surface. Also, if the wind is over 30 knots it's a no-go.

The weather the next day was fine. I watched as Lt. Everett accelerated his plane down the runway. Only in the last 100 yards did the plane struggle into the air and climb slowly away. The hour assigned for the flight passed. After another 45 minutes the Grumman entered our air space, circled, and landed. Against instructions, Everett full-stalled the plane and it dropped down with a dust-driving thump and came slewing down the runway to a shaky stop.

I drove a Jeep to where the pilot was parking the plane. When he walked toward me, I could see fear, relief, and exhaustion on his face.

"What took so long, Lieutenant?" I asked.

"I couldn't get that damn plane off the water," he answered. "It wouldn't fly. About the fifth try, I hit a wave and we bounced into the air."

"Was there any wind?"

"Yes sir, there was a good breeze, and the water was all churned up. You know, that plane flies like a Mack truck. It fell out of the chandelle I tried. It seemed to ignore the controls. Either they are all lousy airplanes or this one has something really wrong with it."

An hour or two later I called Everett to my office and said, "Tell the sergeant what you just told me." After he finished, I said, "Sergeant, I want you and the other mechanics to find out what's wrong with the plane. Is it the engine not revving up and is there something wrong with the controls? If you can't find anything wrong I'm going to have Grumman send a pilot and a mechanic down here to test the airplane."

Late that afternoon the plane captain came into my office. "Captain, we found the problem, he said. "That big pontoon float that the plane uses on the water is full of high octane fuel!"

"How the hell did that happen?" I asked.

"Well you know, every morning we top off the fuel tanks. That plane always took 20 or 30 gallons, and each gallon weighs about 6 pounds. The other two stayed almost full, and it hit us that there must be a leak in the main tank located in the top wing and that the gasoline was somehow running down into the pontoon. It's no wonder Lt. Everett had so much trouble getting that gas-heavy plane off the water, and it's no wonder it flew like a truck."

"OK," I said, "first thing tomorrow, drain that pontoon. Have a fire truck stand by."

As I watched the draining procedure from my office I saw the officious lieutenant commander walk up. He pointed at the pontoon, threw his arms in the air, and stomped around in a tight circle, his fists clenched. I could hear his yells through my closed window. There was no reason, I decided, for me to join him.

Now back to the Alexanders' housing. After several months, the ads I put in the paper brought results: Hermi and I rented a two-room house on a small lot in Morehead City. It wasn't air conditioned, of course, but there were ceiling fans in every room that at least moved the hot, moist air around to give some relief. There was one feature the fans couldn't combat: the cook stove, which was fired by a scorching coal fire under the grill. We became aficionados of cold dishes.

The greatest asset of this house was its location. I could drive to Bogue Field in 45 minutes. Wake-up time was moved from 5:00 to 6:00, and I could get home before dark.

We found two sources of good food. There was then, and still is, a famous Morehead seafood restaurant with the questionable name of The Sanitary Fish Market. We went there for dinner three or four times a week to indulge in the many varieties of crabmeat dishes. The décor was "summer camp classic" with rough wood furniture, smoke-darkened windows, paper napkins, and bare bulbs hanging from a tiered ceiling. It would be a wild exaggeration to call what the hairy waiters performed "service"; but, so what? We went there to eat, not to be waited on.

Sunday night dinner at the Cherry Point Officers' Club was another matter. There was a lush wall-to-wall carpet, comfortable chairs, crystal chandeliers, linen tablecloths, and elegant china and silverware. In their spotless white jackets, the waiters were masters of their craft. But beyond all that finery, and of greatest importance, the cuisine was four-star. Filet mignon and lobster were staples week after week.

Hermi had a problem: There was no limit to the amount you could eat. Having spent most of the week opening cans, when she saw all that wonderful spread she let go of all restraint. Our first Sunday, she reduced three large lobsters to empty shells and completed her meal with long strips of rare steak washed down with red wine.

Picnic lunches became a habit too. Droning around in sloppy circles for four hours to earn flight pay was an endless bore. I started to say it was a "crashing bore" which it might have been when I sometimes let sleep take over. Eventually, I found a way to eliminate the endless circling. It was arranged that Hermi and I would have a picnic lunch together courtesy of the taxpayers. I flew up to New Bern (this was before we moved) and circled the house. Hermi came running out with a basket, leaped into the Buick, waved to me (the top was down), and followed my low-flying plane as I led her in circles to a nearby auxiliary airfield. I landed, cut the engine, and ran to the Buick as it came rolling to a stop. We sat in the shade of an old oak tree and ate a joyous lunch. We soon parted, the groundling in the Buick speeding back to New Bern and the eagle in his war plane back to Bogue Field. I was able to write in my log only 1 hour and 23 minutes – 2 hours and 37 minutes short of that month's 4 hours of required flight time.

Flying over the waters of Bogue Sound, I occasionally saw a dark circle of roiled water caused by a mammoth gathering of large fish. Several commercial fishing boats always had their lines out trolling for fish; I would fly over one of them, wag the wings, and in a series of low zooms lead them to the circle. When they got in the middle of that vast school, it took them only minutes to fill their boat with flopping fish. Seeing this frenzy, all of the other boatmen made fast wakes to catch their share. Using aircraft as the aerial eyes of the fisherman was so successful that after the war they used Piper Cubs to find their quarry.

A "Test Flight" to Bridgeport

For a third diversion I had to get clearance from the lieutenant commander. "Sir," I said, "I want to keep my hand in with cross-country flying using the radio beams. Will you OK a week-end flight to Bridgeport, Connecticut, and back?"

"Why Connecticut, Captain?," he asked.

I thought it would be a mistake to tell him I was going to see my Yale room-mate Edgar Cullman. I might enjoy myself, and that would be unthinkable.

"Following the coast I'll use a series of radio beams for navigation, which will be good training. I could turn around at Floyd Bennett Airfield on Long Island, but there's a lot of air traffic in that area. Bridgeport has excellent run-ways and maintenance facilities, and that's why I picked it."

This was true, but not the whole truth.

"All right, you have my permission. You can leave Friday and be back Monday. That will give you a chance to rest before you return."

The weather was clear when I took off, but it gradually deteriorated. By the time I was west of Atlantic City, New Jersey, I was flying on instruments in a dark cloud. To get in the clear I turned east toward the Atlantic and soon was out in the open. My flight path from there to Bridgeport was plotted over open water, and Manhattan was shrouded in low clouds to the west.

The war in Europe was over. Our soldiers were being brought home to join the upcoming invasion of Japan. Below I saw a huge passenger liner headed through the waves toward New York. I flew down to deck height, some hundred feet over the water. As I approached the ship I saw "HMS Queen Mary" inscribed in large block letters on her bow. She was the renowned flag-ship of Great Britain's merchant fleet. Close by the open deck I circled the Queen; cheering, waving, and leaping American GI's lined her rails. They saw the white star on the wing of my single engine plane and knew it must have flown only a short distance from land, so my plane was a sign that they were almost home.

As I climbed away from that joyous ship, with a huge Union Jack stream-ing from her stern, I felt some of the elation my welcome had given those homesick veterans. I had given them reason to know home was not far away.

My first sight of Coney Island could have been my last. As I approached the famous amusement park on Long Island through low scattered clouds, I suddenly saw an open steel jump tower looming directly in front of me. I pulled back sharply on the control stick and shoved the throttle wide open, clearing the tower by too few feet. The tower was Coney Island's parachute jump. Before the war many brave thrill seekers (I think they were just stupid) were hauled to the top of the tower in a sling chair, cut loose, and parachuted quickly to the ground. For this they paid money. If I had hit the tower my cer-tain death would have been the first (and I think the only) fatality related to the tower. I was glad not to have such a distinction.

Two weeks after my flight, a similar bank of low clouds covered Manhattan. A B-25 (the Air Corps medium bomber) flying low from Floyd Bennett Field on Long Island became blinded by the clouds, and the pilot flew the plane into the seventy-sixth floor of the Empire State Building.

The pilots were killed, probably on impact. One of the engines was hurled through an elevator shaft, cutting the cables and dropping the car to the basement; miraculously, two women passengers survived. Fourteen people died as a result of the crash, but the building was never in danger of collapsing. The tower's structural engineers were designing for unknown forces. With the exception of the nearby Chrysler Building, no skyscraper then erected approached the height of the Empire State. So to be sure the building was safe, the structural engineers far exceeded the prescribed strength for all of the steel structure's components. That over-designing, plus the fact that the B-25 was a relatively small plane with limited fuel capacity, saved the Empire State Building from a 9/11-type catastrophe. Even now I sometimes wonder if I had stayed on my original course over mid-town Manhattan and flown blindly through that heavy cloud mass, I would have smashed into that menacing tower myself.

I was approaching the broad, long Bridgeport runway. My limited flight time in the SB2C (Scout Bomber Curtiss) made me cautious. Because I didn't have the comfortable feel of the plane that comes only after many hours flying it, I wanted to be sure I wouldn't approach too slowly, lose flying speed, stall, and spin in. I came in fast on the wheels and used most of the runway to stop. The "follow me" Jeep led me to the administration building, where Edgar and his wife Louise were waving me welcome. After exchanging hugs and a kiss with Louise and manly hugs with Edgar, I closed out my flight plan at the office desk and then walked with them to the car.

"See that pilot over there?" Edgar asked, pointing to a Naval aviator in his blue uniform. "We were standing together when you landed. When he saw you come in fast on the wheels, he laughed and said 'Your friend must be married. That fast landing was a husband landing. He wasn't taking any chances of stalling that plane and making his wife a widow.'"

It was a great stay at the Cullman farm near Stamford, where Edgar's mother and father gave me an unearned hero's welcome. Early Sunday morning I took off from Bridgeport, first circling the Cullman farm only a few miles south. The family came out and waved me goodbye.

The flight back to Bogue Field had only one unlikely event. As I accelerated down the Bridgeport runway with the canopy pushed back behind me,

I heard a loud crack. When I gained altitude and pulled the canopy shut I saw that one of the Plexiglas panels was gone. When I landed at Bogue, I reported the lost panel to the snippy lieutenant colonel. He grilled me as though I had deliberately damaged his aircraft. My only answer: "Colonel, it happened as I was taking off at Bridgeport. I heard it crack, but I didn't see it. I have no idea how it happened." "Well, I'll have to accept your non-answer." he said. "But you will be charged for replacing the panel." The man I'd come to think of as "Lt. Col. Bull" was not one of the Marines' "few good men."

On to Atlantic Beach and Tennessee

One day an unwanted letter was lying in our post office box. It gave us notice we had just two weeks to vacate the house we were renting. If we couldn't find a place, Hermi would have to go home to New Orleans and I'd move into the Bachelor Officer Quarters at Cherry Point. Every free moment we went out knocking on doors with no luck.

Someone suggested we try Atlantic Beach, a small island just offshore from Morehead City. Just across the two-lane causeway that connected the island to the mainland, we saw a small vacant wooden building perched on a sandy lot. A tattered notice nailed to a post gave the name of the woman who owned the building. We found the owner in Morehead City. She went with us to inspect the paint peeled shack. On the way she told us she had used it as her real estate office and her home. "I'm a lawyer," she said. "I've given up real estate and am returning to practice."

She walked us quickly through the small office, the bedroom with a small bed, the bathroom, and the living room; the kitchen had a two-plate grill, a small oven, and a small dining alcove. The sparse furniture was old and bare. It wasn't inspiring, but it would have to do.

I was very concerned about the exterior's cracked, warped wood siding. A cold wind blew through it, and there was no insulation or heating element that I could see.

"How do you heat this place?" I asked.

"Oh, I'll bring back the electric heaters. I took them home. I was afraid they'd be stolen."

"OK?" I asked Hermi. She said "OK," but with a dubious look on her face.

"All right, we'll take it. Please bring the heaters in tomorrow."

The next day was cold, rainy, and gray, not very kind weather for our move. And our landlady didn't show with the heaters. I called several times, but there was no answer. To create some warmth, we turned the electric oven on high and opened the door. More phone calls and a note left at her empty house brought no response. We kept the oven going 24 hours a day for several weeks.

Soon there came a savage pounding at our door. It was our enraged "landwoman" (she was no lady). I opened the door, and she plunged in and shoved the bill at me.

"Why is my electric bill sky high – what have you been doing?" she growled.

"We've had to leave the oven on to get a little warmth. You never brought us the space heaters you promised. I called you repeatedly and left a note at your house. It's we who should be outraged! Why don't you cool down and just bring us the heaters."

"Well, I understand," she grumbled. "I'll get the heaters."

Just before dark I heard her horn, went out, and took the heaters into the house. They were more efficient than the oven, but just barely.

During our time at Atlantic Beach, news of the most memorable event came to us on our small radio. Franklin D. Roosevelt was dead. America had lost its great president, who optimistically and courageously led the country in peace and war. Harry Truman, the almost unknown vice president had, as he said, "a ton of bricks fall" on his head. This dramatic change was quickly absorbed. Truman faced a terrible decision but ordered the dropping of the two atomic bombs over Hiroshima and Nagasaki. Within a week the Japanese surrendered. He was not Roosevelt (no one could be) but he was a fine president who made world-changing decisions saving Europe from Russian domination.

When I became commanding officer at Bogue, I signed papers acknowledging I was now custodian of the squadron's matériel. Included was a large quantity of hand tools stored in a warehouse. The supply sergeant in charge of the tools assured me they were there. I signed. A week later he was transferred to the Pacific. Several weeks later the sergeant who had replaced the one transferred came to my office and said he thought I'd better go with him to the warehouse.

It was a short, silent walk. When we entered the warehouse and the sergeant flipped on the light, I saw rows of empty shelves and only a few tools scattered here and there.

"Good Lord," I said, "Where are all those tools I signed for?"

"Sir, whenever a Cherry Point squadron was headed overseas, its supply officer would come here and demand hand tools for his squadron. I think the COs that preceded you agreed to the demand, but none of them ever had the paperwork signed."

"Well," I said, "lets keep this quiet while I think about it."

The next day I applied for duty at the Engineering Officers School at the Millington Naval Air Station, a major technical training center about 20 miles northeast of Memphis, Tennessee. My orders there arrived in a week. To my shame and guilt, I left those empty shelves for my successor to explain to the commander, who was, I think, as glad to see me leave as I was.

After I left, Lt. Col. "Bull" was transferred to the Marine Air Station at Ewa, near Honolulu. His duties included fire prevention. A massive fire destroyed the large enlisted men's mess hall. The lieutenant colonel was held responsible, demoted, and sent back to a menial job in the States. For me, that was a happy ending to the career of the Marine's version of Captain Queeg.

The first few days we stayed at Memphis's grand old hotel, The Peabody. Every evening a shepherd (really a bellhop) brought a gaggle of quacking ducks into the lobby and led a waddling parade around the fountain. It was, for the guests, the event of the day.

It didn't take us long to find a new two-bedroom house in the neighborhood called Orange Mound. Only two years ago the area had been a black slum but now was covered with cookie cutter bungalows. Hermi had some snobbish, wealthy cousins in Memphis, and they invited us for dinner at their mansion. They went into shock when she told them we were living in Orange Mound. "What?" they cried. "That's a Negro slum!" We were never invited back.

The engineering course at Millington was challenging and absorbing. Every morning an instructor gave a lecture on the particular aircraft component, complete with slides and the various parts under discussion. After lunch we went to the shop, where we learned to rivet and weld aluminum. We also studied the various parts and systems that had been removed from a plane and often went out on the super-hot ramp to repair war-weary aircraft buckling in the heat. Homework was a heavy assignment. I figured if I could explain a system or part so Hermi understood its function, then I had to understand it myself. We spent many evenings at the kitchen table as I explained carburetors, hydraulic systems, spark plugs, magnetos, and other exciting parts to an alternately attentive and bored Hermi.

Those planes were hot, and tools left in the sun burned your hands. One scorching day I was inside a Corsair fighter replacing worn cables in the tail. In a short time I felt weak and about to pass out. With what strength I had left I banged on the metal skin of the plane, and my pounding was heard. It took two men to pull me out and hold me up as I staggered back to the shop.

One of the subjects covered by our instructor was engine timing. A camshaft activated the valves that opened and closed to let fuel into the cylinders. Timing was set for the engine cruising speed. At other speeds the engine didn't deliver maximum power. "Why not", I asked the instructor, "develop a camshaft that could vary the timing for all speeds?" "Good idea" he said.

I made drawings of my invention and sent them to Owen Welles, one of my MIT roommates, who was an engineer with Pratt & Whitney, which made the top-of-the-line engines for our fighters, bombers, and transports. (Owen was a devout pacifist and was exempt from the draft, but I think that when he saw all his friends in military service he wanted to support them.) Owen wrote me immediately, saying that as a rule such ideas as mine are returned unopened to the inventor. More than likely Pratt & Whitney would be developing a similar invention, but the inventor would think the firm had stolen his idea and consider a lawsuit.

"However, Cecil, since I know you trust me, I showed your drawings to the senior engineer," Owen's letter read. "Pratt & Whitney already has a working model of a variable camshaft identical to yours except for one improvement. You show ball bearing contacts, and ours uses roller bearings that would last much longer. Sorry, but your idea is clear evidence that you are a potential first-rate aeronautical engineer. When the war is over go back to MIT and earn yourself a degree in aeronautical engineering."

I never considered his suggestion; my grasp of mathematics was so tenuous I couldn't have passed the required advanced math courses. Pratt & Whitney never used their timer. The advancement to jets made even their finest reciprocating engines obsolete.

V-J Day At Last

"Atomic Bombs Dropped by U.S. Obliterating Two Japanese Cities" read the headlines. One week after the bombs were dropped on Hiroshima and Nagasaki, the Japanese surrendered. I had a rush of fierce and divergent reactions. First, the war was over: We won it, and I had fought in it and survived. This could be summed up in two words – "profound relief." Second, when I read the scope of the devastation produced by the bombs I felt microscopically small and useless. The 20 tons of bombs I let fall were like a tiny firecracker compared to those explosions; third, I felt I could have stayed safe at home and it wouldn't have affected the war's outcome one iota. My third reaction was fear – fear of another nation getting the bomb, fear of a chain reaction that would destroy the earth. That fear intensified as I learned more, and that even the scientific geniuses who developed the bomb weren't certain its force could be limited.

The fear I shared with all knowledgeable people has been a part of my life ever since. Bryant Conant, president of Harvard from 1933 to 1953 and a chemist who worked on the bomb, somewhat lifted that weight of dread in a talk he gave in Atlanta. He said we shouldn't let fear of the bomb permeate our lives and that our children, grandchildren, and great grandchildren would live in a world where no atomic bombs would have destroyed another city. Hannah and Asher, my great grandchildren, have borne out Conant's prophesy. But if more rogue nations and terrorists prevail in their drive for this fierce weapon, Dr. Conant's optimistic view could evaporate in a flash.

On August 15, 1945, Victory Over Japan Day, better known as V. J. Day, all depressing thoughts were shoved away. It was a day to celebrate the end of the war, a war that saw Germany and Japan in ruins.

Hermi and I heard on our radio about the cheering throngs in downtown Memphis. But we had a problem. All of us engineering students who had automobiles were sure our training at Millington made us expert auto mechanics. Disassembling and assembling and just tinkering with our cars was a pastime we all pursued. On V. J. Day the engine of our Buick was spread out on the floor of the garage, and without the car we weren't going to get to town. I put the engine together with the speed one only sees in the amusing accelerated sequences seen in movies and on TV. By noon we had a functioning vehicle, which we raced down to Memphis.

It was a wild and joyous bacchanal. Anybody in uniform was a hero. The war wouldn't have been won without that drunken sailor over there, that dancing airman in the street, or that Marine firing his rifle in the air. Young women gave kisses in abundance to any and every eligible man. We were all eligible, and I had my share as we crept down the crowded main street in our open car. Hermi too was the luscious target of the GIs' lips.

We stayed until after dark, a dark that sparkled with light from hundreds of torches. Fireworks sent rockets screaming into the night, where they exploded high above in cascades of burning, sparkling color. It was the best of times. The joyous celebration was unabated when we left at midnight.

Meanwhile, the skipper of my squadron, Col. Elmer Glidden, was at a desk in Washington reviewing Marine aviators' service records to see who qualified for relief from active duty. When pilots from his squadron records came up, he ordered the pilots released immediately; I don't think he bothered to see if they qualified. My release came while I had two more weeks to earn my certificate as an engineering officer, and the head of the training program accepted my request to hold my release until I finished. I wanted that certificate. The two weeks passed. Hermi and I were packed and ready to go the day after I finished the course. It was farewell to Millington.

One of the things I would miss was an unexpected perk. Across the street from Millington was a Navy Air Base, and I would go there to get my flight time in. Millington supplied me with transportation. The first time I called for a ride I said, "This is Captain Alexander. Please send a driver to the shop to take me to the air field." "Yes sir! Right away sir!"

Soon a long black Cadillac limousine purred up with a WAVE (the acronym for "Women Accepted for Volunteer Emergency Service") driver who qualified as a sex kitten, the right choice for that purring Cad. She was expecting to pick up a high-ranking Navy officer but instead saw a Marine. "Captain I'm looking for a Naval officer, Captain Alexander." "You've found Captain Alexander," I said, "but he's a Marine captain, not an exalted Navy captain." She giggled and said, "Get in, Captain. This will be our secret. Whenever you call for transportation from now on, ask for Abigail. I'll come get you." Never since then have I ridden in such splendor, albeit in secret.

As Hermi and I passed through the guardhouse as we left Millington for the last time, a sailor standing there asked if we would give him a ride into Memphis. "Sure, I said as I opened the door. "Get in. Glad to have you."

He slung his duffel bag onto the red leather back seat and jumped in after it. I asked if he had been discharged, and he answered, "Yes sir!" "Well, what are you going to do in civilian life to earn a living?" "I'm going to study undertaking. I want to own a funeral parlor." "Hey, I said, what's the big attraction of that career?" We were silent for the rest of the trip as I mulled over his unexpected answer. One of the things about the service was that you meet such interesting people.

Again, Hermi and I made brief stops in New Orleans and Atlanta. (I had had it with Montgomery and the Maxwell Field Hospital). We then drove north to New York because I wanted a summer job before I went back to college.

Summer Job-Hunting in New York

Friends had referred us to the Salisbury Hotel in Midtown Manhattan. It was no Waldorf, but it was nice enough and the price was right. I parked our car in front of the hotel and left it with our baggage while we registered. When we came out, the car door was open and the two suitcases with all my prewar civilian clothes on the back seat were gone. The metal footlocker with my uniforms was still there, as were Hermi's clothes locked in the trunk. The hotel desk told us that calling the police was a waste of the nickel the phone call would cost me.

After we were settled in our room, its view overlooking an alley, I told Hermi I was going to Saks to buy a suit, a tie, and a couple of shirts. The store had one suit in my size, a baggy grayish, three-piece outfit that fit me like a wrinkled prune.

That evening we were to drive up to the Century Club in Westchester; the Cullmans had asked us for dinner and a dance there. I hung my new suit on. Hermi looked at me, grimaced, and asked, "Did you get that thing at Saks or Sacks?" So we decided that even if the war was over I should wear my Marine dress uniform; the elite Century Club might bar me if I showed up in my shapeless Sack (Saks) suit. Once we were at the club, however, my comfort level was low when I saw I was the only person in uniform. But Hermi looked great!

Edgar Cullman's brother Arthur was there and greeted us warmly. "Cecil, Edgar tells me you're looking for a job with an industrial designer. Come to my office tomorrow at 10:00; I think I can help you."

When I met with Arthur he said, "Our firm distributes Parliament cigarettes. On the package is a picture of the British Parliament with 'Made in the USA' in very small type. The FTC, the agency that regulates such things, says the package gives the false impression the cigarettes are made in Great Britain and imported. They have ordered us to change the design. To help in your job search I'm giving you the assignment. If you walk into a designer's office with this job in hand it should open the way to your employment." Once more, the Cullman's were in my corner.

The industrial designer Walter Darwin Teague, who had a long and impressive list of clients he became known as "the Dean of Industrial Design," was my first stop.

When I walked into Teague's office he looked me over, his eyes lingering on my gold Navy wings. He didn't offer me a seat. "What makes you think you want to be an industrial designer?" was his reply to my saying I was looking for a summer job. "Before the war I read an article about industrial design in *Fortune* magazine. It sounded like an interesting and challenging career."

"Oh Christ, that article is full of misinformation," he said. "There's nothing in it that resembles the real thing. Forget it." He tossed aside my agreement with Cullman, ignored my portfolio, and finally offered me a chair. Reaching for his intercom, he called his chief designer. "Come to my office. There's a young man here who wants a summer job. I suppose we should talk to him; he's wearing a Marine uniform." I didn't see what my uniform had to do with my qualifications and should have walked out. The designer came in, shook hands, and did look at my drawings and resume. His only reaction was a deep hum from his chest, raised eyebrows, and compressed lips as he handed back my material. "OK" said Teague. "Give us your phone number we'll call you in a day or two." That was the last I heard from Walter D. Teague.

Henry Dreyfuss was, I thought, the top industrial designer and engineer. His exterior designs reflected the function of the article he was encasing. His designs were honest, adhering to the dictum "form follows function." Dreyfuss greeted me with a smile and a handshake. He wasn't interested in the Parliament package. I showed him my work, he shook his head approvingly, but he had one serious reservation.

"You say you're going to Harvard to get your master's in architecture next fall. I have a position for you, and we'd like to have you – but not if you're going to Harvard. We would devote our time and yours to training you, and then you'd go and we would never see you again. Our time and money would be wasted."

"Mr. Dreyfuss, I would agree to work for you for at least two years after I get my degree," I said. "You would get back your investment in me."

"No," he said. "I don't want to tie either you or us down. Things change. If you change your mind about Harvard, our door is open." Many times since, I've wondered how my career would have turned out if I had taken Dreyfuss's offer.

My last try was with J. Gordon Carr, an architect and industrial designer. The project Arthur Cullman had given me, the redesign of the Parliament package, actually appealed to Carr, and he took me on for the summer. But the design was a money-loser, and Carr was still working on it when I left.

Now my wings were clipped. I was back down to earth, facing new challenges and opportunities and having to adjust to being free of the Marine Corps orders and its directives. I was entirely responsible for my future, and there were no insignias on my collar to assure me how I ranked in the civilian world.

I put my 38-caliber revolver in a box and sent it home to my father.

Chapter 23

A Trip Back to the Islands

The moving finger writes; and, having writ, moves on.

— Edward Fitzgerald, The Rubaiyat of Omar Khayyam

In early 1982 Hermi and I were planning a trip to Hawaii to attend an American Institute of Architects conference. When I looked at the flights Continental offered, there in bold print was "Honolulu to Majuro and Ponape." With a flourish I showed the schedule to Hermi. "We can go to Majuro as easy as flying to New York. We can fly to Majuro after the convention." With a laugh she said, "OK, you win. I'll go."

It also occurred to me that my services as an architect might be welcomed, so I arranged to meet with a Ponape official during our trip. Four decades after my stay in the Marshalls, building structures in the Pacific rather than bombing them had a certain appeal.

Several weeks later we were seated in the rear section of a Continental 747 throbbing its huge way to the Marshall Islands and our destination, Majuro. A latticed curtain stretched halfway up across the spacious cabin, and the space in front was filled with boxes, bags, cans, crates, trunks, suitcases, and one goat – a chaotic and odoriferous collection of the Marshall islanders' personal baggage on its way home.

As the plane circled and descended to land, I looked down through the misty air at Majuro. A beautiful narrow green and white reef surrounded the large lagoon, which spread some 20 miles long and 10 miles wide.

The long islet where surplus planes were parked during the war had been converted to a 10,000-foot runway, more than ample for our big jet to land. At the end of the runway was the terminal, which we taxied to without delay.

To call the rambling, falling-apart, wooden shambles a "terminal" was a wild exaggeration; "overgrown chicken coop" better described it. The cramped space was jammed with people waiting to take off or to greet friends and families when they arrived.

One battered counter sprawled under a cracked sign announcing "Car Rentals." There I found that only Japanese cars were available. (Who won the war?) Rates were reasonable, and the cars were well kept. I rented one for the time we would be on the atoll, and a short drive took us to the adjoining island – the location of our airstrip and squadron headquarters back in the Forties. Along the lagoon was a row of cottages, each with a living-dining room, a small kitchen, and a bedroom. We rented one. A broad view of the lagoon through the large front windows soon came alive with sunset colors reflecting off the sparkling water. Hermi admitted that Majuro deserved every admiring adjective I'd always attributed to it.

Disappointment and Joy

The next day we went sightseeing, first taking in a row of very substantial houses where the mounded coral revetments that surrounded and protected our planes once stood. Then we went to the library, which housed the Marshall Islands History Center, repository to which I later sent some of my wartime documents. Next stops were a general store, a grocery store, and a movie theater. These establishments, along with an ice cream parlor, drew natives from the nearby atolls that had escaped the intrusion of American civilization.

It was sad to see that the natives had built wretched huts of plywood and corrugated siding and shared common bathroom facilities; these shacks were a sorry substitute from the neat thatched-roof homes elevated on palm-tree trunks, the norm when I lived on Majuro. Another major disappointment came when I met a fat American who sold the natives life insurance they obviously couldn't afford, a heartless act that surprised and disgusted me.

Our cocktail hours were spent at the Marshall Island Yacht Club. There were no yachts here, nor even a rowboat. The unpainted wooden building contained a fine mahogany bar brought from Chicago and about ten round tables with uncomfortable wire-backed chairs. The bar opened to the beach littered with broken and rusting airplanes, stoves, a refrigerator, pots, pans, and even a broken and rusting machine gun. The beautiful coral beach I remembered was now covered with junk.

It was at the Yacht Club that we met Jonathan Weisgal, a young Washington lawyer who was at Majuro to represent the natives in their lawsuit against the United States for our government's shabby treatment of them since the war — to wit, subjecting them to fallout from repeated nuclear bomb tests in the Marshalls. Despite his somber mission, Jonathan was a bright and engaging man, and we enjoyed our afternoons with him.

The headquarters for Marshall Islands Airlines was on Majuro. The airline's small transports flew among the surrounding islands loaded with cargo and people, so I booked passage to Mili (Hermi didn't want to go.) When the pilot learned I was a pilot and had bombed Mili, he offered me the empty co-pilot's seat. Then, after we were airborne, he said, "It's all yours. Fly us to Mili."

The 50 miles to the atoll flashed by; ahead was the one remaining runway. My many attacks on Mili, with its deadly anti-aircraft and machine guns, lurched into my brain, making it hard to convince myself that we wouldn't soon come under heavy fire from an assortment of 8-inch coastal guns, 20 and 40 caliber anti-aircraft guns, and a hail of machine gun fire.

Flashbacks aside, I put the plane down on the end of the runway. It came to a stop in front of a crowd of cheering islanders, there to greet a native woman with her newly acquired husband, a white American. As I opened the cabin door, a fat black hand reached in, grabbed me by the ankle, and started pulling me. The hand belonged to a beaming, very stout woman dressed in a loudly patterned blue muumuu. The pilot grinned and said, "She and her sister are queens of Mili. It's her way of welcoming you. Last time I was here one of them grasped me by the hair and tried to fling me around with my feet in the air."

If the queen succeeded in pulling me out, I would fall 5 feet to the ground, so I clung to the plane and with strenuous kicks freed my leg before climbing down. The second queen ran to me with a large basket balanced on her head. Laughing and grinning, she shoved it into my arms.

"Yours", she shouted. "Yours!"

I put the basked filled with bread, pandamus fruit, and live crabs in the plane. Both the queens then took turns hugging the breath out of me. Never had I had such a powerful reception.

The returning newlyweds were hoisted over the heads of their family and carried away. A large Japanese tourist was recording all this frantic activity with his camera.

I had time for a short look around at some rusty aircraft parts half-hidden by weeds before the pilot called out, "We have to leave." As we taxied away the two fat queens, obviously twins, blew us kisses.

In my memory, Mili was now not only a deadly target during World War II but the site of those nearly deadly (but friendly) queens and their subjects.

After I went back to our cottage, the Japanese-American manager greeted me. "Mr. Alexander, the Japanese photographer you saw on Mili wants to talk to you," he said. "We can meet for lunch tomorrow at our dining room, and I'll interpret for you." I accepted the invitation. When I arrived the next day, the dining room reminded me of the one at my summer camp – a long hall surrounded by screened windows. My two lunch companions were seated at a rough wooden table near the entrance. They rose, shook hands, and waved me to a chair.

In answer to my questions, the Japanese fellow said he had been a soldier on Mili, had almost starved, and was badly wounded by an exploding bomb. He pulled up his shorts and pulled down his sock to reveal a bulging scar that ran from his ankle to his hip. It occurred to me that his wound might have been the result of one of my bombs.

I showed him a collection of photos of the Majuro lagoon filled with our battleships, carriers, cruisers, and destroyers. Amazed, he told me that nobody on Mili knew a huge task force had been anchored only 50 miles away. Suddenly, a group of teenagers gathered around us. They looked with astonishment at the vast fleet in the pictures, and then gazed out at the lagoon as if they expected those ships to reappear. They talked excitedly as they left.

The former Japanese soldier's answer to my last question left me shaken. "Were any American pilots captured, and did they survive?" He replied, "Five were taken. None survived." The oft-repeated warning that Japanese beheaded captured airmen was no longer a rumor; it was a reality. This Japanese veteran and his wife were on the same mission Hermi and I were on – returning to see their wartime station. None of his memories could have been pleasant.

A High Point on Laura Island

The most enchanting experience of our trip was unexpected, and came after we drove our rented car down the 20-mile strip on the west side of the lagoon to the large island called Laura. During the war the natives were moved there and to several adjoining islands to isolate them from the service personnel. Hermi and I brought with us the food-filled basket the queens had given me on Mili, and we also had a boxful of packaged peanut butter crackers we bought in Honolulu. Parking our car near the beach, we settled on the hot coral to eat our lunch. For a reminder of the history of Majuro, we needed only to look a few feet down the beach to see the rusting wreck of a Japanese fighter.

In a few minutes we were surrounded by a small group of joyous native children, ranging in age from 16 all the down to 4. They were ready to share lunch with us – not the local delicacies in the basket but the peanut butter crackers. The 4-year-old, holding a package of the crackers in his mouth, easily scampered to the top of a palm tree that bent over the lagoon. There he settled among the fronds, ripped open the package, and had a grand meal.

The 16-year-old boy spoke excellent English. I asked him what his ambition was. "I want to go to college in the United States. I also want to fly and have a career as an airline pilot." He hoped to be awarded a scholarship to Harvard, saying his grades were excellent and his advisor thought his chances were good. So here, on this island lost in the Pacific, was a bright young boy who knew about Harvard and wanted to enroll there. I wished him well.

Hermi and I remembered our picnic on Laura as the high point of our trip. Those bright young kids were the future, not the rusting war relics strewn about the beaches.

An Eventful Side Trip

Our next destination was Ponape (now spelled Pohnpei), a major island miles west of Majuro. Hermi, whose failing health made her very tired at first, said she wouldn't go to Ponape, she would just wait for me at Majuro. "No way, Hermi," I said. "If you won't go with me, I'm not going. We'll fly back to Hawaii."

"All right," she answered. "I can make it. Let's go."

As the plane took off I looked down at my memory of my lost warrior days, my lost youth. You can't go home again they say. Nor, I discovered, can you go back to your war again.

Ponape is a large island dominated by a tall, quiet volcano with a lagoon surrounded by a narrow reef at is base. As our plane descended, the pilot pointed out a series of small cottages set in the trees near the top of the mountain. "That's the best hotel on the island. You should stay there."

It looked all right to Hermi and me, so when we landed we found a representative of the hotel and arranged for a cottage. The hotel rep put us in a truck with few or no springs, and we bounced on our way up a rutted and rocky road.

The hotel more than met our expectations. We were first shown the dining room and bar, which looked out over the lagoon to the ocean. We were then taken to a cottage nestled under mighty trees. The plumbing was new, and the small kitchen was well fitted-out. A thick air mattress beckoned us to lie down. Going to bed would be a pleasure.

The Ponape official I had arranged to meet was the island's top citizen – a senator in the Federated States of Micronesia. I found him scraping paint off a small landing craft he had salvaged and planned to use to haul goods around the lagoon for profit.

"Come on," he said in excellent English. "We'll go up the mountain to the old Japanese airstrip where the government wants to build." Another bumpy ride took us up to a wide shelf, where the outline of the runway could still be seen. My mind wandered back to the plans for a bombing mission trip from Enewetak to this very field; fortunately the mission, which would undoubtedly have run our tanks dry halfway back from the attack, was called off.

The senator pointed to a grassy knoll and asked, "You see that hill at the end of the runway? And do you know what we call it?" I replied, "No. What's it called?" "We call it Chickenshit Hill," he answered, offering no reason for this nasty name for a very beautiful part of the landscape.

We descended the mountain and entered the government center, a large court surrounded with one-story white buildings with red roofs. The court was filled with marching bands assembled from the surrounding islands to compete for the title "First Band."

When the senator's car drove in and I alighted, all the bands broke into the Marine Hymn; our host had arranged this welcome. I had never heard the hymn played with more volume and spirit. It tingled my spine, and I was delighted.

We were then driven to the airport, where Hermi waited for me. As we walked to our plane, the senator promised to keep in touch and tell me of any buildings that I might have a hand in designing. We thanked him, shook hands, and pulled our way up the steps into the plane. (A letter telling me of a potential project eventually arrived in my mailbox, but nothing ever came of it.)

The stewardess standing by our seats pointed to the cluster of buildings. "Our captain always comes this close to that hotel and announces what a fine facility it is – he's a part owner." With a smile, I wondered whether there was a small conflict of interest here.

The long flight back to Honolulu and on to San Francisco went without incident, though jet lag was a long- lasting side effect from flying through all those time zones. Years after, the jet lag was forgotten but the memory of our journey into "paradise" was a source of pleasure and delight.

Epilogue

Among the meditations in Chapter 16 in Part 1 of *Crossing the Line,* "Some Final Thoughts," are those on my family, my history as an architect and civil rights advocate, old-style communication vs. that of today, the nature of man, and religion, Jewish and otherwise. Less than 200 words are devoted to war and peace, and virtually none to my role as a soldier; hence this epilogue for Part 2.

When I think about what I brought back with me from my wartime activities in the Marshall Islands, I find it difficult because what I lived was far from the terrible realities faced by those who served farther south in the Solomon Islands. I guess I can sum up my feelings this way: if I had that war to fight over again, I don't think I could improve on the personal aspect. I regret that I probably killed and wounded many Japanese soldiers in my 60 dive-bombing missions and 100-plus surveillance flights. But that was what I was retained to do, and I did it as well as I knew how.

General William T. Sherman is famous (or infamous) for his statement "War is hell". It certainly was for the citizens of Atlanta, which he burned to the ground. But war wasn't hell on the atolls of Majuro. This island in the Marshalls was a beautiful work of nature, and its long, wide, deep lagoon could handle our entire fleet. I was lucky to survive my many missions, but I never felt I contributed much to the war effort. Of course, if I had been shot down and/or killed, that would have been another story.

My experience as a Marine and Naval aviator taught me to be very conscious of detail and the need to work closely with other people. I believe I largely based my goals for my post-war life on those soldiering days I spent in the Pacific and North Carolina.

Mixed Feelings

To put it directly, when I first experienced dive bombing it scared the hell out of me. Strangely, I later came to enjoy it and was very good at it. In a sense, dive-bombing was a preamble to the guided missile. Of course, when a guided missile hits the ground there is no human on board. That's a very big difference: my bomber and I were one and the same.

I was always conscious that the plane I flew, the Scout Bomber Douglas, or SBD, was the one that won the Battle of Midway. It sounds bloodthirsty now, but I always wanted to get a carrier in my sights. The fact that destroyers throwing up a hail of anti-aircraft fire would surround the carrier didn't seem to bother me at the time. I did sink one ship, but it was a merchant ship that caught fire and was destroyed. I was awarded an Air Medal for that.

As interesting, frightening, transformative, and enlightening as my military service was, I have no illusions: There is no good war. There is no glory in war. The only thing that can be said for war is that it settles some issues that need to be settled. One day, I fervently hope, mankind will figure out how to accomplish this without firearms. If we fail to do so, we are going to self-destruct.

Indexes
Crossing the Line

Crossing the Line – Part 1 – The Awakening of a Good Ol' Boy

D–E

N–P

Q-R

Roosevelt, Pres. Franklin D. 87, 128, 144, 158, 196, 214
Rose, Michael 81
Rosenthal, Bob 264 (photo)
Rosser White Engineers 217
Rothschild, Architect Bernard (Rocky) 87-90, 93, 99-100, 131
Rothschild, Bill 114, 245
Rothschild, Hava 114
Rothschild, Rabbi Jacob 110, 176-177, 246
Rothschild, Janice 177
Round House (Alexander residence) 81, 105–112, 114, 124-125
Design and construction 105–107
Rouse, James 248–249, 259-260
Rowe, Artist Nellie Mae 284
Rudolph, (Architect) Paul 58

S–T

Saarinen, Architect Eero 59, 88
Salina, Annlie x
Samuel, Don 111
Sanders, Gov. Carl 150, 202
Sandler, Roz 283
Sartor, Margaret 253
Schlesinger, Rae 83
Scottish Rite Children's Hospital 223
Scottish Rite Masonry 15
Selassie, Haile 200
Selma, Ala. March on 146
Settle, Cmdr. T. G. W, "Tex" 25
Shanks, Hershel 91
Shanks, Judith Alexander Weil ix, 89
Shanks, Julia ix

Shelton, Jesse 143
Sherman, Gen. William T. 10, 15, 269, 274
Shutze, Architect Philip Trammell 6, 78
Sichalwe, Percy x
Simon, Editor Howard 14
Skandalakis, Dr. John 212
Skidmore, Owings & Merrill Architects (SOM) 202, 204, 205, 207
Slade, Frances Fowler xi
Slaton, Gov. John M. 4–5
Smith, Caitlin Weil ix, 92
Smith College 51, 114, 159, 232
Smith, H. O. 33
Smith, Jed Alexander ix, 90
Smith, Milton M. (Muggsy) 131-137
Smith, Vernon (Catfish) 19
Smyre, State Rep. Calvin 270, 273
Sommerville, Robert (Bob) 176
Sousa, John Philip 265
Southerland, Randy xi, 293
Southern Bell building 203-207
Spalding, Editor Jack 94, 130
Spartacus and the Gladiators 32
Speech and Hearing Clinic, Atlanta 173
Spelman College 161, 172, 231
Squantum Naval Air Station 62
Squinkles 281
Steel, Roy 203, 205-206
Steinberg, Architect Mickey 108
Stephens, Beaupré 224
Stephenson, Dante 232
Stewart, Dr. Preston x
Stone Mountain 61
Stribling, Young 154
Stubbins, Prof. Hugh 56, 109

X-Y-Z

Crossing the Line – Part 2 – The War Years

E-G

H-J

S-V

W-Z

Made in the USA
Lexington, KY
31 July 2013